THE WORST MILITARY LEADERS IN HISTORY

THE WORST MILITARY
LEADERS IN HISTORY

Edited by
John M. Jennings and Chuck Steele

REAKTION BOOKS

Published by
REAKTION BOOKS LTD
Unit 32, Waterside
44–48 Wharf Road
London N1 7UX, UK
www.reaktionbooks.co.uk

First published 2022

Printed and bound in Great Britain by
TJ Books Ltd, Padstow, Cornwall

A catalogue record for this book is available
from the British Library

ISBN 978 1 78194 583 0

CONTENTS

FOREWORD

Vice Admiral (Retd) Sir Jeremy Blackham
Former Deputy Chief of Defence Staff, UK

M uch time and effort has been spent in military training establishments the world over on the study of leadership, frequently examining great leaders of the past who are perceived as successful, analysing the reasons for their success and deriving lessons for aspiring leaders. This approach has its limitations. It is self-evident that no two military encounters are identical, and that the sort of leadership needed against different enemies, in different military environments, as part of differing strategic and political goals and with different technologies will itself be different. Commanding people in the air is obviously a very different task in detail from commanding them in land or sea battles. Leadership at the tactical level may require very different skills from leadership at the operational or grand strategic levels. Some leaders may be very good at one of these functions but much less good at others, so it is important that the right person is chosen at the right level and in the right environment. Success or failure at one level may tell us little about a leader's abilities at another level.

By way of illustration, one might consider that the type of leadership required from General Eisenhower during the 1944 Normandy campaign was very different from that exercised by General Patton. It is quite possible that neither of them could have done the other's job. Does this make them bad leaders? I think not. To take a further example from my own service, discussed in this book, Admiral David Beatty badly failed his country and his commander-in-chief at the battle of Jutland but, as Chuck Steele observes in his essay, Beatty was much more successful as the professional head of his service. Does this make him one of the worst leaders or one of the best? Were those characteristics that made him unfit for one task the same as those that suited him admirably for another? It is common in the military for a person to be promoted to the next level because of success at a lower level. Is this the most sensible process?

This book takes a rather welcome unconventional approach to the subject. It examines leaders across history who may be judged to have failed badly as a result of their own errors, rather than through the brilliance of an opposing leader, sometimes in terms of strategic vision and planning, sometimes in terms of tactical ineptitude, often as the result of serious flaws of character. The assembled essays consider, often in extensive detail, some of the candidates for the title of 'worst military leader in history' and seek to justify the candidature of the subject of the essay. It is for the reader to decide to what extent each one succeeds. I doubt that there will be unanimity. It certainly produces some of the more interesting and contentious views of the complicated subject of successful military leadership that I have come across. It also highlights the very different qualities that can make for success or failure in different circumstances. Any student of the subject who set out a matrix of the errors made by these people might learn something very useful for their own careers.

What, then, should we conclude? The editors sensibly do not provide a definitive answer to this question. It is surely for those reading the book to consider the evidence offered and to draw their own conclusions as to the failures of the leaders here analysed, and the lessons that these might offer in other, different circumstances. There may well be no universally agreed answers. Military leadership is an art as much as it is a skill. Some things can be taught and some things must be learned, which is rather different. Some leaders may be gifted to intuit things which others have to work hard to understand. And leadership must be practised, testing the lessons' use in other circumstances where they may be relevant, and adapting them as appropriate.

Perhaps in the end we might remember that Napoleon was reported as saying, when it was suggested to him that some of his generals won battles by luck, 'I would rather have lucky generals than good ones.' But is luck simply fortuitous? We should also heed the words of the great golfer Gary Player, who said, 'The harder I work (read study), the luckier I get.'

INTRODUCTION

John M. Jennings and Chuck Steele

Military biography is one of the oldest and most prolific sub-disciplines in the field of history. The ancients, such as Thucydides and Sima Qian, readily grasped that one must analyse the decisions made by military leaders in order to understand the reasons for victory or defeat on the battlefield, and in order to analyse those decisions, it is necessary to understand the people who made those decisions. How did their backgrounds and character influence their decision-making? What constraints did they face, and how did they cope with those constraints in the pursuit of victory? Why did they make the decisions they did, and how did those decisions lead to success or failure? These universal questions have fascinated military historians for thousands of years and have led to the writing of countless volumes.

Consequently, a keen awareness of the long and distinguished tradition of military biography placed us in the challenging position of adding another volume to the vast corpus that will offer a new and different perspective on the age-old questions of leadership. In considering this challenge, we drew on numerous informal discussions among the faculty of the history department at the United States Air Force Academy (USAFA). As military history is one of the core courses offered at USAFA, there is never a paucity of faculty or cadets eager to discuss the merits of individual leaders and their influence on fields of battle. Indeed, as USAFA serves as a centre for the education and training of future officers, it is incumbent upon its history professors to illuminate the historic challenges posed to members of the profession upon which they are entering. Generally, conversations of military leadership in the classroom focus on history's greatest com-manders. With limited time to address even a small portion of the history of armed conflict, faculty tend to concentrate on great captains as it is hoped that by examining history's most illustrious command-ers, young officer candidates will find sources of inspiration and, at the least, generate some degree of self-awareness when it comes to recognizing the traits of successful leaders. As faculty, we emphasize the role of leaders in the hope of engaging our students to see them-selves in the stories unfolding before them.

This emphasis on commanders whose greatness is usually defined by victory extends beyond the classroom to the field of military biog-raphy. This is not surprising: history, after all, loves a winner too. Moreover, as confirmed by our experience in the classroom, it is entirely logical that, if the lessons of military leadership are to be studied by present and future leaders for practical purposes, they should study success. However, like *yin* without *yang*, this is a limited approach that essentially ignores the inverse: if one can learn from studying the suc-cesses of the greatest military leaders in history, cannot one also learn equally well from studying the worst military leaders in history? It is to this other side that the present volume is dedicated.

While this project began as something of a flight of fancy, it is an attempt to balance the scales of instruction in military history. The renowned historian Sir Michael Howard provided a set of instruc-tions for those who would make the study of war their business in his essay 'The Use and Abuse of Military History'. In what has become one of the most oft-quoted articles among military historians, Howard admonished readers to study the subject in width, depth and context.[1] However, professors often make poor students, and much of what Howard advised goes unheeded. In this instance, there seems to be an excess of enthusiasm for the study of winners, and very little, or not a corresponding amount, of attention paid to those who make someone else's victory possible. Emphasizing the greatest commanders at the expense of the worst does not hew closely to the need to present history in width and depth. Frankly, without giving ample consideration to the worst leaders, historians fail to examine war fully in context. Although the stories presented here are one-sided appraisals, they are meant to provide a counterweight to the standard in terms of explaining out-comes. At the least, they should help provoke readers to question the causes of command failure as much as the sources of success.

Moreover, as the discipline of military history requires critical evaluations of leadership, it is not surprising that those engaged in its study are likely to have very strong opinions about who did well and who did not while in command. What is surprising is that the liveliest discussions among friends and colleagues over the past twenty years have centred on who did the worst in war. In examining history's great commanders, the same names and well-known arguments emerge, making discussions of such subjects redundant and even tedious. However, discussions of failed commanders inspire a strange passion that verges on competitiveness. Some of the characters discussed in this volume are well known; others may seem obscure. The unifying factor in all these essays is that every leader examined here failed in a noteworthy manner. In fact, their faults have become their legacy – whether it is deserved or not is a judgement reserved for the reader.

War is an adversarial undertaking. For every commander who has won acclaim for solving immense problems in the crucible of war, there is at least one other who has failed to do so. While losing is not always the hallmark of ineptitude, there are some commanders who have managed to fail for various reasons as spectacularly as any who had succeeded. The remarkable individuals whose inability in war has captivated the minds of friends and colleagues are the subjects of the essays in this book. Away from the classroom and its pressure to inspire, the casual conversations of military historians have here been turned into a collection of stories underscoring commanders it is hoped will never serve as role models to future leaders.

SCHOLARSHIP ON BAD MILITARY LEADERSHIP

Although they too focused largely on the great commanders, the ancients seemed to realize that studying the flaws of the losers could offer significant lessons on military leadership. Thus Thucydides not only examined triumphs of great generals such as Pericles, but he devoted considerable attention to the numerous leadership failures of Nikias (who is the subject of James Tucci's chapter in this volume) in the Sicilian expedition of 415–413 BCE. Plutarch devoted one of his *Lives* to Nikias as well, along with other such notable losers as Pyrrhus and Crassus (the subject of Gregory Hospodor's chapter in this volume), in addition to his biographical sketches of the greats, such as Alexander and Julius Caesar.

This understanding seems to have persisted for millennia, as Niccolò Machiavelli echoed the ancients in his exhortation to prospective rulers:

> As to the mental training of which we have spoken, a Prince should read histories, and in these should note the actions of great men, observe how they conducted themselves in their wars, and examine the causes of their victories and defeats, so as to avoid the latter imitate the former. And above all, he should, as many great men of past ages have done, assume for his models those persons who before his time have been renowned and celebrated, whose deeds and achievements he should constantly keep in mind, as it is related that Alexander the Great sought to resemble Achilles, Caesar Alexander, and Scipio Cyrus.[2]

However, modern historical scholarship on the topic of failed military leadership is scanty at best. A notable contribution is Alan Clark's 1962 *The Donkeys*, which describes the disastrous offensives launched by the British Expeditionary Force in the first two years of the First World War.[3] His title refers to the description of British soldiers attributed to various German generals as 'lions led by donkeys', which at the same time was an indictment of the poor leadership of the 'donkeys', namely French and Haig. However, while Clark's book seems to promise a focus on the leaders, he tends to devote more attention to the horrific impacts of their remarkable ignorance and indifference to the soldiers in the trenches, who were slaughtered in the tens of thousands as they tried to carry out operations that were basically impossible.

The theme of incompetent British military leadership in the First World War has been, relatively speaking, something of a mine as it was also the topic of John Laffin's *British Butchers and Bunglers of World War One*.[4] Surveying the entire war, Laffin also devotes considerable attention to the suffering of the enlisted men and junior officers caused by the callous and ill-informed decisions made by their commanders. He is, however, much more explicit in his condemnation of French, Haig, Gough, Hamilton and so on, for not only their gross and seemingly wilful incompetence, but their laziness and dishonesty in refusing to accept responsibility for their catalogue of failures by blaming them on the inexperience of the men, or simply on bad luck.

While Clark and Laffin both explicitly treat military incompetence, their studies are of limited utility to the student hoping to learn lessons on leadership due to a limited focus on a single conflict and an emphasis on describing the incompetence and its consequences, rather than explaining it.

With the emergence of the social sciences in the nineteenth century, the study of leadership increasingly devolved to political scientists, psychologists and sociologists. While the idea that failed military leadership can be instructive has also been lost on social scientists for the most part, they have nevertheless been largely responsible for the two most recent major works that examine failed military leadership as a discrete topic: *On the Psychology of Military Incompetence* (1976) by psychologist Noman F. Dixon, and *Command Failure in War: Psychology and Leadership* (2004) by co-authors Philip Langer, an educational psychologist, and historian Robert Pois.[5]

Dixon's book, which deals exclusively with the British Army, first describes a number of case studies of military failure from the Crimean War to the end of the Second World War, including notable catastrophes such as the Charge of the Light Brigade (Tennyson's ode notwithstanding), Magersfontein, Kut, Singapore and Arnhem. In explaining the causes of these leadership disasters, Dixon argues that they were essentially the product of the symbiotic relationship between the social psychology (or perhaps more accurately, psychopathology) of the British Army and personalities of the officers who achieved success in such a dysfunctional organization. The British Army (and militaries in general, as Dixon implies), as an authoritarian institution, was characterized by rigid conformity, narrow-minded anti-intellectualism, obedience to petty and mindless discipline ('bullshit', as Dixon calls it), adherence to an external code of honour that merely distanced the leaders from the led (the 'officer and gentleman' construct), and the elevation of displays of physical courage over moral courage. In such a stifling environment, it is not surprising that well-connected, superficial and spit-and-polish duffers such as Haig were able to flourish and rise to high command. Rather more surprising is that, occasionally, innovative outsiders like Monash could also join the higher echelons of leadership, but they often did so in spite of the institution.

While *On the Psychology of Military Incompetence* is justifiably regarded as being something of a standard work on the subject it nevertheless has limitations to the historian seeking to draw lessons on military leadership. The book's focus on one institution over a relatively short period of roughly a century raises the question of whether the author's conclusions are more broadly applicable to other militaries and other times. Moreover, as a social scientist, Dixon's methodology was essentially the opposite of that employed by historians. To Dixon, history served to provide case studies to illustrate his theories, whereas for the historian, the history comes first, with models and theories of occasional use in helping to make sense of how and why things happened the way they did. Given this, Dixon's references to the lack of maternal affection in Haig's upbringing and his anal retentiveness to help explain his inept leadership may strike the historian as just a trifle reductionist.[6]

In *Command Failure in War: Psychology and Leadership*, Pois and Langer examine eight case studies in failures of military leadership, including Napoleon's invasion of Russia, Lee's defeat at Gettysburg and Hitler and his generals during the Stalingrad campaign. While they express a greater awareness of the complexity and stressfulness of the context in which military decision-making takes place, they nevertheless argue that the failures examined in the book can largely be explained by the inflexibility of the commanders in question. In other words, Napoleon, Lee, Hitler and his generals, and so on were essentially spoiled by their early successes, and when confronted with a new paradigm were unable to make the adjustments away from what had brought them those successes in the first place.

While Pois and Langer avoid the reductionism of Dixon and are more mindful of the history, their approach too has limited utility for those seeking to learn the lessons of bad military leadership. For one thing, their case studies tend to focus quite extensively on the battles and campaigns themselves, with the result that the narrative sometimes obscures the more important issue of leadership failures. Moreover, while Langer and Pois offer a longer and more varied scope of study than Dixon, their approach is still limited geographically to Europe and North America, and chronologically from 1759 to 1943. A more universal approach, embracing the ancient and medieval world, as well as the non-Western world, would be helpful in distilling the essence of what makes for bad military leadership. Beyond that, while Pois and Langer rightly wish to avoid the reductionism of Dixon, their attempts to psychoanalyse long-dead historical figures based on written records nevertheless lead to occasional pat psychohistory generalizations, such as the impact of Frederick the Great's dysfunctional relationship with his father on his later decision-making at Kunersdorf. Such speculations may make for interesting reading, but they are not necessarily good history.

Nor are all social scientists even convinced that military failure is a product of leadership failure. For example, *Military Misfortunes: The Anatomy of Failure in War* (1990), by political scientist Eliot A. Cohen in collaboration with historian John Gooch, tends to downplay the role of leadership altogether. Focusing on the topic of military failure in its own right, as they illustrate with case studies such as Gallipoli, the Battle of France and the Yom Kippur War, Cohen and Gooch conceptualize it as a sort of mechanical process of various combinations of breakdowns, which they liken to an industrial accident. Consequently, the human factor finds limited place in their largely mechanistic schema, and the role of leadership in military failure is compared to 'operator error when highly complicated machines malfunction'.[7]

Being historians and not social scientists, the authors in this volume do not present case studies to serve as support for particular models of behaviour. These essays were not solicited to demonstrate theories of leadership; they are intended to remain grounded in the reality of war as a quintessentially human activity, and as such, stand as singular examples of ineptitude. Correspondingly, they are meant to be critical in a forceful manner. The limitations imposed by a fairly short word count have driven the contributors to focus tightly on what their subjects did wrong in waging war. Keeping in mind that one of the motives for this work is to share with a broader audience the commanders our authors thought were history's worst, the opinions are quite personal and not intended to abide by the standard practice of seeking balance. Rather, this is a collection of cautionary tales that are intended to make a unique contribution to the study of military leadership.

Sir John Keegan, one of the most influential military historians of the second half of the twentieth century, offered the opinion that the study of battle was clearly a matter for historians. In his most popular work, *The Face of Battle*, Keegan stated, 'For the human group in battle, and the quality and source of stress it undergoes, are drained of life and meaning by the laboratory approach which social scientists practice ... Battle is a historical subject, whose nature and trend of development can only be understood down a long historical perspective.'⁸ In this vein, the authors contributing to this work are offering their thoughts on a small slice of the larger issue of human performance in combat. Specifically, the contributors here have all been tasked with considering the faults in those commanding in war.

In what may be the most popular single volume on the history of military leadership, *The Mask of Command*, Keegan divided his study into four categories to suit his archetype generals. In his estimation, leadership was best measured against concepts of heroism. He started with Alexander the Great as his epitome of heroic leadership, worked his way through the Duke of Wellington as an example of anti-heroic leadership, on to U. S. Grant as his model for unheroic leadership, and finally, he examined Adolf Hitler as an example of false heroic leadership. Keegan created interesting categories, but while they may have suited his intent in writing a book, they do not fit the whole range of actual leadership. The categorizing of leaders, however, can be a risky proposition. Just as every commander is unique as a human being, so too, they are singular in their approach to command. As most historians will attest, history does not repeat itself – every event and person is as distinct as a snowflake. No two events or two individuals will ever be acted upon by the same sets of circumstances. Thus the section headings in this book are largely intended to serve as a convenience to the readers. The chapters do not represent an attempt to prove a larger point about the nature of leadership; the subjects in each chapter share some similarities in context or behaviour and nothing more. If the reader wants to examine these case studies to develop models of leadership, that is an individual prerogative and was not a goal of the editors in developing this project.

DEFINING TYPES OF BAD LEADERSHIP

What are the characteristics that make for the worst military leaders in history? Answering this question is just as daunting and full of contradictions as trying to distil the qualities of the greatest commanders. For example, how do victory and defeat factor into this question? This would seem to be the most basic criterion for distinguishing between the best and the worst. After all, warfare is perhaps the most goal-orientated of human endeavours, with winning equalling success and losing equalling failure. And yet, is it really as simple as that? If the study of the great commanders were reduced simply to focusing on the winners, why is there a veritable library of works on Napoleon and why do aspiring military leaders continue to study him so assiduously? He may have had a good run early on, but his career ended in crushing and ignominious defeats on the steppes of Russia in 1812 and again at Waterloo in 1815. If the victory-and-defeat dichotomy is really the truest measure of greatness, it would be Kutuzov, Blücher and Wellington who are studied and emulated, rather than Napoleon.

As victory and defeat do not necessarily seem to be foolproof criteria for determining the best and worst military leaders in history, perhaps character is a more reliable measure of greatness, or the opposite. Have not some commanders been widely judged as among the greatest for their integrity, nobility of spirit and chivalry, irrespective of the outcomes they achieved on the battlefield? As is the case with victory or defeat, the notion of character as a criterion of greatness has a certain superficial appeal due to its seeming simplicity. Nevertheless, it is also a measure that must be regarded with significant reservations. In this case, one need look no further than the military leadership of the Confederacy during the American Civil War. After the conflict, Robert E. Lee in particular, and to a somewhat lesser extent his lieutenants, such as Stonewall Jackson and J.E.B. Stuart, were praised by some historians for their sense of honour and chivalry as part of the 'Lost Cause' myth, which sought to depict the Confederacy as fighting a noble if ultimately doomed struggle against the aggressive and materially superior Union.

Fortunately, that long-standing myth is now undergoing a much-needed correction in the United States, and increasingly Lee and his henchmen are being seen for what they truly were: people who betrayed the country that they had sworn to defend in order to preserve the vile institution of slavery, and in the process were responsible for the murder of more of their fellow Americans than any foreign enemy. As a result, the current buzz-phrase 'character counts' would seem to have limited utility in establishing who are the greatest and worst leaders, to say the least.

For the purposes of this study, the editors have divided the subject commanders into the following five categories: Criminals, Frauds, the Clueless, Politicians and Bunglers. The authors have played no part in suggesting where their subjects fell in the aforementioned categories; the divisions were based solely on discussions between the book's editors, so any fault in mis-categorization rests on their shoulders.

It is hoped that this introduction and the efforts at explaining the placement of subjects within certain categories will help readers focus their attention on what made these failed commanders worthy of inclusion in such an inglorious list. However, the editors' efforts in this instance are somewhat akin to trying to explain impressionistic art. We are trying to impose order and definition on things that were produced under far less restricted circumstances.

CRIMINALS: BARON ROMAN F. VON UNGERN-STERNBERG, NATHAN BEDFORD FORREST AND JOHN CHIVINGTON

The maintenance of military discipline has been a key to success on the battlefield since ancient times, and at first glance it would seem to be a straightforward issue. Armies, after all, are also legal and bureaucratic institutions with regulations and clearly established penalties for violating those regulations. Nevertheless, for commanders, achieving success in establishing and maintaining discipline is a more nuanced process that requires a sense of balance. On one hand, a military force lacking clear-cut parameters for behaviour on and off the battlefield can degenerate into an unruly mob. On the other hand, a commander who errs in the opposite direction and becomes a martinet type, enforcing often petty regulations with harsh discipline, stifles initiative and incurs the hatred of subordinates. While merely bad commanders may be guilty of following one of these extremes, three of our contributors suggest that some of the *worst* commanders in history actually exceeded them by engaging in criminal conduct and encouraging criminality among their troops. We argue that this is the salient characteristic that best characterizes Roman F. von Ungern-Sternberg, Nathan Bedford Forrest and John Chivington, and therefore place them in a category that we call Criminals.

As proverbial 'loose cannons' more interested in pursuing their own ends than the larger objectives of the armies in which they were serving, all three were guilty of gross insubordination. Operating within the admittedly hazy command and control structure of the White army in the Russian Civil War, Ungern, as John Jennings describes, devoted his energies to an absurd campaign to restore monarchies in Europe and Asia rather than focusing on defeating the Reds. This led him to fall out with his superiors and launch a militarily useless invasion of Mongolia on his own, rather than supporting White operations in Siberia. In his chapter, Christopher Rein notes that Forrest was able to achieve a measure of success leading small raiding forces during the American Civil War, but that his irascible temper and stubborn egotism led to failure in larger commands as he frequently proved unwilling and incapable of executing assignments in more complex operations, to the detriment of those operations. Moreover, his numerous clashes with his peers and superiors, even to the point of challenging a couple of them to duels, undermined discipline in the Confederate ranks. Chivington, the subject of Courtney Short's chapter, was a supremely ambitious officer desperate for military glory that he could then translate into political power. This insatiable hunger for a battlefield triumph led him to contravene U.S. Army policy and attack a peaceful Native American encampment at Sand Creek, Colorado. The resulting massacre was so horrific that it not only managed to shock a public that was otherwise indifferent to the fate of the Native Americans, but played a major role in inflaming the frontier, which in turn necessitated a long and costly pacification campaign.

The most serious charge in the bill of indictment against Ungern, Forrest and Chivington, however, is murder. As Short persuasively argues in her chapter on Chivington, there is a clear-cut distinction between killing in warfare and murder, and all three leaders crossed the line into the latter in various ways. Ungern's fanatical anti-communism and antisemitism led him to order the murder of Jews and accused communists both in large-scale massacres and in the torture and killing of individuals and smaller groups. Forrest, who was already personally acquainted with settling scores with violence before joining the army of the Confederacy, became notorious for massacring surrendered Black and southern Unionist soldiers. And indeed, after the war he continued to indulge his racist and murderous proclivities as the founder of the Ku Klux Klan. While Chivington, for his part, does not seem to have had any more than the usual antipathy towards Native Americans of his contemporaries, his overweening ambition for battlefield success led him to incite the bloodlust of his men and then set them on a peaceful encampment with the admonition to take no prisoners. As Short concludes, 'he intended unlawful murder and massacre.' Sand Creek, in other words, was not so much a battle as a mass murder instigated by Chivington.

The murderous rage that so frequently animated Ungern, Forrest and Chivington was not just directed against the enemy, but sometimes turned inward against their own men. While Chivington only threatened to kill some of his own officers when they justifiably balked at murdering peaceful Native American men, women and children, Forrest actually stabbed one of his own subordinates to death during a quarrel of uncertain origin. Ungern, however, outdid both as his unpredictable and irascible temper led him to lash out at his own men with liberal application of capital punishment in various forms. Most spectacularly, this included burning one of his officers at the stake, which must be a unique application of that particular execution method in the twentieth century. As the authors show, such behaviour hardly endeared Ungern, Forrest and Chivington to at least some of their men, to the detriment of morale and combat effectiveness. Indeed, Ungern's own men mutinied and turned him over to the enemy when they had finally had enough of his maniacal and murderous leadership.

FRAUDS: DAVID BEATTY, GIDEON PILLOW AND ANTONIO LÓPEZ DE SANTA ANNA

Labelling someone a fraud may seem to be an exceedingly harsh judgement for a student of history to fix upon a wartime leader. However, in this instance, the term is meant to draw attention to the gap between the contemporary reputations of David Beatty, Gideon Pillow and Antonio López de Santa Anna as putative exemplars of military effectiveness and their demonstrated inability while in command. This section also treats what might be termed hubris, as all three seemed blinded to their own flaws by exceedingly large egos. While any number of subjects in this volume may be said to have suffered from hubris – Custer and Conrad come quickly to mind – the figures presented in this section had either manufactured reputations themselves, or had reputations foisted upon them that were terribly at odds with their performance as commanders. Indeed, for all the pomp and ceremony that attended the career ascent of Beatty, Pillow and Santa Anna, their actual performance in their most consequential assignments was entirely lacklustre. The fraud perpetrated in these cases is that, by whatever means Beatty, Pillow and Santa Anna came to hold their most significant combat commands, the strain of battle exposed them for being entirely out of their depth.

As Robert Wettemann explains, Pillow was probably the most fraudulent of the three. Coming to prominence at a time when the concept of military professionalism was alien to most in the United States, he was the personification of all that was wrong with a system that allowed amateurs to lead men in battle. He owed his positions (he held significant commands in both the Mexican–American War and the Civil War) to his prominence in civil society and not to any measure of training or demonstrated ability in the field. Santa Anna, as Gates Brown details, was a leader who had experienced some success in minor conflicts and had managed to magnify those small triumphs into a reputation as both a major political and military force in nineteenth-century Mexico. He was not dissimilar to Pillow in that his reputation off the battlefield inspired a degree of confidence that was at odds with his actual martial abilities. In this regard, both Pillow and Santa Anna might just as well be considered as subjects for the sections on political generals or bunglers. However, as the foundation of their failure was set in a fundamental lack of preparedness to lead men in war, which was coupled with an egotism that blinded them to their own ineptitude, they clearly belong in our section on military frauds.

Chuck Steele's chapter makes Beatty the odd man out in this gallery of commanders notable for their misappropriated fame. Beatty is one of the most controversial characters in the history of armed conflict because he had legitimately won the respect and admiration of his peers before failing miserably in the biggest naval engagement of the Great War. Serving at a time of rapidly evolving technologies that proved difficult for the nimblest of minds to master, Beatty was disastrously out of step with technological progress. While he epitomized the daring sort of naval officer long associated with the likes of Drake and Nelson, Beatty did not serve in the Age of Sail, and despite his appeal to those longing for continuity with the iconic figures of the past, Beatty was a man out of touch at the dawning of the Age of Dreadnoughts. He exuded aggressiveness and confidence, earning one biographer's laudatory claim to be history's 'last naval hero'.[9] In appearance and demeanour he was seemingly the quintessential British naval officer. In the defining moment of his career, however, the opening stages of the Battle of Jutland, Beatty acted rashly. His impetuosity was calamitous for thousands of British sailors and nearly delivered the most important victory of the First World War to the Imperial German Navy.

Pillow and Santa Anna also failed in the most important of their military assignments. Pillow, who had benefited from the better efforts of more successful generals, namely Winfield Scott in the Mexican War, would go on to demonstrate as a Confederate general in the Civil War that he was a soldier in name only. Santa Anna, who had gained a reputation fighting against rebels in Mexico, used that reputation to rise to the top of both the military and political ladders in the years before the midpoint of the 1800s. Like Pillow, any reputation that he had burnished in his salad days was to be proven unfounded when he was given greater responsibilities in later years. Specifically, he was earmarked for infamy for his disastrous direction of the main Mexican efforts in both the War of Texas Independence and the Mexican–American War. In these two conflicts, Santa Anna proved that he was truly out of his depth as a strategist and operational-level commander, leaving Mexico greatly diminished in territory and in the lives of its defenders.

A healthy ego is essential to maintaining confidence in a crisis. However, for Beatty, Pillow and Santa Anna, their egos went unchecked, and all three men demonstrated an inability to be self-aware enough to recognize their shortcomings as commanders. They revelled in their fame and went to war with levels of confidence out of proportion to their abilities. They lived the military equivalent of the tale of the emperor's new clothes and thousands of soldiers and sailors paid the price for their fraudulence.

THE CLUELESS: CONRAD VON HÖTZENDORF, LEWIS H. BRERETON AND GEORGE A. CUSTER

Surely, one of the characteristics of the great commanders is a keen situational awareness grounded in the reality of their circumstances. This includes not just an understanding of the environment in which they are operating, but an ability to anticipate and overcome constraints to operations, as well as a broad sense of the capabilities of their forces and how to apply those capabilities most effectively to achieve victory. At the same time, the great commanders seek out as much information as possible on the capabilities of their enemy. While this information is bound to be less than perfect or complete, 'know your enemy' is a time-honoured battlefield maxim for good reason. In this section, however, we have identified three commanders whose common claim to ignominy is that they were, in effect, the antithesis of the situationally aware commander. Wilfully blind to the potential risks of their operations, heedless of the capabilities of their own forces (usually overestimating them) and failing to know their enemy (usually underestimating it), these commanders led their forces to disaster or repeated disasters. For this reason, we are calling Franz Conrad von Hötzendorf, Lewis Brereton and George A. Custer the Clueless.

As Mark Grotelueschen and Derek Varble describe him in their chapter, Conrad seems to have been something of a Renaissance man of cluelessness on both strategic and operational levels. As chief of staff of the Austro-Hungarian Army from 1907, he spent the next seven years lobbying vigorously for war against Serbia, Italy, Russia, Montenegro and Romania, arguing, oddly, that such a war was necessary to the survival of Austria–Hungary. While Conrad's conviction that the Dual Monarchy must wage war against essentially all of its neighbours save Germany was strategically suspect to say the least, his confidence that he could prosecute such a war successfully with the ramshackle army under his command was an even more remarkable display of his lack of awareness. When the war he so eagerly sought finally came in August 1914, Conrad was unprepared for the realities of the conflict. Obsessed with punishing Serbia, he refused to acknowledge, and failed to plan for, the possibility of Russia entering the war, leading him to deploy the bulk of his forces against the former. When the latter did indeed join the war, the now-panicked Conrad ordered a hasty redeployment to the Russian front that left the fragile rail system hopelessly snarled and played no small role in disastrous defeats suffered by the Austro-Hungarian Army in 1914. Conrad's almost sublime cluelessness in the early days of the conflict essentially crippled the Dual Monarchy for the duration of the First World War.

John Abbatiello's chapter on Lewis Brereton describes a different kind of cluelessness. After a chequered pre-war career, Brereton was in command of the u.s. Army Air Force in the Philippines when it was almost completely destroyed on the ground by the Japanese on 8 December 1941. Nevertheless, Brereton continued to move onwards and upwards to preside over other disasters. In 1943 Brereton commanded the disastrous air raid on the Ploesti oil fields in Romania, in which roughly one-third of the attacking force was lost after inflicting minimal damage to Axis oil production. After the Allied landings in Normandy, Brereton's aircraft were responsible for bombing u.s. forces in July 1944, resulting in nearly five hundred casualties. And finally, appointed commander of the First Allied Airborne Army, Brereton oversaw the disastrous Arnhem operation. While Abbatiello argues that Brereton deserves a place in the pantheon of worst commanders in history simply on the basis of being in command during these four disasters, one can also conclude that Brereton was the epitome of the blinkered 'company man', carrying out orders even when confronted with circumstances that called for reconsideration or modification of those orders. Thus, while Abbatiello does not fault him for doing so, the fact is that Brereton dithered for a full day after the Japanese attack on Pearl Harbor waiting for word from MacArthur, rather than adjusting to the opening of hostilities by at least taking measures to protect his aircraft and crews. Nor does Brereton seem to have raised any concerns about the riskier aspects of the Ploesti and Arnhem operations. He simply carried them out, to their disastrous conclusions. At the same time, this may perhaps explain why he continued to rise to higher positions of command despite his abysmal record: unlike noisy troublemakers such as Patton, Brereton could be counted on to adhere to orders, apparently untroubled by independent thought or initiative even when circumstances demanded.

For George A. Custer, lack of initiative was never a problem. On the contrary, as David Mills explains in his chapter, the essence of Custer's cluelessness as a commander stemmed from initiative that bordered on disobedience at times, aggression to the point of recklessness, and a lack of interest in mastering the details of the military profession. During the American Civil War, Custer had been able to rise to the rank of major general at the age of 24 due to his heedless personal courage, single-minded pursuit of the offensive, and flair for self-promotion, but as Mills notes, while such audacity may have served Custer well, his command tended to suffer disproportionally higher casualties than other units. After a mostly lacklustre post-war career spent serving in drab frontier posts, Custer saw an opportunity to regain his wartime fame in 1876, when his regiment was ordered to take part in an operation against a large confederation of Native American tribes in Montana. Reckless to a fault as always, Custer stuck to his usual tactic of ordering an immediate attack on the Native American encampment, ignoring orders to wait for the rest of the army to catch up, failing to study the terrain, and ignoring warnings from his scouts that he was vastly outnumbered. As a result, his particular brand of aggressive cluelessness led to his demise, along with all of the men under his immediate command, at the Battle of Little Bighorn.

POLITICIANS: CRASSUS, NIKIAS, RAYMOND VI

As Clausewitz famously averred, 'war is a continuation of politics by other means', and the great military leaders in history have also been astute politicians. Eisenhower stands out as an example of a political general in the best sense of the term. He is not remembered as a great commander for his triumphs on the battlefield so much as for his extraordinary political skill in successfully formulating grand strategy and directing the complex Allied coalition against Nazi Germany. In the worst sense of the term, political generals may be ambitious leaders whose actions on the battlefield are motivated by a selfish desire to parlay victory into political power, or they may be incompetents who are thrust into positions of military leadership due to political power or influence. In other words, political generals are great military leaders when they are generals first and politicians second, and in the case of the worst military leaders, the inverse is true: they are politicians first and generals second. With this distinction in mind, we have placed Marcus Licinius Crassus, Nikias and Raymond VI, Count of Toulouse, into a category called Politicians.

The Roman general Crassus, the subject of Gregory Hospodor's chapter, has been regarded as a sort of paragon of military ineptitude since ancient times due to his spectacular defeat by the Parthians at the Battle of Carrhae in 53 BCE. Indeed, Plutarch included a biography of Crassus in his *Lives* as a sort of cautionary tale, blaming the defeat on his personal moral shortcomings, especially greed. In Hospodor's chapter, however, Crassus is shown to have been a reasonably successful member of the patrician class, whose greatest military achievement was suppressing the Spartacus slave revolt. While he did possess great wealth and devoted much time and effort to acquiring more, he was not motivated by greed so much as by political ambition. As Hospodor points out, it was standard practice for patricians like Crassus to purchase patronage networks, and then use those networks to enhance their political standing. Nevertheless, Crassus remained in the second tier of Roman leadership despite his efforts, which left him increasingly frustrated. Desperate for a fresh battlefield triumph to realize his dream of joining the top echelon of Roman leadership, Crassus secured the governorship of Syria in order to use it as a staging point for a campaign against the Parthians. More concerned with improving his personal political prospects than with conducting a sound campaign, Crassus led his army to disaster.

Like Crassus, Nikias of Athens achieved notoriety in the ancient world for his military failure, which was first described by Thucydides and then by Plutarch. As James Tucci describes in his chapter, Nikias, as a member of the Athenian elite, was expected to be both a political and a military leader, but he seems to have had little aptitude or desire for either. Despite some minor victories against allies of Sparta in the Peloponnesian War, the habitually cautious Nikias found himself politically and militarily outclassed by more audacious and charismatic rivals, and his caution came to be ridiculed as cowardice. This, according to Tucci, left Nikias with a habitual fear of what the Athenian public thought of him, with disastrous consequences. The timid Nikias not only failed to talk the Athenian assembly out of launching a massive expedition to Sicily in order to attack Sparta's ally Syracuse, but, to his horror, he was appointed to command the expedition. Nikias duly led the subsequent campaign, but in such a desultory manner that his command was essentially wiped out. As Tucci concludes, the failure of the Sicilian expedition was one of the leading causes of the downfall of Athens, for which Nikias bears the lion's share of blame. As a political leader in a democracy, he failed to persuade his fellow citizens of the folly of the expedition, and as a military commander, his ineptitude doomed the expedition to defeat.

Finally, Laurence Marvin recounts the life of Raymond vi, who came into his position of political and military leadership through inheritance as the Count of Toulouse. Despite the impressive-sounding title, however, Marvin points out that in the complex environment of medieval France, the ability of nobles to rule effectively over their domains depended on their personal qualities, and Raymond seems to have been singularly lacking in energy, judgement and courage, both physical and moral. Caught up in the religious and political conflicts of the thirteenth century, Raymond made the mistake of antagonizing the papacy, with the result that he was excommunicated and attacked by a crusading army determined to wipe out the Cathars, a heretical sect that was prevalent in his domain. During this losing conflict, known as the Albigensian Crusade, Raymond displayed a remarkable 'tin ear' politically as he alternated between defying the

Church and supporting the crusade against the heretics, in addition to military incompetence and a proclivity for embarrassing displays of physical cowardice. As Marvin sums up his assessment of Raymond, 'In an era when political and military leadership were intertwined and loyalty was often given to a personality rather than an institution or state, he lacked the charisma to inspire and the ability to defend his lands while remaining in the good graces of the Church.'

BUNGLERS: NOGI MARESUKE, ROMANUS IV AND GARNET WOLSELEY

To be a bungler is perhaps the least offensive indictment made in this volume. Making mistakes is standard human practice. As everyone can attest, a most common response to any self-made error is the ubiquitous defence, 'well, I'm only human.' Yet, as commonplace as missteps are to human nature, war magnifies all faults. Blundering commanders may survive to contemplate their failures in battle, but it is a certainty that many of those whose lives are entrusted to their care will not be so fortunate. The commanders examined in our section devoted to bunglers, Nogi Maresuke, Garnet Wolseley and Romanus IV, were not necessarily unsuccessful generals. In fact, Nogi and Wolseley enjoyed reverence well after their demise. Nonetheless, to our contributors, they all failed to acquit themselves in a manner that was befitting of the enormous responsibilities they shouldered. Specifically, when subjected to scrutiny, these three men mismanaged their forces and courted disaster through their ineptitude. They had advantages and opportunities that could have been exploited to far greater gain, but these commanders were to varying degrees incompetent.

Nogi Maresuke was a commander revered more than reviled by his contemporaries. Furthermore, his career did not end in failure. Yet, Danny Orbach makes a strong case that Nogi was operating beyond his abilities and was a poor student of war. While his efforts in besieging Port Arthur during the Russo-Japanese War were crowned with victory, the operation was hardly a study in efficiency. Nogi himself was astounded by the exceedingly high number of lives he sacrificed to achieve his objective. In many regards, he might have fit well in our list of Frauds, based upon his contemporaries' misplaced confidence in his abilities as a field commander and his inability to justify that confidence. As Orbach argues, the misplaced reverence for Nogi's ability exacerbated the problems evident in his poor management of the siege. Rather than be held to account for his bungling, he was hailed for his martial ardour. So, without scrutiny, Nogi muddled through to victory, and his soldiers paid for his incompetence with their lives. As noted earlier, victory and defeat are not always the measure of a successful commander, nor do they provide a litmus test for bunglers.

Andrew Holt's discussion of the Byzantine emperor Romanus IV Diogenes is perhaps the most obvious or least controversial inclusion in a chapter devoted to bunglers. With his focus on Romanus's defeat at the Battle of Manzikert, Holt illuminates the failings of neglect and mismanagement befitting someone labelled a bungling commander. While he inherited an empire in decline, Romanus failed to take vital initiatives that might have staved off military disaster. As Holt argues, he was oblivious to the state of relations with the Turkish Sultan Alp Arslan and failed to maintain situational awareness of strategic-level developments involving his rival. When Romanus went to war, he stumbled into a fight he was not prepared to win. His failures could just as well have landed him in our collection of clueless commanders, but his maladministration of the resources of an empire and the prerogatives of an emperor makes him a fitting inclusion in a list of bunglers.

Similar to Nogi, Wolseley's inclusion on our list of bunglers requires a more nuanced appreciation of generalship than most of the other studies in this project. Joseph Moretz takes particular care to detail the many layers of effort for which Wolseley was responsible in the Nile expedition to relieve the siege of Khartoum (March 1884–January 1885). Unlike the matter of Romanus, Wolseley does not stand out in military history as a failure. He was well regarded in his time and undoubtedly can claim admirers to this day. However, moving beyond the accolades bestowed upon him by his contemporaries, there is the matter of his last campaign. His part in the failure to rescue Major General Charles Gordon was a sour note on which to end his military career. As Moretz describes, the failures of Wolseley were manifest and to him must be afforded the larger share of blame in the failed operation, insofar as the plan adopted and the force organized were the products of his hands. That he also served as the expedition's commanding general only emphasizes his outsized role and responsibility in the tragedy that followed. In the last instance of his generalship, muddling through failed to save Gordon and those trapped in Khartoum.

SO WHAT?

The chapters that comprise this book are neither synopses of their subjects' lives nor attempts at balanced accounts of what our contributors consider to be history's worst commanders. This is an exercise in subjective history. If the reader desires balance or completeness in the details of the lives of the leaders depicted in this book, then where available, more comprehensive biographies should be consulted. If biographies are not available, then the reader should look into as many campaign and battle histories as can be found detailing the plans and decisions of those commanders that stimulate their curiosity. This project represents what our historians have made of their inquiries into such sources, and upon the request of the editors, they have attempted to craft arguments explaining why these were the worst military leaders in history. While the editors have collected these articles into a single volume, ultimately it still consists of highly personal evaluations of ineffective command.

These essays are not intended to serve as the definitive list of history's worst commanders. Any student of military history is bound to have their own opinion about who did well and who did not when it came to facing the ultimate test. In this sense, the project's highest aim could only be to initiate discussion about the qualities of bad commanders. If this book prompts its readers to scrutinize other military leaders for the casualties they suffered or the inefficiencies of their efforts in the pursuit of victory, it will have achieved a great objective. While this project grew out of informal conversations, it has at its heart the serious business of applying critical analysis to the role of individuals entrusted with the weightiest of matters. As noted by Keegan, the study of battles is a matter for historians, and miscarriages are as much a part of what transpires on the battlefield as is success. It is no less important for students of the past to understand the myriad faces of ineptitude and be able to affix blame as it is for them to know who deserves credit for jobs well done. As untoward as it may seem, neglecting criticism leaves the study of military leadership a quest for only half-truths.

PART I

CRIMINALS

I

ROMAN FEDOROVICH VON UNGERN-STERNBERG

John M. Jennings

The Russian Civil War of 1918–22 was in several respects a sequel to the First World War. Its sheer physical scope was enormous: the battlefronts ranged across a vast area from Archangel in the north to Crimea in the south, from the gates of Warsaw in the west to Vladivostok in the east. The pitiless, fratricidal struggle between Reds and Whites claimed the lives of millions of combatants and civilians. Moreover, it was a conflict with significant international ramifications, as a multitude of foreign powers dispatched armed forces to Russia to aid the Whites, while the Reds for their part attempted to foment a world communist revolution. In this monumental conflict, inept military leadership played no small role in the defeat of the Whites. Lacking the effective command and control structure of the Red Army, the White military was essentially a hotchpotch of local armies led by a motley and ill-disciplined assortment of commanders who often behaved more like warlords than responsible military professionals. Arguably, the worst of these was Roman Fedorovich von Ungern-Sternberg, who led a reckless and ill-fated invasion of the Soviet Union in 1920.

Ungern, a junior officer during the First World War, was thrust by the circumstances of the Russian Civil War into the leadership of a band of White fighters operating along a section of the Trans-Siberian Railroad. A fanatical monarchist, he then launched a foray into neighbouring Mongolia, which he planned to use as the springboard for an offensive to destroy the Soviet Union and restore nothing less than the Russian, Chinese and Mongol empires. Ungern's pursuit of this grandiose military fantasy with a pitifully small army, as

Roman Fedorovich von Ungern-Sternberg under interrogation by the Soviet army, September 1921.

well as his single-minded ferocity in carrying out the struggle against the Reds, which included the torture and murder of both real and imagined enemies, led his contemporaries to dub him the 'Mad Baron' and the 'Bloody Baron'. Despite a distinct lack of enthusiasm among the Mongols for his crusade, due largely to their revulsion at his cruelty, Ungern nevertheless proceeded to invade the Soviet Union in the summer of 1920, with predictably disastrous results. Ultimately his own troops, exasperated by defeat and Ungern's brutal leadership, mutinied and turned him over to the Reds, who duly shot him.

Roman Fedorovich von Ungern-Sternberg was born on 22 January 1886 into a world of aristocratic privilege, but his life was characterized by instability almost from the start. His parents, an Estonian noble and an Austrian baroness, separated in 1891 due to his father's idiosyncratic behaviour.[1] After being expelled from secondary school, Ungern began preparing for a career as a naval officer, but when the

Russo-Japanese War broke out in 1904, the impetuous youth volunteered for army service. Although the hostilities were winding down by the time he arrived at the front, the teenaged baron earned a medal for bravery and a promotion.[2]

After returning from the front, Ungern barely managed to graduate from military school in 1908, and as a junior officer he refused to follow the conventional path of service in an infantry regiment. Instead, in June 1908 he joined the First Argun Regiment of the Transbaikalian Cossacks, which was posted at Dauria station, a stop along the Trans-Siberian Railway.[3] The frontier posting appealed to Ungern, who was most at home on horseback in the wild, living the same rough life as the Cossacks under his command, but who was manifestly uncomfortable in the more socially polished and conventional environment inhabited by his fellow officers. As Baron Peter Wrangel, Ungern's commander during the First World War and a future leader of the Whites, described him:

> He was a man of queer contrasts. He had an original, penetrating mind, but at the same time an astonishing lack of culture, an extremely narrow outlook, the shyness of the savage, a foolish swagger, and an unbridled temper. He was very extravagant, though his means were exceptionally small.[4]

Heavy drinking apparently made Ungern even more hot-tempered and unpredictable, for during one drinking bout the enraged Baron struck a fellow officer, who responded by slashing him across the forehead with a sabre. Ungern was court-martialled and expelled from his regiment. He was subsequently dispatched to the western Mongolian town of Hovd, arriving there in February 1913 to assist with training the new army of Mongolia.[5]

A suzerain of the Qing Empire since the seventeenth century, Mongolia was able to achieve nominal independence in 1911 as Manchu rule in China collapsed. The titular leader of the newly independent Mongolia was the eighth Javzandamba Hutagt, who was believed to be a reincarnation of the Buddha. Despite a personal lifestyle that was far from ecclesiastic, as he was a drunkard and had become blind after contracting syphilis, the Hutagt was an astute politician.[6] In July 1911 he summoned the leaders of the aristocracy and clergy to a conference to discuss Mongolia's political future. Subsequently, a delegation was dispatched to St Petersburg with an appeal to Tsar Nicholas II for Russian aid.[7] Unfortunately for the Mongolian delegation, it arrived at a time when there was little enthusiasm for such a foreign policy adventure among the Tsar's officials and it was sent home largely empty-handed.[8]

Despite Russia's rebuff, the Mongolian revolution proceeded. On 4 December 1911 the Qing Resident in Urga, the capital, fled to the Russian consulate for protection after the demoralized Chinese garrison surrendered.[9] His escort was under the command of Grigorii M. Semenov, a junior officer of mixed Buriat Mongol–Cossack descent who had been posted to Urga with a small detachment of Cossacks to guard the Russian consulate.[10] Semenov, like Ungern, was a courageous junior officer, but was also constitutionally undisciplined and unpolished. Eventually the paths of these two officers crossed during the First World War, and their fortunes would become closely linked during the Russian Civil War.

Ungern's later stay in Hovd coincided with the high point of Tsarist Russian influence over Mongolian affairs. Military advisers like Ungern and Semenov helped to modernize the army, while civil advisers overhauled the finances and administrative structure of the new government. During this period Ungern steeped himself further in the language and culture of Mongolia, spending most of his free time alone in the wild on horseback or in consultations with Mongolian clerics, who apparently fostered his growing interest in mystical Buddhism.[11]

In the summer of 1914 Ungern was dispatched to Europe with the First Nerchinsk Cossack Regiment. His service on the Eastern Front from 1914 to 1916 was characterized by a combination of exceptional bravery in battle, which won him the St George's Cross, the highest medal for valour in the Imperial Russian Army, and wild behaviour away from the battlefront, most notoriously the drunken assault of a hotel porter who had refused his demand for a room. Although he received a light punishment of two months' confinement for that incident – his superiors noted in his favour that he had been injured five times in battle – such eccentricity ensured that the Baron would never rise above the rank of captain.[12]

In early 1917 Ungern's regiment was transferred to Persian Azerbaijan, where the Russian army was fighting against the Ottoman

Turks. By that time he had made the acquaintance of Semenov, who was also a captain in the Nerchinsk regiment. Ungern and Semenov had much in common: they were exceptionally courageous junior officers, as Semenov had also won the St George's Cross; they had both served in Mongolia; and both were keen students of Mongolian language and culture.[13]

In March 1917 Nicholas II abdicated, which must have horrified Ungern. Although the new Provisional Government pledged to continue fighting, army discipline began to deteriorate. As the Russian soldiers began to desert in ever-increasing numbers, Ungern recruited a detachment of volunteers from among the local inhabitants of Persian Azerbaijan, the Aisars, in an attempt to shame the Russians into staying at the front. Although the experiment with the Aisars failed, Semenov pursued the idea of recruiting non-Russian units. He contacted Buriat Mongol acquaintances in his native Transbaikalia (a region of Siberia to the east of Lake Baikal) to sound them out about organizing military detachments, and at the same time he broached the idea to the military chain of command.[14]

Semenov's proposal eventually was accepted by the War Ministry, which ordered him to Chita, the regional capital of Transbaikalia.[15] Ungern subsequently joined him, but they quickly learned that the authority of the Provisional Government was virtually non-existent, and that chaos reigned throughout the region. Although Semenov had begun to make enough headway through the myriad of local revolutionary committees to begin selecting volunteers by the end of September, the Bolshevik seizure of power in November 1917 ended that effort. Semenov and Ungern became fugitives and had to split up to evade arrest by the Soviet authorities.

They eventually reunited in late November at Dauria, a station on the Trans-Siberian Railway in Transbaikalia, where they discovered that the garrison consisted of one company of militia assigned to guard German and Turkish prisoners of war.[16] Asserting his dubious authority with the defunct Provisional Government, Semenov was able to gain tenuous control over the ill-disciplined garrison, aided by some of the prisoners of war, who were formed into a company of military police by Ungern. Semenov dispatched agents to Buriat and Cossack leaders in Transbaikalia with appeals for volunteers and horses, and he contacted General Dmitrii L. Khorvat, the chief administrator of the Chinese Eastern Railway, for assistance in forming a volunteer detachment to protect the region against encroachment by the Bolsheviks.[17]

With little immediate outside support forthcoming, on 18 December 1917 Semenov and a handful of Cossack junior officers and enlisted men moved eastward along the railway to Manchuria station. Finding the garrison there as unruly as the one at Dauria, Semenov decided to disarm and disperse it. Ordering the Baron to come with a train of empty freight cars, Semenov bluffed the Manchuria garrison into disarming by persuading the men that a fully armed battalion was on the way from Dauria. When Ungern and his 'battalion' of four other men arrived, the entire garrison was loaded into the empty freight cars and sent far away to the west. After this success, Semenov and Ungern disarmed and disbanded the Dauria garrison in the same way.[18]

Such activities were part of the emergence of the White movement, which was arising spontaneously across Russia in armed opposition to the depredations of the new Soviet regime, and in the chaotic conditions of the Civil War, previously insignificant figures like Semenov and Ungern could quickly rise to positions of prominence among the Whites. Indeed, by January 1918 Semenov had recruited five hundred volunteers for his unit, which was now known as the Special Manchurian Detachment (SMD). With this force, Semenov and Ungern were able to occupy more and more stations along the railway, further enhancing their power and authority. Semenov appointed Ungern as the military governor of Hailar, a small town on the Russian–Chinese border, but Ungern's efforts to establish order there met with widespread resistance from the garrison, which also had to be disarmed and dispersed.[19]

Moreover, the Allied powers, alarmed that a potential Soviet alliance with the Central Powers might decisively tip the wartime balance of power, had begun to support anti-Bolshevik leaders like Semenov. By February 1918 the British and the French were paying Semenov monthly instalments of cash to purchase arms and equipment.[20] Semenov's most significant foreign ally, though, was Japan. For expansionists in Japanese civil and military circles, the Russian Civil War presented an opportunity to detach Transbaikalia and Primorye (the Russian Maritime Territory), and Semenov seemed amenable to the idea of becoming the regional ruler under Japan's auspices. In October 1918 the SMD, which had reorganized and refitted with Japanese cash and equipment, and was supported in the field by Japanese troops, launched a major offensive northward into Transbaikalia and seized Chita.[21]

The capture of Chita was the pinnacle of Semenov's fortunes in the Civil War. The SMD did not undertake any further offensive operations, but instead remained in Transbaikalia and binged on criminality and drunken debauchery. Gangs of SMD thugs known as the *razvedkas* roamed the railway lines on armoured trains, terrorizing the local population with indiscriminate robberies, rapes and murders in the name of rooting out Red partisans.[22]

The degeneracy of the SMD started at the top with Semenov. He seems to have spent most of his time in Chita enriching himself with bribes and loot, and then drunkenly partying with his lackeys and many mistresses. Having achieved a measure of respectability when he was elected field ataman (chieftain) of the Transbaikalian Cossacks in June 1918, the inflated Semenov refused to subordinate himself to the White 'supreme ruler' Admiral Aleksandr Kolchak, whose regime was based in Omsk. The two eventually reconciled, but their dispute did irreparable harm to the White war effort.[23]

By the end of 1919 a Red Army counteroffensive had dislodged Kolchak's army from its foothold on the western slopes of the Ural Mountains and driven the Whites into a headlong retreat to the east. Kolchak himself was captured and shot by Soviet authorities in Irkutsk in February 1920, but not before appointing Semenov commander-in-chief of the White Far Eastern Army.[24] This proved to be a hollow gesture, as the Far Eastern Army consisted of Semenov's now militarily worthless detachment and the fleeing remnants of Kolchak's army. At the same time, Semenov faced mounting pressure from partisan units that were springing up all across Transbaikalia in anticipation of the Red Army's arrival. The fatal blow to Semenov came when the Japanese Army began to withdraw from Transbaikalia in the summer of 1920. When that process was completed in the autumn, the SMD collapsed. The remnants fled east to Primorye, where the Whites were preparing a last stand.[25]

In the meantime Ungern, who had moved back to Dauria from Hailar, was growing estranged from Semenov: in fact, the paths of the two had begun to diverge from around the time that Semenov established himself in Chita. Although the Baron remained Semenov's nominal subordinate and neither would admit publicly to a rift, Ungern was a 'loose cannon' by nature, while Semenov was utterly incapable of, and uninterested in, maintaining effective command and control over his subordinates.[26] Moreover, Ungern, whose personal asceticism had become even more pronounced during the Civil War, disapproved of the Ataman's corruption and debauched lifestyle. In particular, the notoriously antisemitic Ungern was disgusted with Semenov for having an open affair with a Jewish cabaret performer, 'Mashka' Sharaban. Ungern even named one of his horses 'Mashka' to show his disgust.[27]

Most importantly, while at Dauria the Baron managed to raise and equip a considerable detachment on his own. This unit, known as the Asiatic Cavalry Division (ACD), numbered approximately 1,500 men equipped with rifles, some machine guns, and four artillery pieces as of August 1920. The ACD was a polyglot melange of Russians, Cossacks, Buriat Mongols, Chinese and a small detachment of Japanese organized in units along national lines, but all under the command of Russian officers.[28] Recruits came from a number of sources: original adherents of Semenov and Ungern, leftovers from the failed attempt to create non-Russian national units, remnants of Kolchak's defeated army, desperado *razvedkas* from the SMD, as well as a large number of refugees and riff-raff intercepted and press-ganged into the Baron's service as they attempted to flee to China by rail.[29]

During his stay at Dauria, Ungern's already unstable personality became, if anything, even more manic. While known for his personal courage and honesty, he drove himself and his men with the same ruthless energy, and unlike Semenov, he enforced military discipline with the utmost brutality. For minor infractions, the most common punishment was a beating with a bamboo lash, while the death penalty was applied liberally for more serious infractions.[30]

At the same time, the Baron's fanaticism led him to carry out a campaign of extermination against anyone within his reach suspected of being a revolutionary, communist or otherwise. As a result, Ungern's Dauria became infamous as the worst of the White torture chambers, which was a considerable achievement in the brutal environment of the Civil War. This in turn attracted some of the most twisted sadists from among the Semenovites to join Ungern because of the seemingly limitless opportunities for torture and murder, such as the syphilitic Colonel Leonid Sipailov, a former petty railway official and *razvedka*. Sipailov's most spectacular atrocity was the bludgeoning and drowning of 31 hostages in Lake Baikal in January 1920, but he was also a serial rapist and murderer who took great pride in his nickname, 'the Strangler of Transbaikalia'.[31]

By the summer of 1920 it was clear that no matter how resolutely and cruelly Ungern carried on his personal crusade against the Reds, his position was becoming untenable because of the withdrawal of the Japanese Army and Semenov's collapse. Under the circumstances, withdrawal to Chinese territory, where Ungern's band would have been disarmed and interned, would have been the prudent course of action given its military insignificance and the looming White defeat. Nevertheless, in early August 1920 Ungern ordered his men to make preparations for the infinitely longer and more perilous march south-west towards Mongolia.[32]

Heightening the peril of such a move was uncertainty over their welcome because Semenov's ambitions had conveniently provided the Chinese government with a pretext to dispatch an army to Mongolia and reassert imperial China's traditional position as suzerain. In January 1919 Semenov travelled to Mongolia to sound out his political contacts there about establishing a pan-Mongolian empire. Encouraged by the response and by his Japanese military advisers, Semenov then sponsored two conferences of tribal leaders at Dauria and Chita in February. The Chita conference resulted in a far-fetched scheme to establish a Mongolian empire encompassing Mongolia, Transbaikalia and northern China. Semenov appealed to the Mongolian government to send representatives to the conferences, but the Hutagt and his advisers wisely refrained from entangling themselves in Semenov's chimera. Without the support of the Hutagt, the pan-Mongolian movement collapsed quickly, but not before Semenov threatened to march on Urga in retaliation. In response, the Hutagt's government then appealed for Chinese troops to defend Mongolia from Semenov.[33]

The price for the dispatch of Chinese forces was the abolition of autonomy and the full return of imperial China's political and economic privileges. The Hutagt's advisers were divided on the matter, leading to lengthy and inconclusive negotiations until the arrival in Urga of a regiment of Chinese troops on 27 September 1919, with two more on the way. This display of force intimidated the Mongolian leadership into petitioning the Chinese government to abrogate autonomy in November 1919, and on 1 January 1920 the Hutagt was compelled to bow before a photo of the Chinese president and surrender his seal of office.[34] The Chinese garrison of Urga, now numbering several thousand troops, was under the command of two rival warlords, Gao Zaitian and Chu Qixiang. Over the succeeding months, military discipline began to unravel and Chinese rule became increasingly arbitrary and harsh. The demoralized Chinese soldiers engaged in plundering, raping and murdering the local population, especially the Mongolians and Russians. The two commanders in Urga set the tone for their subordinates: the 'particularly ignorant and uncouth' Gao specialized in extortion, while Chu contented himself with his harem of beautiful young males.[35]

Although Ungern's decision was met with some consternation by the men, as the 'Baron did not inform anyone about his future plans – such indeed was his personal character', the ACD set off at the end of August, accompanied by a long supply column that included a number of carts filled with gifts for Ungern's contacts in Mongolia.[36] After skirting along the border throughout September, the ACD finally crossed into Mongolia on 1 October 1920 and marched roughly south-west across a sparsely populated region of rugged steppe land intersected by a number of rivers. The rough terrain slowed the progress of the detachment, and as autumn set in the men, who were still clad in their summer uniforms, suffered from effects of the increasingly cold weather. At the end of October the ACD reached the outskirts of Urga.[37] At that point Ungern decided to launch an assault immediately on the capital, which was being heavily fortified by the Chinese garrison.

According to Canfield F. Smith, Ungern's decision to march into Mongolia and attack Urga was at least to some extent influenced by his peculiar ideology. In addition to his fervent devotion to the principle of absolute monarchy, Ungern was a 'true believer' in the pan-Mongolian movement. He embraced the Mongolian lifestyle, spent on horseback in the wild steppe land, as well as the language, customs and culture, especially the esoteric Buddhism of the lamas with whom he constantly consorted. It is likely that he was introduced to the pan-Mongolian idea by Semenov, but unlike the fickle Ataman, who quickly dropped it for a new political adventure, Ungern remained faithful to the cause.[38] Hearing nothing further from Semenov, but receiving reports on the situation in Urga, the impetuous Ungern set off to liberate the Hutagt's capital from the hands of Chinese republican troops, which would be the first step towards realizing the pan-Mongolian ideal.[39]

Ungern's men arrived at the outskirts of Urga on the night of 26/27 October and immediately commenced the assault, with one force striking from the east and Ungern himself leading an assault from the north. The Chinese troops, however, not only vastly outnumbered the ACD, but were much better equipped with machine guns and artillery, and were well entrenched. In a confused and often savage battle of Russian attacks and Chinese counter-attacks between the trench lines, the ACD suffered heavy casualties and lost most of its artillery, forcing Ungern to call off the attack. He retreated to a position half a day's march northeast of Urga, where the detachment halted and regrouped. On 2 November Ungern renewed the assault, but in three days of frenzied fighting the Chinese again repulsed the ACD. On 5 November Ungern ordered a general retreat back to the position northeast of Urga.[40]

Following the defeat at Urga, the ACD was in desperate straits. Ungern had lost many of his best men and a great deal of equipment. With winter setting in, the sharp cold was taking its toll on the lightly clad army.[41] The mounting sense of desperation did not improve Ungern's disposition, and one of his subordinates, Lieutenant Chernov, wound up bearing the brunt of the Baron's savage temper at that time. Chernov, who was a favourite of Ungern, had been put in command of the medical unit during the battle for Urga. As he was accompanying the wounded to the rear, Chernov 'perpetrated absolutely unprintable things' against the nurses, most of whom were the wives of other officers, looted Mongolian and Chinese settlements along the way, and ordered the poisoning of all of the wounded because he considered them to be a nuisance.[42] When Chernov returned to the encampment, Ungern found out about his misdeeds and ordered him to be flogged and then burnt at the stake. As the execution was carried out many of Chernov's comrades looked on, at first with grim amusement as he was not terribly popular in the detachment, but then with growing horror as he slowly roasted to death.[43]

As the winter progressed, the situation in Urga was also deteriorating. Because the Chinese had failed to pursue Ungern's exhausted and beaten army in November, the garrison had to remain in a constant state of alert in case he should return, which frayed the nerves of the soldiers. As supplies began to run short and opportunities for plunder dwindled, the morale of the Chinese troops sank even lower. Then, in late 1920, the Chinese authorities in Urga ordered the Hutagt's arrest. Although this was an attempt to 'shock and awe' the residents of Urga into submission, the incarceration of the revered holy man only aroused the disgust and anger of the Mongolians. Eventually, the Hutagt was permitted to return to his palace, but he remained under heavy Chinese guard.[44]

Ungern, meanwhile, had not given up on Urga. He spent much of his time reconnoitring, even personally entering and leaving the heavily guarded city in broad daylight before the surprised Chinese soldiers could react. He further unnerved the Chinese by ordering his men to build many huge campfires in the hills around Urga, which conveyed the impression that his army was much larger than it was in reality, and by instructing his agents in Urga to spread rumours that he was endowed with miraculous powers, including immunity to bullets.[45] Ungern also began to benefit from Chinese heavy-handedness as numbers of Mongolians, angered at the treatment of the Hutagt, flocked to his encampment and boosted the unit's complement to 1,400 men by the end of January 1921.[46]

With the ACD thus reinforced, Ungern decided to launch another assault on Urga on 1 February 1921. Once again there was fierce fighting, but this time the already shaky discipline of the Chinese garrison broke on 3 February. As panic set in, the garrison disintegrated and fled the city. At first the fleeing remnants set off to the north, where they were pursued and cut down by the hundreds in the crossfire of Ungern's machine guns. From there, the desperate Chinese turned west and south to skirt around Urga, then east towards Chinese territory, with Ungern's men in hot pursuit all along the way. In the end, only some of the cavalrymen made it back to China. On the afternoon of 3 February, Ungern entered Urga in triumph.[47]

After enduring months of Chinese oppression, the residents of Urga at first welcomed Ungern as a liberator, but he quickly wore out his welcome by unleashing a reign of terror. The men of the ACD, crazed by the months of privation, bloodlust and looted liquor, went on a rampage of pillage, rape and murder. In a frenzied state himself, Ungern ordered a pogrom against Jews and communists: on the nights of 4–5 February the Baron's men dragged some 37 men, women and children out of their homes and hacked them to death with sabres. Urga's tiny Jewish community essentially ceased to exist.[48]

Once this initial bloodletting was accomplished, Ungern set about refitting and re-equipping with captured Chinese supplies, and then expanding his army. Initially he did this in two ways. First, he dispatched punitive detachments led by some of his worst henchmen to force other White bands in Mongolia to submit to his control.[49] Second, he ordered a call-up of White refugees in Urga and elsewhere in Mongolia. While these actions did increase the size of the detachment, they also began to cause strains between the Baron and his longtime followers on one hand, and the new recruits on the other. Ungern was openly suspicious of the political reliability of the draftees, while many of the draftees thought that Ungern was a maniac surrounded by a gang of brigands and murderers.[50]

The conquest of Urga also made it possible for Ungern to start realizing his dream of creating a vast empire that would unite the peoples of Central Asia from the Caspian Sea to the Amur River under the absolute theocracy of the Hutagt. As Ungern wrote, only then might it be possible to carry the pro-monarchical crusade to Europe:

> It would be impossible to aspire for the general restoration of European Monarchs, owing to the deterioration of the public mind and science, and the influence of socialism, which has driven the nations out of their minds. We are left no margin at present but to begin our work in the Central Empire and the tribes touching it on the boundaries of the Caspian Sea, after which the problem of restoring the Monarchy of Russia could be ventured upon, but on the condition that the Russian people would regain their common sense, otherwise they would be subjected to acknowledge such necessity. I have no personal ambitions in life and am ready to die for my devotion to Monarchy, no matter whether it be realized in my native country or anywhere else.[51]

The first step was completed on 15 March 1921, when the Hutagt was enthroned as Great Khan of the Mongols at a ceremony in Urga, followed by the inauguration of an autonomous government.[52] As was the case with Semenov's abortive pan-Mongolian venture, the Hutagt's participation was vital to the realization of Ungern's grand vision. But like Semenov before him, Ungern saw his dream immediately evaporate when the Hutagt and his advisers showed no enthusiasm for the idea. Innately cautious, the Mongolian leaders temporized as long as their unwelcome guests remained in Urga, but they had no wish to bind themselves to Ungern, who was sure to be expelled either by the Chinese or the Soviets. Accordingly, in April 1921 the Hutagt sent a letter to Beijing in which he disavowed Ungern's actions and requested a restoration of the old relationship, namely Mongolian autonomy under China's suzerainty.[53]

The Hutagt's rejection not only ended Ungern's dream of creating an empire in Central Asia, but it meant that Mongolian material aid would only be given grudgingly. Without the active support and participation of the Mongolians, the Baron's army would not be able to sustain itself for long. Therefore, over the next several months, Ungern looked for a patron outside of Mongolia, but his options were limited. One possibility was Japan, which had supported Semenov so lavishly. Although the Soviets were convinced that Ungern was a Japanese agent, Japanese Army intelligence officers were extremely sceptical of the viability and utility of the Baron's tiny army. Moreover, his obstinacy and unpredictability compared unfavourably to the pliable Semenov.[54]

If his surviving correspondence is any indication, Ungern most assiduously courted a number of northern Chinese warlords for support. This necessitated, from the Baron's point of view, considerable contortions of the truth regarding the attack on Urga, in which he had just slaughtered several thousand Chinese troops. When none of the warlords showed any interest in his crusade to restore absolute monarchy, Ungern's desperation intensified. At one point he even proposed to install Zhang Zuolin, the warlord ruler of Manchuria, as the khan of an empire that would unite Manchuria and Central Asia. Zhang, who was busily engaged against other warlords in the struggle for domination over China itself, was not interested in Mongolia and ignored the offer.[55]

As his sense of frustration grew, Ungern became even more arbitrary and prone to vicious outbursts of temper, while the occupation of Urga degenerated into violence and chaos. The psychotic Colonel Sipailov, who was appointed the commandant of Urga, was able to take advantage of the Baron's pathological suspicions to create an atmosphere of terror among the White refugees, in which a single word of denunciation could lead to death. In this way, Sipailov and his henchmen were able to loot, rape, torture and murder at will. The looting was especially profitable, as Ungern awarded the looter with one-third of the booty as a commission. For example, Sipailov reportedly received a sizeable bounty for appropriating the property of a wealthy and well-known merchant named Noskov. After arresting Noskov on false charges, Sipailov tortured the merchant for eight days until he became a mindless 'sack of bones'. When the torturers were finished, they threw Noskov's corpse out on the garbage heap.[56]

The lawless savagery of his detachment further soured Ungern's relations with the Mongolians. For their part, the Mongolians could not understand why the Russians were turning on one another with such brutality, and they were disgusted by the wanton killings being carried out by the Baron's men. Furthermore, as Ungern was increasingly resorting to forced requisitions to keep his army supplied, his demands were straining Mongolia's already limited economy. Especially difficult for the Mongolians to bear was the requisitioning of their horses, which were still the principal measure of wealth. Finally, with few Mongolians enlisting voluntarily, a general mobilization of the male population began, 'which amounted to a simple seizing of the men who had come to Urga to pray at the holy shrines or on business'.[57]

By the spring of 1921 Ungern was facing a grim future. He could not remain in Mongolia much longer. Not only was he wearing out his welcome among the Mongolian population, but the Soviet regime, which had been preoccupied with tying up loose ends of the Civil War elsewhere, was now able to concentrate on his destruction. In order to accomplish this, there was a significant build-up of Red Army forces in the region, and at the same time the Soviets, after much hesitation, began to provide military and political support to the partisans of the nascent Mongolian Communist Party.[58] If Ungern stayed in Urga, it would only be a matter of time before this powerful force overwhelmed his tiny army.

Perhaps the most logical course of action would have been to march east, cross into Chinese territory for a brief internment, and then move on to Primorye to join the last stand of the Whites there. However, Ungern likely had two objections to doing so. First, with the blood of so many Chinese troops on his hands, it would be difficult to predict how he would be received by the authorities in China. Second, Ungern, to whom the cause of monarchy was sacred, did not want his unit contaminated by association with other White forces, even at the end.[59]

As always the Baron's instinct was to attack. On 8 May he left Urga quietly with half of the ACD, while the other half departed on 9 May.

Both columns headed north, but Ungern's intentions were not made clear until 21 May 1921, when he issued his Order No. 15 to all of the White detachments in Mongolia and Siberia, calling for a general offensive against the Soviet Union. In the first section of this bizarre document, Ungern spelled out his political aim, which was nothing less than the restoration of the Romanov Dynasty. His operational plan, based on wishful thinking to say the least, called for the ACD and the other units in Mongolia to advance northward independently, supported by Ataman Semenov's army in the Ussuri region. The operation was to be a strictly Russian affair, for it was not possible to 'depend on our foreign allies, who are enduring a similar revolutionary struggle'. Rather, since 'war is fed on war', Ungern directed the commanders of the White detachments to mobilize the local inhabitants and to confiscate supplies along the way.[60]

In this final struggle against 'the criminal destroyers and defilers of Russia', there was to be no pity. Ungern ordered individual detachment commanders not to get in the way of pogroms against communists in the liberated areas, where 'commissars, communists and Jews' were to be killed, 'along with their families'. Detachment commanders were given free rein to apply the death penalty, and indeed Ungern ordered them to show no mercy: 'the old basis of justice is changed. It is not "truth and mercy". Now it must be "truth and ruthless severity" . . . remember that evil is to be destroyed forever.'[61]

On 30 May 1921 Ungern ordered the advance to begin in accordance with Order No. 15. While the Baron and his troops moved into Transbaikalia via the border towns of Kyakhta and Troitskosavsk, a second column followed the west bank of the Selenga River into the same region, and the other White detachments moved north from their respective positions across Mongolia. After less than two weeks of bitter fighting, though, it was clear that the offensive was a disastrous failure. Not only were the Whites facing a vastly superior foe, namely the powerful Red Fifth Army and numerous partisan detachments, but Ungern's decision to divide his already meagre forces simply made it easier for the Soviets to defeat them piecemeal. Ungern himself was defeated at Kyakhta on 9 June and forced into a hasty retreat, losing all of his artillery and most of his machine guns. On 29 June he linked up again with the second column, which had fared slightly better, and they encamped along the Selenga between Mongolia and Transbaikalia.[62]

Over the next few weeks the morale of the ACD eroded precipi-
tously as defeat, harsh living conditions in the camp, Red harassment
and Ungern's arbitrary cruelty took their toll. The most disgruntled
were the recently mobilized officers, who bore the brunt of not only
the combat, but the Baron's ferocious outbursts of anger, which often
resulted in beatings and occasionally in summary executions. To make
matters worse, on 15 July the men of the detachment received another
blow when news reached them that the Red Army, with a small
Mongolian partisan force, had taken Urga. This meant that their retreat
to the south was cut off, and many of the men worried about their
families, whom they had left behind there.[63]

Ignoring the growing discontent in the ranks, Ungern launched
another offensive northward on 17 July. On 30 July the detachment
reached the northern shore of Gusinoe Ozero (Goose Lake), southeast
of Lake Baikal, despite heavy losses in desperate, no-quarter combat.
But on receiving information that Red troops were massing between
himself and Lake Baikal, the Baron decided to retreat southwest back
into Mongolia. While that line of retreat made it possible to avoid the
bulk of the Red Army, it meant that the already exhausted and hungry
men had to cross rugged terrain of mountains, rivers and steppe.
Desertions and acts of insubordination increased along the march.
Finally, when word got out that Ungern was planning to march the
men across the Gobi Desert and enter the service of the Dalai Lama
in Tibet, a group of recently mobilized officers began plotting to mutiny
and assassinate the Baron. On 19 August 1921 the mutinous officers
struck. While a number of his most hated subordinates were killed
during the uprising, Ungern managed to escape into the night after
his tent was peppered with machine gun fire.[64] The next day Ungern
made his way to the nearby camp of his Mongolian auxiliaries and
ordered them to arrest the mutineers. The commander of the Mongolian
detachment agreed to do so, but instead he and his men grabbed the
Baron, tied him up, and turned him over to Red partisans.[65] From there,
Ungern was taken to Novonikolayevsk (now Novosibirsk), where he
was briefly interrogated by the local Soviet authorities. After that he
was tried and shot on the same day, 15 September 1921.[66]

Despite its grotesque trappings, resembling the plot of a Joseph
Conrad novel, Ungern's campaign proved to be something more than
a militarily insignificant tangent of the Russian Civil War as it had a
significant impact on the geopolitical terrain of northeast Asia. As

Canfield F. Smith argues, while his attack on Mongolia was successful in the sense that he eliminated the Chinese military presence, it merely created a vacuum and provided a convenient pretext for the Red Army to fill that vacuum by occupying Mongolia in pursuit of Ungern's detachment. As a result, not only did Ungern fail abjectly in realizing his dream of destroying the Soviet Union and restoring imperial rule in Russia and Asia, but ironically, his atrocity-laden and implausible campaign wound up facilitating the expansion of world socialism as the People's Republic of Mongolia became the first Soviet satellite in 1924.[67] Therefore, Roman F. von Ungern-Sternberg has richly earned a prominent place among the worst military leaders in history.

2

NATHAN BEDFORD FORREST

Christopher M. Rein

Recently published military histories of the American Civil War continue to extol the virtues of Nathan Bedford Forrest with such quotes as 'arguably the most capable cavalryman produced by the war', and 'undoubtedly the most outstanding combat commander in the war', perpetuating a myth of military effectiveness that has made the southern cavalryman an enduring icon of the Lost Cause.[1] One of his biographers, Andrew Lytle, even believes the South could have won the war had Confederate President Jefferson Davis only recognized Forrest's 'genius'.[2] And Robert E. Lee, upon being asked to name the 'greatest soldier' the war produced, is alleged to have responded, 'A man I have never seen, sir. His name is Forrest.'[3] Despite detailed re-evaluations by Brian Steel Wills, David A. Powell and others, Forrest remains overrated militarily, especially his operations during the 1864 campaign season, when he was unable to adapt to a focused strategy designed to prevent crippling raids on the Union logistic infrastructure that had highlighted his earlier service.

By examining Forrest's later military career, including his inability to work effectively with his peers and the devolution of his military command into a loosely organized society of armed raiders, it is possible to offer a reappraisal of Forrest's military career that will overturn the false narrative that still dominates both popular and scholarly histories of the war.[4] Despite whatever untutored tactical genius and magnetic personal attraction Forrest may have possessed, he undoubtedly failed at the operational and strategic levels of war, and his brutal treatment of his captured opponents, coupled with the damaging legacy he left for future military leaders, make him a strong contender for the title of worst military commander ever.

An analysis of Forrest's military career brings to light a familiar dilemma for those responsible for assessing and selecting military talent. Certainly, competence is an essential attribute for higher command: officers must have mastered their craft and have demonstrated the professional ability to successfully lead and accomplish assigned tasks. Raw talent and professional competence are the bedrock of many successful military careers, from Alexander to Napoleon to Eisenhower; but talent, as the saying goes, will only get one so far. Alongside professional competence, there are the personal intangibles that also contribute to the career of a successful leader. Most critical among these are the interpersonal skills demanded for harmonious working relationships with peers, supervisors and subordinates. Often, leaders who possess great technical competence develop a hubris that blinds them to their flaws, causing them to become a prima donna, guilty of 'drinking their own bathwater'. Senior commanders seem to expect a modicum of vanity when selecting subordinates, as self-confidence remains a highly valued virtue. But commanders also know that an officer who alienates peers, berates subordinates and infuriates superiors will be a hindrance rather than a help to any military organization, no matter how talented the officer is personally. Teamwork remains an important, even critical, component of any successful military career, making the 'plays well with others' box one of the most important to be checked on any evaluation form. Forrest's brief military career demonstrates clear and repeated evidence of his inability to do so. Thus the argument against Forrest's greatness rests on three legs: his personal failings as a man, his inability to provide the Confederacy with capable military leadership above the tactical level, and the flawed example he set for future generations, thereby inflicting continuing and sustained damage to his nation.

Nathan Bedford Forrest was born in the summer of 1821 in a rugged area of Middle Tennessee 48 kilometres (30 mi.) south of Nashville. The recently settled frontier, and the clannishness of Forrest's Scots-Irish ancestry, ensured that the young southerner's life was filled with violence. In many ways, Forrest's ancestry and the predominant culture in that region of the United States both created the conditions that fuelled Forrest's meteoric rise to the highest levels of Confederate leadership and simultaneously guaranteed that he would ultimately

Nathan Bedford
Forrest, *c.* 1862–5.

fail at the highest level of war. As several chroniclers of Anglo-American
Scots-Irish society have argued, some of the defining aspects of the
culture are soaring ambition and penchant for hard work, coupled
with short tempers and a willingness to escalate conflict to a violent
conclusion, often followed by remorse and regret. Forrest's life clearly
demonstrates all of these attributes.

In addition to his genetic material, Forrest came of age in an environment where these aspects coloured his early life. The frontier lacked
established and stable social institutions, leading to frequent recourse
to violence rather than litigation to settle disputes, occasionally in the
form of duels. Forrest's pre-eminent biographer, Brian Steel Wills,
asserts, 'Not only were these frontier folk willing to employ violence
against each other, they saw such activity as a natural part of social life.'
It also fostered an intense pride and loyalty, both to family members
and those perceived as fellow members of the clan, as well as a heightened sensitivity to any slights to its honour. Of Hernando, Mississippi,
Forrest's first home in the Memphis area, Wills wrote, 'Violence and
honor continued to be much a part of daily life. Men fought over real

and imagined grievances in the streets, usually settling their differences by blood.'[5]

On 10 March 1845 four men came to settle a score with Forrest and his uncle and mentor, Jonathan, with whom he had entered into a business partnership in Hernando. The altercation turned violent, with Jonathan falling mortally wounded from a bullet intended for his nephew. Forrest continued the struggle, shooting and killing two of his attackers, and, with his ammunition exhausted, chasing the other two off with a Bowie knife. The act was so within the norms of southern upcountry society that the townspeople later made Forrest both constable and coroner, as well as a lieutenant in the state militia. In 1851 he relocated to Memphis and moved naturally from trading livestock to selling real estate and slaves. Memphis was then ideally situated between the surplus slaves of the Upper South who were 'sold down the river' from their 'Old Kentucky Home' to the hellish cotton and sugar plantations in the Delta, and Forrest prospered, socially and financially, from the increasing demand. Throughout his antebellum career, which included a term as a Memphis city alderman, Forrest's ambition, popularity, business acumen, lack of formal education and temper were all on full display. They remained so during Forrest's apparently successful but ultimately failed military career.[6]

For Forrest, as for other southern secessionists such as William Lowndes Yancey, any threat to slavery was a personal attack to their prosperity and threatened to return them to the poverty that was never far from their doors.[7] When the South seceded, Forrest volunteered his services as a private, but quickly earned a commission as a colonel in his own regiment. But his famous temper, resulting in an almost immediate and uncontrollable rage that he later regretted, led him to abuse the men under his command. Even Forrest's more sympathetic biographers relate accounts where Forrest bashed a scout's head against a tree for bringing him false information, slapped a lieutenant into a river because he would not roll up his sleeves and join his men in building a bridge, knocked another out of a boat with an oar for refusing to help paddle across the Tennessee River, and beat a soldier with a branch and shot a colour-bearer for fleeing a rout.

In one of the clearest examples of Forrest's 'inharmonious' relationships with his subordinates, on 14 June 1863 Lt Andrew Gould, who had served as an artillery commander during Forrest's successful

pursuit of Streight's raid across northern Alabama, requested an audience with Forrest at his headquarters in Columbia, Tennessee, where
Gould confronted the general about his transfer from Forrest's command. Unhappy with Gould's performance during the Battle of Day's
Gap, Forrest had relieved him from command and selected him for
reassignment. The confrontation became heated and, although the
sequence of events is unclear, Forrest emerged with a bullet from
Gould's pistol in his abdomen while Gould suffered a stab wound
that penetrated his lung and proved fatal. Regardless of who launched
the first blow, allowing a conflict with a subordinate to escalate to the
point where one either kills or has to take another life in self-defence
is not a hallmark of effective military leadership. His defenders circu-
lated accounts that Forrest had been 'attacked', either verbally or
physically, to justify the general's actions, and Forrest retained his command, but the incident is a serious blot on his military record. Forrest's
quick temper and willingness to use violence against his own men both
undermined his claims to innocence in the confrontation with Gould
and seriously and repeatedly compromised his ability to lead effectively.
In some cases, men and officers who disapproved of Forrest's profli-
gacy with their lives and brutal treatment of prisoners refused to serve
under him. One even claimed, 'I object to a tyrannical, hotheaded
vulgarian's commanding me.'[8]

Forrest's relationships with his peers were equally squally. On
3 February 1863 Forrest cooperated with General Joseph Wheeler's
cavalry in an attack on the town of Dover, Tennessee, adjacent to Fort
Donelson. In the action Wheeler ordered Forrest's command in an ill-
advised attack on the strongly defended town, resulting in heavy
casualties among Forrest's men. After the battle, Forrest told Wheeler
that he would 'be in my coffin before I will fight again under your
command'. During the retreat from Nashville, Forrest allegedly threatened General Benjamin Cheatham with a pistol in a dispute over
whose troops would cross a ford first. In April 1863 Forrest cooperated
with General Earl Van Dorn in a raid on Thompson's Station, Tennessee,
but during the raid Forrest felt that Van Dorn had failed to provide
adequate support. In keeping with Forrest's nature, the dispute became
heated and led to the men challenging one another to a duel, before
the situation was eventually defused. A jealous husband killed Van
Dorn a month later, suggesting further character flaws on Van Dorn's
part, but the incident became yet another in a pattern of behaviour

that made it more difficult to excuse Forrest's many transgressions as isolated incidents.[9]

Worse, the interactions had a significant effect on future operations. During the summer and autumn of 1863, when Confederate General Braxton Bragg depended on his cavalry to keep him apprised of Union General William Rosecrans's movements, Forrest's and Wheeler's inability to effectively support the army with accurate and timely intelligence led indirectly to the loss of Chattanooga, one of the South's strategic rail centres.[10] As Bragg's army retreated into North Georgia, he repeatedly tried to take advantage of Rosecrans's dispersed formations in the mountains to surround and destroy one of the isolated commands, but could never secure sufficient intelligence of Union dispositions and intentions in a timely fashion, preventing an effective counter-blow. In the ensuing battle along the banks of Chickamauga Creek, Forrest clearly failed in his role as a corps commander of cavalry, allowing himself to be sucked into the whirling fray of combat to the detriment of his duties in locating the Union lines and pursuing the defeated force, assisting the Union Army's escape into the defences of Chattanooga.

On 18 September a stout Union defence at Alexander's Bridge and Reed's Bridge provided Rosecrans early warning of Bragg's attempt to turn his left flank, pushing him away from his base at Chattanooga and potentially leading to his destruction on one of the mountain coves of northern Georgia. Bragg had ordered Forrest to screen the advance and secure the crossing but Forrest had singularly failed to do so, instead transferring most of his available force to meet an imagined threat farther north.[11] As a result, Confederate infantry had to fight for the crossings, costing precious time and enabling Rosecrans to shift more units to the threatened sector. That night Forrest again failed to effectively screen the army's right flank and gather information about Union dispositions, intelligence that would have revealed a yawning gap in the Union lines. According to David Powell, this was 'the most significant intelligence oversight of the entire battle'.[12]

The following day Forrest initiated a major engagement in the same area, commandeering rebel infantry and feeding them, along with his own cavalry, into an imbalanced fight piecemeal, wrecking several regiments. As a result, 'Forrest left Bragg blind that morning.'[13] The fighting further delayed Bragg's planned counterstroke and gave additional time to strengthen the Union centre. Powell judged that

Forrest continued to perform as if he was still a brigade or division commander rather than a corps commander in charge of Bragg's entire right flank. He made little or no effort to send out more extensive patrols that might report on the overall Union dispositions, a mistake that would affect Bragg's subsequent decision-making.[14]

On 20 September Confederate reinforcements from Lee's army in Virginia and an incredibly poorly timed Union shift opened a hole at the exact moment and location of Bragg's attack, enabling him to split Rosecrans's army and drive it from the field. A stout defence by General George 'Pap' Thomas on Snodgrass Hill covered the Union retreat, but Forrest's lack of aggression enabled the strung-out columns to reach the safety of Chattanooga without serious pressure. Leading from the front often ensured that Forrest was absent from his headquarters and unavailable for consultation with his superiors or subordinates and unable to direct actions on distant parts of the field. As Powell found, 'Forrest struggled to meet the rigorous challenges of his increased responsibilities ... Too often, Forrest found himself in the thick of the action and unable to avoid making tactical decisions better left to others,' because 'Forrest was too often unable or unwilling to resist the lure of personal adventure and/or delegate minor missions.'[15]

Forrest was undoubtedly a skilled and inspirational tactical leader, but he had been promoted out of his depth. He could not adapt to the increased responsibility of command at higher levels and thus deprived a more competent commander of a vital post with the Confederate forces defending Tennessee and Georgia. While conventional wisdom has heaped blame on Braxton Bragg for the incomplete Confederate victory, recent reappraisals of Bragg, especially Earl Hess's, highlight just how often Bragg's subordinates failed him, either through direct insubordination and intrigue, or indirectly by failing to perform assigned tasks or collect essential intelligence and relay it in a timely manner.[16] Chickamauga was perhaps the most notable of those examples. Though relieved of his command and sent back to western Tennessee to resume his raiding and raise new formations, Forrest escaped greater censure only because Bragg's other cavalry commander, General Joe Wheeler, had performed even worse. But, in a classic case of the Confederacy's inability to manage its poor crop of commanders,

Wheeler earned a promotion and command of most of Forrest's units, leaving the latter embittered.

After the Confederate concentration and victory at Chickamauga, Bragg sent his cavalry north in an attempt to sever Rosecrans's constrained supply lines leading into Chattanooga, but Forrest allowed his command to be pulled off in the direction of Knoxville, permitting the Union forces to retain control of the city. After this incident, Bragg reportedly said, 'He is nothing more than a good raider,' and arranged for Forrest's transfer to western Tennessee, where Forrest could use his personal popularity to attract new recruits to his banner. Before leaving Bragg's command, Forrest allegedly confronted Bragg in his tent and told him,

> I have stood your meanness as long as I intend to. You have played the part of a damned scoundrel, and are a coward, and if you were any part of a man I would slap your jaws and force you to resent it. You may as well not issue any orders to me, for I will not obey them.

The story is probably apocryphal, as the evidence is poorly supported in the literature, but Forrest's admirers and supporters repeated it in their flattering biographies, often with Forrest's approval, suggesting that it was an accurate reflection of Forrest's opinion of Bragg.[17]

During the ensuing campaign in western Tennessee, Forrest's troops, either under his orders or because of his failure to restrain them, massacred over half of the African American garrison at Fort Pillow, killing most after they had surrendered. The affair followed a bloody repulse at Paducah, Kentucky, when soldiers of the U.S. Coloured Troops (USCT) successfully held a fort near the town and inflicted heavy casualties on Forrest's command. To prevent the loss of men in costly frontal assaults, Forrest often resorted to bluff or bluster, suggesting that, if he was forced to storm a defence work, he could not be responsible for the actions of his men in the heat of combat. The affair at Fort Pillow lent weight to his threats, though he never repeated them, and thus he had much to gain from the affair. Though Forrest apologists repeatedly claim that the astronomical Union casualties, which fell disproportionally among the USCT troops defending the post, were somehow consistent with taking a fortress by storm, every reputable analysis has clearly demonstrated that a massacre did indeed occur.[18]

Forrest's men retained a reputation for atrocities against both former slaves and southern Unionists in the u.s. Army, murdering one of the surrendered commanders of a loyal Tennessee cavalry regiment and returning captives to slavery in violation of the articles of war. Black soldiers earned a measure of revenge during the retreat from the Battle of Brice's Crossroads in June 1864, when they inflicted heavy casualties on Forrest's command and prevented a rout of the Union column, permitting another foray into northern Mississippi a month later. As Tom Parson has demonstrated, Forrest did not perform well at the Battle of Tupelo, likely sulking because General Stephen D. Lee had been placed in overall command.[19] Forrest led an ill-advised charge against strong Union defences at Tupelo, then suffered a serious wound in another futile personal attack on the Union rearguard. Though his defenders cited his personal bravery and willingness to 'mix' with his foes, these are attributes best displayed among senior enlisted men and junior officers, not men in high command responsible for large formations. Robert E. Lee, despite his many failings, at least had the good sense not to lead 'Pickett's charge' in person.[20]

By virtue of his having been banished to essentially an independent command, Forrest was unable to coordinate his efforts directly with the Confederate defence of Atlanta. At a point when Confederate cavalry raids could have disrupted General William T. Sherman's vulnerable rail logistics through Tennessee, Forrest found himself fending off, successfully in most cases, a series of expeditions from Memphis organized with the sole purpose of keeping him occupied. In reporting his actions to Secretary of War Henry M. Stanton, Sherman wrote, 'I will order them to make up a force and go out and follow Forrest to the death, if it cost 10,000 lives and breaks the Treasury. There will never be peace in Tennessee until Forrest is dead.'[21] By the time Forrest finally disengaged in early September and marched into northern Alabama and southern Tennessee, Atlanta was already in Sherman's hands, though the threat did influence Sherman's decision to send part of his army back to Nashville and bring the rest on a highly publicized 'March to the Sea'. Forrest's inability to effectively disrupt Sherman's supply line during the 1864 Atlanta campaign, coupled with his ineffectual defence of the now-worthless interior of Mississippi, was a major contributing factor in the defeat of Confederate arms in the decisive year and theatre of the war. If the South had any chance of victory, it was in using its hard-riding cavalrymen to disrupt Union supply lines, as they had successfully done in 1862, to stymie the efforts of the North's superior arms. But Forrest's failure to adapt led directly to southern defeat.

In September 1864, after recovering from his wounds and finally disengaging from the wasteland of northern Mississippi, Forrest led another of his patented raids designed to disrupt Union supply lines and keep his famished and underequipped command supplied. Crossing the Tennessee River near Florence, Alabama, he invested Athens and again bluffed the Union commander into surrendering, profiting from his earlier actions at Fort Pillow by claiming not to be able to restrain his men if they had to attack a fort garrisoned largely by Black soldiers. Another Union outpost at Sulphur Trestle did not succumb so easily, forcing Forrest to expend much of his valuable artillery ammunition before surrendering, ensuring that the raid could not penetrate deeply into Tennessee. Though he did cut one of the two rail lines leading from Nashville to Chattanooga, he was unable to seriously threaten the other, meaning that Sherman's army in Atlanta remained adequately supplied.

By late in the war Confederate supply difficulties and logistics failures meant that Forrest's command often had to meet their subsistence needs by frequent requisitions from the Confederate home front, which undoubtedly affected support for the war, and by raiding Union outposts for military supplies. One of the most successful examples came in October 1864, when Forrest took his mounted force into Tennessee and emplaced his artillery along the western bank of the Tennessee River in an attempt to interrupt steamboat traffic to Johnsonville on the opposite bank. From that point, the newly constructed Nashville and Northwestern Railroad brought supplies into the city, circumventing the low water on the Cumberland River at that time of year and augmenting the capacity of the Louisville and Nashville Railroad. Forrest's men captured one supply ship, appropriating a large quantity of uniforms and equipment to meet their needs, and succeeded in inducing a conflagration at Johnsonville that destroyed millions of dollars' worth of Union property destined for Thomas's army at Nashville. But the raid served only to replenish Forrest's command. The temporary logistics interruption and previous stockpiles meant that the raid had no effect on Thomas's ability to repel Hood the following month, and Forrest's independent raid actually delayed Hood's advance into Tennessee, facilitating Thomas's ability to concentrate his force and oppose the invasion. While Forrest effectively cooperated with John Bell Hood's attack on Nashville in December 1864, by then the depleted Confederates had little prospect of success and Hood's army left Tennessee virtually destroyed. Yet again, self-serving raiding and poorly coordinated operations had been costly for the Confederacy.

In a final command, in defence of the vital Confederate manufacturing and logistics centres at Selma, Alabama, and Columbus and Macon, Georgia, Forrest signally failed to protect the cities from a massive Union cavalry column led by Major General James Wilson. Though a numerical disparity diminished the likelihood of success, Forrest could not prevent Wilson from isolating his dispersed columns, sealing Selma's fate. Again, Forrest demonstrated commendable personal bravery at Ebenezer Church, personally killing an attacking Union cavalryman, but while he was 'mixing', he was not directing the defence of Selma, and the powerful Union column rode into the city almost unopposed the following day and levelled the vital Confederate factories and warehouses.[22]

Tactically, Forrest fared much better in a number of smaller engagements, but even here he showed his vulnerabilities. His victory at Murfreesboro in the summer of 1862 had been a close-run affair, and he wasted time and lives attacking troops barricaded in buildings in the town. At Parker's Crossroads faulty reconnaissance almost caused his command to be crushed between two converging forces, before he barely made his escape. And many of his victories relied on bluff or inferior or untrained opponents, which masked his command's vulnerabilities. An untutored officer, Forrest apparently never bothered to learn the cavalry manual of arms, leaving such 'minor details' to his subordinates. Thus his vaunted tactical acumen stemmed largely from a personal aggressiveness and often violated sound military concepts.[23]

Additionally, most of Forrest's most notable victories, including his raid on Murfreesboro in July 1862, and the skirmishes at Lexington and Thompson's Station, Tennessee, in 1863 and at Brice's Crossroads in Mississippi in the summer of 1864, came in minor actions that had little influence on the larger course of the war. He was undoubtedly a skilled tactical commander, but had little success in translating these operational victories into strategic successes. But his actions and campaigns have spurred a virtual cottage industry of Forrest-worshippers, many within the ranks of the u.s. military.[24] This has been one of Forrest's most unfortunate legacies as a military commander. In focusing on tactical expertise, the Department of Defense has, at times, neglected the operational art or strategic capabilities that bring success in armed conflict. In Vietnam, the army won an unbroken string of tactical victories that could only delay the eventual strategic defeat. In what some have described as a 'strategy of tactics', the service focused excessively on the flawed metric of 'body counts', without developing a more effective counter-insurgency strategy that might have altered the strategic situation. More recent conflicts mirrored this pattern, as u.s. forces typically prevailed in their encounters with insurgents in Iraq and Afghanistan, yet failed to craft a military strategy that led to a strategic resolution. Just as Forrest raided to keep his command supplied, without necessarily concentrating on how it might best impact the Confederate war effort, the recent emphasis on winning battles has often come at the expense of winning wars.[25]

Forrest's actions at Fort Pillow foreshadowed both a post-war episode when he personally killed one of his hired freedmen with an axe handle, and his future sponsorship and support of night-riding Ku Klux Klansmen, an organization in which Forrest played a prominent, if secretive, role, at one point even threatening to call the organization out to battle the Tennessee state militia. Though he later issued an order for the organization to disband, this was most likely an attempt to disassociate himself from its activities, which continued unabated.[26] Forrest apologists have pointed to his 'final order', issued at the close of the war, in which he advised his men to submit to Union authority and work to rebuild the nation, as evidence that Forrest did not advocate for continued resistance against federal authorities. In that directive Forrest lectured his men to 'submit to the "powers that be", and to aid in restoring peace and establishing law and order throughout the land', and to 'obey the laws' of the 'Government to which you have surrendered'.[27] But, at the time, he could hardly have done otherwise. The Confederacy was defeated and prostrate, and further resistance, at that time, would have been futile and only led to more bloodshed. But, as Radical Reconstruction proceeded and ex-Confederates sought to resist Black enfranchisement and equality, Forrest offered his support in opposition to these programmes mostly through his surreptitious support of the Ku Klux Klan. Whether he served as 'grand wizard' of the secretive organization or not (though the evidence suggests that he did), he was undoubtedly a member and worked to further the organization's goals of terrorizing African Americans and suppressing both their vote and their role in helping to rebuild the shattered region. His veneration among both members of the Sons of Confederate Veterans and Klansmen is ample testament to his feelings for supporters of their shared cause of restoring and preserving white supremacy.

So why has Forrest had such an enduring appeal, especially among professional military officers? One possible explanation is Forrest's reputation as an 'untutored genius' in a military culture that fosters rampant anti-intellectualism. Forrest himself is said to have claimed, 'I ain't no graduate of West Point, and never rubbed my back up against any college.' In 2001 Court Carney argued that this was a major element of Forrest's enduring appeal, as 'the quintessential Confederate hero, whose rough-hewn, unschooled martial style reflected the virtues of the southern "plain folk"'.[28] In a 1934 paper at the Command and General Staff College at Fort Leavenworth, Capt. Neil S. Edmond, an infantry officer whose family lived in Alabama during the Civil War, wrote a paper extolling the virtues of Forrest's military leadership. In alleging that Forrest possessed military vision, he argued it was 'strange that an unlettered unmilitary man could see where experts, so called, were blind', and that 'finished education is not always essential where the dominant traits [of leadership] are present'. Edmond believed that, during the First World War, 'officers for high command were selected by reputations made in the class room and in many instances with disastrous results'. Comments such as these highlight the frequent use of Forrest's military career to assert that education and the effort of serious and sustained study were somehow unnecessary for a career as a successful military officer if one possessed innate qualities of command, providing a shortcut past the hard work of military professionalism. It is not surprising that these observations were most often advanced by adherents to the 'Myth of the Lost Cause', who, not coincidentally, might find their academic background deficient when compared to their peers from other sections of the country. Edmond closed his thesis by arguing that Confederate authorities did not recognize or appreciate Forrest's genius (despite promoting him to major general!), which would be 'always regretted by those whose sympathies are with the South'. In 2006 another serving officer, this one a student at the Air Force's Air Command and Staff College, likewise found that Forrest's 'controversial issues' did not preclude his being awarded the title of 'Great Captain'. He argued, 'Forrest's leadership skills might have been a little ruff [*sic*] around the edges, but they worked and ultimately led to victories against great odds.' He concluded, 'Someday, once America sees past the causal issues of the Civil War and deals directly with the individual's accomplishments, Forrest will be seen, as he should be, a great military leader.'[29]

While certainly a dynamic *leader*, and, Brian Steel Wills has argued, an expert *cavalryman*, perhaps even the Confederacy's best, Forrest was certainly not a great *commander*. He was more than capable of inspiring his fellow rough-hewn backwoodsmen to join his command and of leading them into battle, often to their detriment, but great leadership is only one aspect of command. Forrest was certainly a skilled *tactician*, but great commanders must have *strategic* vision, or some semblance of how their tactical victories translate into successful *operations* (known as 'operational art') and, ultimately, into strategic victory. Otherwise, the commander runs the risk of falling into the same traps set for American commanders in Vietnam and Iraq: winning an unbroken string of tactical victories but never translating these successes into the strategic conditions necessary for a decisive victory. Thus Forrest best fits the description of a *warrior* (in Carney's words, a 'warrior-king of the "plain people"'), befitting his ancestors who led their clans in the Scottish Highlands, and others who have fought in resistance movements around the globe.[30] But, as critics have argued, historically the great warriors have all been defeated by professional militaries, including the English forces that broke the power of the Scottish clans, led by skilled and capable *commanders*. And so it was with Nathan Bedford Forrest.

Forrest's military career, despite personal courage and tactical acumen, is, at best, a mixed bag of success in unimportant battles and failure in those that proved decisive. As one more recent assessment found, 'most historians agree that his handful of successes failed to have any real impact on the future of the Confederacy'.[31] But Forrest's actions and legacy, as a flawed exemplar who has continued to do damage to his nation well after his passing, places him firmly in the category of 'failed military leaders'. By lending his name and considerable prestige to the founding of an organization that continues to do as much as any other to encourage racial strife and violence in the South, and by providing a flawed example for future military officers charged with the defence of their nation, Forrest has continued to do harm to the nation whose banner he lived under for 52 of his 56 years, despite that nation providing an unlettered son of the frontier with the opportunity for substantial social and economic advancement. Forrest's misguided sense of duty and honour to a false and treasonous regional authority rather than the nation of his birth, and his remarkable ability to persuade others to do likewise, helped plunge the nation into its bloodiest conflict, and his post-war career, despite his protestations to the contrary, provided additional obstacles to sectional reconciliation and progress. Viewed holistically, Nathan Bedford Forrest's failed military career offers a strong case for the title of 'worst military commander in history'.

John M. Chivington, *c.* 1860s.

3

JOHN M. CHIVINGTON

Courtney A. Short

On the morning of 29 November 1864, the 1st and 3rd Colorado Volunteers, led by Colonel John M. Chivington, attacked a Cheyenne and Arapaho village at Sand Creek and massacred the unsuspecting Native Americans. The massacre at Sand Creek ignited a divisive response throughout the local area and caught the attention of federal officials. Editorials written in the *Rocky Mountain News* celebrated the valour of the army in a just campaign; yet reports from soldiers who knew of and witnessed the attack contradicted the images of glory and forced military and government officials to inquire into the brutality of the offensive and the conduct of the troops.[1] News that the Colorado Volunteers had attacked a village of mostly women and children who had petitioned for peace left the community unsettled, even in an era when attacks at dawn against sleepy Native American villages stood as the tactic of choice.[2]

Violent encounters between the Native Americans and whites, like the Sand Creek massacre, pre-date the birth of the United States; settlers and tribes along the East Coast clashed for centuries with varying outcomes. By the nineteenth century, exploration and expansionist ambitions, backed by like-minded presidential administrations, led to government treaties that dislocated the Native populations to make space for pioneers. Legislation, such as the Indian Removal Act of 1830, forced tribes that once resided in mid-western or southern territories to find new land west of the Mississippi. By the 1840s, discovery of precious metals and fertile lands in the western territories spurred massive white migration. Government policy first sought to simply protect wagon trains as they travelled towards their western destinations, but soon, treaties urged tribes to stay on reservations and adopt agriculture.[3]

To prevent any trouble, soldiers deployed along the western frontier to military outposts. Their responsibilities varied from enforcing government policy towards the Native Americans, to protecting commerce and rail investments, to eradicating crop infestations. Soldiers simultaneously protected vulnerable citizens while balancing their efforts to curb the violent tendencies of aggressive civilians who maintained their right to defend themselves and their families. Across the wide expanse of prairies and formidable mountain ranges, the u.s. Army also contended with the unpredictable disposition of numerous Native American tribes; the soldiers lived lived with the constant possibility of violent engagement.[4]

Compounding the friction, each tribe maintained its own rules for conducting war and seeking peace. The variance in behaviour confused the soldiers, who grew to distrust the motives of all Native Americans. Darwinian scientific theories, popular in the mid-nineteenth century, that categorized Native Americans as an inferior race destined for eradication, magnified the ever-present wariness soldiers felt towards the tribes. The u.s. military approached its adversaries under a veneer of legitimacy; it regarded the Native Americans as irregular fighters and tribes as insurgent forces who did not deserve civil treatment according to the rules of war, which justified arbitrary treatment of their warriors and civilians alike. Classifying the Native Americans as racially inferior guerrillas encouraged soldiers in the West to kill their enemies with less conscience and pursue military advantage with little thought to greater consequences.[5]

The events at Sand Creek occurred within an environment where white settlers and soldiers alike viewed Native Americans as inferior, disposable and dangerous. Yet, when Chivington rode into the Cheyenne and Arapaho encampment along Sand Creek that morning with seven hundred men under his command, he ordered an attack so horrific that it tarnished his military reputation and extinguished his political ambitions. With no regard for the agreement between the Native Americans and agents of the u.s. government that had designated the Sand Creek area as a refuge for friendly tribes, the 1st and 3rd Colorado Volunteers slaughtered the Native Americans. Chivington's brutality and disregard for treaties exceeded the acceptable limits of military behaviour in the Indian Wars to the extent that, soon after the attack, both the military and Congress launched investigations into the Sand Creek massacre.[6] As the leader of the massacre, Chivington stands as one of the worst military commanders in history due to his ruthlessness towards the Native Americans, which appalled his contemporaries in an era when bigotry towards non-whites was widespread.

In addition to his criminal brutality, Chivington's leadership at Sand Creek also demonstrated his fundamental incompetence as a commander. His ambition led him to make military decisions based on self-promotion, and his selfishness manifested itself in insubordinate behaviour that undermined strategic objectives. Callously disregarding the cautions of his subordinates and threatening them with violent retribution, Chivington incited his men to engage in wholly disproportionate brutality. The extreme violence of Chivington's attack not only caused an outcry among the settlers and the u.s. government because it contradicted their sense of self-righteousness, but incited a substantial Native American uprising that cost the government considerable difficulties in the West.

When Chivington arrived in the Colorado Territory in 1860, he did so as a Methodist minister, not as a soldier. Appointed the presiding elder of the Rocky Mountain District of the Kansas–Nebraska Conference, he enjoyed popularity among the unruly gold seekers. With the sound of the guns on 12 April 1861 at Fort Sumter, however, Chivington began to consider another calling. He soon joined the 1st Colorado Volunteers as a combat soldier, not a chaplain, and pinned on the rank of major.[7]

As the Civil War expanded westward, Chivington had an opportunity to gain fame. During the Battle of Glorieta Pass in 1862, he successfully attacked a Confederate supply train, an action that earned him a reputation as a skilled and brash military leader. Newspapers and official reports lauded Chivington and his men for their bravery, which encouraged him to aggressively pursue promotion in the military. Motivated by public applause, he campaigned for promotion to brigadier general by collecting endorsement letters, drawing upon the influence of his associates in the ministry, and meeting with Secretary of War Edwin Stanton in Washington. He gained widespread support among influential civic leaders. Senators Samuel Pomeroy and James Lane of Kansas, Hiram Pitt Benet (the Colorado delegate to Congress) and Colorado Governor John Evans all patronized Chivington's advancement. The desire for promotion was an initial step in his plan for a seat in Congress. A naturally driven man who even in the ministry ruthlessly fought for personal advancement, Chivington had also expressed strong political views for more than a decade; since 1856 he had regularly advocated the Republican Party platform. With Colorado Territory flirting with statehood as Chivington began to enjoy fame for his achievements, he did not hesitate to exploit his military success for political advantage.[8]

Though Chivington earned public acclaim for his performance in battle, he had offended many of his fellow soldiers through his insolent and callous behaviour. Outspoken and defiant, he spent much of his military career in conflict with subordinates, peers and superiors alike. His efforts to secure a promotion failed largely because his consistently insubordinate behaviour hindered his chances. He did, however, rise to the rank of colonel and take command of the District of Colorado.[9]

Chivington saw the failure to gain greater rank as a minor delay in his journey towards holding influential positions in government and the military. The romanticism of battlefield victory allowed him to retain the firm support of the public, as well as that of congressional delegates and the Governor. In 1863 President Abraham Lincoln even listed his name on a promotion roster submitted to Congress. His fast rise from major to military district commander with a brush at a general's star propelled him to push harder for what he perceived as his rightful level of power. Central to his motivation was his understanding of the role of his performance at the Battle of Glorieta Pass in the success that he found afterwards. Stopped short of brigadier rank but with increased authority as the commander of the District of Colorado, he actively sought another opportunity to deliver a glorious victory and demonstrate his superior military skills.[10]

In early 1863, as Chivington ascended the ranks, tensions increased between Native American tribes and settlers across Colorado Territory. U.S. military leaders lacked a sufficient force to contend with warring tribes across the wide expanse of the frontier. Sprawling routes, like the 645-kilometre (400 mi.) Santa Fe Trail, posed a serious challenge to the small numbers of U.S. troops.[11]

Native American raids cost the white settlers dearly in cattle, horses, guns, ammunition and food. Their fierce attacks also led to killings and kidnappings of the pioneers. The gruesome murder of a ranch family, the Hungates, at their home in June 1864 alarmed settlers, who felt ill-prepared for an encounter with hostile tribes.[12] Nonetheless, the army desperately attempted to protect goods and livestock, and to safeguard the settlers.

By late summer, government officials regarded the frontier as being in a state of war. Chivington considered the Kiowas and Cheyennes as tribes 'determined on war' and Major General Samuel R. Curtis, commander of the Department of Kansas, wrote to Major General Henry W. Halleck, chief of staff, that 'the Indian difficulties west of this point are serious.'[13] Governor John Evans petitioned for both the transfer of more troops to his territory and the authority to raise a regiment of men to serve on temporary duty for one hundred days. 'Extensive Indian depredations, with murder of families', Evans wrote to Stanton. 'It is impossible to exaggerate our danger.' Chivington directed his own requests to Curtis. 'Can easily raise a company for 100 days,' he wrote, 'Can I do it? Needed immediately for defense against the Indians.' The War Department granted Evans the authority to raise the 100-days men, designated the 3rd Colorado Cavalry.[14]

Chivington saw war as an opportunity. Commanding a unit tasked 'to punish the Indians and to put a stop to their hostile operations in the territory', he hoped to demonstrate his military genius, and thus reinvigorate his campaign for promotion and political advancement.[15] However, his efforts to build his base of political support alarmed his superiors, who thought he was neglecting his military obligations.[16] Aware of critical reports in the press about Chivington's behaviour, military officials directly questioned his ability to properly command his forces. Chivington defended himself in a letter written to Curtis in August. He wrote, 'I assure you, general, that I have not spent an hour nor gone a mile to attend to other matters than my command ... I shall continue to give unremitting attention to my duties of a military character.'[17] His travel to Denver, however, under the guise of responding to the Hungate massacre, placed him in close proximity with potential constituents. As a lead advocate for statehood and a nominee for Congress, Chivington's engagement with Denver crowds undoubtedly gave him an opportunity to present himself as a civic leader as well as a military man.[18]

Politics distracted Chivington from his command, warped his view on military matters, and led to decision-making that favoured his personal ambitions over the best solutions to strategically stabilize the frontier. As a military commander, he led his formation with his own interests in mind, rather than those of his troops or those of his higher headquarters, whose orders he had a requirement to follow.[19]

In September 1864 tensions subsided and the army softened its approach to dealing with the Native Americans. Curtis, for example, prompted by the Department of the Interior, considered assisting the peaceful tribes in buffalo hunts. The quiet did not dispel distrust, however; the military as well as the settlers remained apprehensive about the renewal of hostilities. Any peace overtures required careful evaluation to ensure their truth and reliability; Curtis feared that acquiescing too early might create vulnerability when spring conditions favoured Native American attacks.[20]

Correspondingly, troops across Colorado Territory found themselves less actively engaged in confrontations with Native Americans. Official government policy, while encouraging punishment of warring tribes, opposed engaging friendly tribes. General Field Orders No. 1, published 27 July 1864, further identified lawful targets as 'Indians at war with us ... but women and children must be spared'.[21] The policy backed the belief that attacks against Native Americans camping peacefully would incite a level of violence that the short-handed frontier troops could not handle. Even earlier in the summer, distressed at the rising tensions, the government urged de-escalation, if possible. Charles Mix, the acting commissioner of Indian affairs, Department of the Interior, gave Evans instructions to 'use every endeavor to keep the peace with the Indians'. Chivington himself received $3,000 to use for treaties with the Cheyenne and Arapaho.[22] Each military officer, therefore, had a requirement to carefully review the actions of the Native Americans, and then counter the threat in an equivalent and appropriate manner: avoid war, if able, but fully prosecute war once declared. Aligned with these policies, Governor Evans designated Fort Lyon, Fort Larned, Fort Laramie and Camp Collins as refuges for friendly tribes.[23]

The dwindling prospects for conflict dismayed Chivington as the government made decisions that favoured caution, and his men's 100-day enlistments were nearing expiration, which put his plans of demonstrating his worth for higher office in jeopardy. Chivington, however, had a tendency to defy military rules to secure what he desired.[24] As conditional obstacles challenged the possibility of

Chivington achieving his ambitions, he grew more apprehensive and determined to have his fight. As he would later explain in a speech at the annual meeting of the Colorado Pioneers in Denver in September 1883, 'what must be done, must be done quickly.'[25] His inclination towards insubordination, and his resistance to established military procedures and rules, made him an unpredictable and unreliable commander, whose actions jeopardized the strategic objectives of the u.s. military in the West.

As the weather turned colder, Cheyenne chief Black Kettle wrote a letter, delivered to Fort Lyon, which asked for peace. Major Edward W. Wynkoop, commander of the post, was interested in the prisoner exchange offered in the letter, but, also aware that he lacked the authority to accept the peace offer, he arranged for a meeting in Denver with Evans.[26] Chivington reacted with alarm, partly because Wynkoop, his subordinate, had not brought the matter to him first, but also because any motion towards peace delayed his desired battle. 'Winter approaches. Third Regiment is full, and they know they will be chastised for their outrages and now want peace,' he appealed to Curtis. 'I hope the major-general will direct that they make full restitution.' Curtis held the authority to make any peace arrangements, but Evans entertained the travel party.[27]

On 28 September 1864 Evans hosted a council at Camp Weld between the Cheyenne and Arapaho chiefs and u.s. military leaders, including Wynkoop and Chivington. The council proceeded under great strain. Evans viewed the chiefs with misgivings and repeatedly scolded them for attacks committed in the previous months. As the chiefs made their case for peace, he barely listened. In frustration, White Antelope, a chief of the Cheyenne, asked plainly how they could receive 'protect[ion] from the soldiers on the plains'. Evans replied curtly, 'You must make that arrangement with the Military Chief . . . Whatever peace you make must be with the soldiers, and not with me.'[28]

With Evans removing himself from the negotiations, the meeting then belonged to Chivington, who gave instructions to Black Kettle and the Arapaho chief, Left Hand, about how to submit to the army. He spoke only once at the council and explained, 'My rule of fighting white men or Indians is, to fight them until they lay down their arms and submit to military authority. You are nearer Major Wynkoop than anyone else, and you can go to him when you are ready to do that.' With Chivington's words, the council closed.[29]

Wynkoop believed that Chivington had given him the responsibility, as commander of Fort Lyon, to handle the situation further, and that he 'would act toward [the tribes] according to [his] best judgment'. With Wynkoop's approval, Black Kettle and Left Hand brought their village to an area outside of Fort Lyon.[30] Notably, however, Wynkoop did not offer peace. He acknowledged that he lacked the authority to commit the u.s. military to formal arrangement with a warring tribe. Instead, he allowed the Native Americans to reside under his protection until higher military officials could engage the chiefs themselves. Wynkoop acted in accordance with Chivington's orders as stated at the Camp Weld council. The interim refuge he created, however, tested the boundaries of his position and created the appearance that he sought to pursue peace unilaterally. The assumption that Wynkoop aimed to defy his superiors and act independently proved false, but he lost his command to Major Scott J. Anthony, who arrived at Fort Lyon on 2 November.

As the new commander, Anthony classified the Cheyennes and Arapahos as prisoners, not as peace-seeking Native Americans, but he continued Wynkoop's policy of allowing them to camp unharmed. Anthony did not share Wynkoop's belief in the good intentions of the tribes, despite acknowledging that Black Kettle and Left Hand had asked for peace. He based his decision to allow the tribes to stay encamped on his observation that the tribes appeared too weak to fight. By the time Wynkoop departed from Fort Lyon on 25 November, the Cheyenne and Arapaho had settled along Sand Creek, a location approved by Anthony. The tribes received regular trade visits from the post.[31]

Black Kettle and Left Hand believed they were camping in a protected area, an arrangement rooted in the outcome of the Camp Weld council. The chiefs then waited for army officials to initiate peace negotiations. In addition to Wynkoop and Anthony, both of whom granted the tribes permission to camp safely in the area outside of Fort Lyon, other soldiers who had attended the Camp Weld council concurred with the tribes' understanding of the purpose of the encampment. Black Kettle and Left Hand had followed the instructions given to them by Chivington himself; they had returned to Fort Lyon and willingly conformed to Wynkoop's demands.[32] Curtis also validated the arrangement made by Wynkoop and Anthony with the Cheyenne and Arapaho. In correspondence with the Department of New Mexico, he stated his intention to consider the tribes' desire for peace. 'The Arapahos and Cheyennes have come into Lyon begging for peace,' he wrote, 'The hardest kind of terms are demanded by me and conceded by some of these Indians ... They insist on peace or absolute sacrifice ... Of course, they will have to be received.'[33]

With full knowledge of the disposition of the tribes along Sand Creek, Chivington then planned an expeditious attack against them.[34] Referring to the Cheyennes and Arapahos as 'hostile Indians' in his reports, he sent the 3rd Colorado towards Fort Lyon first, followed by the 1st Colorado. The combined force fell under his command; a purposeful alignment intended to ensure he retained control over the coming attack.[35] With the 100-day enlistments still active, he had the larger and stronger force. Black Kettle and Left Hand's tribes, which were unaware that Chivington was hoping to re-create the military glory of Glorieta Pass and advance his political ambitions at the cost of their lives, were unprepared for the impending strike. Only a victory could catapult Chivington into yet a higher position of power and, with his current term of enlistment expiring in late September 1864, he had no time for errors. He made every effort to ensure he and his men could not lose.

His aggressive plans directly contradicted the intent of his commanding officer. Curtis wrote to the Department of New Mexico about possible peace with the Cheyenne and Arapaho on the same day that Chivington staged at Fort Lyon in preparation for the next morning's attack. The planned raid against a known peace-seeking opponent exposed something more sinister about Chivington than mere disobedience. Even on the minimally regulated battlefield of the West, policies governed behaviour as a way to contain war and protect the stability of the growing nation. The violence that Chivington sought to inflict extended beyond the reasonable boundaries of even nineteenth-century warfare; he intended unlawful murder and massacre.

As Chivington travelled towards Fort Lyon, he received consistent confirmation that Black Kettle and Left Hand had not changed their intentions nor moved camp. As he met men along the road, he probed them for information about the activities around Fort Lyon and the tribes nearby. Specifically, he asked if Anthony had continued the policies of Wynkoop. The men he encountered confirmed that Black Kettle and Left Hand had permission to camp by Sand Creek, that interactions between the tribes and the u.s. military continued agreeably, and that the Native Americans acted 'very friendly'.[36] The reports sat well with Chivington; the present docile behaviour of the unsuspecting Cheyennes and Arapahos made them attractive targets. The conditions he had painstakingly arranged remained in place. Riding into Fort Lyon on the morning of 28 November, Chivington felt confident of victory.

Anticipating opposition from the officers at the post, he quickly had his men set up pickets to deny both entry and exit. Anthony greeted Chivington, told him where Black Kettle and Left Hand were camping, and reiterated the tribes' demand for peace. Encouraged by Anthony's eagerness as well as his information, and anxious to stifle dissenters, Chivington arrested soldiers with reputations for assisting the Native Americans.[37]

He soon faced more resistance than expected. Numerous officers refused to attack the village that they had fed and traded with for over two months. Captain Silas Soule, who had attended the Camp Weld council, attempted to rally his fellow officers in protest. 'Any man who would take part in the murders, knowing the circumstances as we [do]', he asserted, '[is] a low-lived cowardly son of a bitch.' Lieutenant Joe Cramer, also present at Camp Weld, argued with Chivington that attacking the friendly tribes amounted to murder. Cramer and Soule did not stand alone; other young officers also expressed disgust at the forthcoming attack. Chivington responded by threatening to hang Soule for trying to incite a revolt and chided the others by insulting their service. 'Damn any man or men who are in sympathy with them,' he replied, 'Such men as you and Major Wynkoop better leave the u.s. Service.'[38]

Throughout his military career Chivington lacked tact and an ability to build meaningful relationships with superiors or subordinates; he consistently bristled at any challenge to his ideas, even when such input might have led to more effective decisions. Chivington did not care to change his intent to attack peace-seeking tribes as a means to propel his ambitions at the expense of Army strategy in the West. His failure to respect and listen to subordinates grew from more than simple incompetence; his commitment to slaughter required him to disregard any rational input provided by others.

At daybreak on 29 November, the men of the 1st and 3rd Colorado, along with a small contingent of New Mexico cavalry, descended on the still village of Black Kettle and Left Hand. The surprised warriors hastily put up a defence that wavered against the pressure of the attack, and then broke. Retreating towards the Creek, they staged a second stand and braced for the continued assault. U.S. infantry, cavalry and artillery swept cleanly through the encampment; the soldiers killed all who lived there and destroyed the lodges. Despite a gruelling fight, the unremitting onslaught of Chivington's force routed the Native Americans, who fled under the terror of charging U.S. troops. Over six hours later, the commotion fell silent, and hundreds of men, women and children lay dead across the ground.[39]

Chivington's troops easily overpowered the village, which consisted of more women and children than warriors. The slaughter, however, did not occur simply because a larger force with more combat power overtook a weaker group. The brutality of the soldiers exceeded the level of violence seen in other raids and battles between U.S. troops and Native Americans in the West. Women begged and screamed on their knees as soldiers hacked off arms and ripped scalps. Troops mutilated bodies by cutting out genitals and tearing off fingers; they disembowelled a foetus from the womb of a pregnant woman. The men acted with bloodthirsty abandon, as if they had gone mad.[40]

The crazed violence of the men was incited by the orders Chivington had issued to them before they rode for the village. He instructed his soldiers to kill every person found in the camp. To his subordinates, he voiced a longing for bloodletting and made flippant comments about cannibalism.[41] Anthony further encouraged the murderous violence by screaming abhorrent battle cries. As hundreds of women ran towards the charging soldiers on horseback, pleading for their lives, Anthony yelled, 'kill the sons of bitches.'[42] The soldiers, nerves at high pitch at the onset of combat, ignored the appeals.

Conditioned by their superiors to see only enemies before them and with adrenaline electrifying their nerves, some soldiers failed to notice white flags hoisted in the air or carried by Native Americans and traders. White Antelope, along with John Smith, an interpreter, and two others from a trading party sent by Anthony days earlier, rushed to greet the approaching troops in hopes of defusing the conflict. Other chiefs stood calmly in front of the soldiers, unarmed. Determined in their attack, the soldiers shot at them and thus set the course for indiscriminate slaughter.[43] The slaughter was exacerbated by the use of two 12-pound howitzers. After shattering a hastily constructed defensive line, the guns bombarded the Native Americans 'while they were running' towards the creek.[44]

Beyond the creek, the fighting dissolved into a melee of individual encounters. Spurred on by Chivington and Anthony's orders to take no prisoners, the soldiers maimed and dismembered living and dead alike. Chivington watched the violence, but did nothing to interfere. Soldiers beat the brains out of children. They tossed a baby into the feedbox of a wagon to starve for days before discarding the still-living infant along the road. They methodically shot at the back of a young child who trailed his fleeing family. They chased down women attempting to escape to the expanse of the prairie and watched as mothers sliced their children's throats hoping to save them from murder and torture. With riotous screeches, the troops sawed the scalps off their victims in an act that even Anthony, an advocate for the unchecked violence, called 'a barbarous practice'. The men acted in accordance with Chivington's orders: they 'killed and butchered all they came to'.[45] The extreme violence, incited and condoned by Chivington, undermined the moral bearings of the soldiers, impacted the execution of other military endeavours of the U.S. Army in the West by supposing an extreme capacity for brutality, and called into question the legitimacy of the overarching strategy of the U.S. government in the region.

Some soldiers, such as Soule and Cramer, stood their ground and refused to fire. Though they lacked the authority to stay at Fort Lyon, they demonstrated courage once on the battlefield by steadying the hands of all the men under them. Silencing their rifles put their lives at risk; they knew such disobedience could lead to hanging and they could not hide their actions. Chivington did take notice of the defiance and reported their behaviour to his superiors. Soule, Cramer and their soldiers later became damning witnesses to the massacre at Sand Creek.[46]

As the frenzied violence dissipated late in the day, Chivington sent out a short report to his higher headquarters. In a few lines he told a hurried story of glory and complete victory. Rich with descriptive statistics and self-praise, his note told the story of a unit that had overcome the fatigue of distance, the discomfort of snow, and the wrath of an overwhelming enemy to deliver a spectacular triumph. Chivington crafted the report to stir up excitement and capture the interest of his superiors and the public. He believed that news of Sand Creek as a magnificent success would elevate his reputation and launch his promotion. 'All did nobly,' he reported, with confidence and high spirits.[47]

Chivington's indifference towards the violence and destruction went beyond the usual emotional hardening caused by combat experiences; he not only planned a massacre, but revelled in its aftermath. Good military commanders, responsible for using controlled force to achieve government objectives, display aggression; yet they also possess compassion and the ability to understand the impact of their missions. A military commander without empathy can unleash unchecked brutality and undermine discipline. Chivington failed to control his troops or himself, and coldly incited a massacre for his own purposes. The absence of humanity in his military performance at Sand Creek exposed his shortcomings as a leader, rather than demonstrating his skills, as he had hoped.

On 13 March 1865 the Joint Committee on the Conduct of War, a congressional commission, began its investigation into the events at Sand Creek. A parallel effort, the Special Joint Committee on the Conditions of the Indian Tribes, examined broader Native American policy, and included an account of the actions of the 1st and 3rd Colorado. An investigative military commission had begun the month prior that involved testimony from men such as Soule and Wynkoop.[48]

Throughout the investigations Chivington steadfastly defended his actions. He never wavered from arguing that Black Kettle's and Left Hand's tribes posed a serious threat to settlers, and that they were to blame for many depredations that had occurred over the previous summer. His attempts to defend his reputation contradicted the correspondence, conversations and orders that he had given before the attack. Before his peers and superiors in military and government hearings, he never showed remorse.[49]

He found few allies. When news of Sand Creek reached Curtis and Halleck, they both condemned the conduct of Chivington and his soldiers. Curtis found that his subordinate had 'transgressed [his] field orders ... [and] acted very much against [his] views' by attacking a peace-seeking village of mostly women and children. Chivington's refusal to honour the agreements that identified Sand Creek as a temporary refuge undermined Curtis's authority to handle strategic concerns within his department, and ran counter to the intent of his superiors.[50] Halleck decried not only the brutality towards a peaceable tribe, but the depth of the cunning involved in the planning. He concluded that 'the conduct of Colonel Chivington's command towards the friendly Indians has been a series of outrages calculated to make them all hostile.'[51]

In addition to causing his downfall, Chivington's actions ignited the spread of retaliatory violence that government policy had sought to avoid. Halleck and Curtis now faced an increase in raids and depredations from Native Americans throughout Colorado Territory and the greater West. In January 1865 the War Department relayed information to Halleck about 'active hostility of the Indians, incited mainly by the recent attack of Colonel Chivington at Fort Lyons', and concurred with a need for additional troops. Curtis at first dismissed the correlation between Sand Creek and the surge of Native American aggression, but he could not deny the increase in attacks. The U.S. government, over the course of almost a year, committed 8,000 soldiers and spent more than $40,000,000 to contain the fighting. The duration and intensity of the raids caused General Ulysses S. Grant, general in chief of the U.S. Army, to consolidate the western military departments into the Division of the Missouri under General John Pope. The warring parties signed the Treaty of the Little Arkansas River in October, but it barely held into the new year. Conflict began again in early 1866 and fighting continued for over a decade.[52] Chivington's tactics at Sand Creek derailed the U.S. government's strategic and operational objectives at such a high cost that his reputation was forever tarnished.

Chivington spent decades after Sand Creek defending his leadership and decision-making. He spoke at public conventions and denied any wrongdoing in an attempt to restore his image. In some places, he found sympathetic audiences. The Methodist congregation initially believed that Sand Creek justly punished the Native Americans for the deaths of white settlers. At least thirty supporters enthusiastically donated to the State Historical and Natural History Society in 1898 for a display of a portrait of Chivington in the state capitol building in Denver. The group, who described Chivington as a Colorado defender and 'the Sand Creek Hero', included his grandchildren.[53]

Many throughout the United States, however, agreed with the findings of the Joint Committee on the Conduct of War that held Chivington responsible for 'deliberately plann[ing] and execut[ing] a foul and dastardly massacre . . . having full knowledge of their friendly character'.[54] The men of the 1st and 3rd Colorado faced condemnation by an appalled public and opportunity-seeking politicians who linked the event to their platforms. The soldiers turned against each other in recriminations and excuses.[55] For Coloradans, who faced the uncertainty of violence across the wide expanse of the territory, there remained a careful balance between their fear of attack and condemnation of the excessive brutality demonstrated at Sand Creek. The settlers did not have sympathy for the Native Americans, but Chivington's disregard for rule of law endangered all who resided in the West, settlers and tribes alike, because it encouraged an abandonment of limits on warfare.

While the controversy of Sand Creek did not signify a positive change in attitudes towards the Native Americans, the extermination of the tribes at Sand Creek was so gratuitous and unjustifiable that it shocked even the relatively lax moral sensibilities of Civil War-era Americans in this regard. The level of savagery at Sand Creek even managed to horrify white settlers, who were otherwise inured to violence on a brutal frontier. As a result, Chivington became a pariah and saw his military and political ambitions crumble.

Chivington's greatest failure, however, and what arguably made his massacre abnormal in a time when such brutality more typically caused celebration, lay in his neglect of military ethics and his shortcomings as a military commander. Pursuing his ambitions at any cost, he defied the U.S. government and ruthlessly dismissed his subordinates' insights and protests. In doing so, he derailed the larger military campaign plan that aligned with government initiatives to settle the West and gradually push out the Native Americans at a rate that the smaller U.S. Army could handle. His merciless descent on a recognized peaceable encampment set off a sustained wave of retaliatory incidents to the dismay of the U.S. military that had worked to prevent such an outbreak. Chivington's military and moral failings made his attack at Sand Creek indefensible.

Chivington orchestrated the slaughter of hundreds of surrendering Native Americans, destabilized the frontier for many years to follow, and incited tense and prolonged controversy throughout Colorado and the nation. His despicable behaviour did not even gain him the promotion he sought; he never became a general nor served in Congress. Instead, he lived out the rest of his life as a polarizing figure who is a fitting candidate for the title of the worst military commander in history.

PART 2

FRAUDS

Vice Admiral Sir David Beatty, *c.* 1915–16.

4

DAVID BEATTY

Chuck Steele

At first glance David Beatty appears to be an unlikely figure to end up in a study of history's worst commanders. However, beyond his rakish good looks, commanding presence and the acclaim garnered from contemporaries, he proved to be a disastrously bad wartime commander.[1] At the turn of the last century he was known throughout his service for being both courageous and charismatic. Beatty was a popular and wilful officer who seemed to be the embodiment of all that was best remembered from the Age of Nelson, when audacity was the most prized trait of a Royal Navy officer. Indeed, his immense popularity and the perceived resemblance to Nelson were so great that it caused one of his subordinates, Rear Admiral William Pakenham, to confide to First Lord of the Admiralty Winston Churchill that, with Beatty, 'Nelson has come again.'[2]

However, the lion's share of Beatty's heroics and reputation were the products of service removed from the sea and alien to the strains of fleet command. Regardless of the laurels acquired in his youth, Beatty was also the British admiral responsible for leading the Battle Cruiser Fleet in its disastrous encounter with Germany's High Seas Fleet at the Battle of Jutland. Inopportunely for Beatty, and those serving under him in the First World War, he was unable to adequately prepare for and control large-scale engagements featuring the advanced technology of the industrial age. Despite participating in all three of the Grand Fleet's battles in the North Sea, Beatty proved a poor student of the first two of those engagements, and his inability to translate his experiences into meaningful lessons to be shared throughout his command subsequently led to misfortunes befalling his squadrons in their most important fight. Particularly, Beatty's leadership of the largest concentration of cutting-edge naval technology at the Battle of Jutland demanded innovative and technologically savvy direction that was utterly missing from his repertoire as an admiral. The failure to capitalize on the superiority of technology available to him, and to prepare for the opportunity of battle in May 1916, mark Beatty as one of the worst commanders in the annals of war at sea. Churchill wrote that Admiral John Jellicoe, Beatty's superior and the officer commanding the Grand Fleet at the Battle of Jutland, 'was the only man on either side who could lose the war in an afternoon', but it was David Beatty who most nearly made that reflection a reality.[3]

David Richard Beatty was born on 17 January 1871 in Stapeley near Nantwich, Cheshire. For the Beattys, military service was a family affair. His father had been a light cavalryman, serving in the 4th Hussars, and all three of his brothers served as soldiers. Despite his father and brothers being drawn to the army, young David set his mind on a career in Britain's Senior Service: the Royal Navy. Embarking on his remarkable career at age thirteen, he entered the Naval College at Dartmouth in 1884. Despite an unremarkable time as a cadet, when he was more infamous than admirable as a student after having been punished more than two dozen times for minor offences and three times for more serious lapses in judgement, Beatty was destined for greatness.[4] Possessing a wealth of physical courage, cultivated in part through a lifelong love of fox hunting, Beatty would be recognized for his bravery and resolve under fire during military campaigns in Sudan (1896–8) and China (1900).

Passing out from Dartmouth without distinction in 1886, he nonetheless found himself posted as a midshipman to the flagship of the Mediterranean Fleet, HMS *Alexandra*. This choice assignment would bring Beatty into daily contact with many of the Royal Navy's rising stars.[5] Personal connections are often of the utmost importance in advancing military careers, and Beatty would enjoy the support of many influential persons throughout his tenure in the navy. One such benefactor was Stanley Colville, who helped propel the young Beatty into the limelight when he selected him to be his second in command of the flotilla accompanying General Herbert Kitchener during his expedition in Sudan.[6] In the campaign of 1896 Beatty proved cool in a crisis, going so far as to personally extricate and jettison an unexploded enemy shell from his gunboat while under fire. When Colville was injured, Beatty took charge, pressed on, and made a name for himself in action during the fighting at Dongola, winning the Distinguished Service Order (DSO) and the admiration of Kitchener. Following his extraordinary service with the gunboats, Beatty was promoted to commander, in about half the time as the other officers of his commissioning year group.[7]

Beatty's meteoric rise continued as a result of his service during the Boxer Rebellion in 1900. Having followed Colville to the China Station, Beatty was once again at the right place at the right time to distinguish himself while under fire. Serving as executive officer to Colville, then commanding HMS *Barfleur*, Beatty led a contingent of sailors in combat at Tianjin. As in the fighting four years earlier, Beatty won praise and promotion for his courage and composure. Leading by example, Beatty was out front with his men when he was wounded in the left arm and wrist. The young commander discharged his duties in a manner that would have been quite familiar to his brothers and father. Following his heroism in China, he made captain at the remarkably early age of 29.[8] Thus, at the dawn of the new century, David Beatty had become one of the most celebrated officers in the Royal Navy, without having done anything of note while at sea.

Following his tour of duty in Asia, Beatty returned to England, where he engaged in two of his favourite activities – hunting foxes and chasing women. Specifically, Beatty sought the affections of Ethel Tree, the sole heir to the fortune of Chicago department store mogul Marshall Field. Tree had been married when she first caught Beatty's eye, before his deployment to China, but a divorce from her husband Arthur on 12 May 1901 left her free to marry Beatty ten days later.[9] At a stroke, Beatty had secured the hand in marriage of the woman he loved, and she, in turn, had liberated him from the financial and service limitations of deriving his income exclusively from the navy. Theirs, however, was a turbulent and complicated relationship, giving Beatty another point of comparison to the navy's idol of the previous century in the form of Nelson's celebrated and convention-defying love affair with Emma Hamilton.

With his hard-won fame and Ethel's fortune behind him, Beatty was able to be discerning in his acceptance of assignments, if not outright demanding. Despite a dearth of time in command at sea, at the beginning of 1910, Beatty attained the rank of rear admiral; his promotion to flag rank made him the youngest officer to be so promoted in over a century.[10] When offered a position suitable to his rank, second in command of the Atlantic Fleet, Beatty declined the offer, as he preferred service elsewhere. For an ordinary officer, such a refusal would probably have meant the end of a career, but Beatty's heroics, his wife's wealth and a bit of good luck made him an exception to the rule. At this time, fortune continued to smile on Beatty with Winston Churchill's arrival at the Admiralty as First Lord in October 1911. Despite warnings concerning Beatty's youth and impertinence, Churchill was thoroughly taken with the young admiral and decided to make him his naval secretary at the start of 1912.[11] Churchill's favour ensured that Beatty's rise to prominence would proceed unabated and that following the war his reputation would be protected.

When it came to Beatty, Churchill recognized the obvious, namely that the young admiral was a very bright star in a constellation dimmed by a lack of meaningful naval activity. Without fleet actions, there seemed no better way to take the measure of officers than to consider their performance under whatever fire had been thrown against them, even if that fire did not come from ships. Indeed, Churchill saw Beatty's heroics on the field of battle as being beneficial to his service as an admiral. According to Churchill,

> It became increasingly clear to me that he viewed questions of naval strategy and tactics in a different light from the average naval officer: he approached them, as it seemed to me, much more as a soldier would. His war experiences on land illuminated the facts he had acquired in his naval training. He was no mere instrumentalist.[12]

Unsurprisingly, in 1913 when the position of commander of the British Battle Cruiser Squadron became vacant, Churchill filled it with Beatty. The appointment would eventually lead to Beatty's command of the Battle Cruiser Fleet and to his becoming one of the most controversial figures of the Great War.

Churchill, as a trained and battle-tested soldier, might have been influenced by personal bias in lauding Beatty's unconventional professional record. Regardless of the sources of affection for Beatty, or of Churchill's potential for excessive pride in the superiority of the judgement of soldiers, the First Lord was wrong to have discounted the importance of being technologically orientated for members of the sea service at the dawning of the twentieth century. In fact, the Royal Navy of Beatty's time was transformed in a few short years by First Sea Lord, Admiral of the Fleet John 'Jacky' Fisher and a pair of revolutionary ship designs that he championed. With the launching of HMS *Dreadnought* in 1906, Fisher and Britain had ushered in a new age in naval architecture and fleet capabilities. In addition to new battleships, another impressive and innovative ship type was making its debut in the first years of the twentieth century: the battle cruiser. In both instances, it was clear that the performance of the new ships was markedly superior to what existed previously. Both ship types were bigger, faster and capable of striking much harder than anything present at the Battle of Tsushima in 1905. More importantly, *Dreadnought* and her battle cruiser analogue *Invincible* were merely the first iterations of rapidly changing manifestations of sea power.

At the Battle of Tsushima, Admiral Togo Heihachiro flew his flag from the British-built battleship *Mikasa*. At that time, the Japanese flagship was state-of-the-art technology. She displaced slightly more than 15,000 tons, her main armament consisted of four 12-inch guns, her power plant could deliver 15,000 horsepower, and she could attain a top speed of 18 knots.[13] A little more than a year later, the British launched *Dreadnought*. The newer battleship displaced nearly 22,000 tons when fully loaded, her main armament consisted of ten 12-inch guns, her turbine engines could deliver 23,000 horsepower, and she could steam at 21 knots.[14] By the time of the Battle of Jutland, ten years later, Beatty had available to him four Queen Elizabeth-class battleships – the state of the art in 1916. The newest battleships displaced 33,000 tons fully loaded, the main armament was upgraded to eight 15-inch guns, their turbine engines could deliver 75,000 horsepower, and they could steam at 24 knots.[15]

While Beatty had battleships under his command at the Battle of Jutland, this was only a temporary arrangement, as his standing with Churchill before the war had won him the enviable command of the more romanticized battle cruisers. These ships packed the punch of battleships but had even greater speed. As Churchill remarked, the battle cruisers were 'the strategic cavalry of the Royal Navy, that supreme combination of speed and power to which the Admiralty were continuously directed'.[16] The first of the British battle cruisers were the Invincible class (*Invincible, Indomitable, Inflexible*). These ships, launched in 1907, displaced a little over 20,000 tons fully loaded and mounted eight 12-inch guns, their turbine engines delivered 41,000 horsepower, and they could steam at 25 knots.[17] By May 1916 Beatty was flying his flag from HMS *Lion*, the lead ship in a class of battle cruisers that included *Princess Royal* and the *Queen Mary*. The new ships displaced 29,700 tons fully loaded and mounted eight 13.5-inch guns, their engines could generate 70,000 horsepower, and they could steam at a remarkable 26.5 knots.[18] However, the increases in speed for the battle cruisers came at the expense of additional defensive armour. They were fast ships, but they would prove to be vulnerable.

The net result of these rapidly changing developments was that naval engagements would involve ships capable of firing at greater ranges with heavier shot, while also moving faster to contact. In other words, technology was driving an accelerated pace and range of battle. According to Norman Friedman, Fisher was fascinated by the need for attaining simultaneous increases in gunnery ranges and ship speed: 'Only higher speed would enable a British fleet to choose its battle range so as to force an enemy to submit to a pounding he could not effectively return.'[19] To his credit, Fisher oversaw the development of ships capable of the dramatic increases in speed and firepower he desired. However, in the First World War, Beatty would prove an incapable maestro when it came time to coordinate the new instruments in the race to meet their full potential in battle.

Although it has been argued that the Royal Navy had forgotten how to fight in the years between the Napoleonic Wars and the Battle of Jutland, such assertions miss the more significant point that Britain's actual struggle was in learning from its experiences in the First World War as the crisis unfolded. A particularly egregious affirmation of this historic deceit was recently offered by a U.S. Naval War College professor, who tried to make the case that Britain's performance in battle in 1916 was a result of some form of institutional amnesia. According to the professor, 'by 1916 the Royal Navy had in effect forgotten about the rigors of war against a peer competitor.'[20] Of course, by May 1916 the Royal Navy had engaged in four substantial actions against the Imperial German Navy: the battles of Coronel and the Falklands fought in the South Pacific and South Atlantic Oceans in November and December 1914, and the battles of Heligoland Bight and Dogger Bank fought in the North Sea in August 1914 and January 1915. The problem confronting the Royal Navy, and David Beatty, in May 1916 was not that they had forgotten how to fight, it was that they proved incapable of learning appropriate lessons from their own recent experiences in war. If anything, Beatty, the most heralded combatant of his generation, remembered too much about how battles were fought on land, or in an era far removed from that requiring his services as a fleet commander.

In the course of the First World War Beatty had three opportunities to display his ability as a squadron/fleet commander. The first instance in which ships under Beatty's command saw battle was 28 August 1914, off Heligoland Bight. Although it was Commodore Roger Keyes, the commander of Britain's submarine service, and not Beatty, who was the architect of the operation that became the First World War's first major naval engagement, the timely intervention of Beatty resulted in considerable damage to German naval forces, and a clear-cut victory for the Royal Navy. However, poor information-sharing before the battle, and poor communications throughout the fight, deprived the British of what might have been an even greater success. It also presaged a string of problems that would plague the Royal Navy and Beatty throughout the remainder of the war.

Specifically, in late August 1914 Keyes came up with a plan to set an ambush near Heligoland Bight after his submarines observed regular German naval activity in the area.[21] Beatty's part in the battle would be critical, but unscripted. Keyes's plan was shared in only the vaguest terms with Jellicoe, who feared that Keyes and his operational partner Commodore Reginald Tyrwhitt, commanding the First Light Cruiser Squadron out of Harwich, might find themselves facing overwhelming odds. Consequently, Jellicoe implored the Admiralty to inform him of the plan and allow for the Grand Fleet's participation. As historian James Goldrick noted, 'although Jellicoe acted swiftly, dispatching Beatty and Goodenough [the commander of the 2nd Light Cruiser Squadron] at 0500 on 27 August and following with the battle squadrons shortly after, neither he nor his subordinates knew precisely what was happening.'[22] Confusion reigned supreme at Heligoland Bight. Not only were Jellicoe and Beatty unaware of the details of Keyes's plan, but Keyes was unaware of the movements of the other forces participating in the action.[23] Disaster was averted, and the British managed to avoid sinking their own ships, but more importantly, Beatty's battle cruisers *Lion*, *Queen Mary*, *Princess Royal*, *Invincible* and *New Zealand* appeared in the nick of time to rescue Tyrwhitt's force, which was being drawn down upon by a trio of German cruisers.

Beatty's arrival led to the sinking of two of the cruisers, *Cöln* and *Ariadne*, and sent the other (*Strassburg*) to flight.

Beatty and the Royal Navy had emerged from their first experience of battle in the Great War with fresh laurels, but the battle should have been less celebrated and better studied for it was rife with valuable lessons. The battle was a confusing mess and a complete mismatch once the battle cruisers arrived on the scene. As Beatty wrote to Keyes, 'our disappointment was great when we got there and only found Light-cruisers [*sic*] to compete with, poor devils.'[24] Though Beatty wished for an encounter with a comparable foe, the ability to engage with relative impunity was undoubtedly a boon to the Royal Navy. Unfortunately for the British, even though the communications problems were acknowledged, the easy victory may have dampened the sense of urgency necessary to keep from making the problems chronic rather than acute.

Perhaps more significantly, in the time between Beatty's first two sea battles, the Royal Navy fought two more engagements, the battles of Coronel and the Falklands, the latter of which showed how effective the battle cruiser concept was – if properly employed. After the German East Asia Squadron, commanded by Maximilian von Spee, had destroyed two of Britain's old armoured cruisers at the Battle of Coronel on 1 November 1914, reinforcements were rushed to the South Atlantic, specifically the battle cruisers *Invincible* and *Inflexible*, and at the Battle of the Falklands on 8 December 1914 Britain was avenged. Again, a relatively painless victory may have prevented a sense of urgency from gripping the Royal Navy's senior leaders, this time concerning the problems of matching the advantages of speed and the range of heavy-calibre guns with the difficulties of plotting targets and directing accurate fire. As one historian noted,

> the *Invincible* and *Inflexible* exploited their superior speed to hold the hopelessly outgunned armoured cruisers *Scharnhorst* and *Gneisenau* at ranges varying from 12,000 to 16,000 yards (6.8 to 9.0 miles) and sank both with negligible damage to themselves, but it took them four and a half hours and 1,180 shells, and they scored approximately 6 percent hits.[25]

In Beatty's next action, the Battle of Dogger Bank on 24 January 1915, poor communications and inefficient shooting would once again hinder the Royal Navy. Relying on superior signals intelligence from the Admiralty in London, Beatty took two squadrons of battle cruisers out from the Firth of Forth to meet with additional lighter British naval forces to intercept Franz Hipper's First Scouting Group. The British had a five to three advantage in battle cruisers (*Lion, Tiger, Princess Royal, Indomitable* and *New Zealand* against *Seydlitz, Moltke* and *Derfflinger*). Hipper, who had put to sea in anticipation of intercepting inferior British forces, let discretion serve as the better part of valour, recoiling into headlong retreat once the disparity in forces became apparent. Meanwhile, Beatty's battle cruisers spared no effort in trying to close the distance with the fleeing Germans. Owing to their generally superior speed, and the Herculean efforts of British stokers, Beatty's squadrons steamed ever closer to the Germans. Once *Lion* (Beatty's flagship) was within 22,000 yards of the armoured cruiser *Blücher* (the last and slowest ship in Hipper's line) the British opened fire.[26]

However, as the British pressed on, problems in communications and fire control became manifest. *Tiger* failed to target the appropriate ship (*Moltke*) and instead directed its fire on the *Seydlitz*, which was already being targeted by *Lion*.[27] Compounding problems for the British was the fire being poured onto *Lion*. The flagship was hit several times and suffered significant damage. As *Lion* slowed, Beatty was quickly out of position to lead, resorting solely to signal flags to direct his squadrons. Worsening the situation, the signals being issued were not clear in establishing the Admiral's intent. Beatty's signals resulted in the remaining fully serviceable British battle cruisers concentrating their fire on the badly damaged *Blücher*. As the commander of the Second Battle Cruiser Squadron, Rear Admiral Archibald Moore, attested, 'the Vice-Admiral [Beatty] made a general signal: "Attack the rear of enemy bearing NE"; this was apparently the *Blücher* (she bore approximately NE from *New Zealand* at the time).'[28] At the end of the battle, the unfortunate armoured cruiser had drawn the overwhelming attention of Beatty's battle cruisers and was the only one of Hipper's ships sunk.

In addition to poor communications, British gunnery was abysmal, with only 1 per cent of rounds hitting home at ranges between 16,000 and 18,000 yards.[29] Beatty had not done well in preparing or controlling his forces. The battle was a lost opportunity for the British that highlighted poor communications and ineffective standard operating procedures. Nevertheless, in its aftermath, Beatty was honoured for having routed the Germans. Indeed, it was at this point that Pakenham made his proclamation of admiration for Beatty to Churchill.[30] Obviously, Britain thirsted for a hero of Nelsonic proportions, but unlike Nelson, Beatty neither comprehended the strengths and weaknesses of the technologies at his disposal nor did he enjoy a demonstrative qualitative advantage in sailors and commanders over his foes. The First World War was not merely a struggle between a sea power and a land power; this was a contest between two highly industrialized nations – with fleets that were technological marvels representing the full measure of both belligerents' mechanical prowess.

A failure to understand rapidly changing weapons and communications systems was not Beatty's only fault in being unable to meet historic expectations; he had not cultivated a group of competent and audacious subordinates, similar to Nelson's famous band of brothers. Beatty was brave and ambitious, but neither of those qualities obviated the need for him to develop a team that shared an understanding of how a modern sea battle should be fought. A case in point was Moore, who for his efforts to point out the confusion caused by Beatty's poor communications was reassigned by Churchill and replaced by Pakenham. The Royal Navy had spent centuries developing a unique warrior ethos, and Beatty seemed to be its exemplar in 1915. Rather than scrutinize his failure to prepare for the chaos of battle and produce a victory worthy of the assets under his command, the Admiralty sang the praises of its anointed hero and left the weight of his mistakes to be borne by Moore. As Beatty confided to Jellicoe not long after the battle, '1st Lord [Churchill] was in a disturbed frame of mind and wanted to have the blood of somebody. I gather this is the First Sea Lord's [Fisher] idea also; they settled on Moore.' Adding his condemnation to that of the Admiralty, Beatty wrote, 'well frankly between you and I he is not of the right sort of temperament for a BCS [battle cruiser squadron].'[31]

Perhaps fearing that Beatty was feeling too much pressure to be a modern-day Nelson, or that he might not be the most assiduous student of naval affairs, Jellicoe wrote the following to him in March 1915:

> I am starting to write a difficult letter. I should imagine that the Germans will sooner or later try and entrap you by using their battle cruisers as a decoy. They must know that I am

– where I am – and you are where you are, and they may well argue that the position is one which lends itself to a trap to bring you into the High Seas Fleet, with the battle cruisers as bait. They know that if they can get you in chase, the odds are that you will be 100 miles away from me, and they can under such conditions draw you well down to the Heligoland Bight without my being in effective support. It is quite all right if you keep your speed, of course, but it is the reverse if you have some ships with their speed badly reduced in the fight with the battle cruisers, or by submarines. In that case the loss of such ships seems inevitable if you are drawn into the vicinity of the High Seas Fleet with me still too far off to get to your help or to their help, so as to extricate before dark.[32]

Jellicoe's note was prophetic. Reinhard Scheer, the commander-in-chief of Germany's High Seas Fleet, set the very trap Jellicoe feared at the end of May 1916. At the Battle of Jutland on 31 May–1 June 1916, Beatty played directly to German expectations. However, with the Grand Fleet anticipating Scheer's course of action, Beatty was not merely the victim of well-reasoned German planning, but also the bait in a far more extensive engagement that would feature the full might of the Grand Fleet. Sortieing once again upon receiving signals intelligence from London, indicating Hipper's Scouting Group was putting to sea, Beatty once again led the Battle Cruiser Fleet to search for Hipper's forces. Once outlying elements of the two fleets came into contact with each other, the larger ships of the battle cruiser forces were drawn together. In short order, a heated moving battle took shape between the two groups of battle cruisers. The fighting was intense and extremely costly for the British. Beyond getting the better of Beatty in combat, Hipper was playing his part in leading Beatty on a chase toward Scheer in what is known as the 'Run to the South'.

Beatty's force consisted of six battle cruisers (*Lion, Queen Mary, Princess Royal, Tiger, New Zealand* and *Indefatigable*) and Rear Admiral Hugh Evan-Thomas's Fifth Battle Squadron of four Queen Elizabeth-class battleships (*Barham, Valiant, Warspite* and *Malaya*). Beatty's fleet ordinarily did not include Evan-Thomas's battle squadron, but Horace Hood's Third Battle Cruiser Squadron (*Invincible, Inflexible* and *Indomitable*) was temporarily attached to the Battle Fleet, and the

Queen Elizabeths were sent south to serve Beatty in their stead.[33] Not surprisingly, in the short time that Evan-Thomas had traded places with Hood, communications between Beatty and the Fifth Battle Squadron commander were poor at best, and there was a lack of understanding over Beatty's operating procedures.[34] These discrepancies could not be cleared up under fire and at full speed. In his rush to come to grips with his old adversary, Beatty not only outstripped the support of Evan-Thomas's immensely powerful battleships, but in driving on so quickly he surrendered the advantages of superior gun range that his battle cruisers held over their five German counterparts (*Lützow*, *Derfflinger*, *Moltke*, *Seydlitz* and *Von der Tann*). Instead of engaging at more than 20,000 yards, it was estimated that Beatty opened fire at a range inside 18,000 yards – possibly as low as 16,000 yards. Seemingly, the British solution to the problem of ineffective gun ranging was not to be found in firing more rounds from longer ranges but firing more rounds from shorter ranges. Rather than meet the intent of the battle cruiser's design, to combine greater speed with the ability to engage at a relatively safe distance, Beatty's ships were well within the range of Hipper's battle cruisers when the fighting began at approximately 3:45.[35] The British were in a dire predicament concerning their vulnerability to German fire that was exacerbated by being silhouetted against the western sky, thus allowing for easier target acquisition by their foes.[36]

Additionally, as the distance between the disparate parts of Beatty's command grew, it became more difficult to maintain communications between the battle cruisers and the battleships. While Moore had been replaced after voicing his concerns over the confusing signals at Dogger Bank, Beatty had nonetheless retained his signals lieutenant, Ralph Seymour. Despite more than a year intervening between the battles, matters were unimproved in terms of the clarity of communications between *Lion* and the other ships under Beatty's command. Indeed, as the battle cruisers formed into line, they once again failed to target all of Hipper's battle cruisers. Having a one-ship advantage over Hipper, Beatty had called on HMS *Princess Royal*, the ship immediately behind his own, to concentrate fire on Hipper's flagship, the *Lützow*. Regrettably for the British, the next ship in the German line, *Derfflinger*, was initially left unmolested by the *Queen Mary*, the third ship in Beatty's formation.[37]

The consequences of Beatty's haste were disastrous. At 4:02 the British lost the battle cruiser *Indefatigable*, and at 4:26 they lost *Queen*

Mary.[38] In the span of less than half an hour, Hipper had sunk a third of Beatty's battle cruisers, and the Germans had taken the lives of more than 2,000 British sailors. Beatty's battle cruisers and Evan-Thomas's battleships were thoroughly drawn into the trap Jellicoe had foreseen. Following Hipper's First Scouting Group was the main force of Scheer's High Seas Fleet. Like sharks drawn to blood, Scheer's battleships pressed on to complete the destruction begun by Hipper. Knowing that Jellicoe and salvation were behind him, Beatty turned his forces north to lead the Germans into a broader clash with the entire Grand Fleet. Again, distance and communication proved difficult, and Evan-Thomas's battleships passed Beatty and his remaining battle cruisers before making their turn to the north under very heavy fire from the High Seas Fleet. According to naval historian Eric Grove, 'The effective defeat of the Battle Cruiser Fleet in the "Run to the South" was caused not just by poor shooting but flawed tactics that did not take advantage of his gunnery superiority, and by an unwillingness to concentrate with the Fifth Battle Squadron.'[39]

It is somewhat ironic that regardless of the misfortunes that had befallen Beatty's fleet, the German hunters were on a course to become the hunted. At least one historian, Andrew Gordon, has posited that Beatty's escape to the protection of Jellicoe's guns was 'a tribute to his [Beatty's] leadership, single-mindedness and stamina', yet even in this Beatty was not beyond reproach.[40] Again, poor communications from Beatty, or rather non-existent communications, left Jellicoe without proper situational awareness. Earlier in the day, the commander-in-chief of the Grand Fleet was aware that battle had been joined between the battle cruiser forces of the two fleets, and then that the High Seas Fleet had entered the fray. However, while Jellicoe knew that Scheer and his fleet were in pursuit of Beatty and the Battle Cruiser Fleet, the senior British commander was aware of little else until the two parts of the British fleet made visual contact shortly before 6 p.m. When Beatty finally was in sight of Jellicoe, the latter pressed Beatty for the course and bearing of the Germans – he received the bearing, but not the course.[41] Still, Jellicoe's battleships manoeuvred expertly to steam into line firing full broadsides into the bows of the German High Seas Fleet when contact was made at approximately 6:30 p.m. As evening turned to night, the Grand Fleet's twice crossing of the German T placed Scheer in an untenable position, making retreat his most attractive option. Scheer would succeed in his efforts to escape, aided by night and more communications problems – this time throughout the Grand Fleet. The battle ended in the early hours of 1 June, but the controversy was just beginning.

Remarkably, Beatty's reputation as an admiral was not ruined by the response his fleet made to the German challenge. Almost immediately after the battle, Beatty and his supporters sought to cast the fight in a new light. To Beatty and his partisans, the battle was not a failure because of the losses to the Battle Cruiser Fleet, but because Jellicoe failed to annihilate the German Fleet. In the words of Beatty's adoring subordinate Pakenham: 'To us it looked as though all was over with the Germans but the killing ... If there had been a David [Beatty] in the battlefleet, we should have had a different tale to tell.'[42]

Though Jellicoe received the lion's share of criticism for failing to deliver an industrial-age Battle of Trafalgar, it was the losses to Beatty's battle cruisers that gave Germany its greatest claim to success at Jutland. Despite his earlier exposure to battle in the North Sea, Beatty failed to capitalize on his experiences and neither improved procedures for clearer communications nor engaged in practices facilitating more effective gunnery. Indeed, British efforts to increase their rates of fire led to dangerous practices for the stowing and handling of ammunition throughout the Grand Fleet. However, the problems associated with those practices were most acute in the battle cruisers, owing to their diminished ability to sustain a pounding from heavy-calibre guns. The advantages of the battle cruiser's superior speed and gun range, as envisioned by Fisher, were lost on Beatty at Jutland. Perhaps a mere instrumentalist would have fared better. After all, it was the battle cruisers, the weapons platform Churchill thought ideally suited to the command of Beatty, that were at the heart of the losses among the British at Jutland.

As they had been after Dogger Bank, Beatty's shortcomings were overlooked in favour of pinning the blame for an incomplete victory, or worse, on an officer less attuned to seeking celebrity. Far from being held accountable for any of his failings at Jutland, Beatty was rewarded for his service, replacing Jellicoe as the commander of the Grand Fleet, once the latter was made First Sea Lord to deal with the U-boat menace. At war's end Beatty took the greatest of laurels, retaining command of the Grand Fleet during the surrender of the High Seas Fleet. In November 1919 Beatty became First Sea Lord, a position he would hold for eight years. His performance as First Sea Lord during the 1920s was far more laudable than his efforts as a fleet commander. Beatty proved to be an adroit advocate for the Royal Navy, maintaining its standing at the fore of world navies regardless of the austerity brought on by the end of the First World War. According to Andrew Lambert, it was Beatty's time as First Sea Lord that showed his 'true greatness as an admiral'.[43]

Beatty's efforts to achieve a favourable interpretation of his role at the Battle of Jutland put him at odds with many who fought at Jutland and several notable historians, not the least of whom was Julian Corbett, the author of *Some Principles of Maritime Strategy* and the *History of the Great War Naval Operations, Based on Official Documents*. When Corbett's official history was published, the Admiralty, firmly under Beatty's influence as First Sea Lord, saw fit to distance themselves from criticism and issue a disclaimer stating, 'Their Lordships find that some of the principles advocated in this book, especially the tendency to minimize the importance of seeking battle and of forcing it to a conclusion, are directly in conflict with their views.'[44] Furthermore, in the years after the battle other accounts of the fighting were written by partisans of both Beatty and Jellicoe. Beatty for his part actively sought to change the historical record concerning his actions, despite many of the battle's participants and chroniclers being aware of the disingenuous nature of Beatty's editorial efforts. The inevitable verdict of the attempts to rewrite history was that Beatty knew how poorly he performed in command.

Beatty's career was long and illustrious, and if the Battle of Jutland had not resulted in such terrible losses to the ships and crews under his command, he might be thought of as one of the many gifted naval officers in British history. While it may seem untoward to judge Beatty so harshly more than a hundred years after his struggles at Jutland, there is no denying that by 31 May 1916 Beatty should have been the most knowledgeable war fighter in the Royal Navy; yet, for all of his experience in battle, his last effort in a fighting command was his worst. Moreover, in the aftermath of the battle, Beatty and his partisans tried to shift blame, making Jellicoe the subject of the criticism they deserved. He could not let the record go unaltered, not if he expected to retain his pre-eminent standing in naval and national circles. Perhaps for all the praise heaped upon him over his career, Beatty had conflated his reputation with that of the Royal Navy. Perhaps it was more important to sustain the image of Beatty as an incomparable warrior admiral than to risk diminishing the ethos created by men such as Drake, Anson, Rodney and Nelson. Regardless of these considerations, Beatty proved himself to be not only a poor fleet commander but a thoroughly ignoble man for his efforts to escape accountability for his actions.

5

GIDEON J. PILLOW

Robert P. Wettemann Jr

The annals of military history are filled with the names of commanders whose mark of distinction was a singular leadership failure or inadequate display of martial acumen as demonstrated in one war. Rarer are those whose claim to fame is ineptitude in two conflicts, such as Tennessean Gideon Pillow, who gained a lacklustre reputation during the Mexican–American War (1846–8) for his 'puerile imbecility', partisan politics and 'despicable self-puffings' that alienated him from other American officers who distinguished themselves with their martial skill and personal valour during that conflict.[1] Hanging up his general's uniform for civilian mufti when the conflict ended, Pillow returned to command twelve years later as a general officer in the Army of the Confederate States of America during the American Civil War. There, too, he became known for his ineptitude, prompting the future commander of the Union armies, Lieutenant General Ulysses S. Grant, to later write, '[I] judged that with any force, no matter how small, I could march up to within gunshot of any entrenchments [Pillow] was given to hold.'[2] Gideon Pillow was the nadir of a martial system that valued personal ambition, party loyalty and the supposed innate martial abilities of the American citizen over military professionalism, general knowledge of military art and science, and the ability to inspire and lead men into battle. These failings earn Gideon Pillow a place among the ranks of the worst military leaders in history.

Born on 8 June 1806 in Williamson County, Tennessee, Gideon Pillow was raised in a well-connected and propertied family that admired and respected the citizen-soldier tradition. For Tennesseans,

General Andrew Jackson was a household name, as he had led a mixed force of U.S. Army, Tennessee volunteers and others to victory in the Battle of New Orleans in 1815. The Pillow family possessed close ties to this tradition as William Carroll, one of Jackson's trusted lieutenants, was a cousin to Gideon Pillow by marriage. Carroll had joined the Tennessee militia as a captain in 1812, ending the war as a major general under Jackson's command. Succeeding Jackson as commander of the Tennessee militia, Carroll went on to a successful political career as governor of Tennessee. The soldier-turned-statesman served as a role model for young Pillow, who witnessed at first hand how a capable and charismatic leader could translate martial prowess into a successful political career, and he undoubtedly looked to follow in his kinsman's footsteps.[3]

An 1827 graduate of the University of Nashville, the young Pillow read the law for three years before passing the bar and advertising his services as a lawyer in 1830. His legal work connected Pillow with other influential Tennesseans, first among these being his fellow lawyer James K. Polk. Although he was never Polk's law partner, Pillow and 'Young Hickory', as Polk came to be known, were close associates, with Pillow later becoming a law partner with Polk's nephew, J. Knox Walker.[4]

While he developed close ties to Polk, it was, however, his cousin William Carroll who provided Pillow with his entrée into military service. In 1833 Carroll, now governor of Tennessee, named Pillow, a military novice, to serve as adjutant general of the state's militia, awarding to him the single star of a brigadier general at the age of 27. While such an appointment might shock modern martial sensibilities, such practices characterized the so-called 'Era of the Common Man'. Pillow's appointment, however, came at a time when a contrary trend was emerging to challenge the citizen-soldier orthodoxy. In the decades that followed the War of 1812, American politicians and military leaders who had witnessed the destruction of the nation's capital at the hands of the British Army reformed the American military establishment. Recasting the U.S. Military Academy as a school of engineering and the military arts, a new generation of American officers were reinventing the U.S. Army. Following the lead of General Winfield Scott, who became commanding general of the army in 1841, they embraced military professionalism defined in terms of technical expertise and a shared identity as members of a larger military

Gideon J. Pillow, early 1860s.

bureaucracy that valued service over self. Pillow's appointment ran counter to such notions, and while the new brigadier professed to have read the military manuals of the day, there is little evidence he ever drilled Tennessee troops during his three years as adjutant general. Despite the exalted title, his was largely a state patronage position that he hoped to use as a path to higher office.[5]

After three years' service as brigadier general, Pillow returned to his law practice in 1836. He soon acquired Clifton Place, a plantation near Columbia, and over the course of the next two decades transformed it into one of the largest estates in Tennessee. As his wealth grew, so did his political influence. In 1844 Pillow played an 'important role' in the nomination of his friend James K. Polk to the presidency. Pillow's support of Polk earned him the appreciation of the future president, a position that would soon place the ambitious, lawyer-turned-adjutant general in a position to pursue martial glory.[6]

Following a skirmish between U.S. dragoons and Mexican lancers along the Rio Grande, Polk's claim that 'American Blood had been shed on American soil' offered him the justification to ask Congress for a declaration of war against the Republic of Mexico, which he received on 13 May 1846. In the wake of this declaration, coupled with news of General Zachary Taylor's successes at the battles of Palo Alto and Resaca de la Palma, Pillow and hundreds of other patriotic Tennesseans flocked to the colours, hoping to gain glory through martial pursuits in Mexico. Partially because of his 'eminent qualifications' as former adjutant general, but largely because as a stalwart Democrat he could keep an eye on Taylor and other officers of a Whiggish bent who dominated the regular army, Polk therefore extended to Pillow a commission as brigadier general, with instructions to 'place yourself at the head of your command within the shortest possible period'.[7]

Arriving at Lomita, Mexico, to assume command of the Second Brigade in Major General Robert Patterson's Second Division of Volunteers, the political general's actions soon exposed him as a military novice. First, Pillow suspended the onerous task of daytime guard duty, which was welcomed by his soldiers, but potentially threatened the security of his brigade's encampment. Less than a month later, he proposed reorganizing the Tennessee brigade by transferring two companies from the First Regiment Tennessee Volunteers to the Second Regiment Tennessee Volunteers. Considering that the men in the respective units had already elected their officers and took immense pride in their respective organizations, Pillow's unpopular proposal, designed only to balance the number of companies in each regiment (the First Tennessee contained twelve while the Second Tennessee contained eight), ultimately required the intervention of Taylor to maintain unit integrity. It prompted Colonel William Campbell of the First Tennessee to comment that Pillow's command capacity was 'one of the smallest caliber that has ever been elevated to so high a command'.[8]

After these botched efforts, Pillow dug himself into a ditch from which it would take years to escape. Lieutenant Cadmus M. Wilcox, an 1846 West Point graduate who served in the Fourth Infantry, wrote in his *History of the Mexican War* that while at Camargo, Pillow ordered his troops to fortify their encampment by digging an entrenchment in the direction of a possible enemy approach. In doing so, however, Pillow instructed his men to pile the excavated earth on the wrong side of the ditch, rendering it totally ineffective as a military fortification. Pillow's lack of military acumen would be galling to any officer educated at West Point, for nearly all regular officers serving at the company level during the Mexican War were familiar with the design and construction of military fortifications. In the aftermath of the War of 1812, Superintendent Sylvanus Thayer had transformed the u.s. Military Academy into the nation's premier school for military engineering. In 1836 instructor Dennis Hart Mahan had authored *A Complete Treatise on Field Fortifications*, which became the principal text on the subject.[9]

Pillow's actions earned him little favour with Taylor, who regarded him as one with 'much to learn as regards to his new profession'. When the victor of Palo Alto and Resaca de la Palma led troops against Monterey, he left the Tennessee politician-turned-general behind with one of the regiments from his home state. Pillow moved only as far south as Tampico, remaining there until February, when he received orders for Veracruz. From the outset, Pillow understood his role in joining Scott on his proposed overland campaign. As had been the case with Taylor, Pillow effectively functioned as Polk's eyes and ears, taking whatever steps necessary to monitor the behaviour of Scott, another emerging Whig political rival.[10]

Landing at Veracruz on 9 March 1847, Pillow and his Tennesseans engaged in a few minor skirmishes until the city capitulated on 26 March. Pillow went to great lengths to ingratiate himself with Scott and his second-in-command, General William Jenkins Worth, prompting Campbell to label Pillow as part of 'a sort of triumvirate'. While Pillow undoubtedly believed that his posting was a product of confidence, Campbell did surmise, however, that Scott was 'simply paying Polk for letting him [Pillow] come here', as Pillow continued to demonstrate the same lack of military ability that had plagued him from the outset.[11] Shortly after landing, he ordered a company of Pennsylvania volunteers to stand as night guard, ordering half the company to sleep on one side of the road while the remainder stood guard on the other side. While this was a sound deployment in his mind, Pillow was oblivious to the fact that if aroused, they would have 'inevitably killed as many of our own men as the enemy', a fact recognized by a private in the company in noting the 'little generalship of our commander'.[12]

With Veracruz secured, the first order of business was to attempt to end the war without further bloodshed. In early April Polk had dispatched Nicholas B. Trist to Veracruz in order to negotiate with elements of the Mexican government. When Trist arrived bearing instructions from the president to include Pillow in any treaty negotiations, u.s. troops had reached Puebla, about 280 kilometres (175 mi.) from Veracruz. British agents quickly informed Trist that Mexico might be willing to settle for a bribe and the chief clerk of the State Department negotiator approached Pillow, who quickly endorsed the proposal in hopes of establishing himself as a key player in the negotiations. A reluctant Scott gathered Pillow and fellow generals John Quitman, James Shields, David Twiggs and George Cadwalader to discuss the possibilities, with Pillow taking a lead role in advancing the proposition. Little came of the attempted bribe, despite an initial deposit of $10,000 on the part of the United States.[13]

With the Mexican government rejecting American efforts to negotiate a settlement, Scott began preparing the campaign to conquer Mexico City. He ordered Brigadier General David E. Twiggs's division of regulars to leave the city and they began their march on the National Road towards the capital. Pillow followed a few days later, with his brigade of the First and Second Tennessee Volunteers and First and Second Pennsylvania Volunteers forming part of Patterson's Volunteer Division. If Pillow's previous exploits had not been enough to prove his martial ineptitude, he would soon have another opportunity to prove his incompetence. Recognizing American intentions to march towards Mexico City, Mexican General Antonio Lopez de Santa Anna had dug in near Cerro Gordo, where the National Road passed through a narrow defile dominated by high ground known as El Telegrafo on the right, with three significant promontories rising from the valley floor on the left. Santa Anna hoped that by constructing batteries at the end of each ridge, coupled with fortifications constructed atop El Telegrafo, such 'impregnable' works could stop any force marching towards Cerro Gordo on the main road towards Mexico City.[14]

Scott, recognizing the folly of a frontal assault, quickly looked to his West Point-educated engineer officers to discover an alternate route.

Following skirmishes on 11 and 12 April, Scott ordered Captain Robert E. Lee and Lieutenant Pierre G. T. Beauregard of the Corps of Engineers to scout the area, which led to the discovery of an old goat trail leading to the rear of the Mexican positions. They surmised that it could be widened to allow passage of men and artillery, potentially allowing Scott's army to avoid a frontal attack. With this knowledge in hand, Scott carefully prepared his orders to outflank the Mexican positions, hopefully minimizing the casualties inflicted upon his 10,000-man invading army.[15]

Choosing to manoeuvre instead of launching a frontal assault, Scott divided his army, giving each wing distinctly different objectives. Trusting the ambitious, yet militarily inexperienced Tennessean with what could be interpreted as the main attack, Scott ordered Pillow and his brigade to assault the three fortified ridges south of the National Road. Pillow considered his attack to be the most important. In reality, his division was to fight a holding action designed to concentrate the enemy's attention on American movement coming directly up the National Road from Veracruz. The most significant part of the American offensive fell to Twiggs and his division of approximately 7,000 regulars. Having set off on the morning of 17 April, their task was to widen the existing goat trail, outflank the Mexican positions atop El Telegrafo, and render the Mexican positions untenable. If successful, Scott's careful planning would result in a complete envelopment of the Mexican Army and its surrender. If he failed, the possibility existed for the Mexican forces to concentrate on each wing of the u.s. Army while divided and defeat it in detail.[16]

An old adage states that no military plan survives first contact with the enemy, and Pillow quickly took it upon himself to make that a reality. Although he had joined Lieutenants Zealous Tower and George McClellan in scouting the primary route of advance on 13, 15 and 16 April, when his brigade began its march on the morning of 18 April, Pillow set out along a new route, much to the chagrin of Tower. The new route was shorter, but much narrower, requiring the volunteers to deploy in single file, greatly delaying their ability to move into position. At the same time it lacked effective cover, providing the enemy with a greater opportunity to see the approaching Americans. Before Pillow's volunteer brigade could hack out a new path and attack the enemy, they heard gunfire to the west of El Telegrafo. The Battle of Cerro Gordo had begun, and Pillow's reckless impetuosity had prevented his men from serving as the diversionary force that Scott had intended.[17]

Pillow's first bad decision was compounded by his second. Tower's original route would have brought Pillow's volunteers into action below the Mexican position nearest the National Road, out of sight of the other two fortified promontories that dominated the left (south) side of the National Road. Instead, Pillow's disregard of Tower's proposed route brought his men into action under fire from all three Mexican positions, which collectively mounted nineteen pieces of artillery. Moving into position in single file, Colonel Francis Wynkoop's First Pennsylvania, Haskell's Second Tennessee, Campbell's First Tennessee and Roberts's Second Pennsylvania struggled to form their lines of battle with alacrity and dispatch. Shouting to Wynkoop to move his men forward, Pillow carelessly alerted Mexican gunners to the American movements. With carefully cleared and prepared fields of fire, the Mexican gunners quickly capitalized on Pillow's poor decision, and enemy fire soon rained down on the confused Americans. The Second Tennessee moved forward shortly thereafter, with Haskell's men struggling to support the attack of the Pennsylvanians. As a result, the two volunteer regiments attacked piecemeal, suffering significant casualties, with all four regiments under Pillow's command forced to form up while under constant fire from the Mexican batteries.[18]

Hoping to restore order to the chaos of a diversionary 'attack' now in danger of failing, McClellan sought out the Tennessee politician-turned-general, only to find Pillow in the rear taking cover behind a bush. Hoping for orders to clarify the situation, McClellan was disappointed when an errant canister round broke Pillow's right arm, forcing him and an aide to withdraw further to the rear to get medical assistance. En route, Pillow encountered Campbell of the First Tennessee, and ordered him forward to take command and press the attack. Campbell's efforts were for naught, for when he ordered Wynkoop to move his regiment forward, the Pennsylvania commander refused to recognize the Tennessean's authority. Lacking orders to the contrary, Haskell had his men fall back. His troops responded gladly, adding to the chaos by rushing through the lines of advancing Pennsylvanians. In the course of his retreat, Haskell encountered Pillow, who by this point undoubtedly recognized how his reputation might be damaged by a premature departure from the battlefield, a broken arm notwithstanding. Pillow accused Haskell of failing to complete his attack, then directed his venom towards Wynkoop's Pennsylvanians, who by then were also retreating in disarray.[19]

Believing his brigade to be in trouble, Pillow turned to McClellan, ordering the young engineer officer to find Scott and request reinforcements to bolster his faltering attack. McClellan rode off to find Scott. When he finally located the commander, McClellan dictated the concerned Tennessean's request, but Scott tersely responded that 'he had no regulars to spare'. While Pillow had ignorantly disregarded Scott and the engineers under his command, Twiggs's division had enjoyed considerable success, and by this point in the battle Santa Anna and most of his army were fleeing from Cerro Gordo in disarray. The 5,000-odd enemy that remained in opposition to Pillow would probably soon surrender, and Scott was, in McClellan's words, 'not much surprised and not much "put out" that Pillow was thrashed, and attached no importance to his future movements'. McClellan returned to find Pillow, by which time the Mexican troops manning Pillow's objective were already raising white flags of surrender, giving up not because they had been defeated by the valour of Pillow and his brigade, but because they had been abandoned by Santa Anna and the rest of the Mexican Army.[20]

Scott's assessment of Pillow's brigade was damning with faint praise. He noted the 'great daring' with which the brigade had assaulted the Mexican batteries, as 'they contributed much to distract and dismay their immediate opponents'. Scott's accolades to the contrary, Pillow's first major command was a disastrous failure, in McClellan's words, simply a product of 'puerile imbecility'. Believing himself to be a capable commander, Pillow made decisions on his own, and he failed. He chose the wrong route of march and ordered his men to attack the wrong position. As a direct consequence of his decisions, he not only caused unnecessary casualties, but ran the risk of dooming the entire American attack to failure.[21] These facts, however, were lost on Pillow, who believed himself to be a great commander.

Returning to Tennessee to recover from his wounds, he faced criticism by volunteers from his home state, who were returning home at the end of their enlistment. Leadership from both regiments excoriated their former commander for his conduct, prompting the arrogant Pillow to publish his own version of the battle, which predictably depicted his leadership in a much more favourable light. Although it shocked many regular officers when Polk promoted Pillow to major general, it was understandable politically as the president would have someone on the inside to monitor Scott's campaign into central Mexico, especially as 'Old Fuss and Feathers' Scott was under consideration as a potential presidential candidate in the election of 1848.[22]

Pillow's promotion to major general and command of a division only inflated his own sense of martial prowess. As had been the case previously, however, Pillow's acumen continued to be called into question. His orders to artillerymen to train their six- and twelve-pound cannon on Mexican positions mounting artillery with greater range and firepower led 1842 West Point graduate Lieutenant Daniel Harvey Hill to refer frequently to 'the ass Pillow' in his diary.[23]

As the American Army approached Mexico City in August 1847, Scott ordered Pillow and men of his division to cut a road through the *pedregal*, a lava field blocking the approach of the American Army, though he cautioned them against seeking a general engagement. Encountering Mexican troops defending Padiernia, the impetuous Pillow ignored the orders of his superior, feeding additional troops into a fight at Contreras that he could have avoided. Later that day an angry Scott appeared on the scene, only to discover that General Persifor Smith, a brigade commander in Twiggs's division, had flanked the Mexican force and was in position to attack, which he would with success the next day. When Scott finally confronted Pillow, who by that point was more than a mile and a half away from his troops, the American commander suggested to the Tennessean that he might want to be in closer proximity to his troops. Later that evening Pillow returned to Scott's headquarters and confessed that he had been unable to find his command. Already deep in preparations for the next day's attack on Mexican positions at Churubusco, Scott ordered Pillow to remain at headquarters. While Pillow undoubtedly interpreted this as a testament of his importance to the American offensive, for the diplomatic Scott it represented a way of keeping the troublesome Tennessean out of the way.[24]

In the next day's attack, Scott had not intended for Pillow to assume a significant role, but the battle's development led to his troops joining the fray, attached to General William Jenkins Worth's division in attacking a vital river bridge and forcing a Mexican withdrawal further to the north. During the course of the fighting, Pillow encountered a group of Mexican officers riding in his direction. Although the exact circumstances of their movement are unclear based upon contemporary reports, Pillow nonetheless shot one of them, forcing the rest to scatter, further emboldening Pillow in his belief that he was an effective commander.[25]

After taking Churubusco, Scott agreed to Santa Anna's request for an armistice, believing it to be a preliminary step towards ending the war. Unbeknownst to Scott, Santa Anna had no intention of capitulating, forcing Scott to attack Molino del Rey, which the American general believed contained a Mexican cannon foundry. Pillow opposed the attack, and when no cannons were discovered, he privately informed Polk of his commander's poor judgement, with respect to both the armistice and the cannons.[26]

By early September only the Mexican citadel of Chapultepec prevented the American Army from entering Mexico City. When Scott summoned his generals in preparation for the attack, the audacious Pillow, emboldened by his own perceived record of martial success, arrogantly put forth his own battle plan, which Scott promptly rejected. Instead, Scott, after carefully reviewing the objectives for each officer in the forthcoming battle, named Pillow to attack Chapultepec from the west, with Quitman's brigade driving towards the Mexican positions from the south. Pillow objected to Scott's plan, believing that his forces would suffer heavy casualties, and if successful, they would be left outside the city and away from all the glory, though Scott was nonplussed at the concerns raised by an officer for whom he had little professional respect. Shortly after the attack commenced the next day, Pillow was wounded when a Mexican grapeshot round struck his ankle and broke a bone, and he spent the remainder of the battle under a tree. After American troops swept the castle, Pillow had his men carry him up the hill. There he encountered a sergeant from the Second Pennsylvania who still harboured a grudge from how Pillow had treated his regiment at Cerro Gordo. When the soldier reminded Pillow of his regiment, the arrogant general castigated the sergeant for his impudence.[27]

With the fighting at an effective conclusion, Pillow took up the pen in efforts to assert his valour and prowess as a commander. In the aftermath of the fighting at Contreras, Pillow had penned a version of the battle later leaked to two New Orleans newspapers, which published the account under the name of 'Leonidas'. In Pillow's version of the final campaign, he commanded all the troops except the division commanded by Worth, and it was through his efforts alone that the American Army was rescued from 'gloom' and led to victory. 'Leonidas' likened Pillow to Napoleon, and of his martial acumen wrote, 'He evinced on this, as he has done on other occasions, that masterly military genius and profound knowledge of the science of war, which has astonished so much the mere martinets of the profession.'[28]

It took a few weeks for Leonidas's account of the battle to reach Mexico. In the meantime, relations between Scott and Pillow continued to deteriorate. When Pillow forwarded his official accounts of the battle to Scott, the bold Tennessean's version had him assuming command and issuing orders attributable to Scott, at the same time condescendingly commending his superior for his role in the battle. Responding diplomatically, Scott called upon Pillow to set the record straight. Pillow continued to claim that his was the correct account, then impudently called upon Scott to meet with him to discuss the discrepancies, citing a need to recover from wounds that limited his own movement.[29]

Scott's discovery of the Leonidas letter widened his growing rift with Pillow into a chasm. Despite the pseudonym, it was not difficult to ascertain the account's true author, which incensed Scott. When the general discovered that Pillow had also written directly to Polk claiming mistreatment during the Veracruz campaign, as well as informing him about the failed bribery attempt with Trist, Scott had Pillow arrested and charged with violating the chain of command by writing to the president. Anonymous letters penned by other officers followed, and a flurry of charges and countercharges soon flew back and forth, with Scott decrying these 'despicable self-puffings' in official orders.[30] Seeking a resolution, Polk ordered Pillow released, relieved Scott of his command, and called for a court of inquiry to investigate the circumstances surrounding Pillow's arrest. Convening in Mexico City in March, the trial was soon suspended, and reconvened in Frederick, Maryland, later that June. There the Tennessee lawyer proved his mettle in the trivial matters of the courtroom, launching a successful inquisition that destroyed Scott's hopes for a presidential bid in 1848. In doing so, Pillow crippled his own reputation in challenging an officer whom no less than Arthur Wellesley, Duke of Wellington, had lauded as 'the greatest living general'.[31]

Believing that the court of inquiry had established his place as a hero of the Mexican War, Pillow vaingloriously remained active in Tennessee politics, but could not translate his supposed military successes into a significant political post. In 1850, he passed on the opportunity to follow cousin William Carroll into the governor's office, believing that the 'deranged condition in which I found my private affairs after so long an absence in Mexico' would prevent him from giving the utmost to the position. Expanding his agricultural holdings into Arkansas and Mississippi, he assumed a voice of moderation in Tennessee and throughout the South as the Compromise of 1850 heightened sectional tensions. Meeting as a delegate to the first 1850 Nashville Convention of Southern states, Pillow spoke out against the 'sting and venom' of radical opponents to Henry Clay's omnibus bill. When a second convention met, Pillow continued to be a voice of moderation, though as a Tennessee Unionist he soon found himself alienated by emerging radical sentiments throughout the South.[32]

In the decade that followed, Pillow continued dabbling in national politics. Committed to the defeat of his wartime adversary Scott in the presidential election of 1852, he lobbied to join fellow Mexican War general Franklin Pierce on the Democratic ticket, but once politicking began at the Baltimore convention, Pillow soon found himself on the outside looking in. Four years later, he joined a declining number of pro-slavery Jacksonian Unionists in supporting James Buchanan, but failed to win a posting in Buchanan's administration. He soon found a new friend and ally in future Tennessee Governor Isham Green Harris. Remaining active in Tennessee, he narrowly missed election to the Senate in 1856. After being a critic of Stephen Douglas in the election of 1860, Lincoln's victory prompted him to call for a convention of slave states, though he remained personally opposed to secession.[33]

As the secessionist movement swept across the South, Pillow remained a player in his home state. Governor Harris commissioned Pillow senior major general of the Provisional Army of Tennessee in May 1861 and tasked him with organizing, training and motivating the future Confederate Army of Tennessee. Pillow's administrative ability and energies were perfectly suited to such a post. Recognizing the importance of the Mississippi River as a lifeline for the Confederacy, Pillow soon began balancing his time between further preparations for the Army of Tennessee and defending the river, anticipating a field command. His efforts, however, were for naught, as the Confederate

Army incorporated the Army of Tennessee into its order of battle and Pillow was demoted to brigadier general. Instead, Confederate President Jefferson Davis extended command of the newly formed Western Department to General Leonidas Polk, with Pillow serving as his second in command.

Pillow found his new rank insulting, as the vast majority of Mexican War veterans who returned to command did so at a higher rank than they had enjoyed in the previous conflict. Pillow never recognized how his actions during and after the Mexican War had damaged his reputation, and that West Pointers like Polk, even after he had left the army for a career in the Episcopal Church, were viewed as more suitable for command. Undaunted, Pillow soon plagued his leadership with the same problems he had caused in Mexico. Pressing Polk to take action, he violated Kentucky's neutrality by occupying Columbus, pushing the state into the orbit of the Union, and failed to take advantage of a superior position in his first battle against Union Brigadier General Ulysses S. Grant in the impromptu Battle of Belmont, Missouri. These exploits, however, would pale in comparison to the damage done to his reputation by the disastrous surrender of Fort Donelson in February 1862.[34]

As 1861 ended, Pillow had submitted his resignation because he felt that other officers were receiving more accolades, though he ultimately chose to remain in service after pleading with Davis and withdrawing his resignation. In anticipation of a Federal offensive down the Mississippi River, General Albert Sidney Johnston tasked Pillow with gathering men and materiel at Clarksville, Tennessee. After Federal forces under Grant captured Fort Henry, Pillow began reinforcing nearby Fort Donelson. Ordered to take command of the garrison on 9 February, Pillow soon clashed with brigadier generals Simon Bolivar Buckner and John B. Floyd, who had recently arrived to mount a defence at Donelson. The presence of these Confederate generals meant little to Grant, who later wrote he had few concerns while 'Floyd was in command . . . he was no soldier, and I judged he would yield to Pillow's pretensions.'[35]

Grant's army of 25,000 Federals surrounded Fort Donelson on 13 February. Fighting off an attack by Union gunboats on 14 February, Floyd proposed a breakout from the fort and withdrawal towards Nashville. To these ends, Pillow, vowing to defend Tennessee against the invading Union army, called for an attack against the Federal right beginning on the morning of 15 February as a preliminary action to a general withdrawal. By mid-morning the next day, Pillow was well on his way to winning the battlefield glory he desperately sought, rallying his troops, driving the Union force forward, and triumphantly reporting to Johnston that the 'day is ours'. A Federal counter-attack, however, soon turned the tables and inexplicably Pillow ordered the Confederates back into their old positions. That night, Pillow, Floyd and Buckner had to choose between fighting on and capitulation. Recognizing that if he surrendered, he would certainly be tried for treason, the formerly brave Pillow struggled to protect his reputation. Publicly professing a willingness to stay and fight, he made plans to flee at the same time. Floyd did the same, leaving Buckner with the dubious distinction of surrendering to Grant on 16 February 1862.[36]

With his reputation in tatters, Pillow struggled to find a command. At the Battle of Stones River he led a Tennessee Brigade attached to General Braxton Bragg, and while he displayed aggressive tendencies, observers reported that he was cowering behind a tree in the midst of an attack. Capitalizing on his organizational skills, he commanded the Volunteer and Conscript Bureau for most of the Confederacy in 1863 and 1864, though these duties kept him off the battlefield. In 1864 he returned to the field, briefly commanding a raid against General William T. Sherman's lines of communications near Lafayette, Georgia. Again, Pillow failed to restrain his ego, delivering a telegraphic lecture to Bragg, the notional commander of the Confederate Army. Bragg largely ignored him, and after another failed effort, Pillow soon found himself on recruiting duty for the rest of the war.[37]

Although Pillow had been one of the wealthiest men in Tennessee prior to the beginning of the Civil War, the conflict resulted in the destruction or confiscation of much of his property. In the decades that followed, he attempted to meet with his old enemies Grant and Sherman, but neither received him, leaving him even more embittered. He died in the 1878 Memphis yellow fever epidemic, and he is buried in Elmwood Cemetery.[38]

Gideon Pillow was a man of dreams. Growing up in the literal shadow of one of the great citizen-soldiers of his day, he had immeasurable martial ambition, and went to great lengths to translate these aspirations into a glorious reality. These ambitions notwithstanding, his own ego ultimately failed him. When questioned or criticized, he rarely found fault with himself, and would go to whatever lengths necessary to cast himself in the best possible light. This arrogance proved to be his undoing, and on repeated occasions his reputation suffered damage that he himself simply could not see. Though he should have recognized his own faults, hubris led to his downfall as a military commander. While a leader of men should be brave and bold, success comes to those who are also humble, and this was a lesson that Gideon Pillow never learned.

6

ANTONIO LÓPEZ DE SANTA ANNA

Gates Brown

ntonio López de Santa Anna is a controversial figure in
Mexico, even today. He is commonly blamed for losing half
of Mexico's territory to the United States in two disastrous
conflicts. Although Santa Anna's gambles made him successful in domestic politics and in some of his military endeavours, he
struggled against foreign enemies, most notably in his defeat by U.S.
immigrants in the Texas Rebellion of 1835–6 and his failure during
the Mexican–American War of 1846–8. There is more to placing Santa
Anna on the list of worst military leaders in history, however, than just
losing to stronger enemies, which oversimplifies the outcome of most
conflicts as either winning or losing. Rather, this chapter will focus
on the following qualities that make Santa Anna a candidate for the
worst commander in history: his unwillingness to take subordinates'
advice or recommendations in critical situations, ignoring significant
enemy capabilities in defensive plans, accepting too much risk, ignoring logistical considerations and not understanding the context of the
campaign. These failings are most clearly on display in his two most
disastrous conflicts, those of 1835–6 and 1846–8.

It is not just the fact that Santa Anna lost these conflicts, but how
he lost them, that is so telling. In the Texas Rebellion, his cruelty gal-
vanized those fighting for Texan independence and his inability to
maintain security led to a quick collapse of what had been, until then,
a successful campaign. In the Mexican–American War, Santa Anna's
unwillingness to take counsel from subordinates, fundamental errors
in logistical planning and inability to judge risk increased the difficulties for the Mexican Army when it could least afford errors. Thus

Antonio López de Santa Anna, engraving from Brantz Mayer, *Mexico; Aztec, Spanish and Republican*, vol. II (1853).

Mexico's defeat in both conflicts was not just a matter of losing to a superior foe, but a result of Santa Anna's faulty leadership.

Prior to fighting the rebellion in Texas, Santa Anna took part in rebellions himself. In 1828 he led one against the election of President Manuel Gómez Pedraza and helped install Vicente Guerrero, who had come in second place. At the end of 1829 Gómez Pedraza was ousted by his own vice president, Anastasio Bustamante. In 1832 Santa Anna accused Bustamante of wanting to overthrow the federal system of government then in place in Mexico and took up arms, forcing the resignation of Bustamante's government. As a result of his previous actions, Santa Anna built enough support to win the election of 1833 and became the eighth president of Mexico.[1]

Santa Anna did not enjoy governing and deputed his vice president, Valentín Gómez Farías, to govern. However, the Mexican Congress and Gómez Farías instituted radical reforms that sought to secularize Mexico, as well as reduce the size of the Mexican Army and end the practice of having a special legal code for the clergy and soldiers. Santa Anna felt compelled to return to power and stop these reforms because they disadvantaged the Catholic Church in Mexico and the army. The Plan of Cuernavaca, written by José María Tornel, a supporter of Santa Anna since Mexico gained its independence from Spain, called for Santa Anna to take emergency measures and reverse what Tornel and others considered illegal legislation. Returning to the capital, Santa Anna dismissed both the Congress and his vice president, and reversed the laws that had angered the army and Catholic Church. Although it would have been possible for Santa Anna to become a dictator, he did not; rather, he exercised emergency powers with a new Congress. The tension between Gómez Farías and Santa Anna concerning the best way to govern was emblematic of the political conflict in Mexico at the time. Those who supported a more liberal and secular Mexico, such as Gómez Farías, were at odds with the conservatives who supported the position of the Church and the army. This factionalism re-emerged in the Mexican–American War in the next decade.[2]

Santa Anna's actions at this time were indicative of his political capability, which allowed him to exploit opportunities in periods of political instability. He was able to build a sizeable faction of supporters. Although he did not want to rule as president, he did accept the results of the election and did stand for election. This is what makes Santa Anna such an interesting person; he was clearly adept at reading the political winds in Mexico and he was capable as a military commander. However, Santa Anna's presidency and his use of emergency powers alienated the growing number of United States immigrants in northern Mexico.

The specifics of the entire Texas campaign are outside the scope of this chapter; what is important is how Santa Anna chose to fight it. Santa Anna ignored one of his first chances to mitigate the political damage from his victory at the Alamo, which was a foregone conclusion given the overwhelming superiority of Mexican forces. However, his decision to kill all of the defenders only stoked the anger of the rebels, and his unwillingness to treat the rebels with mercy confirmed their fears about what to expect under his rule.

The Texan forces had occupied the Alamo in order to claim its cannon. The first commander of the Alamo, Lieutenant Colonel James Neill, wanted to maintain the garrison because the rebels could not move the cannon from the mission, even though the revolutionary Texas government could not reinforce the position. Santa Anna quickly marshalled his 6,111-man force to destroy the revolution, as success offered the opportunity to solidify his power in Texas and Mexico City. Although William Barret Travis, who had taken command at the Alamo, expected Mexican forces to arrive in the middle of March, Santa Anna's army appeared in San Antonio on 23 February.[3]

Santa Anna's rapid build-up of his force and movement into Texas were indicative of his capability to inspire men to fight for him. However, inspiring men to march in a campaign is not sufficient for victory. In this case, there was more to leadership than the purely military aspects of the campaign. Mexican law stated that the president could not personally lead troops, so Santa Anna resigned his office. Although he was not president when he was leading the troops, he well understood the political objective that his campaign sought to achieve. This was where he faltered in the Texas campaign and his inability to mitigate his violence had catastrophic repercussions for Mexico.[4]

In addition to weighing the political impacts of a campaign, commanders also must balance the risk of offensives to their own forces. This was a campaign in which Santa Anna held the advantage of time. Although he faced logistical problems due to the long lines of communication that supported his forces in the field, his forces were still operating in friendly territory; there were rebels but it was still Mexico. Yet Santa Anna decided on a quick tempo of operations in San Antonio.

Given his advantages, Santa Anna had no reason to force a decision by attacking. The longer he waited, the weaker the Alamo defences became. Santa Anna also failed to build up his own logistics base in San Antonio to make projecting force farther north into Texas more feasible. Over the course of several days, it was clear that there were no reinforcements coming for the besieged garrison, further decreasing the need for Santa Anna to launch an attack. Time was the best weapon that Santa Anna had. Each day that he forced the beleaguered defenders to continue to stand at their posts was another day that the men in the Alamo had to contemplate the disparity between their situation and that of the Mexican forces. Eventually the defenders had to choose either to starve to death in the Alamo, try to escape their surrounded position, or surrender and plead for mercy.

Santa Anna, however, made surrender more difficult because one of the first things he did when he reached San Antonio was to fly a red flag over his headquarters, signalling that there would be no quarter given to the rebels captured in battle. Santa Anna gave the defenders of the Alamo one chance to surrender and made it clear that their choice at the time sealed their fate: if they declined to surrender immediately, they faced death; if they surrendered, they could expect clemency. The rebels refused to surrender immediately and remained in their defensive positions. The Texan rebels knew they faced a dire choice and more time would not improve their position. However, they did not have to decide, as Santa Anna chose for them by assaulting the garrison.[5]

When Santa Anna called his officers to a meeting on 5 March, the twelfth day of the siege, he shocked most of the subordinate commanders by informing them that they would soon lead an assault on the Alamo. By this time the outer curtain walls of the mission fort were falling under fire from Santa Anna's light field guns and the heavy guns were only a few days away. The garrison was small in number, estimated at 189 to 257 defenders. When the Mexicans assaulted the Alamo, they found the defenders, although tired, ready to fight. The Mexicans advanced in four Napoleonic attack columns, which were useful when employing ill-trained soldiers. Veterans made up the perimeter of the attack and the new soldiers were on the inside, which gave them little choice but to stay with their unit and move to the fight. When the Mexican assault forces moved within artillery range, they received devastating anti-personnel artillery fire. The Alamo defenders filled their cannon with any small bits of metal they could find in order to maximize the damage to the infantry formations. This fire halted the Mexican columns for a short time, but could not overcome the numerical advantage of Santa Anna's 1,500-man force. Although the Mexican soldiers killed every defender of the Alamo, which Santa Anna claimed was necessary in order to bolster the morale of his men, the siege had cost six hundred dead and wounded soldiers. He had sacrificed over a third of his force at San Antonio to take a garrison that had to fall, with or without this assault. Few military forces can sustain many victories like this.[6]

Santa Anna's decision to offer no quarter did make sense in that he wanted to eradicate the threat to Mexican authority. However, when using violence to achieve a political objective, military commanders must take into consideration the second- and third-order implications of their actions. He ultimately wanted a stable status quo in Texas, with the region still under Mexican authority. He had to find a way to incorporate the legal settlers into this new status quo and gain their loyalty. One of the ironies of the Texas Revolution was that the legal settlers did not, in large part, actively support the armed rebellion against Mexican authority before the Alamo. It was the fall of the Alamo and the brutal treatment meted out by Santa Anna that stirred many more settlers in Texas to support the cause of Texas independence and not just Mexican reform. So instead of fighting a disorganized group of foreign insurgents trying to build support for their minority cause, Santa Anna transformed the Texas cause into a more broad-based fight against a brutal dictator who had ordered wanton killing and who promised to continue his campaign of brutality throughout Texas.[7]

Santa Anna's brutality continued in Goliad after the surrender of a group of more than three hundred Texas fighters. Although they had surrendered expecting to be treated as prisoners of war, the Texans were executed on the orders of Santa Anna, who regarded them as insurgents. In doing so, Santa Anna again missed an opportunity to show his humanity and make it more difficult for the Texans to raise support for their cause. If Santa Anna had merely returned these defeated fighters to the United States, it is hard to see how their experiences in Texas could inspire others to follow. Instead, the Goliad massacre, like the Alamo, became a galvanizing force that inspired Texans to rally and continue to fight for their independence.[8]

Santa Anna's mercilessness is not surprising. He did not show mercy to his own people in Zacatecas when he allowed two days of raping and pillaging. However, his massacres at the Alamo and Goliad spurred the revolutionaries to take more aggressive action instead of cowing them into acquiescence. The Texas government voted to declare independence and made Sam Houston the commander-in-chief. However, Houston needed Santa Anna to make a mistake if he was going to prevail over the superior numbers of the Mexican forces. Houston had a stroke of good fortune when he intercepted letters addressed to Santa Anna that made it clear that if Houston moved quickly, he could attack Santa Anna without having to face the entire Mexican contingent. To rally the Texans, Houston reminded them of the horrors of the Alamo and Goliad with the battle cry 'Remember the Alamo, remember Goliad.'

The Texans met the Mexican forces at the San Jacinto River near New Washington, where Santa Anna failed in a bid to capture the rebel government. The problem with Santa Anna's position at San Jacinto was that it did not suit the Mexican forces well and did not offer many options in terms of egress if the planned fight turned out poorly for the Mexicans. Santa Anna isolated his forces by his own decision. His lines of communication were at their breaking point but his enemy's lines of communication were short and resilient, since they were fighting in their own land and had an increasing number of supporters.[9]

Although Santa Anna was reinforced with a contingent commanded by General Martín Perfecto de Cos that made the total Mexican force 1,250 strong against Houston's 910 men, the march had exhausted Cos's new recruits. Moreover, veterans were in short supply after the bloody battle of the Alamo, another problematic consequence of Santa Anna's poor decision to storm the Texas mission. Santa Anna expected the Texans to attack on the first night he made camp but this did not happen. Santa Anna knew that Houston had seen Cos's forces ride into the Mexican camp, so it seemed that the period of greatest danger had already passed. In addition to waiting for reinforcements, Santa Anna ordered his troops to build earthen breastworks over the first night in camp in order to further strengthen their position, showing Santa Anna understood the importance of improving his position while in the defence. After the Texans failed to attack when Santa Anna thought it most likely, he gave his men orders to rest, including Cos's exhausted troops.[10]

While it was reasonable that Santa Anna wanted to give his troops time to rest, he was still within small-arms range of the enemy, who remained in the area. His decision to rest his men, moreover, neglected security by reducing his defences and allowing most of his soldiers to sleep while the enemy was still nearby. Santa Anna assumed that the arrival of his reinforcements had discouraged a Texan attack. He did not anticipate Houston's audacity to attack with a numerically smaller force.

When the battle began, the Texans quickly lost their unit cohesion and broke ranks to assault the Mexican positions. The Texas artillery barrage ruptured Mexican lines and allowed the disorganized assault to proceed, and it quickly devolved into hand-to-hand combat. The quick tempo of the Texan assault made it almost impossible for the Mexican commanders to form their troops and stop the attack. The Mexican position quickly fragmented and the troops retreated.[11]

Houston gained another lucky break when his troops captured Santa Anna, who offered to order the withdrawal of his army from Texas. Although many of the Texans wanted to hang Santa Anna for his cruelty, Houston, who understood that Santa Anna's value was in his authority to order the withdrawal of the Mexican troops from Texas, refused to do so. Santa Anna ordered his subordinate, General Vicente Filisola, to move his troops south to San Antonio. Filisola did withdraw, but went much further, retreating south of the Rio Grande instead due largely to the poor logistical situation that the Mexican forces faced in Texas. They had limited ability to resupply themselves, the seasonal rains made manoeuvring difficult, and the troops were too far from their base of support to make holding their position tenable even in San Antonio. This lack of logistical support was, in part, exacerbated by Santa Anna's desire for a rapid campaign. He did not build a base of support in San Antonio to prepare for further force projection and his forces paid the price for this lack of preparation.[12]

Ultimately, neither Sam Houston's military skill nor the heroic sacrifice of those at the Alamo or Goliad led to the success of the Texas War of Independence. Rather, it was the poor decision-making by Santa Anna to detach his force from the larger army in order to try and capture the rebels' government that brought him to San Jacinto. Instead of building his capacity to project forces into Texas, Santa Anna decided to attack the Alamo, which left him with fewer veteran troops when he needed them most and an inadequate logistical base. In addition, his merciless treatment of the defenders of the Alamo and Goliad spurred more enthusiasm for Texan independence than it had commanded previously. Once at San Jacinto, Santa Anna ordered the Mexican forces to take up a position that left few viable routes of retreat. Finally, it was Santa Anna's order to allow his troops to rest and relax their defences because he assumed that the Texans were not going to attack that created the critical vulnerabilities that Houston exploited. All of these failures were indicative of Santa Anna's larger failure to adapt to the new context of the Texan rebellion. What had worked for him previously, assuming risk and moving with audacity, worked against him in this campaign. Santa Anna, through his own failures, did much to nullify many of the advantages over an initially small band of malcontent settlers with which he had begun the campaign in Texas. His capture sealed the fate of Mexican rule in Texas.

Nevertheless, Santa Anna's failure in the Texas Revolution did not end his political career. After a period of exile, he returned to Mexico in 1837 and his leadership of the successful defence of Veracruz in the First Franco-Mexican War of 1838–9 provided Santa Anna with an opportunity to return to military and political relevance.[13] Meanwhile, tensions between the United States and Mexico were high after Texas gained its independence because many Mexicans thought that the United States had supported the rebels to claim the territory for itself. The desire for territory was at the heart of the war between the United States and Mexico that broke out in 1846. The conflict was Santa Anna's second major failure.[14]

At the beginning of the Mexican–American War, Santa Anna was in exile in Cuba after domestic unrest had forced him from the presidency in 1845. Santa Anna sent a message to u.s. President James Polk offering to act as a mediator and Polk replied by allowing Santa Anna passage into Mexico and paying him a sum of not more than $2 million with the expectation that Santa Anna would form a new government and negotiate a peace agreement. However, when Santa Anna arrived in Mexico, he instead set about organizing defences against a possible u.s. invasion. After his return Santa Anna once again was elected president, but, as was the case previously, he largely ceded his political power to his vice president in order to focus on military matters.[15]

Santa Anna's first concern was organizing a campaign against u.s. General Zachary Taylor's army, which had crossed the border and was occupying a position at Saltillo. Santa Anna was able to raise an army of about 20,000 soldiers, mainly infantry, and marched north as quickly as possible as he knew that Taylor had sent his regular forces to support General Winfield Scott's advance into Mexico from Veracruz. This meant that Taylor only had volunteer soldiers, who were new to soldiering and had little idea of the realities of combat. In order to ensure that his forces' movement was rapid, Santa Anna ordered his troops to take with them food rations to cover three days because they had to move quickly and could not wait for a large logistics train for daily resupply. This meant that Mexican forces had to move 385 kilometres (240 mi.) through a desert in the winter with limited supplies, and as a result, losses from death and desertion mounted along the march.[16] More concerned with speed than with logistics, Santa Anna told his soldiers that they could resupply themselves from the captured goods they were sure to get from the u.s. forces.

Despite the hardships of the march north, Santa Anna was comfortable with the risk because a victory over Taylor might bring the war to an end before Scott's invasion even began. While Santa Anna's willingness to accept risk made strategic sense, he was unable to overcome the tactical imbalances that his forces faced in the Battle of Buena Vista. Faced with the need to force a rapid battlefield decision, Santa Anna chose to attack Taylor's army, which was located on favourable terrain for defence, rather than attempt to wait Taylor out by isolating his army and cutting its lines of communication. This meant that Santa Anna had to attack an enemy that was in terrain that nullified his numerical advantage.[17]

The Battle of Buena Vista lasted two days. Although Santa Anna claimed that more than 2,000 u.s. soldiers were killed to a loss of 1,000 Mexican troops, the reality was that Santa Anna's forces lost about 2,100 men compared to approximately 900 u.s. soldiers. The majority of Taylor's losses were in the form of 1,500 desertions among his largely green volunteers. Santa Anna had to retreat after two days of fighting because he could not logistically support his forces. His decision to operate with a reduced logistical train forced this decision on him. Unfortunately for Santa Anna, the march back towards Mexico City was just as brutal as the combat and when he returned to the capital his forces were roughly half of what they had been when he started the campaign. Santa Anna's decision to force a quick victory exacerbated an already difficult situation for Mexico.[18]

Although war can unite a country, the Mexican–American War did not unite Mexico. While Santa Anna was fighting Taylor's forces, his political rivals were working to overthrow the government of his vice president, Valentín Gómez Farías, who had assumed the presidency during the war. The rebels joined with moderate critics of Gómez Farías and called on Santa Anna to return to the presidency and save Mexico. This was indicative of the problems of national will that Mexico faced in the mid-nineteenth century. In the middle of the conflict, the political factions fought each other instead of uniting against the u.s. invaders. This lack of national will continued to be a problem during the Mexican–American War.[19]

When Santa Anna began to organize the defences against Scott after Buena Vista, he again showed his skill in building an army, and when the government was unable to supply his army with food or gunpowder, Santa Anna personally supplied these provisions.[20] Santa Anna then decided to build a defensive position at Cerro Gordo, near Xalapa, the state capital of Veracruz. This hilltop position was above the yellow-fever belt that had made Veracruz such a forbidding place, and Santa Anna was hoping that a stay there would weaken Scott's army before any fighting took place. Other than that, Cerro Gordo had much more to recommend itself as a defensive position. It was a relative high point and had good visibility of the surrounding terrain. It commanded the road that lay between Veracruz and Mexico City, and if Santa Anna could hold this position, he could frustrate Scott's advance into Mexico.[21]

Scott planned to attack Mexican artillery on the hills around Cerro Gordo. Once Santa Anna learned of the position of Scott's troops, he took action to reinforce his men. However, he discarded the recommendation of Lieutenant Colonel Manuel Robles Pezuela, who was in charge of planning the initial defences of the Mexican position. Robles Pezuela recommended that Santa Anna reinforce the position on the hill of Atalaya with more men and heavy artillery to prevent Scott from taking the hill. Santa Anna thought that the position was impregnable because of the surrounding dense forest and a steep ravine that impeded movement. Also, Santa Anna thought that if the Americans took the position, then the Mexican batteries at Cerro Gordo could destroy the invaders on the hilltop. Santa Anna's estimate of the situation was incorrect, and once the Americans took the hilltop they were able to use this position to support subsequent attacks that caused a complete disintegration of the Mexican forces in the field. This defeat was the last attempt to halt the u.s. advance until the u.s. forces arrived almost at the gates of Mexico City.[22]

The defeat at Cerro Gordo was troubling for Santa Anna. He had lost his army, his munitions and the payroll. For Santa Anna personally, the location of the loss was upsetting. Cerro Gordo was close to one of Santa Anna's haciendas and it was in the region of his birth. He had grown up in this area and made his name fighting against insurgents who opposed Spanish rule before switching sides and joining the revolutionaries. For Santa Anna, the defeat at Cerro Gordo was a significant personal humiliation.[23]

As Scott's forces advanced and began to lay siege to Mexico City, Santa Anna then proposed a ceasefire, which Scott accepted.[24] During the negotiations Santa Anna demanded that the United States pay all costs of the war, forgive Mexican debts, recognize all of the land grants in Texas made before 1836, end the blockade of Mexican ports and evacuate all occupied territory in Mexico. In exchange, Santa Anna agreed to recognize the independence of Texas with the Nueces River, rather than the Rio Grande, as its southern border and to consider granting the United States trading privileges in California. Scott rejected these unrealistic terms and the war continued, but Santa Anna had bought his forces time.[25]

Santa Anna tried to make good use of this pause in the fighting. He worked within the capital to rouse the people to defend their country, which was facing a dire situation. Santa Anna also attempted to persuade u.s. soldiers to desert and join the Mexican side with the promise that they could live among a truly free people who were equal, with no slavery. However, these efforts failed. There was little sense of national spirit for Santa Anna to rouse among the Mexican people at the time because of the country's fractured political state. Although Santa Anna gained support from both the radicals and the moderates, he was uninterested in serving as president and instead focused on organizing the defence of Mexico.[26]

Although Santa Anna intended to keep fighting the war, he was unable to rouse support for a guerrilla war. He moved south to Oaxaca in order to reorganize his forces, but his army suffered from desertions and a lack of enthusiasm. Santa Anna's final battles of the war, a raid on Huamantla and an attack on a u.s. supply train at Puebla, failed. After the departure of the army and the government from Mexico City, a new government formed and removed Santa Anna from command. The Treaty of Guadalupe Hidalgo, which the new government signed on 2 February 1848, ceded half of Mexico's territory to the United

States by recognizing the Rio Grande as the southern border of Texas and agreeing to sell the land that now makes up Arizona, California, Colorado, Nevada, New Mexico, Utah and Wyoming.[27]

After the war Santa Anna became the focus of blame for Mexico's defeat. Many Mexicans believed that he had worked with Polk to ensure U.S. victory. Even today, many Mexicans consider him a traitor because of wartime conduct. Santa Anna, however, was merely incompetent, not a traitor. Nevertheless his incompetent leadership had proven nothing short of disastrous for Mexico.

Although there were few options for Santa Anna to create a viable strategy to win the Mexican–American War, given the inferiority of his army to that of the United States and the lack of popular support for the war, Santa Anna's leadership actually facilitated the U.S. victory. His hasty decision to move north to fight Taylor without establishing a supply line cost the Mexican army precious time and men. Santa Anna attacked Taylor, thinking that this opportunity was worth the risk, but it required moving across a desert with limited supplies and then fighting a well-entrenched enemy that used the terrain to great effect. Santa Anna risked too much in trying to defeat Taylor quickly and had to rebuild his forces and deal with political instability as a result of his defeat at Buena Vista, hampering his ability to defend against Scott's invasion.

Once Santa Anna retreated south and restored peace to Mexico City, he then turned his attention to Scott's forces, but his decisions at Cerro Gordo were also faulty. He neglected to heed the recommendation of his subordinates and reinforce the hill at Atalaya, allowing U.S. forces to seize the hill and destroy his army in short order. Santa Anna's unwillingness to listen to subordinates had also plagued him in fighting the Texas Revolution, when he ignored their cautions against an attack on the Alamo and pleas to show mercy to the Texans at the Alamo and Goliad. The latter failure in particular cost Mexico dearly as the rebel leaders used the Alamo and Goliad as a rallying cry to their supporters after a string of early defeats. Moreover, after the Alamo, Santa Anna's decision to divide his forces provided the opportunity for the Texans to fight the Mexicans on a more numerically equal footing.

At San Jacinto, Santa Anna displayed another failing, namely his neglect of defensive preparations. He failed his troops by neglecting to ensure that they were being protected while at rest, because he incorrectly assumed that the enemy had missed its best opportunity to attack. However, his lack of preparation wound up inviting an attack that was the undoing of the Mexican campaign in Texas.

Santa Anna deserves to be on this list, but he was not completely inept. He displayed courage and was effective in command against Native Americans, unorganized peasant rebels and Spanish colonial forces. His political acumen, willingness to accept risk and leadership abilities thrust him into pivotal roles at key moments in the early history of Mexico. However, none of this translated into success in battle against the Texans or the United States. What earns Santa Anna a place on the list of worst military leaders in history was his inability to understand the political ramifications of his actions in the broader political context of the Texas War of Independence, his losing gamble in choosing to focus on attacking Taylor's forces while Scott was preparing an invasion, and his unwillingness to heed the recommendations of his subordinates at the Battle of Cerro Gordo. These faulty decisions were instrumental in the military defeats that cost Mexico half of its territory and thus earn Santa Anna a place of infamy in the history of his country.

PART 3

THE CLUELESS

7

FRANZ CONRAD VON HÖTZENDORF

Mark E. Grotelueschen and Derek Varble

In a conflict notorious for failed generalship, Austro-Hungarian field marshal and chief of staff Franz Conrad von Hötzendorf repeatedly demonstrated that he was the worst of a bad lot during the First World War. His incompetence preceded the conflict and continued its damage until nearly the war's end. In the seven years prior to 1914, he recommended more than fifty times that his government declare war on various neighbouring states, without any special provocation and despite his army's unpreparedness.[1] As the Austro-Hungarian Imperial and Royal (*k.u.k.*[2]) Army's senior officer from 1906 to 1911, and again from 1912 to 1917, he was responsible for that army's competence and capability, and First World War campaigns along the Serbian, Russian and Italian fronts revealed terrible weaknesses in the military organization he led for so long, and was so eager to employ. His most recent, and most impartial, biographer Lawrence Sondhaus noted, 'in no other country had one general so dominated the shaping of pre-war tactics, strategies, and war plans, then led his army to disaster in the opening campaign, then managed to remain at his post for most of the war.'[3]

These two basic facts alone – his unwavering bellicosity despite the abject unpreparedness of the army he led – warrant Conrad's inclusion as one of the worst military leaders in history. Moreover, he mismanaged Austro-Hungarian mobilization after his government finally followed his incessant recommendations to declare war on its neighbours. Unable to decide whether to send a crucial swing force to either the Russian or the Serbian fronts, his incompetence ensured those critical units influenced neither, leading to serious defeats on both fronts in 1914 and 1915. After Italy declared war in 1915, his forces failed against that poorly prepared and led army.[4] By 1916 horrendous casualties on three fronts left the *k.u.k.* a shattered military force. In 1917 the new Austro-Hungarian monarch, the young Kaiser Karl, finally replaced Conrad as chief of staff, and sent him to the Tyrol sector of the Italian front to command an army group, where, after failing again, his ultimate dismissal took place in mid-1918.

The demands of Great War command found Conrad lacking, and he typically blamed others, especially his allies, for his forces' failures, which was an outlandish claim since these allies defeated the same enemies who routinely defeated Conrad. Whenever German forces took the lead in the Eastern and Southern Fronts, as they did at Gorlice–Tarnow against Russia in 1915, against Romania in 1916 and against Italy at Caporetto in 1917, they proved that Austro-Hungarian defeats on those fronts were due to the ineptness of the *k.u.k.* and its leaders, not the invincibility of its opponents. Much of the overall responsibility for these failures necessarily belongs to Conrad, who served as that army's chief for nearly eight years prior to the war, and worked harder than anyone to ensure that a major war would occur, and thus expose the Dual Monarchy's unprepared, ill-led and over-matched army on the fields of battle.

Franz Xaver Josef Conrad von Hötzendorf was born on 11 November 1852, the son of retired Austrian colonel Franz Xaver Conrad von Hötzendorf. An assignment to the General Staff Corps of the Austro-Hungarian Army followed education at Hainburg, the Theresian Military Academy at Wiener Neustadt, and the *k.u.k. Kriegsschule* in Vienna, leading to postings at the headquarters of the 6th Cavalry Brigade, the 4th Infantry Division and the 47th Infantry Division. After service as the chief of staff for the 11th Division in Lemberg (now Lviv, Ukraine), he became a faculty member at the *Kriegsschule*, where he taught tactics and developed a reputation as an engaging instructor and an innovative tactical thinker. Like many other leading military professionals in that era, he advocated the attack 'at all costs'.[5] He then commanded infantry units from battalion to division, insisting on realistic training and exercises, and also asserting offensive superiority.[6] He emphasized military modernization and suggested that offensive, 'preventative' wars against Italy and Serbia – Austria–Hungary's rising, irredentist neighbours – might be necessary. Soon he attracted the attention of Archduke Franz Ferdinand, who

Franz Conrad von
Hötzendorf, 1915.

in 1906 recommended Conrad to Kaiser Franz Joseph as the chief of Austria–Hungary's general staff.[7]

Austria–Hungary faced serious security challenges when Conrad took office that November. He was not the man to resolve them, for, as Sondhaus noted, his 'expertise was as a tactician, not a strategist'. His subsequent performance led historian Holger Herwig to conclude that Conrad 'was no match for the position'.[8] Although he was an exemplary linguist (literate in nine languages) with first-hand experiences where his forces later fought, Conrad's planning disregarded important human, geographic and climatic factors. Equally disconcerting was Conrad's growing commitment to aggressive, social Darwinist views of statecraft and foreign policy recommendations based on them. Conrad resorted to war *first* rather than last.

In 1907 newly installed chief Conrad proposed war against 'Austria's congenital foes' Italy and Serbia. A year later he added Russia to Austria's supposed enemies, and in subsequent years Montenegro and Romania joined Conrad's list as well.[9] This bellicosity appears to have been a direct outgrowth of Conrad's Darwinian convictions and world-view, which shaped his views of geopolitics and international affairs. Conrad once wrote:

> The recognition of the struggle for existence as the basic prin-
> ciple of all events on this earth is the only real and rational
> basis for policy making . . . Whoever remains blind to the
> mounting danger, or whoever recognizes it but remains too
> indolent to arm himself, and is too undecided to deliver the
> blow at the proper moment, deserves his fate.

In essence, as Sondhaus has stated, Conrad 'believed in a "will to win" in the international arena no less than on the battlefield'.[10] To Conrad, these were not just theoretical views; rather, the implications for Austria–Hungary were existential: 'Only an aggressive policy with positive goals can save this state from destruction.'[11]

Conrad's incessant recommendations for aggressive war were generally unsolicited. Meddling in diplomacy contributed to Conrad's temporary dismissal in 1911. Conrad believed that 'the friend of humanity likes to dream of the possibility of eternal peace, but the leading politicians . . . must take things as they are and draw their conclusions from the inexorable struggle for existence.'[12] Furthermore, Conrad rejected Clausewitz's famous assertion that war was 'not merely an act of policy but a true political instrument, a continuation of political intercourse, carried on with other means'.[13] Instead, according to Sondhaus, war 'replace[d] politics' for Conrad, who believed that 'politicians and diplomats were to create conditions favorable for victory in war, then step aside while the military men did their job'.[14] As Conrad wrote, 'The fate of nations, peoples, dynasties is decided not at diplomatic conference tables but on the battlefield.'[15] While chief of Austria–Hungary's general staff, Conrad did all he could to turn his assertion into a prophecy; in the end, battlefield fate brought disaster for him, his army and his empire.

Before they precipitated all-out war in 1914, various crises in the Balkans between 1908 and 1913 showcased Conrad's private views and official actions. When in 1908–9 the Dual Monarchy faced a crisis in Bosnia and Herzegovina, Conrad failed to convince political leaders to shatter 'expansionist [Serbian] aspirations', resulting in his profound disappointment.[16] He contemporaneously confided to a friend, 'with this resolution of the Balkan crisis a thousand hopes . . .

are buried for me. I have also lost the joy in my profession, and thus lost that which has sustained me in all circumstances since the age of eleven.'[17] For years after, Conrad bemoaned that 'lost chance' and railed against what he called 'this foul peace which drags on and on'.[18] Similar disappointments transpired in 1911 and 1913, wherein he made 'relentless' but unsuccessful attempts to undertake war against Serbia. Franz Joseph told him that 'the government's duty is to preserve peace'. Conrad caustically replied, 'but certainly not at any price'.[19]

Accompanying this advocacy for war, Conrad's endeavours included specific plans for attacking Austria–Hungary's individual neighbours. The general staff also had to consider the possibility that Austria–Hungary would fight multiple enemies simultaneously, especially Serbia and Russia, as well as engage in a general European war, making cooperation with Austria–Hungary's closest ally, Germany, of tremendous importance. Cooperation between them, however, was neither open nor intimate, a failing for which Conrad bears substantial responsibility.[20]

In his seminal study on that hesitant cooperation, Graydon Tunstall notes that Conrad reached just 'two general points of agreement' with his German counterpart, Helmuth von Moltke, in the five years prior to the war. Should a general European war ensue, Germany would direct its main forces against France, with a subsidiary effort against Russian Poland, while Austria–Hungary would make its major attack in the east to resist Russian pressure. When war arrived in the summer of 1914, 'both leaders expected more from each other than they got and gave less than they had "promised"'.[21] This mismatch was particularly egregious for Conrad, who consistently demanded more support against Russia than Germany had pledged, while he clearly failed to deliver on his Russian commitments.

By the summer of 1914, events at last gave Conrad his best chance to secure the war he so desired. After Serbian terrorists assassinated Habsburg heir Franz Ferdinand, Austro-Hungarian political leaders once again contemplated war with their Balkan neighbour. The Dual Monarchy's foreign minister Leopold Berchtold summarized Conrad's position in this crisis: '*Krieg, Krieg, Krieg.*'[22] Indeed, by 1914, Conrad had developed what Herwig calls a '"war-at-any-price" mentality' and a determination 'not to let the last moment slip by "to settle [Serbian] accounts"'. So committed was Conrad to hostilities as the only means of maintaining Austria's place in Europe that he advocated armed conflict even with a clear understanding that war risked destroying the Austro-Hungarian Empire and its nearly four-hundred-year-old Habsburg monarchy.[23] Conrad privately, and clairvoyantly, admitted that war would be 'a hopeless struggle, but nevertheless it must be because such an ancient monarchy and such an ancient army cannot perish ingloriously'.[24] Of course, both did perish without any particular glory, and under Conrad's military leadership the *k.u.k.* perished with a shocking degree of ineptitude.

A particularly troubling dimension of Conrad's reckless belligerence comes from the reasonable suspicion that personal goals of a romantic nature help account for his rashness. Conrad, a 55-year-old widower, began wooing Virginia 'Gina' Reininghaus, the 28-year-old wife of Viennese businessman Johann von Reininghaus, in 1907. By 1914 Conrad's undeniable affection and persistence, as well as Gina's own marriage difficulties, resulted in a complicated affair between the two. Conrad was obsessed with Gina. Between 1907 and 1915 he wrote her 3,000 letters, including some more than fifty pages long. He almost lost his position due to a lack of discretion in his pursuit.[25] He was desperate to make Gina his own wife, but her Catholicism, and the prevailing religious, political and social sentiments of the time, required extraordinary measures to secure the necessary divorce for Gina. Conrad apparently believed that, were he a war hero, the myriad restrictions standing in the way could be overcome. In a private letter to his mistress, Conrad openly confessed that he longed for a 'war from which I could return crowned with success that would allow me to break through all the barriers between us . . . and claim you as my own dearest wife!' Such success, Conrad believed, 'would bring the satisfaction in my career and private life which fate has so far denied me'.[26]

The influences of Conrad's world-view and personal life in advocating war can never be fully ascertained, but his role in helping to push his state, and nearly all of Europe, into the greatest war in its history to date is clear. In 1925 Otto Bauer, a prominent Austrian Social Democrat, stated: 'If we are listing the five or six men in all of Europe who bear the primary guilt for the outbreak of the war, one of these five or six men would be Field Marshal Conrad.'[27] Some scholars go further. The leading historian of the role of Austria–Hungary in the origins of the First World War, Samuel R. Williamson Jr, has labelled Conrad 'the single individual probably most responsible for the war in 1914'. His consistent calls for war, buttressed by his 'confident assessments of military success', helped lead his civilian masters over the brink.[28] Although many at the time, and since, adjudicate imperial Germany as primarily to blame for the the First World War, Herwig properly notes that 'the initiative for war lay in Vienna', and that 'Habsburg and not Hohenzollern decided to settle accounts by military rather than diplomatic means. Both the direction and the pace of the July crisis were dictated by Vienna.'[29] And in Vienna, Conrad was the war party's undisputed leader. While all major players in Berlin and Vienna, from heads of state, to senior ministers, to military leaders, had by mid-July 1914 'accepted [war's] calculated risk', even a general European war, Conrad not only *wanted* war, but was practically *desperate* for it.[30]

Yet for all Conrad's optimistic bellicosity, 1914 found his army and his state unprepared for war. Austria–Hungary had for years spent less, on a percentage basis, than other major European powers, while also training a smaller portion of its population than its enemies. Herwig offers a reason for this unfortunate reality: 'The truth is that Habsburg military forces were designed not to fight a major war but rather to maintain a delicate political balance in the Empire.'[31] In the words of historian Norman Stone, 'In Vienna there was always a large gap – perhaps larger than anywhere else – between ideals and reality. The Austro-Hungarian army was not strong enough for the role [Conrad] cast for it.'[32] And yet, Conrad urgently desired to field this inadequate force. As army chief, Conrad was responsible for understanding its strengths and weaknesses, and for providing sound military advice to his political leaders on how best to use that force. Conrad failed to discharge these duties.

Conrad's culpability for Austria–Hungary's future military failures is particularly significant because, more than in any other national European army, the *k.u.k.* bore the stamp of its energetic, long-serving chief. He had written his army's manual for infantry tactics, educated many of its officers at its staff college, helped secure promotions and important positions for those he liked, and designed the strategic plans that would guide campaigns. As Sondhaus has stated, Conrad was 'a unique star in the constellation of personalities involved in the origins and conduct of the First World War ... Among the men responsible for shaping the tactics, strategies, and war plans that led old Europe to destruction in the unprecedented bloodletting of 1914–1918, he had no equal.'[33] Not only did Conrad fail in his duty to balance the demands facing Austria–Hungary's army against its actual capabilities, when war finally came, his strategic decisions proved incompetent.

Conrad's long-desired war for which his army was so ill-prepared arrived in the summer of 1914; circumstances now demanded crucial command decisions, important strategic direction, and critical oversight of his staff and the fielded forces. He failed in all respects.

Most serious were Conrad's flawed troop deployment decisions during Austro-Hungarian mobilization. The empire's annually updated war plans included those for war against Serbia alone (War Case B, for Balkan) and Russia alone (War Case R). However, as far as the extant records show, Conrad had failed to plan for what increasingly had become the likeliest scenario: a multi-front war against *both* Russia and Serbia (namely, War Case R+B).[34] In subjecting the staff to extraordinary time pressures while scrambling to redesign complicated mobilization and deployment details in July 1914, Conrad's omission proved disastrous.

War planning led Conrad to organize the *k.u.k.* into three parts. *A-Staffel* would operate against Russia in southern Poland with 27 infantry divisions and nine cavalry divisions, along with 21 'hastily formed and poorly equipped supplementary (or third-line) reserve infantry brigades'.[35] *Minimalgruppe Balkan,* nine infantry divisions and seven supplementary reserve brigades, was dedicated to Serbian operations. *B-Staffel,* a strategic reserve swing force comprised of eleven infantry divisions, a cavalry division and six additional reserve brigades, provided the key element in Conrad's strategic scheme.[36] For War Case B, *B-Staffel* was to join *Minimalgruppe Balkan* in its offensive against Serbia. War Case R, or any general European war, directed *B-Staffel* north to join *A-Staffel* in its invasion of Russian Poland. These arrangements required a timely, accurate and dispassionate assessment of any given crisis's actual strategic situation so that *B-Staffel* would proceed to the proper front.[37] Assessing the crisis that emerged proved too much for Conrad, whose earlier failure to plan for War Case R+B now placed him in a terrible position.

Contrary to plentiful evidence in late July suggesting Russia would intervene were Austria–Hungary to attack Serbia, thereby necessitating the non-existent War Case R+B plan, Conrad, obsessively committed to punishing what he called that 'dog Serbia', initially ordered a mobilization against Serbia alone.[38] Even when numerous reports indicated that Russia was actually mobilizing its forces along the Galician front, Conrad stuck with his initial assessment that *B-Staffel* should train south towards Serbia.[39] Despite repeated calls from Berlin for Conrad to execute War Case R, targeting Russia with Austria–Hungary's mobilization, Conrad refused, instead persisting with War Case B and orders that the four critically important *B-Staffel* army corps were to train south, in the face of all evidence that war with Russia was imminent, leaving *A-Staffel* grossly overmatched without the crucial reinforcement from the swing force. There exists only one reasonable explanation for Conrad's inexplicable reluctance to execute War Case R as it was designed, which is what Herwig calls 'Conrad's visceral hatred of Serbia and his determination to destroy it'.[40]

This obsession deluded him in three important ways. First, Conrad continued to believe that Russia might abstain, despite firm contrary evidence by late July.[41] Second, he assumed that were Russia to enter, its mobilization would take so long that the *k.u.k.* would crush Serbia in a 'lightning stroke' and then redeploy north to meet the slowly emerging Russian threat.[42] Finally, when in a state of near panic he realized that Russian entry was imminent, with Russia mobilizing more quickly than expected, he made the disastrous decision to continue the *B-Staffel* deployment already under way to the Serbian front, have those forces detrain there, wait ten days doing practically nothing, and then re-deploy back towards Galicia in the hope that they could join *A-Staffel* in its grand offensive into Russian Poland.[43] Conrad proved to be terribly wrong on all accounts. He simply could not control his own emotions and employ his forces rationally, despite Moltke's regular reminders to concentrate against Russia, the much greater threat. Not for the last time, Conrad's calculations were, in the words of Holger Herwig, based on 'wishful thinking'.[44]

Another disastrous decision that summer positioned Conrad's fielded forces for failure. In early July, as he pushed for war against Serbia irrespective of Russia's response, he ordered his staff to adjust the plan for a future *A-Staffel* deployment. War Case R originally transported *A-Staffel* units in tandem with the *B-Staffel* swing force as far forward as possible into the Galician frontier via rail to initiate a deep offensive strike against Russian forces still organizing themselves in Russian Poland. But in mid-July, ostensibly because he learned that Romania was almost certainly not going to join the Central Powers and put its forces on the right flank of the *k.u.k.*'s field armies, Conrad directed his planners to have his northern field armies detrain along the San–Dniester river line, nearly 160 kilometres (100 mi.) to the rear of the original drop-off locations.[45] Only the cavalry divisions would proceed to the frontier. Railway planners informed him that this change could be accomplished without any serious difficulties, as far as the railway scheme was concerned. This arrangement, known as the *Rückverlegung*, became the new plan.[46]

Had Conrad intended his northern forces to defend against invading Russian divisions in newly prepared positions, his new plan might have made some sense, especially if he intended to focus on Serbia consistent with War Case B before pivoting against Russia. However, doing so would have been a massive deviation from all pre-war planning as well as from his own obsession with waging offensive warfare whenever possible. Most significantly, it would have been a flagrant breach of his firm agreement with Moltke to begin any Russian war with an invasion of Russian Poland in order to guard Germany's eastern front from Russian forces while the main German field armies attempted to crush France in just seven weeks with Moltke's modified version of the famous Schlieffen Plan.[47]

In the event, *Rückverlegung* proved calamitous. Austro-Hungarian forces did not defend their new, rearward San–Dniester line positions, instead marching forward – on foot – towards their originally designated deployment positions in a grand offensive against Russian Poland as initially planned. As with his mishandling of *B-Staffel*, Conrad's indecisiveness and vacillations made the *k.u.k.*'s challenging situation much more difficult. When the Austro-Hungarian infantry divisions ultimately engaged their Russian enemies, they did so exhausted from a hundred additional miles of marching routes that could have been travelled via rail.[48]

These two terrible mobilization decisions by Conrad – initially sending *B-Staffel* to the Balkan front to do nothing before training them back north to join *A-Staffel*, and halting *A-Staffel* forces well to the rear of the frontier but then having them march forward on foot towards their originally planned deployment locations – contributed to the horrific defeats the *k.u.k.* suffered on both fronts in August and September 1914. Of all the major belligerents, Austria–Hungary suffered the most disastrous defeats in the First World War's opening campaigns. The *k.u.k.* failed to achieve any operational or strategic goals against either Serbia or Russia, while suffering tremendous losses on both fronts.

Conrad's opening offensive against Serbia began on 12 August, some two weeks after Austria–Hungary's war declaration. Conrad's choice to command this offensive, the well-connected General Oskar Potiorek, proved a poor one. Potiorek's overall manpower superiority, with his 460,000 soldiers matched against 400,000 Serbian troops, did not translate to Austro-Hungarian success.[49] Serbian Field Marshal Radomir Putnik, who used his experiences and successes in the two recent Balkan wars to good effect, outfought Potiorek. Putnik, who knew that much of the *k.u.k.*'s Second Army (the bulk of the *B-Staffel* forces) then deployed on his northern frontier would soon withdraw for Galicia, ignored the hollow threat. After Potiorek's Fifth and Sixth Armies (namely, *Minimalgruppe Balkan*) crossed into Serbia, Putnik's surprise counter-attack inflicted a costly and humiliating defeat on the *k.u.k.*, resulting in 100,000 casualties and its ouster from Serbian territory by the end of August.[50] As usual, Conrad put all the blame elsewhere, even though his horrible mismanagement of the *B-Staffel* deployment reduced Potiorek's available forces and, contrary to War Case B assumptions, he approved Potiorek's understrength attempt to initiate a major invasion of Serbia without the full use of the *B-Staffel* forces (namely, the Second Army).

Greater disasters awaited further north against the Russians. In mismanaging the general mobilization so that it started late and de-trained the *A-Staffel* forces far to the rear of the frontier, Conrad passed the initiative to his enemy. Nevertheless, he ordered the First and Fourth Armies, on his western flank, to drive north towards Russian Poland without any knowledge about the Russian forces opposing them, and without a clear understanding of what those armies were to achieve.[51] The Third Army, on the eastern flank, was to wage an 'active defence' supporting the armies on its left, but in a display of opera-tional incoherence Conrad let its aggressive commander Rudolf Ritter von Brudermann also advance east into the unknown, and away from the two armies to its west. As alluded to above, by the time the Austro-Hungarian troops made contact with Russian forces, they were worn out from many days of forced marches in the summer heat.[52]

Of equal significance, these forces were considerably smaller than pre-war plans expected, since the Second Army (namely, *B-Staffel*) had yet to arrive in theatre, and the Germans had informed Conrad that their forces would stand on the defensive in East Prussia. But Conrad decided to attack anyway.[53] Making matters worse, Conrad's supply lines proved inefficient, staff-work was bungled, the infantry shot down at least three of their own aircraft and telephone communications turned chaotic. To add to the confusion, Conrad sent his massive cavalry force sweeping through the Polish plains, where they accomplished nothing except to provide targets for Russian infantry that slaughtered them with accurate rifle fire. By late August half their horses were *hors de combat*, and the remainder nearly so. As Norman Stone has concluded, 'the army's deployment' – which was Conrad's decision – 'did not offer much promise of success'.[54] As would occur time and again, Conrad provided insufficient men and resources for the missions he assigned them, and the assigned missions were the wrong ones in any case.

Had Conrad's forces been facing any other major European power, the results might have been uniformly catastrophic from the very beginning. But Russian leaders engaged in what Norman Stone has labelled a 'competition in blundering' with Conrad, giving the *k.u.k.* some brief, initial success on the western flank, what Conrad himself called 'a happy beginning'.[55] After stumbling into superior forces from the Austrian First Army, part of the Russian Fourth Army retreated towards Lublin. The *k.u.k*'s Fourth Army similarly prevailed in an initial clash with the Russian Fifth Army, even securing 20,000 prisoners and one hundred guns. But that was the last success the *k.u.k.* would achieve on this front for the year, and even here, broken supply lines precluded exploitation of these initial victories.[56]

Conrad's initial mistakes soon caught up with him. In late August superior Russian forces on the eastern flank sent the Austrian Third Army in headlong retreat to the west. Just days later, Second Army troops, worn out from their rail travel and subsequent foot-marching to the southern flank of the Northern Front, succumbed to Russian forces nearly twice their number.[57] With both of his eastern field armies defeated and retreating, but believing that his western armies had won great victories, Conrad ordered his Fourth Army to assist with the action to the east. This was a mistake, as this force was too late to prevent Russian forces from hitting the Third Army in the rear, while its weakened elements on the western flank were soon overwhelmed. Adding to the disaster, the First Army then collapsed under massive Russian attacks. With all four armies defeated and in danger of being destroyed, Conrad showed his operational incompetence by ordering an implausible counter-attack rather than preparing to retreat. Conrad even made an extraordinarily rare visit to the front to encourage his troops, arriving only in time to learn how shattered his forces were. Russian cavalry was raiding some divisional headquarters. Finally, Conrad ordered a retreat, but his mishandling of his forces and his failure to make any arrangements for the withdrawal led to chaos and confusion for 240 kilometres (150 mi.), all the way back to the Dunajec and Baila rivers east of Cracow. During this debacle *B-Staffel*'s Second Army units finally arrived from their useless excursion into the Balkans. Only the Russians' slow follow-up prevented a complete rout.[58]

Nevertheless, the opening campaign against Russia was disastrous enough. Conrad's forces had suffered horrific losses and failed completely in their operational goals. Four field armies had lost 450,000 men (nearly twice as many as the victorious Russians) and three hundred artillery pieces. Combat units were at half-strength, with particularly high casualties among experienced officers and NCOs.[59] Operational failures and enormous troop losses resulting from Conrad's decisions had strategic repercussions.[60] According to Herwig, 'It would not be too far off the mark to state that the twin disasters in Serbia and Galicia deprived Austria–Hungary of any chance to score a military victory against its adversaries.' Predictably, Conrad blamed others for his failures.[61]

Although Conrad's mistakes had led to operational defeat and catastrophic losses – he privately admitted that Franz Ferdinand would have had him shot had the Archduke still been alive – Conrad returned to his traditional love of the offensive, regardless of his forces' condition, the terrain surrounding them or the weather.[62] He initiated a major attack in late September 1914 to recapture Galicia and break Russia's siege of the massive fortress complex of Przemyśl and its garrison of 120,000 men, 21,000 horses and 30,000 civilians, an effort that consumed Conrad, and much of his army, into the new year.[63]

The last major *k.u.k.* advance of 1914 in the east, the so-called Battle of Ivangorod, was a joint offensive with the German Ninth Army to the north. Both forces advanced easily in early October, and the *k.u.k.* even briefly freed Przemyśl. While both Conrad and his German allies portrayed this as a victorious offensive, in fact, the Russians had merely withdrawn to a better line along the Vistula River. In mid-October a massive Russian counter-attack drove back both the German and

Austro-Hungarian forces. While the Germans skilfully conducted a planned withdrawal, after Conrad's ill-conceived counter-attack failed, Austro-Hungarian forces suffered terrible losses as they retraced their steps in their second major retreat of the young war, leaving Fortress Przemyśl under siege a second time.[64] By the end of 1914 the *k.u.k.* was nearly broken. The Austrian war minister reported losses of nearly 700,000; Herwig suggests that casualties were closer to a million.[65]

With his own forces shattered, a frustrated and increasingly bitter Conrad suffered additional embarrassment through his German ally's successes. Fresh conquests in November followed early German victories at Tannenberg and the Masurian Lakes. The Lódz offensive, in which August von Mackensen's German Ninth Army drove the Russian First and Second Armies back nearly 130 killometres (80 mi.) to Warsaw, taking over 135,000 prisoners during the advance, was too much for Conrad. 'Sick and tired' of his 'egotistical ally', and fearing the humiliation of having to submit to overall German command of the Eastern Front, he submitted his resignation. Sadly for the *k.u.k.*, it was rejected, as was any hope of a truly unified Eastern command for German and Austro-Hungarian forces.[66]

Conrad consoled himself by enjoying the luxuriant comforts of his command post in Teschen, writing self-pitying letters to his mistress, and planning more grandiose offensives for his increasingly fragile armies. These included subsequent, and horrific, efforts at Przemyśl's relief, despite the challenges of exhausted troops, winter weather and favourable Russian positions in the Carpathian Mountains that blocked any direct approach.[67] Undeterred, and delusional in the belief that his upcoming campaign would be 'short and swift', Conrad ordered his already-damaged Third Army to attack along the shortest and most direct route – through the Carpathian Mountains.[68] According to historian Richard DiNardo, Conrad's scheme was 'based on a weak foundation': he allocated only 1,000 guns to support 175,000 attacking troops who had to 'attack through some of the harshest terrain in Europe, in freezing cold and with Russians objecting every step of the way'.[69] Tunstall is even more critical: Conrad 'order[ed] his badly shaken armies to undertake what amounted to a suicide mission'.[70] Even before the offensive began, sub-freezing temperatures caused massive casualties among troops still in summer uniforms who lacked shelter and hot meals.[71] Then a blizzard hit just before the attack. The results of the attack were predictable: 89,000 casualties in just two weeks, with no appreciable gains to show for these losses.[72] Unfazed, Conrad called for a second effort in February and moved his Second Army into the line to conduct it. The Second Army lost 40,000 of its 95,000 men, with climatic conditions so severe that only 6,000 casualties were due to enemy fire; the preponderance resulted from cold and disease. Conrad ordered a third attempt for March, but a series of 'severe winter storms', a 'lack of artillery shells', 'numerical inferiority' and a ferocious Russian counteroffensive finally made Conrad's forces shift to the defensive just to hold current positions.[73]

Nevertheless, the damage was done. Conrad's callous indifference to terrain and weather contributed to as many as 800,000 casualties in his misguided efforts to relieve Przemyśl.[74] Despite these costly and foolish efforts, the fortress – low on food and ammunition – surrendered in late March, yielding nine generals, 93 staff officers, 2,500 officers, 117,000 soldiers, 20,000 civilian workers, nine hundred guns and tons of other materiel.[75] As Tunstall has shown, the campaign was doubly tragic in that Conrad ordered offensives with no chance of success in pursuit of an objective that had already 'lost much of its strategic significance'.[76] Conrad's disastrous efforts to wage winter offensives through the Carpathian Mountains destroyed what remained of the *k.u.k.*'s military capability. After eight months of combat, Conrad's incompetence had, in the words of Tunstall, 'driven the Austro-Hungarian army to the brink of annihilation'.[77] Thenceforth, virtually the only Austro-Hungarian military successes would be achieved by cooperative attacks in which German forces took the lead.

As noted above, Conrad's failures cannot be explained away by asserting that his opponents were simply too powerful. In 1914, while the *k.u.k.* struggled to earn any significant and lasting successes against either Serbia or Russia, the Germans defeated the Russians decisively in multiple battles: Tannenberg, the Masurian Lakes and Lódz. In 1915 the massive Gorlice–Tarnow offensive, arguably the most operationally successful campaign of the war, proved this point yet again. By the spring of 1915 many perceptive observers realized that Austria–Hungary would collapse soon without major German assistance.[78] Therefore, German chief of staff Erich von Falkenhayn determined to make his major effort on the Eastern Front that year. He chose Germany's finest army commander, August von Mackensen, to lead the offensive. He also decided to keep Conrad 'in the dark for as long as possible' to minimize his unhelpful involvement, only notifying him three weeks prior to the start by requesting that the *k.u.k.*'s Third and Fourth Armies be made available to provide flank support for the main effort by forces under German command.[79]

The offensive succeeded when Mackensen's attack in early May achieved total surprise, leading to repeated advances of 16 kilometres (10 mi.) a day and a transformed Eastern Front. The Russians lost 210,000 men in the first week, including 140,000 prisoners. A Bavarian division even liberated Przemyśl. By mid-May the Russians had retreated more than 160 kilometres (100 mi.) along a vast front that ran from the Carpathians in the south to a line north of the Vistula River. The Russians had 412,000 casualties in May 1915 alone. The offensive continued throughout the summer, and was expanded to the north and south, until the lines finally settled near Vilna in the east, after a 485-kilometre (300 mi.) advance. In total, some 850,000 Russians were captured.[80] It was the greatest victory of the war on the Eastern Front.

Desperate for any good news, Vienna promoted Conrad to the newly created rank of colonel-general, but his involvement in the success was minimal. When Mackensen met with Conrad prior to the offensive, he confirmed that Conrad understood that any orders he wanted to issue to Mackensen would have to be pre-approved by Falkenhayn, while for his part, Mackensen had complete authority to issue his own orders to the Habsburg units involved in the campaign.[81] Even Conrad admitted this tremendous success was bittersweet because it had been won, primarily, by an ally he increasingly viewed as a competitor: 'I cannot at all express how distasteful the infiltration with German troops is, but the heart has to follow the head.'[82] At the time and later Conrad and his acolytes have tried to give him credit for developing the concept of the Gorlice–Tarnow attack, but recent scholarship has shown that Falkenhayn made the strategic decisions and that Mackensen provided all significant operational leadership, a pattern of German control that continued throughout the war.[83]

German leadership and combat forces defeated Serbia in late 1915 and Romania in 1916, and led the one successful offensive against Italy, at Caporetto, in late 1917. The smaller Conrad's role, the more successful the campaign. As at Gorlice–Tarnow, the Germans consistently worked to minimize his involvement in their joint campaigns, while they unfailingly avoided getting involved in his unrealistic and grandiose operational schemes.[84]

Throughout the remainder of the war, Conrad continued the pattern of incompetent strategic and operational leadership that he demonstrated in the first year of the war. He mismanaged the Habsburg campaigns against Italy along the Tyrol and Isonzo fronts. In his passionate desire to punish 'perfidious' Italy he left his forces on the Eastern Front weakened and unprepared for the massive Brusilov offensive of 1916, which led to enormous losses of men and land. Conrad begged Berlin for German reinforcements, which, along with Russian logistical problems, saved his army from complete defeat on that front.[85]

By that point in the war, politicians throughout Austria–Hungary began to work for Conrad's removal, and his sacking was only delayed by the difficulty of settling on an agreeable replacement.[86] Kaiser Karl, Franz Joseph's successor upon his November 1916 death, reorganized the army by removing Conrad and taking personal command. Inexplicably, he then dispatched Conrad to Italy to command an army group in the South Tyrol.[87]

Once there, Conrad immediately reverted to form, disregarding troop numbers, resources, terrain and weather in the course of designing massive envelopment offensives.[88] Thankfully for the Habsburg forces, German expertise arrived later that year to take the lead in developing and conducting the hugely successful Caporetto offensive, with which Conrad had no involvement.[89]

However, in late January 1918 Conrad sent the first of a series of proposals for his army group to wage an all-or-nothing offensive against the Italians in the Tyrol. As usual, Conrad's plan was not based on reality: he needed fifteen more infantry divisions and two cavalry divisions to add to his current forces. As might have occurred with Douglas Haig's command in Flanders, his own superiors, in this case the new Habsburg chief of staff, General Arz von Straussenburg, actually worked to deny Conrad any reinforcements.[90] Yet, in the spring of 1918, Arz finally gave in to Conrad's pleas for a variety of reasons. Conrad's last grand offensive of the war ended, like the first, in disaster. Within two days, his Eleventh Army attack, launched on an 80-kilometre (50 mi.) front between the Astico and Piave rivers, ended with the survivors back where they started, achieving nothing but a new casualty list of more than 45,000 officers and men. Finally, on 15 July 1918, the day on which the German Army initiated its final offensive of the war along the Marne, Conrad was dismissed for good.[91]

Conrad's negative impact on the Italian front outlasted him. As Herwig describes it: 'The Battle of the Piave, while not a decisive battle in terms of territorial gains and losses, nevertheless destroyed what remained of the *k.u.k.* Army.' Over the next few months, Austro-Hungarian desertions reduced troop strength from 406,000 to 238,900. Herwig concludes that 'the Austro-Hungarian Army began to disintegrate immediately after Conrad's last offensive',[92] a fitting legacy for the commander who so stridently pushed his unprepared empire into war, botched its mobilization and repeatedly mismanaged its army's campaigns.

A curious historiography attends Conrad's life and career. Conrad himself contributed a massive five-volume memoir, its concluding volume being published in 1925, the year of his death at age 72.[93] His former mistress and second wife Gina proved to be a loyal defender of her husband, as were many of Conrad's protégés, who wrote hagiographic accounts of the general. During Austria's First Republic, Conrad became a symbol for nationalist historians, especially former army officers, who conflated Conrad and 'the honour' of the old imperial Habsburg army.[94] One such writer and former officer called Conrad 'the greatest Austrian commander since Prince Eugene'.[95]

In recent decades, however, leading historians, including Herwig, Tunstall, DiNardo and Sondhaus, among others, have assessed Conrad much more negatively. These scholars criticize Conrad's pre-war bellicosity as well as his wartime strategic and operational guidance. Their accounts note Conrad's many failures in developing strategies, designing plans and directing operations realistic for the forces and resources available. They also confirm that over the course of the war he became increasingly detached from the realities at the various fronts where his armies operated; in his obsession with hurling grandiose offensives at his enemies, he habitually disregarded such crucial factors as proper force ratios, sufficient firepower, terrain, weather, logistics, intelligence, unit training and troop morale. Evaluating Conrad's leadership in the First World War becomes a case study in the disastrous results of overestimating one's own capabilities, while underestimating those of one's enemies and failing to take into account the 'fog and friction' of war. Far from being one of history's 'great captains', evidence overwhelmingly suggests that Conrad was one of the worst.[96]

8

LEWIS BRERETON

John J. Abbatiello

L ewis Brereton emerged from the Second World War as one of its
most controversial airmen largely due to his post-war dispute with
Douglas MacArthur over the events surrounding the destruction
of the Far East Air Force in the Philippines. Brereton had
been MacArthur's air commander since early November 1941. A month
after he arrived, Japanese aircraft destroyed approximately one-third
of Brereton's B-17 bombers and two-thirds of his fighter force, with
most of those aircraft caught on the ground. The controversy over this
defeat became public when Brereton published *The Brereton Diaries* in
1946, in which he defended his reputation by providing his interpretation of those events and implying that MacArthur and his chief of
staff, Richard Sutherland, exercised excessive caution and delay. The
debate continued until both men passed away in the mid-1960s.

The debacle in the Philippines, however, was not the only military
disaster of the Second World War for which Brereton was responsible. In August 1943, as commander of 9th Air Force in North Africa,
he sent five groups of B-24 bombers against the Ploesti oil fields in
Operation Tidal Wave, losing 53 of 177 aircraft on a raid that inflicted
only temporary damage to Axis oil production.[1] In July 1944, as commander of 9th Air Force supporting Allied operations in Normandy,
some of his aircraft bombed friendly American infantry during
Operation Cobra.[2] Finally, in September 1944 Brereton found himself in command of the First Allied Airborne Army, a force of Allied
airborne divisions and their supporting air transports that ultimately
failed to take and hold the bridge across the Rhine at Arnhem during
Operation Market Garden.

As the responsible commander in these four disasters, Brereton surely bears the blame. Interestingly, few historians examining these battles place Brereton in the chain of decisions leading to defeat. Most accounts assign blame to Brereton's superiors or to his subordinate commanders. For example, a recent re-examination of the 1943 Ploesti raid barely mentions Brereton and instead criticizes several of his subordinates for mistakes made in planning, intelligence gathering and over-the-target leadership.[3] These accounts are misleading. In the end, senior commanders are responsible for their organizations' defeats and victories, and Brereton rightfully deserves a place among the worst commanders in military history simply because he commanded four important engagements that either failed in their objective or suffered severe casualties that detracted from any positive gain.

After a short biographical sketch, briefly covering Brereton's service and role in the Philippines, Ploesti and Operation Cobra, this chapter will focus on Operation Market Garden in more depth and his leading role in that operation's failure. Throughout these battles it is important to understand the decisions that Brereton made, the command relationships in which he worked, and the role of fog and friction that was and is always present in military operations. It is also important to note that in an environment where George Marshall, Dwight Eisenhower and Henry 'Hap' Arnold relieved commanders for incompetence or poor leadership ability, often without hesitation, Brereton was never targeted for dismissal.[4] An unfortunate fact about American air leadership during the Second World War was that there were few senior commanders possessing the requisite experience to lead large air organizations. Additionally, those who did achieve high rank had to be preserved in order to contend with their often more senior British counterparts.[5] A combination of these factors likely protected Brereton from being sent home, and instead led to his being 'kicked upstairs' even after several major failures.

Brereton's military career began when he graduated from the u.s. Naval Academy and was cross-commissioned into the Coastal Artillery Corps of the u.s. Army in 1911. While at Annapolis, he apparently discovered that he was susceptible to seasickness, but that did not prevent him from pursuing an assignment with the Aviation Section of the Signal Corps, which sent him to flying school in 1912. Brereton was one of the first fourteen army pilots to qualify for the military aviator badge. The American entry into the First World

Lewis Brereton,
1943.

War provided Brereton with an opportunity to serve in important command and staff positions in Washington and in France, where he became an expert in artillery spotting. William 'Billy' Mitchell soon noticed him, promoting Brereton from squadron commander to wing commander and finally to serve as Mitchell's operations officer at Headquarters, Air Service, Group of Armies. During the war he earned a reputation for superb combat leadership and courage under fire; he was decorated for adjusting artillery fire and for conducting reconnaissance while being chased by enemy fighter aircraft.[6]

The interwar years were not as kind to Brereton. As an air attaché in Paris he proved careless with money and appeared to not get along with the military attaché who supervised him. In the 1920s Brereton commanded the 3rd Attack Group, instructed at the Air Corps Tactical School, commanded the 2nd Bombardment Group and attended Command and General Staff School. Throughout this period he also had marital troubles, financial problems and anxiety attacks, and in the case of the last he sought medical assistance.[7]

Indeed, his reputation suffered from these issues as well as from his association with Billy Mitchell, whom he assisted during the famous court martial proceedings of late 1925.

Service in the Panama Canal Zone and on the faculty of Command and General Staff School in the 1930s helped resuscitate Brereton's career. He was promoted to full colonel in August 1936. Two wing commands during 1939–41 brought him much ground cooperation experience when he supported a series of exercises with army divisions. In June 1941 he took command of Third Air Force as a new major general and led his command during the Louisiana manoeuvres of September, where many ground and air leaders gained experience that would later prove valuable in future campaigns against Axis forces.[8]

In early October 1941 Hap Arnold and Carl Spaatz ordered Brereton to Washington. Brereton assumed the purpose of this summons would be his relief for poor performance during the manoeuvres. Brereton and his fellow airmen had learned many difficult lessons in Louisiana in a massive military exercise that exposed a severe lack of training and preparation for combat conditions as well as an absence of air–ground cooperation arrangements.[9] Instead, he was told to pack his bags for overseas duty. Douglas MacArthur had requested that Brereton take command of the Far East Air Forces, where Brereton's Louisiana experience with preparing facilities and keeping air units supplied and maintained would be extremely useful as the army built up its aviation forces in the Philippines.[10]

Brereton arrived in Manila on 2 November 1941 and immediately got to work reorganizing his command, developing facilities, and demanding more aircraft, pilots, spare parts, radar sets and anti-aircraft artillery. These resources were vital in defending airfields planned to accommodate a large force of B-17 bombers, which were meant to deter Japan from aggression in the Far East.[11] But as the Pacific War erupted, twelve of Brereton's nineteen B-17s at Clark Airbase, along with 34 of his brand new P-40E fighters, were destroyed on the ground by Japanese bombers and fighters at midday on 8 December 1941.[12]

According to William Bartsch in his book *December 8, 1941: MacArthur's Pearl Harbor*, Brereton made good decisions given the circumstances and lack of contact with MacArthur on the morning of 8 December. Like all senior leaders in the Far East, Brereton was notified of the Pearl Harbor attack at about 4 a.m. and immediately directed his subordinate commanders to put their aircraft on alert.

He tried and initially failed to gain permission from MacArthur's headquarters to attack Japanese airfields and other installations on Formosa, as the new RAINBOW 5 War Plan directed.[13] After finally being granted permission to attack Formosa later that morning, Brereton's airmen at Clark suffered a devastating air attack as they readied their aircraft with bombs and fuel for a mission that they never launched. According to Bartsch, 'it would appear that the FEAF commander did all within his power to launch an all-out bombing strike on Japanese airbases on Formosa on the morning of December 8, which the men under his command expected of him.'[14] However, as the commander of a combat organization, Brereton was responsible for this terrible defeat despite his efforts to prepare his forces and his vocal attempts to argue for a better strategy.

After several weeks of attempting to interdict Japanese landings in the Philippines, Brereton received orders from MacArthur directing him to Australia with his remaining aircraft. Brereton served as a senior commander in American, British, Dutch and Australian command and then went on to stand up the 10th Air Force in India in support of U.S. operations in China and Burma. In summer 1942 the War Department ordered Brereton and his few remaining B-17s to North Africa to support British operations against Erwin Rommel's Afrika Korps. Here Brereton established the Middle East Air Force, soon to be renamed 9th Air Force, where he absorbed new U.S. Army Air Force units arriving from America and learned a great deal from the RAF's close cooperation with British Army units. Brereton's fighters, medium bombers and heavy bombers supported General Bernard Law Montgomery's El Alamein offensive, helping to turn the tide of the North African campaign.

By summer 1943 Brereton's 9th Air Force, along with 12th Air Force operating from northwest Africa, was conducting bombing operations against Sicily and Italy in preparation for Operation Husky. However, as Christopher Rein relates in *The North African Air Campaign*, only two weeks into the battle for Sicily, Allied leaders pulled Brereton's two B-24 groups, reinforced him with three more B-24 groups from the UK-based 8th Air Force, and began an intensive training programme for a planned low-level attack against the Ploesti oil refineries in Romania.[15] Low-level attacks were not standard doctrine for American heavy bomber operations in Europe, due to a higher susceptibility to ground fire and difficulty in visual navigation.

The Ploesti plan came directly from 'Hap' Arnold and his Army Air Forces Plans Division, which considered Axis oil production an essential Combined Bomber Offensive target. The lead planner for Operation Tidal Wave was Colonel Jacob Smart, who convinced Eisenhower and the Combined Chiefs of Staff of the need for a low-level attack in June 1943.[16] Thus Brereton essentially served as a force provider for a plan originating from his superiors in Washington and directed from the highest levels of Allied leadership.

As mentioned earlier, the Ploesti raid was only partially successful and resulted in heavy losses of bomber aircraft and crews. A number of factors contributed to the heavy casualties, including foul weather that forced the attacking groups to fly higher and therefore into German radar coverage, navigational errors by two of the B-24 groups, and an aggressive defence by now-alerted German fighters and flak guns. The 98th Bomb Group alone lost 26 of 31 aircraft that reached their targets. Of the 532 aircrew that did not return from the mission, 330 were killed, seventy were interned in Turkey and the rest became prisoners of war.[17] While the raid damaged important facilities at Ploesti, it is important to note that the complex was not operating at full capacity. The Axis easily made up for the destruction by increasing production in the undamaged areas; that is, within the existing cushion.[18]

What, then, was Brereton's role in the Ploesti disaster? Christopher Rein blames Brereton for not agreeing with his subordinates that the low-level plan was ill-conceived. Brereton theoretically had the authority to override Smart's low-level concept and develop his own more conventional high-altitude plan for the attack. It is important to note, however, that the 9th Air Force commander was personally committed to the plan emanating from his chief in Washington. Brereton believed that the element of surprise would be an important advantage of the low-level concept.[19] In the end, as Craven and Cate mention in their official history of the Army Air Forces, the Ploesti raid was 'one of the most outstanding air operations of the war' and was 'an example of brilliant conception, painstaking preparation, and heroism during execution[;] the operation [had] few if any equals.' It was the first large-scale low-level American bombing mission of the war and was a longer mission in terms of distance than any previous bombing raid.[20] As Arnold wrote in his 1949 memoir, 'No mission in the war was more carefully planned, with full knowledge of the odds against it, nor carried out despite mishaps in identifying the target, with more amazing courage.'[21] Regardless of the post-war accolades, Ploesti was a failure, and Brereton again was responsible.

About a month after the Ploesti raid, Brereton took a portion of his 9th Air Force headquarters to England, where it would serve in a ground support role in preparation for the Normandy invasion.[22] Brereton built up facilities and a force of fighter-bombers, medium bombers and troop carriers, the last to be used in airborne operations. In late 1943 the Allies stood up the Allied Expeditionary Air Force (AEAF) to support the upcoming invasion, of which Brereton's 9th Air Force was the major component. Commanded by RAF Air Marshal Trafford Leigh-Mallory, who reported to Eisenhower, the AEAF comprised Brereton's 9th Air Force and the RAF's 2nd Tactical Air Force, Air Defence of Great Britain (formerly Fighter Command), and No. 38 Group, which was a force of several air transport squadrons for airborne troops.

Brereton trained his command, to include a number of exercises with American airborne divisions, and conducted preliminary combat operations in preparation for Operation Overlord. On the night of 5/6 June 1944, Brereton's 9th Troop Carrier Command deposited the 82nd and 101st Airborne Divisions across the base of the Cotentin Peninsula in a poorly executed night operation in bad weather. Poor weather further hindered his close air support operations on 6 June. Brereton's initial performance in support of Operation Overlord further damaged his reputation among American Army generals.[23] However, as the Normandy lodgement expanded, he established 9th Air Force advanced airfields in France and provided important air–ground cooperation to American forces struggling to dislodge German forces from the Bocage.

In mid-July senior Allied commanders conceived a plan to use their overwhelming advantage in air power to rupture German defences in Normandy. The new offensive, called Operation Cobra, would employ heavy bombers from 8th Air Force as well as tactical air power from the AEAF, including Brereton's 9th Air Force, to break the stalemate through saturation bombing of the German lines. Weather interfered with the original launching of the offensive on 24 July and General Omar Bradley and Leigh-Mallory cancelled the operation at the last minute. Unfortunately for the Allies, some of Brereton's P-47s and a formation of 8th Air Force bombers did not receive the recall order and dropped their bombs on infantry of the

30th Division.[24] These mistakes killed and wounded several dozen U.S. soldiers.[25] The next day, the weather cleared and Allied leaders launched the full assault with 1,500 heavy bombers, 380 medium bombers and almost six hundred fighter-bombers. Once again, friendly casualties resulted. In one case, 42 of Brereton's medium bombers dropped their bombs on American positions. The total American casualties due to fratricide on 25 July were 102 soldiers killed and 380 wounded. Among those killed was Lieutenant General Lesley McNair, commander of Army Ground Forces Command, who was in Normandy as an observer.[26]

As 9th Air Force commander, Brereton directly bore the responsibility for these American casualties. It would be inaccurate, however, to state that he was personally blameworthy in this case. All short bombing incidents were classified by U.S. Army investigators as aircrew error.[27] All parties involved in the planning, including senior leaders, knew of the deadly risks associated with targeting enemy positions in close proximity to friendly forces. Planners took this into account by pulling back U.S. infantry from the front line just before the assault and by meticulous preparation of the timing and target boxes of wave upon wave of bombers. Again, the plan came from a higher headquarters, not Brereton's. It is important to note that Brereton himself was among the senior Allied commanders who were almost wounded by friendly bomb fragments on 24 July.[28] Most Allied leaders accepted the American casualties as regrettable but in line with the costs of doing the business of industrialized world war.[29] Nevertheless, Brereton was responsible for his aircrews' training, planning and execution of their portion of the operation.

Brereton's fighter-bombers, led by Brigadier General Elwood Quesada of 9th Tactical Air Command, assisted with the subsequent breakout from Normandy and developed communication and procedural innovations that made close air support and armed reconnaissance extremely effective, adding momentum to the armoured advance. Following these successes, on 8 August 1944 Brereton assumed command of the First Allied Airborne Army, a new formation comprising American, British and Polish airborne forces, two airborne corps headquarters, and American and British troop carrier units to transport them to battle.[30] During the summer of 1944, Generals George Marshall and 'Hap' Arnold had pressed Eisenhower to use his well-trained airborne forces, both American and British, in bold strategic operations that it was hoped would shorten the war.[31] Eisenhower responded by establishing the First Allied Airborne Army (FAAA) and insisted that an American airman command it. Brereton was the ideal fit, given his experience with standing up new headquarters and with airborne operations, and his good relations with the British. The FAAA was unique; it was a standing headquarters in Eisenhower's Expeditionary Forces that was both joint, that is, with forces of land and air services, and combined, comprising forces of different nations. According to Phillip Meilinger, there is evidence showing that Brereton's apparent promotion demonstrated Arnold's and Spaatz's disenchantment with his leadership of tactical air forces.[32] In any case, Brereton immediately focused his energy on preparing the new organization for combat.

After several cancelled airborne operations following the Normandy breakout, Brereton's FAAA would finally see action in mid-September 1944. On 10 September Montgomery, commanding the 21st Army Group on the northern flank of the Allied advance, convinced Eisenhower to allow him to employ the FAAA in a bold offensive in eastern Holland. All intelligence estimates showed that German forces were broken and in full retreat;[33] in Montgomery's opinion the Allies must strike before the Germans could regroup on the German border. In Operation Market Garden three of Brereton's airborne divisions would secure several river crossings as British XXX Corps' 20,000 vehicles advanced along a single road. MARKET was the codename for the airborne portion and GARDEN the name for the XXX Corps ground assault. The final objective, 103 kilometres (64 mi.) inside enemy lines, was the bridge over the Rhine at Arnhem. From there XXX Corps would make a right turn, followed by the rest of the British Second Army, and break out into the north German plain – excellent terrain for Allied armoured forces. Montgomery envisioned an offensive that, if successful, would end the war in Europe by Christmas 1944.

Though the drops on 17 September 1944, the opening day of Market Garden, were extremely accurate with minimal losses of transport aircraft to the enemy, the operation ultimately failed. The Germans unexpectedly reacted fiercely, rushing in counter-attacking forces that pressed – and at times pierced – that narrow corridor. Poor weather, starting on the second day of operations and continuing throughout the battle, hindered the lift of airborne reinforcements, their supplies, and their expected close air support by Allied tactical air forces. On the night of 25/26 September, fewer than 2,000 British airborne soldiers withdrew across the Rhine, signalling an end to the operation. The British and Polish airborne units at Arnhem had lost approximately 1,500 killed and left behind over 6,500 POWs and evaders, about a third of them wounded. Of the 1,743 men who jumped in with the British 1st Parachute Brigade, only 136 were evacuated safely. Additionally, the two U.S. airborne divisions, the 82nd and 101st, suffered about 3,500 casualties over the course of one week of fighting.[34] However, as army historian Charles MacDonald writes, there was little acrimony or controversy over this failure, largely because the operation failed by the narrowest of margins.[35] It was a bold and risky operation that if successful promised tremendous dividends for the Allies. And the decision to launch it was completely out of character for both Montgomery, whose typical modus operandi was to employ overwhelming forces after lengthy and meticulous preparations, and Eisenhower, who favoured a broad-front strategy instead of single thrusts with exposed flanks. Apologies aside, Market Garden was still a failure.

So again, it is important to understand Brereton's role in this disaster. The overall concept of the assault belonged to Montgomery and his staff, and again Brereton found himself in a position where he had to make the best of a plan directed from above. As FAAA commander, what were Brereton's responsibilities? In this rather unusual organization, his role was chiefly in planning, and Brereton was responsible for five major planning decisions that affected the outcome of the campaign. Brereton was not responsible for selecting drop zones, deciding which forces would go in first or choosing the tactical objectives for the airborne troops. Those decisions were left to the troop carrier commanders and the airborne division commanders, and overseen by Brereton's deputy, Lieutenant General Frederick Browning. Browning was the senior airborne soldier in the British Army and would command the airborne corps once on the ground in the Netherlands.

Brereton's staff, and the staffs of his subordinate units, had less than a week to plan this operation. Fortunately, they had recently planned a smaller operation involving only one British division to be dropped near Arnhem in Operation Comet, which was subsequently cancelled, and they leveraged those existing plans as much as possible. At the army level, Brereton wrestled with the following issues.

First, should the drops be conducted during the day or at night? Brereton decided on a daytime drop for a number of good reasons, and this decision proved correct. Daylight would afford more accurate navigation, which had been a hard lesson learned the night before D-Day in June. More accurate drops would allow airborne troops to form up faster and set off for their objectives much sooner, vital when attacking river crossings that needed to be seized immediately. Additionally, at this time during the war, German night fighters seemed to be more of a threat to large aircraft than their day fighters. On the first day of the operation, more than 1,000 fighter aircraft sorties escorted the C-47s of IX Troop Carrier Command and provided close air support and flak suppression, the latter being very effective on Day One.[36] This could not have happened at night.

Routes to the drop and landing zones were another area where Brereton exercised decision-making as the FAAA commander. In September 1944 troop carriers and their airborne soldiers were all based in southern England, and the routes of troop carrier groups had to be carefully planned to avoid German flak concentrations and provide obvious ground features for visual navigation. One option was to fly over the North Sea and then across the Netherlands, where German flak concentrations were relatively low. This was known as the 'Northern Route' and was the most direct route in overall distance from England. About 130 kilometres (80 mi.) of this route would be over enemy-held territory.

The second option was to fly across the English Channel and then over Allied-controlled territory in Belgium, and then head north to the target areas. This 'Southern Route' limited exposure to German-held territory in distance and time – only between 32 and 96 kilometres (20 and 60 mi.) depending on the location of the assigned drop and landing zones – but had the disadvantage of having the troop carriers fly over the front lines where the Germans had anti-aircraft artillery readily available. Brereton judged the two routes to be equally hazardous and decided to use both simultaneously to assist in the de-confliction of aircraft formations and reduction of congestion.[37]

The reader may wonder why the FAAA did not forward deploy to France in order to decrease the flying distance between troop carrier bases and the Market drop zones. The chief reason was a severe lack of transportation capacity required to establish new air bases for the C-47s and gliders as well as basing arrangements for the airborne divisions. Supplying the advancing Allied divisions moving towards the German border was already under severe strain, and there was little capacity to add more to the supply burden of Eisenhower's forces in France. And such a move would require weeks of planning and several months for execution. The FAAA would move its first C-47 squadrons to France in late September and would not move the bulk of its components to the Continent until February 1945.

Returning to Market, Brereton's first two decisions contributed to excellent results on the first day of the landings. Troop carrier formations were tighter in daytime and drops were subsequently more concentrated. Flak suppression by U.S. and British tactical airpower was effective. Troop carrier formations carrying U.S. airborne forces lost only 33 troop carrier aircraft and thirteen gliders on the first day of Market; the British lost none. This amounted to a 2.8 per cent aircraft loss rate, which was much lower than the expected 30 per cent casualty rate.[38] Airborne division commanders lauded the first day drops, with Brigadier General James Gavin of the 82nd stating that the landings were the best in the division's history.[39]

The next three of Brereton's important decisions in Operation Market dealt with what he chose not to do. Brereton could have directed that his troop carrier units fly two round-trip missions on the first day, but instead he decided to execute only one per day. This recommendation came from Major General Paul Williams, who commanded Brereton's IX Troop Carrier Command. The round-trip sorties to the drop zones were between five and six hours in duration. Two of those in one day, plus the loading process in between, would require some night flying. Williams feared that his crews, notoriously unskilled at night navigation, would not be able to launch and form up during a pre-dawn launch or recover to their bases after dark. He also feared that his maintenance crews, undermanned due to the rapid expansion of his troop carrier forces, would not be able to perform required battle damage repairs and routine refuelling and maintenance in time for two lifts. Finally, he was wary of the impact of aircrew fatigue during combat operations; two lifts in one day would be too much to ask of his pilots.[40] And Brereton accepted Williams's recommendation.

Brereton also decided during the planning process to not employ double-tow techniques for gliders. Troop carrier crews had only experimented with double-tow, which is towing two gliders behind one C-47. As a pilot, Brereton understood the dangers of this technique.

Tow-pilots and co-pilots would have to relieve each other at the controls every fifteen minutes due to the sheer physical challenges of maintaining control in the propeller wash of formation flying as the engines strained to keep the aircraft aloft. Double-tow formations would also be much more susceptible to collisions.[41] For such a lengthy flight to the landing zones, Brereton ruled out double-tow for safety reasons.

Finally, Brereton directed that Allied tactical air units based in France would not fly close air support missions whenever troop carriers were near the target area, to avoid the threat of fratricide. No doubt his memories of Operation Cobra influenced this decision. Given weather delays at troop carrier bases in England, difficulty in communications with Allied tactical air force headquarters in France, and poor weather over the drop and landing zones, this meant that close air support was severely lacking after the first couple of days of the operation. Brereton had warned Eisenhower during the planning phase that weather conditions in England and on the Continent could be vastly different.[42] Adding to the challenges of coordination, Brereton's decision to visit the battlefield on 19–20 September, a time when he should have been making key close air support and airlift decisions, put him out of contact with his staff. A poorly timed visit to Eindhoven during an aggressive German counter-attack made Brereton temporarily unreachable by radio.[43]

These last three planning decisions demonstrated Brereton's aversion to risk in an already risky operation. A key feature of airborne operations was, and still is, boldness of execution to achieve surprise with the maximum force available to secure key objectives, in this case, geographic features such as bridges and relatively high ground. It was not the time for Brereton to be conservative. No doubt, the requirement to rapidly plan the operation, for a headquarters that had only been in existence for about 45 days, proved too much to ask of his staff.[44]

In the end, Hap Arnold's review team concluded that Market Garden was ill-advised from the start due to 'overly optimistic intelligence estimates' and poorly aligned ground forces relative to the assigned mission. In the view of Craven and Cate, the American official air historians, 'the air phases of Market Garden were decidedly the most successful of the entire operation'.[45] Eisenhower's efficiency report on Brereton, covering the period 2 August 1944 to 31 December 1944 and including the Market Garden operation, ranked him fourth for air or airborne commanders and tenth among field commanders from a population of 32 army lieutenant generals 'personally known' to him. Eisenhower rated Brereton's performance as 'superior' and remarked that he was 'a serious, hard-working officer of considerable experience in air–ground cooperation and in airborne operations'.[46] This was faint praise indeed. Perhaps Brereton's own views, immediately following Market, are most telling. In a letter to Hap Arnold's chief of staff, several weeks following the operation, Brereton expressed his frustration with the command arrangements under which the FAAA operated:

> I tried to explain in my letter to him [Arnold] that up until now the planning of an operation has not been confided to this Headquarters, but that we are placed under the domination of the Army Group Planning Staff and it seems likely this will continue to be the case. Until the time comes when the planning of the First Allied Airborne Army and the planning of the Ground Staff is on a purely co-equal and coordinating level, I see little chance of any great latitude in forcing my own ideas of properly conceived airborne operation[s].[47]

Here Brereton attempted to deflect blame from his own responsibility to Montgomery's headquarters.

After Market Garden Brereton continued in command of the FAAA, where his U.S. airborne divisions contributed to defending Allied lines during Hitler's Ardennes offensive. His final major combat operation of the war was Operation Varsity, where once again he employed a daylight drop in support of Montgomery's Rhine-crossing operation, this time near Wesel. Brereton trained his troop carrier crews carefully between Market and Varsity, and ensured that lessons learned from Arnhem were incorporated in all stages of the March 1945 Varsity operation.[48] Varsity was the most successful airborne operation of the Second World War, but the cost of this victory was a string of previous failures.

After the war, Brereton led air commands based in the continental United States, including the 1st Air Force and 3rd Air Force, and served on various advisory boards and councils, retiring as an Air Force Lieutenant General on 1 September 1948.[49] He died on 20 July 1967.[50] During the years following the war, Brereton devoted a great deal of energy to protecting his reputation. He was the first Second World

War American general officer to publish his memoirs. His personnel folder is filled with correspondence enquiring about decorations and other recognition, with a clear intent to ensure that his official records reflect an accurate account of his service.[51]

Lewis Brereton does not rank highly among the great air leaders of the Second World War. Air power historian Phillip Meilinger referred to Brereton as a 'capable though not outstanding combat leader'.[52] He was a loyal subordinate who executed plans directed from above to the best of his ability. As a general officer who commanded large air organizations, he chiefly played the role of organizer and planner. Though what we might call Clausewitz's fog and friction of war influenced the outcome of his major failures in the Philippines, Ploestri, Cobra and Market Garden, Brereton ultimately fell short and only the commanding general could bear the blame of defeat.

The terms 'leadership', 'management' and 'command' often seem to be synonymous to those unfamiliar with military operations, but they have significantly different meanings. Leaders, in any context, tend to be defined as those people who influence – whether formally or informally – other members of the organization to meet the organization's goals. Managers tend to be seen as those who employ resources efficiently to meet the organization's goals. On the other hand, the Department of Defense defines 'command' as 'the authority that a commander in the armed forces lawfully exercises over subordinates by virtue of rank or assignment'.[53]

In other words, commanders exercise leadership and management functions, but they are ultimately responsible for their unit, their subordinates and their assigned mission. As a commander, Brereton was responsible for the units over which he had authority, the men he led and the missions assigned to him. He was responsible for the men and aircraft of the Far East Air Force in the Philippines, the 9th Air Force in North Africa and northwest Europe, and the First Allied Airborne Army, again in northwest Europe. He was responsible for important missions assigned to him by MacArthur, Arnold, Eisenhower, Montgomery and other Allied leaders. And as a commander of not just one, but four major Allied failures of the Second World War, he is the worst military commander in history.

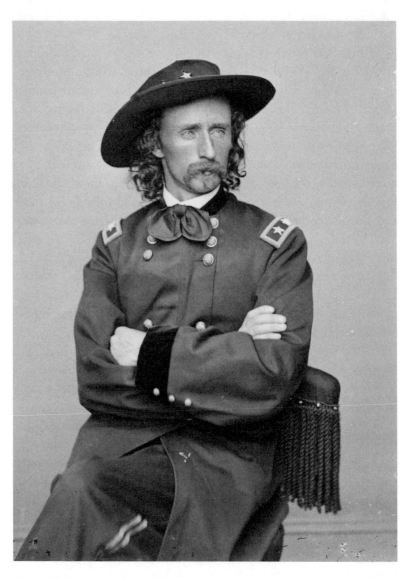

George A. Custer, 1865.

9

GEORGE A. CUSTER

David W. Mills

George A. Custer is perhaps one of the best-known generals in American history, whose renown was generally attributed to a number of factors. The first was his notoriety as the youngest general in the volunteer army during the American Civil War, earning the rank of brigadier general at 23, and major general a year later. The second factor was the level of media attention that he received, making Custer a celebrity in his day. The press aggressively pursued Custer, who actively sought their attention and gave them much to write about. Finally, as a fighter against Native Americans after the Civil War, he perpetuated his image as a war hero, seeking to use his fame as a stepping stone to positions of greater responsibility and financial reward.[1] His subsequent death at the Little Bighorn in 1876 elevated him to legendary status in the eyes of the American public.

As a soldier, he was tactically competent, calm under fire and intelligent, but he was not a good officer. No one would ever accuse Custer of cowardice, as he proved repeatedly that he was a brave soldier, willing to take risks to accomplish his mission or to scatter his enemies before him. Attacking was his signature move, which made him a feared adversary, but one who lost more men than most other cavalry commanders.[2] He was courageous to the point of recklessness, and he took unnecessary risks, endangering not only his own life but the lives of his soldiers.[3] Custer was lucky rather than good, and it was only a matter of time before his carelessness caught up with him. His greatest blunder at the Little Bighorn, where he attacked a superior force without a proper reconnaissance to determine the size and location of the enemy, was the worst defeat of the u.s. Army in the frontier wars, leading to the deaths of 268 officers, enlisted soldiers, civilians and Native American scouts. For these reasons he was one of the worst generals in military history, despite his posthumous fame.

Custer's impetuous behaviour began at an early age. Appellate judge and fellow student at the Creal School in Scio, Ohio, Richard M. Vorhees, remembered that young Custer was a leader among his peers, but showed signs of impulsiveness, especially when challenged. The future general was constantly involved in rough play and fights with other pupils.[4] Even during his tenure at West Point he was reckless. Entrance into the Military Academy was the ticket to a free college education to most aspiring cadets, but represented an opportunity for Custer to match wits with a faculty and administration determined to keep him in line. Custer was not a stupid or untalented cadet, but he decided to graduate last in his class academically in order to push the limits of the administration's tolerance for dismissal, while simultaneously preserving as much time for fun as possible. During his tenure at the Academy, he accumulated 726 demerits, the most in his class. Almost unbelievably, his worst academic performance was in cavalry tactics in his senior year. He was successful in his goal, graduating last in his class of 34 cadets, after many had left the institution for the Confederate Army. Historians have chalked up his ability to survive the West Point years as 'Custer's luck', which allowed him to earn a commission in the u.s. Army and saw him through many difficult times.[5]

Following the attack on Fort Sumter, the remaining 45 members of the class of 1861 reported to the War Department for assignments. Custer's class of 1862 was graduated early to serve in the war, and the cadet who barely passed his course in cavalry tactics was assigned to the 2nd u.s. Cavalry Regiment. He arrived in Washington in time to join his regiment and to participate in the First Battle of Bull Run.[6] Custer held a variety of assignments in the early days of the war, choosing ones that gave him the freedom to go where he pleased. One of his most challenging assignments was as the assistant division engineer, when he was supposed to ascend to 300 metres (1,000 ft) in a balloon under the supervision of Thaddeus Sobieski Constantine Lowe, Lincoln's chief of army aeronautics. Riding in the balloon one day, Lowe observed that Custer was white and shaking like a leaf. 'I saw at a glance that he had courage,' Lowe observed, 'but that his courage was impulsiveness.' Custer may have been assigned to the engineers, but this disassociation with any particular unit allowed him to insinuate himself into battle. He volunteered to reconnoitre enemy positions or to manoeuvre around obstacles for the division and otherwise attach himself to units going into the thick of battle.[7]

General George B. McClellan took note of Custer's bravery and asked to see the young lieutenant. Although his uniform was a disgrace after weeks of campaigning, Custer was thrilled to meet the general that he so admired. At the conclusion of the interview, McClellan offered Custer a staff position. Custer accepted, and rose to assistant aide-de-camp with a rank of captain in the volunteer service. McClellan admired his new aide and became quite attached to him, sending him to the front in order to get a clear picture of the fighting there. As McClellan later wrote, 'Custer was simply a reckless, gallant boy, undeterred by fatigue, unconscious of fear, but his head was always clear in danger and he always brought me clear and intelligible reports of what he saw under the heaviest fire.'[8] Psychologist Duane Schultz writes that Custer was driven by an intense ambition to succeed, and an unquenchable lust for glory and fame. One of the easiest but most dangerous ways to achieve glory was to lead his men from the front. He shared every danger that they did, but he seemed to lead a charmed life on the battlefield, surviving impossible situations. For his bravery, his soldiers loved him.[9] These risks to himself and his soldiers were unnecessary, however. The same traits that his soldiers so admired later got many of them killed at the Little Bighorn.

Custer hoped to serve on a senior staff rather than experience the war in a small unit, and he began cultivating the patronage of the commander of the Army of the Potomac, General Joseph Hooker, and General Alfred Pleasonton, the commander of a division in the newly formed cavalry corps. In fact, in early May he went to work for both men, carrying out instructions on either staff as circumstances warranted, at the rank of captain in the volunteer forces. By the end of May, the young officer's reputation was growing by his routine accomplishment of difficult missions.[10]

In the shake-up following the resignation of Joseph Hooker, Pleasonton was promoted to command the newly organized cavalry corps, consisting of three cavalry divisions and a reserve brigade.[11] To complete the reorganization, General George G. Meade agreed to Pleasonton's request for the promotion of three new brigadier generals to command cavalry brigades, including Custer. Custer, at 23 years of age, became the commander of the Michigan Cavalry Brigade and the youngest general officer in the army. This was an interesting selection, as Custer had no combat command experience and numerous officers in the unit believed that they were entitled to command over the young outsider. He seemed to have risen to the occasion, however, taking command as if he were born to the position, barking orders, and expecting to have them obeyed.[12] For his new command, Custer dressed the part. His uniform consisted of black velvet trousers and coat trimmed in gold lace, with a navy blue shirt and red kerchief knotted at his throat, and a large black hat. Custer intended to stand out on the battlefield, both to his own troops and to the enemy.[13]

Custer took command just in time to see action near Gettysburg, where he prevented Confederate cavalry general J.E.B. Stuart from entering the battle. The Union cavalry guarded an important crossroad, and despite the Confederates outnumbering the Union forces, Custer launched a bloody attack on Stuart's cavalry. Neither side could claim a decisive victory, but Stuart's force was halted in its efforts to attack Meade's from the rear that day. Custer's tactics were unorthodox, but his bravery had perhaps saved the Union Army. His actions came at a heavy price, however, with 29 officers and men killed, 123 wounded and 67 missing. Custer lost six times more men during the battle than Brigadier General David Gregg, another Union cavalry commander present at the battle. According to Edward G. Longacre, who wrote about Custer's performance in the Civil War, Custer had a penchant for acting boldly when conditions seemed to warrant it. When he did commit troops, however, he always led them from the front, possibly sharing whatever fate his soldiers did.[14]

With the defeat of the Confederates at Gettysburg, the new commander in the East, Ulysses S. Grant, determined to take the fight to the South, where the Union Army had only known defeat. The Shenandoah Valley was vital to Southern interests, however, as it was fertile cropland that supplied the Southern army. Experiencing defeat early in the 1864 campaign, Grant placed Philip Sheridan in charge, giving him many forces, including Custer's brigade. The young general was again at the forefront of the fighting, and was nearly killed when an enemy soldier fired at him at short range. Custer reared his horse at the last moment, and the bullet grazed his leg. 'He was perfectly restless in his contempt of danger, and seemed to take infinite pleasure in exposing himself in the most unnecessary manner,' recalled one of Custer's staff officers.[15] This battle was the first Union victory in Virginia and set the stage for the end of the war.

Far to the south, William T. Sherman's march required replacement officers, and Grant selected Custer's division commander, James Wilson, to command Sherman's cavalry. Never popular with the division after assuming command, this was a good move for him. Sheridan then selected Custer to command the division, which devastated the Michigan Brigade. The soldiers loved their commander, under whom they had fought hard and performed their duties well. The unit lost many soldiers, however, with over 350 killed and 1,275 wounded. No other cavalry brigade had suffered such losses. Custer, however, had never ordered them into a fight where he had not led them. He was a determined and popular commander, but his brand of warfare demanded a heavy price. With it, honour and victory followed his brigade. In thanks for his impeccable leadership, Sheridan recommended to Grant that he promote Custer to brevet major general.[16]

When campaigning began in the spring of 1865, the Union force again pursued Lee through Virginia, where Custer again distinguished himself in the fighting at Waynesboro, Dinwiddie Courthouse and Five Forks. Custer's force blocked Lee's retreat, and he received the first flag of surrender from the southern force when Major Robert Sims, a Confederate staff officer, carried a white towel on a stick. Sims stated that General Lee requested a cessation of hostilities, and Custer replied that he could not accept the surrender unless assured that Lee intended to surrender unconditionally, and he sent Sims back to ascertain the answer. Instead of waiting for Sims to return, Custer rode into the enemy lines. He found General James Longstreet and demanded the surrender of the army, but Longstreet refused to comply. Custer, embarrassed, rode back to Union lines cowed by the experience.[17]

Peace may have descended upon the nation, but Custer was a soldier, and he found himself in New Orleans as part of the Reconstruction occupation. Sheridan had orders to eliminate Confederate raiders still operating in Texas, and he sent for Custer to assist in that mission. Sheridan ordered Custer and 4,000 cavalry troopers, comprising five veteran regiments (1st Iowa, 2nd Wisconsin, 7th Indiana, and 5th and 12th Illinois), to Houston. The troopers hated still being in the army, as they thought they should have been mustered out, and they hated the South. Above all, they were in no mood for discipline, and several infractions set the commander against many of his men. In any event, on 8 August 1865 the command left Louisiana for Hempstead, Texas, near Houston.[18] In Texas, the rations were not fit to eat and Custer ordered whippings for several soldiers accused of stealing food from local farmers. The command universally hated Custer for his uncaring and detached attitude, and blamed him for incompetence and neglect of his soldiers. He was not prepared to have his soldiers loathe him after experiencing the adoration of his troopers during the war.[19]

The 5th Illinois mustered out of the army and went home in September, and in October the command left for Austin, with the exception of the 12th Illinois, which stayed in Hempstead. The command patrolled the city while Custer enjoyed life there. In December a number of generals were mustered out of the army, including Custer, who reverted to his regular army rank of captain of the 5th Cavalry Regiment. They left Texas in January, bound for Monroe, Michigan, but he quickly left to testify before Congress on the state of Reconstruction, then to New York City to investigate a career in business. He also considered a career in politics, but set that aside, at least on a temporary basis. Finally, his future was resolved when Congress authorized the creation of four additional cavalry regiments, the 7th through the 10th, in July 1866. He accepted a position as temporary commander of the 7th Cavalry Regiment with the rank of lieutenant colonel, and was dispatched to Kansas.[20]

Custer spent much of the time between his Reconstruction duties and his demise at the Little Bighorn patrolling throughout the Great Plains, with orders to protect settlers, miners and railroad officials, while moving hostile bands of Native Americans towards the reservations. Custer arrived at Fort Riley, Kansas, in October 1866, and shortly after Colonel Andrew J. Smith arrived to command the regiment. In February of the following year, however, Smith took command of the District of the Upper Arkansas, giving command of the regiment back to Custer. The force at Fort Riley had a difficult if simply stated task, to move Native Americans off the Plains and onto reservations so that white settlers and railroad companies could populate the region in safety. Custer's force took to the field with the 37th Infantry Regiment in March 1867, to move the southern tribes south of the Arkansas River.[21] Perhaps the greatest example of Custer's recklessness occurred at this time, when he left his command without permission in October 1867. General William T. Sherman ordered Custer, under the command of Major General Winfield S. Hancock, to preserve the peace and to protect settlers in the area of western Kansas. He had shown up at Fort Wallace, the westernmost outpost in Kansas, where he found the fort under siege; short of food, medical supplies and ammunition; and enduring an outbreak of cholera. Nevertheless, in the midst of the siege, Custer left the fort with 75 of his soldiers on 15 July, destined for Fort Harker, 360 kilometres (225 mi.) east.[22]

Custer claimed that he left to seek aid for Fort Wallace, but his real reason for departing was to find his missing wife, who had travelled to Kansas to meet him. Therefore, the impetuous Custer simply left his post to search for her, pushing his soldiers to the limits of exhaustion and causing a number to desert. On the way to Fort Harker, Custer heard that Native Americans had killed two of his soldiers, but concerned solely with locating his wife, he did not bother to search for their bodies. He finally found her at their home at Fort Riley, and they returned to Fort Harker, where Custer was arrested. On 27 August 1867 Grant ordered Custer held for court martial at Fort Leavenworth, scheduled to convene in mid-September. Testimony began on 17 September and lasted until 11 October. In the end he was found guilty of several charges, including being absent without leave, and sentenced to a one-year suspension of pay and rank.[23]

While Custer was absent, Hancock had failed to bring peace to the Plains region, and Sherman relieved him of his command. Major General Philip Sheridan had not won any friends with his Reconstruction policies in the South, so he was brought in to fill the role that Hancock vacated in the West. Like Hancock, Sheridan was charged with securing the peace between the Platte and Arkansas rivers and moving the Native Americans located there to reservations. Sheridan was unable to find anyone else who could successfully remove the Native Americans from the Plains, so he requested that Custer be returned to active duty two months before the end of his suspension. He arrived at Fort Leavenworth on 30 September 1868.[24]

Sheridan had little luck finding the Native Americans during the summer of 1868, and was determined to continue campaigning into the winter season. The reasons for this are straightforward: the warriors in the summer rode well and they were difficult to find, but when they settled in with the women and children during the winter, they were easy to find, and were not used to campaigning at that time of year. Sheridan sent Custer and the 7th Cavalry Regiment out in a winter campaign against the Indians starting in November 1868, reaching Camp Supply on the seventeenth. Scouts found a trail heading north, presumably to Kansas, where the Native Americans were attacking isolated settlements. Custer left Camp Supply with eight hundred soldiers and scouts, following the Native Americans until he came upon their large encampment on the Washita River. The chief of this village was Black Kettle, whose tribe had been the victims of the massacre at Sand Creek led by Colonel John Chivington in 1864.[25]

Custer attacked Black Kettle's encampment in the same manner that he would employ later at the Little Bighorn. Without ascertaining the size of the encampment or the number of warriors within it, Custer split his command in two, with each group attacking the village at opposite ends while smaller units completed the encirclement. Custer's force attacked just after daybreak on 27 November, killing an estimated fifty of the enemy. When some of the Native Americans managed to escape, Major Joel Elliot and twenty of his troopers attempted to chase them down. Unknown to Custer or Elliot, a camp of Cheyenne, Arapaho and Kiowa was just a few miles down the river. A group of warriors from that camp met Elliot's force, a skirmish ensued, and Elliot and the troopers were all killed and mutilated. Custer did not know this back at the Washita River camp, and the warriors that had killed Elliot's group, plus hundreds of other warriors, began encircling the troopers still in the village. Custer, not knowing the fate of Elliot but assuming he was fine, withdrew from the camp and marched back into Camp Supply on 2 December, finding the remains of Elliot's command on the march.[26] Upon his return, Custer's command received enthusiastic adulation for a great victory.

While Custer deserves praise for extricating his command from a potentially deadly situation, he should have answered for his rash decision to attack an enemy force of an unknown size through unknown terrain. Had he conducted further reconnaissance, he would have discovered the existence of the other camp a few miles away, and probably would have executed the attack differently, perhaps saving the lives of Elliot and his men. For Custer, the Washita victory reinforced his confidence in surprise and audacity, and he viewed his actions as glorious, rather than reckless. This sentiment was echoed by the American general public, who regarded Custer as a hero who had driven the Native Americans from the Washita to reservations and kept the settlers safe.[27]

The setting for the next confrontation with Native American tribes was over the Black Hills, a region sacred to the Sioux but an opportunity for quick cash for white miners, as gold was discovered there. Thousands of prospectors had descended upon the region and demanded protection. In the autumn of 1875 key members of the administration of President Ulysses S. Grant gathered to discuss the situation in Dakota Territory. They had tried to purchase the land but failed; the only way to get the Sioux to give up the Black Hills was to send a military unit as a show of force, which Grant agreed to do. Custer led an eight-week expedition into the Black Hills in July 1874, the purpose of which was not to engage the Sioux, but to identify the potential for gold and other resources found there. His mission was a success, and he reported to his superiors that the region held vast quantities of precious metals and timber.[28]

The campaign season of 1874 and 1875 was quiet, but that was about to change. Grant had spent much of his first two years in office trying to negotiate a peaceful solution with the Native Americans in the West, but by the winter of 1875-6 he had lost patience and decided on a confrontational approach. Although the miners who had flocked to the Black Hills were trespassing on sacred lands that the government had ceded to the Lakota, in December 1875 Grant issued orders that all Lakota and Cheyenne bands must return to the Great Sioux Reservation by the end of January 1876. After that date, the army could take whatever action was necessary to compel them to return to the reservations. Sheridan and another legendary frontier fighter, General George Crook, devised the plan with the help of several talented officers, including Custer. However, during the planning process, officials in Washington called Custer to testify before Congress.[29]

A scandal had been simmering for a while in Washington, as Secretary of War William Belknap was accused of corruption by abusing his role as the supervisor of Indian Agency trading posts in the West. The businesses were quite lucrative, and competition for a trading post licence was intense. When Belknap pulled all of the licences issued previously and offered new ones for a hefty price, a howl of protest arose when the president's brother, Orvil Grant, began securing licences for anyone who paid him a bribe. The House of Representatives decided to hold hearings on the matter, and called Custer to testify as a regimental commander at Fort Abraham Lincoln, one of the posts involved in the scandal. Custer testified several times, and although he had little more to offer than rumours and hearsay, the media soon painted Custer as a star witness due to his illustrious reputation. Critics of President Grant then used the scandal to discredit him and then to discredit Custer, whom the media condemned for corruption and slandering Orvil Grant. The president was so incensed with Custer that he relieved him of any command responsibilities in the forthcoming campaign. Sheridan placed General Alfred H. Terry in charge of the command coming out of Fort Abraham Lincoln, although Grant eventually relented and allowed Custer to accompany, but not command, the eastern prong of the attack.[30]

The campaign plan was simple enough. The enemy tribes were somewhere west of the Black Hills, hunting in southeastern Montana. Thus the offensive called for a three-pronged attack that would surround the enemy, leaving them no avenue of escape. Terry's column, augmented by Custer's 7th Cavalry, would set out from Fort Abraham Lincoln in present-day North Dakota, travelling west. General John Gibbon's Montana column, with infantry and cavalry, would converge from the east. Finally, Crook's Wyoming column would attack from the south. However, Crook's command encountered a contingent of Native American warriors eight days prior to the Little Bighorn battle, forcing the army to retreat, but Crook never sent word to the other commanders that he was withdrawing his force. Perhaps the greatest flaw in the plan, however, was the assumption that the tribes would not be able to stay together as a large force because they would run out of food.[31]

The force spent much of May and half of June looking for the enemy, when Terry divided the command. Terry ordered Custer to travel up the Rosebud River and then up the Little Bighorn River, while Terry would accompany Gibbon's search up the Yellowstone River to the mouth of the Bighorn, then to the Little Bighorn. The two commands should meet up around 26 June. Terry offered his two Gatling guns, with a rate of fire at 350 rounds per minute, but Custer considered these too cumbersome. Custer and his men also left their sabres behind, as they rattled when the horses trotted. Terry offered Custer four companies from the 2nd Cavalry Regiment to augment his command, but Custer turned down the reinforcement. It is unclear whether he refused due to a desire to keep all of the glory for the 7th Cavalry Regiment or because of his strained relation with Terry, but it was assumed that each unit was large enough to defend itself if they found the Native Americans while separated. Contrary to much popular opinion, Terry allowed Custer to take any action he deemed necessary should he strike the enemy's trail. He was not required to wait for Terry, although Terry advised him, calling out as they separated, 'Now Custer, don't be greedy, but wait for us.' 'No, I will not,' Custer shouted back.[32]

For several days Custer and his command had found trails and followed them to a convergence point somewhere on the Little Bighorn. Custer's men rode all through the night of 23/24 June 1876 to get within the vicinity of the enemy camp; the plan was to rest all day on 25 June, and then launch a pre-dawn attack against the camp on 26 June. Gibbon was also expected to arrive on 26 June, which would augment Custer's regiment. Custer estimated that there were eight hundred warriors in the camp, when in fact the camp had between nine hundred and 1,200 lodges, with a total of some 7,000 people within it, including approximately 2,500 warriors.[33]

On 25 June 1876, after the all-night march, Custer's chief of scouts sent word that they had located the enemy camp, and they reported that the valley contained the largest Native American village anyone present had ever seen. When one of the scouts remarked that there were enough enemy warriors there to keep them fighting for two or three days, Custer arrogantly remarked that the battle would be finished in one day. He viewed the camp from a long distance away, but the scene was hazy and he could make out few details. Without further reconnoitring and ignoring the warnings of his scouts, in true Custer fashion, he decided to trust to luck and attack the camp immediately. Despite the lack of intelligence about the size of the opposing force or the size of the encampment, he feared that the enemy would escape if he waited for the other units to arrive.[34]

He was counting on 'Custer's luck' to aid him again. As he had done so many times during the Civil War, and again at the Washita in fighting Black Kettle's band, Custer hastily ordered his command into battle, simply assuming that his men could defeat any enemy force that they encountered. The 7th Cavalry Regiment at the time consisted of 31 officers, 566 troopers, and fifty scouts and civilians. Of particular note, Custer had several relatives with him, including his two brothers, Tom and Boston, his brother-in-law Lieutenant James Calhoun, and his nephew, Autie Reed. Also accompanying the command was Mark Kellogg, a reporter from the *Bismarck Tribune*.[35] They would all die with him at the Little Bighorn.

At 11.07 a.m. Custer split his command into three attack columns and one support column. The three attack columns would ride abreast towards the encampment, slowly spreading out until the columns were no longer within sight of one another. Custer led the right column, which consisted of 213 officers and men of companies C, E, F, I and L. His mission was to ride east of the river until he was centred on the enemy camp, then turn into it and attack. Major Marcus Reno commanded the centre column, with 140 officers and men of companies A, G and M, plus 35 scouts. His mission was to strike the southern end of the camp, preferably at the same time Custer was attacking the centre. Captain Frederick Benteen commanded the column on the left, with 115 officers and men of companies D, H and K. He was to cross the river and ride along the west side of the camp, preventing any hostiles from escaping. Then he would cross the river again and support Custer in the camp. Captain Thomas McDougall and one company were assigned to escort the pack train and therefore were not participating in the attack.

While Custer had used this same approach in attacking Native American camps before, including the Washita, the village he was about to attack was two or three times larger than the four-hundred-lodge villages that he had encountered in the past.[36] This would have been the time for caution since terrain and the opponent's strength, disposition and intent were all unknown; moreover, his own forces were scattered, and he could only assume that they were still following his plan. Caution, however, was anathema to Custer.

Reno's command was the first to encounter the enemy, and it did not go well. Although his presence surprised them, the Native Americans quickly recovered and mounted an attack that sent the troopers in full retreat. Reno's men were rendered completely combat ineffective for the rest of the day. Throughout his life, Reno faced charges of cowardice and of allowing Custer's command to fall. Benteen's reputation also suffered, as he was accused of deliberately delaying in coming to Custer's aid. He reconnoitred the area to the south, found no encampments, and stopped to water the horses twice. At the second watering hole, the command heard gunfire, and soon Benteen had orders from Custer 'to come quick'. Benteen's command moved out slowly, at a walk or a trot at times, when Benteen got another message to hurry to Custer. Benteen met up with Reno's men, who had been routed in panic and confusion. Reno and Benteen discussed going to Custer, but seemed to dismiss the idea until other officers spurred them on. However, due to the enormous number of warriors between themselves and Custer's detachment, they abandoned the idea of trying to meet Custer and took up a defensive position instead.[37]

Although Custer's scouts had repeatedly warned him of the large number of Native Americans in the valley, their warnings fell on deaf ears. When one of the scouts advised Custer not to divide his force because of the large number of enemy warriors, Custer replied, 'You do the scouting, I'll do the fighting.'[38] One of the scouts even invited Custer to look upon the enemy village from a nearby rise, but seeing the settlement, Custer merely remarked 'We've caught them napping. We've got them!' Custer then ordered his adjutant to send a message to Benteen, telling him to hurry and join forces, but Benteen did neither as he and Reno had already formed a defensive position and were fighting for their lives. They repelled the last attack early the next morning, and by noon the Native Americans had drifted away.[39]

No one can say what happened to Custer on 25 June 1876 as none of Custer's men survived to tell the story. Two days after the battle, Gibbon's column advanced up the Bighorn Valley. First, they found the abandoned village and then the naked and mutilated bodies of what remained of Custer's detachment. Even the horses were horribly mutilated. The survivors of Benteen's and Reno's detachments then arrived at the scene of the battle and buried their dead. Diaries recorded the treatment of the bodies: some men were only identifiable by a necklace worn about the neck, a tattoo or fillings in the teeth. The reporter Mark Kellogg was identified by a shoe. Nearly all of the bodies were ill-treated, except for Custer. He was shot twice, once in the chest and once in the temple, but there were no powder burns to suggest suicide. Why he was not dismembered remains a mystery.[40]

Custer became a popular hero at the time, but his disastrous demise was not unforeseen. Although Sheridan praised Custer's personal courage, he maintained that Custer always needed someone to restrain him, noting that he lacked the ability to analyse a situation and was too quick to attack. Sherman described Custer in 1867: 'Young, very brave even to rashness, a good trait for a cavalry officer – but he had not too much sense.' When Sheridan heard of Custer's fall at the Little Bighorn, he wrote to Sherman, 'I feel it was an unnecessary sacrifice, due to misapprehension and a superabundance of courage, the latter extraordinarily developed in Custer.' Finally, Grant, who was by no means a Custer supporter, wrote to Sherman, 'I regard Custer's massacre as a sacrifice of troops brought on by Custer himself that was wholly unnecessary.'[41]

Custer's tactic of choice, which had always worked for him in the past, was to attack aggressively in the face of unknown odds and circumstances. He had gained the adoration of his soldiers during the Civil War by always leading his men from the front. Fortunately for Custer, he was almost always able to turn his attacks into decisive victory, leading him to the erroneous conclusion that this tactic was always successful. However, personal bravery and unthinking aggression are no substitute for careful consideration of the enemy's disposition; nor is luck a substitute for competence. While the phenomenon known as 'Custer's luck' had rescued him from some tight situations in the Civil War, many of his men paid the ultimate price along the way. Eventually, the odds caught up with Custer at the Little Bighorn, and hundreds more soldiers died due to their commander's arrogance and recklessness. Thus Custer was one of the worst commanders in military history.

PART 4

POLITICIANS

Roman bust of Marcus Licinius Crassus.

10

MARCUS LICINIUS CRASSUS

Gregory S. Hospodor

lthough ancient military leaders often shared the horrific consequences of catastrophic defeat with the soldiers they led, the Fates seemed especially unkind to Marcus Licinius Crassus, Roman commander at the Battle of Carrhae in 53 BCE. He witnessed the Parthians parade his son's severed head in front of his army on the tip of a lance. Later, Crassus walked to a parley with his mounted enemies. That one of Rome's most influential men found himself without a horse manifested just how far his fortunes had fallen. After Crassus' assassination at the meeting, Surenas, the Parthian commander, degraded his remains, removing the right hand and head, pouring molten gold into the dead man's mouth, and sending both as trophies to the Parthian king.[1] They arrived after King Orodes II and the Armenian king, Artavasdes II, agreed to a peace treaty and as they were watching Euripides' *The Bacchae* in celebration. Improvising quickly, an actor seized Crassus' head and used it as a stage prop in one of the tragedy's closing scenes. Meanwhile, Surenas staged a mock Roman triumph in Seleucia, a city with pro-Roman leanings, led by a prisoner resembling Crassus dressed in women's clothes and answering to *Imperator*, a title bestowed upon successful Roman generals.[2]

Crassus' reputation fared little better back home. Given the facts that the defeat was Rome's greatest in an offensive war and that Crassus had been one of its most powerful citizens, Carrhae commanded attention and demanded explanation. Although Crassus must certainly have had defenders, crushing defeat remained an unworthy handmaiden. History and the public favour winners. So, too, did Crassus have political enemies who delighted in savaging his performance in the East. Furthermore, assigning responsibility to the commander obviated uncomfortable reflection upon deeper causes of the calamity. Thus a narrative placing the blame solely on Crassus quickly emerged. The surviving sources generally portray a leader driven by greed, hungry for glory and lacking judgement. To most writers, history revealed moral lessons. Accordingly, the debacle unveiled Crassus' character flaws.

Like ancient writers, it is tempting to explain the cataclysm in terms of Crassus' decision-making. Indeed, Crassus was in an ideal position to bring about defeat entirely on his own, combining both political and military authority on the fringe of the Republic's empire. It is a truism that leadership holds any military together and that, correspondingly, leaders are accountable for the success or failure of those under their command. The greater the failure, the worse the leadership, and vice versa. Interpreted this way, Crassus should join a long list of military incompetents. However, this would be a mistake.

Eliot A. Cohen and John Gooch called the natural human tendency to assess a single human point of failure 'little more than a concealed confession of perplexity . . . a cry of despair masquerading as an explanation'.[3] Although Crassus correctly bears much of the responsibility for the crushing defeat, blaming him alone oversimplifies the reasons for the result at Carrhae. Instead, Crassus' failure exposes far more, both the strengths and the weaknesses of the Roman military system during the late Republic. Marcus Licinius Crassus was not idiotic or ruled by his passions. He proved a generally competent, if ordinary, product of Rome's approach to warfare. Against Surenas, a Parthian commander of true genius, ordinary was decidedly not good enough.[4] The roots of the stunning debacle of the Carrhae campaign, then, rest in a mixture of individual and collective failure.

Marcus Licinius Crassus' military expedition against the Parthians in 54–53 BCE reflected the Republic's cultural attitudes towards war, a Roman way of war. Three aspects particularly stand out. First, war and politics were indivisible. Second, Roman warfare was hyper-aggressive and sought decisive battle. Finally, it was profoundly regular.

In Republican Rome, war and politics were intimately linked. Military glory won in the service of the state served as a litmus test of worthiness for higher public office. Along with wealth and political acumen, it was indispensable for any who wished to accumulate power within the Republic. Thus Marcus Licinius Crassus strove to acquire it in order to satisfy his desire to join the first rank of Republican citizens.

As a young patrician of the senatorial class, he gained military experience while supporting Lucius Cornelius Sulla Felix. Crassus raised and funded a personal army, and garnered a reputation as an effective commander, especially for commanding the right wing of Sulla's victorious army at the decisive Battle of the Colline Gate in 82 BCE.[5] However, his command during the Spartacus War (or Third Servile War) of 73–71 BCE served as the singular jewel in his military crown. Only after the defeat of several legions did Crassus receive a special appointment from the Senate and people of Rome granting nearly unlimited power to suppress the slave rebellion.[6] He outfitted thousands of troops with his own money, which he added to those already in the field. Against Spartacus, Crassus proved an effective if cautious general.

His first task was to restore the morale of the army. Despite coming from one of Rome's pre-eminent families, Crassus was a hard man and had led a grim life in his youth, having seen his father's head hung from the rostrum in the Forum.[7] As a commander, he manifested his toughness through uncompromising and rigorous training, and decimating units that performed badly in battle. Decimation was an ancient practice in which one out of ten men were chosen by lots and executed publicly by their comrades. The disgraced legionaries who survived the decimation bivouacked outside the army's main camp and subsisted on barley, basically animal feed, until they had redeemed their honour. Clearly, Crassus meant business and his methods worked.

His operational approach was sound as well. He constantly harassed Spartacus' forces, giving battle only when the conditions favoured the Roman army, such as attacking smaller, isolated enemy forces or fighting on open ground that favoured the legions. Crassus effectively won the war in the Battle of the Silarius River in 71 BCE. Afterwards, he ordered thousands of prisoners crucified as an object lesson for slaves who might consider rebellion in the future.

The goal of all this was political advantage. Crassus hungered for military glory and the popularity it brought. He possessed incredible wealth and considerable political skill. What he lacked was a military reputation as lustrous as his rivals', the critical third leg of political power in Rome.

Between his military exploits, Crassus focused on building both his fortune and his political influence.[8] He acquired his riches through the same practical, tough-minded approach he displayed during the Spartacus War. At a time when the most acceptable patrician income came from landed estates, Crassus unashamedly profited from Sulla's proscriptions by acquiring property far below market value.[9] He also purchased, trained and then rented out slaves, owned mines and became a real estate mogul in Rome.[10] Although Plutarch averred that Crassus' sole vice was avarice, he was no different to many ambitious men in Rome, although certainly more successful and single-minded than most.[11] Personally abstemious, Crassus used his wealth and provided other assistance to further his political influence. He assiduously cultivated clients by supplying interest-free loans, employing his potent oratorical skills as an advocate in lawsuits and dispensing other forms of patronage.[12] Accordingly, he built a formidable informal network of political support, including, at one time, Gaius Julius Caesar. In addition, he pandered to the people of Rome, having on one occasion provided three months' sustenance out of his own pocket to every citizen in the city, as well as feasting them.[13]

The politics of the late Republic were complex, and the details rest beyond the purposes of this chapter. The key for students of these events is the struggle for power among three men: Pompey the Great (Gnaeus Pompeius Magnus), Julius Caesar and Crassus. In 59 BCE the three men formed an unofficial power-sharing alliance, the so-called First Triumvirate, which dominated Rome. In April 56 BCE they met in Luca (modern-day Lucca), where they renewed their alliance. The most important result of the conference was that Crassus became governor of Syria with the right to make war. For him, military success was essential to at least secure and, more significantly, advance his political position.

If the indivisibility of war and politics in Republican Rome led to Crassus making war on Parthia, the Roman expectation that their generals would aggressively seize, retain and exploit the initiative shaped his operational approach to the campaign. Militarily this makes sense because one's actions force the enemy to react, rather than the opposite. Put more parochially, the Romans ordinarily sought to make their opponents dance to their tune, removing the opportunity for them to act as they preferred. There was also a political imperative to act quickly and decisively. Simply put, Rome expected her generals to fight. Although final victory might take years, Roman generals had to show that they were vigorously working towards it.

Crassus surely understood all of this as he considered how to prosecute a war with Parthia. The imperative for victory was, of course, a given. But more than that was required; the people of Rome awarded style points for rapid and decisive action. To maximize the glory gained, speed was essential. On the other hand, Crassus' critics would surely capitalize on any perceived reluctance to take prompt and direct measures as a sign of timidity. Thus balancing the probability of a favourable outcome with a desire to maintain the tempo of operations proved a fundamental problem during the campaign. Crassus sought decisive battle at what he considered the first reasonable opportunity.

Crassus' calculation of a 'reasonable' probability of success was no doubt shaped by his confidence in the Roman military as well as his own experience. Although flexible in execution when in the hands of a gifted commander, the Roman military system relied on standardized organization and tactics. Therefore, the very strength of the system could also breed overconfidence. Roman military history is replete with commanders who appear to have believed that their primary job was to manoeuvre their army close to the enemy, assuming that this alone would deliver success. Such was the excellence of the system that this was often quite good enough. Against enemy commanders of the calibre of Hannibal, Vercingetorix and Surenas, it was not. What was required when adversaries avoided Roman strengths while maximizing their own was agile leadership capable of adapting to meet the challenge.

One of the most important decisions a Roman general made was to determine the appropriate type and number of forces needed given the specific military threat and terrain. An army tailored for the operating environment furnished a commander with a multitude of options to respond to unforeseen circumstances. Overconfident commanders underestimated the importance of fine-tuning their force structure, seeing the problem as a matter of deploying the maximum number of legions available and relying on the heavy infantry to muddle through. And muddle through the legionaries frequently did. But the wars of the Republic were marked by repeated initial defeats, followed by Roman recovery and adaptation to the specific context of the threat, leading to an eventual triumph. The cause in almost every case was overconfidence, hubris even, that the system alone was good enough to prevail. This was the siren's call of regularity, of an excellent system, to which Marcus Crassus was not immune.

The Roman way of war played an important role in determining the outcome at Carrhae and Marcus Licinius Crassus' part in it. First, the intimate connection between war and politics ordained that Crassus needed military glory to remain competitive with his political rivals, which set his date with the Parthians at Carrhae. Second, having gained the authority to wage war, the cultural expectation for rapid and decisive action meant that a showdown would come sooner rather than later. Crassus went to Syria itching for a decisive battle that would reap the laurels he lusted after. Finally, Crassus had supreme confidence in the heavy-infantry-based Roman military system. His faith was not misplaced, but caused him to discount the significance of conditions in his chosen theatre for military adventure, most of all the cavalry-centric character of his Parthian opponents. Despite all this, culture alone does not determine the outcome of a campaign. Instead, it defines the box within which military operations take place. Truly gifted commanders readily adapt within the cultural limitations imposed by their society; less talented ones do not. In any case, final responsibility for success or failure rests with the individual.

In 56 BCE Crassus and Pompey strong-armed the results of the conference at Luca upon Rome. Both were proclaimed consuls, the two most powerful public positions in the Republic; Caesar's *imperium* to prosecute the war in Gaul was renewed for five years; Pompey received two provinces in Spain.[14] A law proposed by the tribune Gaius Tribonius gave Crassus the province of Syria for five years, the authority to declare war and make treaties, and seven legions.[15] Although Crassus was at least sixty years old and his last significant military service was in the Spartacus War of 73–71 BCE, he was giddy with excitement at the prospect of gaining martial glory as well as the riches that victory would bring.[16] He also turned to recruiting the seven legions authorized by law. His recruiting efforts were successful, yielding a force primarily composed of inexperienced men with a core of veterans of Pompey's eastern campaigns in the 60s.[17] Despite opposition to the expedition, Crassus departed Rome to meet his army, brimming with confidence.

Parthia's military potential troubled Crassus little as he travelled south to the port city of Brundisium in early November 55 BCE. Indeed, overconfidence coloured his actions during the entire campaign. This sin, rather than incompetence, framed his decision-making.

Crassus' first task was to stage his seven legions into the theatre of operations. Strategic mobility, the ability to deploy and maintain forces on or beyond the frontiers of the empire, was an outstanding characteristic of the Roman military system and one that Crassus managed well. Getting to Syria was a complex task that involved moving approximately 34,000 legionaries with all of their gear roughly 2,400 kilometres (1,500 mi.). For example, simply providing the standard daily ration for a force this size required at least 33,900 kilograms (74,800 lb) of food.[18] Crassus accomplished this aspect of the deployment professionally as there were no reports of supply difficulties. Getting to Syria was another matter. Travelling by sea was faster than marching but entailed risk as the weather in the Mediterranean is unpredictable in winter. Desiring perhaps to minimize this risk, but to also accomplish the move with maximum alacrity, Crassus used ships to transport his force to Greece, whence they marched to the crossing into Asia Minor and then through the client kingdom of Galatia to Syria. The sea gamble was costly, with the fleet losing 'a great number' of vessels, according to Plutarch.[19] Regardless, attrition was not so large as to prevent the army from undertaking operations soon after its arrival by the middle of 54 BCE.[20]

If the deployment to Syria was largely successful, other aspects of the opening stage of the campaign were not. Crassus appears to have conceptualized military operations during 54 BCE as the shaping phase of the war, the period during which a commander conducts activities to set the conditions for the success of the decisive operation. During this phase, he made several mistakes that were to bear bitter fruit later on. Crassus incorrectly judged the importance of maintaining momentum once he arrived in the theatre, allowing the Parthians critical breathing space to react to the attack. He generally neglected the collection of intelligence.[21] He also failed adequately to appreciate the necessity of building a strong political and military coalition. In these, Crassus acted as one who believed that victory was a given.

Initially things went well once Crassus arrived in Syria. He promptly marched his army to the Euphrates River, integrating auxiliary light infantry and local cavalry as he did. Then, he bridged the river and entered Parthian western Mesopotamia. Crassus' movement from

Roman Syria rather than through the client kingdom of Armenia further north suggests that his strategy was to take the fight to the Parthians via the quickest and most direct route. Moving through the rugged Armenian terrain would have been slower, but would have solidified Rome's alliance and added the Armenian army to his own, especially its cavalry. Conversely, invading western Mesopotamia promised to maximize the campaigning season, offered the shortest path to Mithradates III, who served as a useful distraction as he fought against his brother for the Parthian crown, and would demonstrate boldness and decisiveness, which would play well politically back in Rome. Furthermore, this course of action did not rely on allies as Roman forces would conduct the operation, reflecting perhaps a degree of cultural arrogance.[22]

Whatever the reason, Crassus marched into western Mesopotamia, where he sought battle with the satrap of the region, Silaces, defeating him easily near the town of Ichnae. Success in this minor action can only have increased Crassus' conviction that his Parthian adventure would be an easy one. So, too, did the Greek-dominated cities of western Mesopotamia quickly come over to the Roman side. Only the city of Zenodotium resisted. Crassus swiftly sacked the city, providing both a lesson in Roman power and loot for his soldiers and himself. The Romans, it seemed, were unstoppable.[23]

But stop they did. Crassus evidently viewed operations in 54 BCE as only the prelude for a decisive effort to be made the following year: he garrisoned the conquered territory with 7,000 infantry and 1,000 cavalry and withdrew the rest of his troops to winter quarters in Syria. There were several valid reasons for doing so. Although he had been uniformly successful, he had yet to meet a major Parthian army in the field. His army was inexperienced in major combat operations; defeating Silaces' outnumbered forces and taking Zenodotium had been excellent for morale, but hardly tested the legionaries. Winter quarters, garrison duty and minor operations in Roman-controlled territory would allow time for training. Furthermore, Publius, Crassus' son, was on his way from Gaul with 1,000 picked horsemen and a sterling military reputation. The cavalry was sorely needed given Parthian strength in this department. So, too, would Crassus have looked forward to adding his son to the command echelon. In sum, the campaigning season of 54 BCE portended an even more effective Roman army the following year.[24]

Plutarch, however, assessed Crassus' failure to press on to Seleucia and Babylon as one of his greatest blunders.[25] There were benefits to pushing harder. Crassus' aggressive move into western Mesopotamia caught the Parthians by surprise, and it would take time for them to mobilize an effective army. However, Crassus manifested a methodical approach to operations against Spartacus years before, fighting only when the cards were stacked in the Romans' favour. Playing the game this way had worked then, and possibly, he thought that it would now as well. Even so, boldly marching into central Mesopotamia to link up with Mithradates III when the Parthians were unprepared might just have convinced them to sue for peace, achieving the goals of the campaign and showering Crassus with glory. The Parthians would definitely be ready to welcome the Romans the following year. So, too, did Mithradates III lose both the civil war and his life during the winter of 54–53 BCE. With his death, a valuable Parthian distraction and a potential Roman ally disappeared. Time would prove to Crassus that it waits for no man.

Crassus also disdained to develop accurate and timely intelligence, a cornerstone of military success. His greatest failure in this regard was to ignore making a realistic appreciation of Parthia and its military potential. This was largely due to overconfidence, but also to the fact that the Romans traditionally did not place much emphasis on intelligence activities.[26] He seems to have thought that the Parthians were like the Armenians, and would be as easy to defeat.[27] The Romans had conducted successful operations in the theatre before, and Crassus could easily have garnered valuable insight into his adversary and the operating environment had he been interested in doing so.[28] But he did not. Consequently his decision-making reflected more what he and his army planned to do to the Parthians rather than what the Parthians might do in response. One direct result of this was that his army possessed an inadequate number of auxiliary cavalry and missile troops at Carrhae. Intelligence failures did not cause the disaster, but ill-informed decision-making certainly contributed.

Crassus, furthermore, failed to build an effective political and military coalition prior to the Battle of Carrhae. This, too, was most likely due to his overconfidence in Roman military superiority as well as his distrust of Rome's existing allies. The best example of this involves Rome's new allies, the Armenians. Sometime in the spring of 53 BCE King Artavasdes II of Armenia rode into Crassus' camp with 6,000 cavalry. We have little information about the meeting that took place, only six sentences in Plutarch.[29] It seems that Artavasdes II offered military assistance totalling 16,000 cavalry and 30,000 infantry plus logistical support, but only if Crassus marched his army through Armenia. According to Plutarch, to sweeten the deal, Artavasdes II

> tried to persuade Crassus to invade Parthia by way of Armenia, for thus he would not only lead his forces along in the midst of plenty, which the king himself would provide, but would also proceed with safety, confronting the cavalry of the Parthians, in which lay their sole strength, with many mountains, and continuous crests, and regions where the horse could not well serve.[30]

Crassus, however, refused to alter his plan of advancing through recently conquered western Mesopotamia, and Artavasdes II rode away.

Given what would happen at Carrhae, Plutarch clearly intended that this should be interpreted as another of Crassus' blunders, but the exchange is curious for a couple of reasons. First, the Armenian king dictated the terms of his assistance and quit when he did not get his way. Artavasdes was in a dangerous position, caught between two powerful neighbours. It was in his interest to hedge his bets, but to prescribe the conditions for military cooperation seems rash given the potential for Roman retribution. Second, in Plutarch, Crassus acquiesced to the behaviour. As one of Rome's leading men, he was used to getting his way and would, or should, have been jealous of the prerogatives of his position. No Armenians joined the Roman army during its advance into Parthia. Why did Crassus not demand some tangible measure of support, at the very least a portion of the 6,000 cavalry accompanying the Armenian king? One is led to the conclusion, yet again, that Crassus' overconfidence caused him to dismiss the significance of adding as much allied cavalry to his force as he could. He must have believed that he could win without Armenian help, although it is also possible that he simply did not trust the Armenians because of their relationship with his rival Pompey or rate their military prowess highly. Crassus was well versed in the practice of high-stakes power politics. He was also an old hand at managing client–patron relationships. It is difficult to imagine that Artavasdes could have refused had

Crassus insisted that an Armenian contingent march into western Mesopotamia with him.[31]

As it stood, the Armenians and Romans would wage war separately. While this forced the Parthians to deal with two separate problems if both were aggressive, it also divided the efforts against them because the communication methods of the period made close coordination impossible. There was every reason to question the commitment of the Armenian king to the Roman cause. If Artavasdes hedged his bets, Crassus' army would advance alone into the heart of the Parthian Empire. From an Armenian perspective, there was little to be gained by spilling much Armenian blood in a war that would only decide which power would dominate them.

In sum, it seems clear that Crassus had not done all that he might have to set the conditions for success before marching into the heart of Parthian Mesopotamia in May 53 BCE. He prepared for the impending showdown armed with the certainty of success. Had he been less self-assured or more attuned to the fickleness of Mars, he would have considered more deeply the significance of surrendering the initiative during the autumn of 54 BCE, of discovering as much as he could about the Parthians and their plans, and of cementing an effective coalition, securing additional troops in the process. As it was, his overconfidence led to over-optimistic assumptions, expectations and calculations.

The Parthians used the respite provided to brace themselves for the coming storm. King Orodes II appreciated the seriousness of the Roman threat.[32] Consequently, he collected intelligence by sending an emissary to Crassus' camp, nominally to make a last-ditch effort to avoid war. Predictably, the diplomat returned empty-handed except for valuable insight into Roman plans and preparations.[33] So informed, Orodes developed a straightforward strategy to defeat the Romans and Armenians in detail. He would take the main field army into Armenia to deal quickly with the less dangerous threat from that direction, leaving a smaller force under the command of a leading noble, Surenas, to delay the Romans. With the Armenians subdued, the two forces would unite for the conclusive battle with Crassus.[34]

In the spring of 53 BCE Crassus crossed the Euphrates at Zeugma in blissful ignorance of careful preparations to receive him. Gaius Cassius Longinus, who had a date with Julius Caesar nine years later on the Ides of March, and Publius Licinius Crassus rode with him at the head of approximately 40,000 men: seven legions of heavy infantry,

4,000 auxiliary light infantry and missile troops, and 4,000 cavalry, including 1,000 picked Gallic horse.[35] After crossing the river, Crassus faced a choice to take a more southerly course towards Ctesiphon, Babylon and Seleucia or to head west directly into the heartland of Parthia.[36] He decided to march west. Plutarch castigated him for this decision, claiming that an Arab chieftain tricked him into marching into a desert against the advice of Cassius.[37] However, Crassus' march followed a major caravan route towards a river swollen with spring runoff and passed through several garrisoned towns, most notably Carrhae.[38] Far from marching through a trackless desert, Crassus followed a well-travelled route that promised the decisive battle he craved at the earliest possible moment. Furthermore, the Arab chieftain offered this sage piece of advice, 'if you intend to fight, you ought to hasten on before all the king's forces are concentrated and he has regained his courage; since, for the time being, Surena and Sillaces have been thrown forward.'[39] This can only have played upon Crassus' desires and preconceptions.

Having identified Crassus' line of march, Surenas deployed his army on the far side of the Belikh River upon chosen ground. Crassus' scouts had consistently reported that Parthians shadowing the army as it marched fled from combat, which only affirmed his belief that any coming fight would be an easy one.[40] All this changed on the morning of 9 June in 53 BCE, when members of the Roman reconnaissance screen arrived to report that the scouts had been routed and that a large army comprised of cavalry was quickly approaching. This was only the first of a series of cognitive shocks that Crassus would experience this day.[41]

Initially he reacted relatively well. The enemy was not passively waiting to be swept from the battlefield. One can but wonder what ran through Crassus' mind as it became clear that the Parthians meant to fight. Crassus held a brief leadership conference with his wing commanders, Cassius and Publius, in which Cassius recommended that the army be deployed in standard formation, a long line across the plain with cavalry stationed on the flanks. At first, Crassus concurred, but, upon quick reflection, changed his mind and ordered the army to form a hollow square with twelve cohorts on each side and a squadron of cavalry interspersed between each; the logistics train and a reserve assumed position at the centre of the square.[42] Despite the hesitation, Crassus undoubtedly passed his first battlefield test since the Spartacus War, for forming a square was a classic response when infantry confronted cavalry, yielding no flank for the horsemen to attack. Furthermore, the allocation of cavalry evenly within the formation meant that every portion had cavalry support and would benefit from combined arms.[43]

More circumspect was the decision to advance. Apparently, the Roman formation arrived at a small stream while marching forward. Most of Crassus' officers recommended stopping to rest and assess the situation, engaging in battle the following day. Encouraged by his son, Crassus ordered the army to press on.[44] In light of what happened afterwards, taking a more cautious course of action seems prudent. Perhaps Crassus feared that the enemy would withdraw, denying him the battle he sought so ardently. He knew that back in Rome any pause would be judged harshly because Rome expected her generals to fight. Significantly, no source suggests that anyone proposed moving to ground more suitable for infantry to confront cavalry, much less a withdrawal. Even those advising discretion were committed to a stand-up fight, just at a later time. Combat was part of the Republic's cultural DNA.

Surenas' army closed on the Romans sometime during the afternoon to the deep thrum of war drums. Out of a massive dust cloud, a host of light cavalry emerged. The throng parted into two, riding towards either side of the Roman square. At this point, Surenas' cataphracts (heavily armoured cavalrymen), heretofore screened by the horse archers, removed the robes and skins covering their burnished armour, which now glittered brightly in the sun, and trotted towards the front of the Roman formation as if to charge. All this was calculated to unsettle the Romans.[45]

It did not. Confronted by a solid wall of interlocking shields, the heavy cavalrymen drew off. Crassus reacted by sending his light infantry forward. They were met by a torrent of arrows and withdrew within the square.[46]

With the initial engagement completed, Surenas men began to execute his plan and the fighting settled into a rhythm. The 9,000 Parthian light cavalry worked to encircle the Romans, firing volleys into the tightly packed legionaries as they did. The horse archers were careful to stay out of the throwing range of Roman *pila* as they poured forth a galling fire. The legionaries quickly learned the power of the Parthian composite bow, which penetrated their shields and body armour and, in some cases, nailed limbs to the ground. The effect of suffering punishment without being able to strike back – essentially the heavy infantrymen could only stand firm and take it – eroded morale.[47] If the Romans thought that their suffering would soon end, Surenas' foresight to provide mobile resupply for his archers guaranteed that it would not. His horsemen simply rode to the nearest camel to pick up another quiver filled with deadly contents.

Seeing this, Crassus recognized that defeat stared him squarely in the face. Only a few hours ago, he had ridden at the head of a 40,000-man Roman force parading towards an inevitable victory. Now, unless he did something, the Parthians would inflict death by a thousand cuts upon his army. The impact of the sudden and dramatic shift in fortune played havoc with emotions. Crassus was no more immune than a frontline legionary to the effects of this shocking turn of events.[48] Desperate situations often call for desperate measures, and what happened next was nothing if not a desperate effort to snatch victory from the jaws of defeat. Crassus ordered Publius to attack with 1,300 cavalry (including all of the elite Gallic horse), five hundred archers and eight cohorts, perhaps 5,000 men in total.[49]

In response to Publius's sortie, the Parthian horse archers opposite him withdrew in seeming disorder, but in the direction of Surenas' 1,000 cataphracts who sat in reserve. Buoyed by the prospect of reversing the tide of battle and the apparent flight of the Parthians, the Romans pursued beyond the supporting distance of the main army, whereupon Surenas committed his cataphracts. Despite the frenzied efforts of the Gallic cavalry during the ensuing melee, the heavily armoured Parthians proved too much. The remnants of Publius' corps retreated to a hillock, where they were wiped out, primarily by arrow fire. Only five hundred were taken prisoner; Publius and the aristocratic members of his staff committed suicide rather than suffering the indignity of surrender. The Parthians removed Publius' head, mounted it on a lance, and rode back towards Crassus' army to renew the attack.[50]

Concurrently, Crassus took advantage of the abatement of pressure to move the army onto sloping ground to better defend against cavalry. Only after doing so did messengers arrive informing him of the crisis involving Publius' isolated contingent. If he had expected his son to return triumphant, those hopes were now dashed. Plutarch tells us that 'Crassus was [now] a prey to many conflicting emotions, and no longer looked at anything with calm judgement.'[51] But before he could order his troops forward, war drums announced the return of the Parthian horse archers.

The spectacle of Publius' head affixed to the point of a lance marked the denouement of the Battle of Carrhae. All that was left before nightfall was more bloodletting as the Parthians resumed their ranged missile assault on the demoralized legionary square. Roman victory was unattainable; defeat was assured. In this his darkest hour, Crassus, however, settled his nerves and rose to the occasion, preventing an immediate rout by riding up and down the ranks shouting encouragement. This was all that was left to him, demonstrating the bravery expected of a patrician when faced with adversity.[52]

Whatever inspired Crassus to heights of charismatic leadership during the closing stages of the battle left him at nightfall. According to Plutarch, failure and the loss of his son caused him to fall into a listless depression. The Parthians, who rejected night fighting, pulled back to bivouac. They would return in the morning. Cassius and a legate, Octavius, vainly attempted to rouse Crassus from his funk. There remained grim decisions to be made concerning how to save the remainder of the army, but it now lacked firm direction. Cassius and Octavius stepped into the void and ordered a withdrawal towards the garrisoned city of Carrhae, abandoning 4,000 wounded. To the sound of the pitiful cries of their disabled comrades, who well knew the fate that awaited them when the Parthians returned, the once proud army marched away from the battlefield as a largely disorganized rabble. It had ceased to exist as an organized entity.[53]

Crassus' failure to manage the retreat into Roman Syria stands as his greatest failure as a tactical military leader. Withdrawing under pressure after a defeat is a difficult, perhaps the most difficult, military operation. It requires firm leadership to mitigate the tendency towards chaos. At the very least, a commander should maintain close control over the operation by doing things such as specifying the timing for and route of march, providing for route security and designating assembly areas. All of this was absent during the two days after the battle, which was characterized by false starts and disorganization. Consequently the withdrawal was a shambles. Plutarch leaves us with the distinct impression that Crassus was carried by events rather than attempting to shape them.[54]

The Parthians followed up their victory by slaughtering the Roman wounded left on the battlefield, rounding up stragglers, and dispatching isolated groups of Romans. Surenas recognized that the Romans might return should Crassus escape with a reduced, but still coherent, force. Consequently, he made taking Crassus a priority. In the end, Crassus, one of Rome's most powerful men, died in an ignominious scuffle at a parley.[55]

The Carrhae campaign of 54–53 BCE stands as Rome's worst defeat in an offensive war. Around 10,000 of the 40,000-man army made it back to Roman Syria, 10,000 became captives and 20,000 died.[56] Among the senior leadership, only Cassius survived. After the catastrophe, Rome's eastern empire lay open to invasion had the Parthians decided to do so. Crassus' death also ended the First Triumvirate, which left Caesar and Pompey to compete for dominance and contributed to the Republic's demise. For this if no other reason, Crassus deserves to be listed as one of history's worst military commanders. Rightly or wrongly, leaders are judged primarily by results. Thus the magnitude of the defeat at Carrhae weighs heavily upon Crassus' reputation.

This being said, Rome's culture of war set conditions for the disaster. Although we may hold Crassus to account for mismanaging the retreat, which magnified the result of the battle, he made no unconventional decisions prior to that, at least from a Roman perspective. In the end he lost because he was too orthodox, too much a reflection of the Roman way of war. The political importance of a military reputation made him lust after the opportunity to command troops in a major conflict. The time that Crassus spent cultivating the other pillars of political power in Republican Rome – wealth and political influence – meant that a relative amateur would command a Roman army. Two centuries of eventual, if not immediate, Roman military success created an unquestioned faith in a system based upon heavy infantry and focused on decisive battle. Rome's historical triumphs, then, haunted Crassus as an albatross, creating unrealistic expectations and overconfidence tending towards hubris. This, rather than incompetence, led him to underestimate his enemy. In retrospect, Carrhae possesses the classic elements of tragedy: as a protagonist, Crassus' virtues, which allowed him to rise to near mastery of Rome, contained the seeds of his eventual downfall.

In the end, the case of Marcus Licinius Crassus reminds us that an unreflective trust in a culturally acceptable, systems approach to war and warfighting can lead to a debacle. Social systems evolve within a cultural context and work best when addressing problems that they are designed to solve. The best systems attend to a wide range of common problems. When operating at scale, military institutions also require systems and processes to function efficiently. However, war is a dynamic human pursuit requiring the application of both reason *and* art. Gifted leaders recognize this and tailor solutions to the specific context of the mission they set out to accomplish. The example of the Carrhae campaign calls attention to the fact that war is a hard school-house, and, when the headmaster possesses the talents manifested by Surenas, it is harder still. One forgets that the enemy gets a vote at one's peril. These lessons are no less relevant today than they were on 9 June 53 BCE.

Joachim von Sandrart, *Nikias*, 17th century, engraving.

II
NIKIAS

James Tucci

Ismenias the Theban used to exhibit both good and bad players
to his pupils on the flute and say, 'You must play like this one',
or again, 'you must not play like this one'; and Antigenidas
used to think that young men would listen with more pleasure
to good flute-players if they were given an experience of bad
ones also. So, I think, we also shall be more eager to observe
and imitate the better lives if we are not left without narratives
of the blameworthy and the bad.

Plutarch, *Life of Demetrius*, 1.6[1]

I n his *Lives of the Noble Greeks and Romans*, Plutarch typically pairs
similar subjects, characters who offer variations on the same theme;
for example, Alexander the Great and Julius Caesar. As examples
of men whose fatal character flaws doomed them as field commanders, Plutarch matches up the Athenian politician and general
Nikias with Crassus, the Roman patrician known for his avarice and
for leading a failed expedition against the Parthian Empire, which
culminated in defeat at the Battle of Carrhae in 53 BCE, at the time
the worst defeat of Roman arms since Cannae (216 BCE). In his *Life
of Nikias*, Plutarch reminds the reader that Aristotle called Nikias one
of the three best citizens of Athens, citing his goodwill and paternal
affection for his city's people.[2] However, the tone of his biography is
clearly a condemnation of Nikias as both a military commander and
an individual, culminating in Plutarch's description of Nikias' disastrous command of the ill-fated Athenian expedition against Syracuse
in the Peloponnesian War.

By Plutarch's standards, Nikias was judged a very poor commander, and, given Plutarch's range of subjects from the mythical roots of ancient Greece through to the end of the Roman Republic, he is clearly one of the worst commanders of the ancient world. But does that mean he is one of the worst commanders in all of history? This summary of Nikias' career and account of the Sicilian expedition illustrates the strategic impact of his political and tactical incompetence.

Nikias came to political maturity at the peak of Athens's wealth and power during the Peloponnesian War (430–405 BCE) as a member of the great Pericles' political party. Nikias had what at first glance appears to be a successful record as a military commander early in the war, capturing the island of Cythera off the Laconian coast in 424, seizing several Thracian towns in 423, taking the islet of Minoa off the coast of Megara in 427, leading a successful raid on Corinth in 425, and another off the coast of Boeotia in 426.[3] Most of these operations were either seizing lightly garrisoned islands or brief raids designed to cause destruction. They were all part of Pericles' strategy, designed to extract an economic and political cost on the Peloponnesian League and improve Athens's strategic situation. However, Plutarch goes so far as to claim Nikias' successes were due to good fortune, not skill: 'Nikias therefore tried to evade problematic or lengthy commands, and whenever he went out on an expedition himself, he made safety his primary concern; consequently he was, of course, usually successful.'[4]

Plutarch proves his point in his description of Nikias' behaviour in the Pylos campaign in 425 BCE, suggesting that Nikias' refusal to face the Spartans was characteristic of his timid generalship.[5]

In 425 BCE, as part of a continued raiding strategy against Sparta's coalition, an Athenian task force found itself in the small harbour of Pylos on the southwest corner of the Peloponnese. Realizing the ideal location of the base on Athens's line of communication to western Greece, they began to build a fort.[6] This was intolerable to the Spartans as any enemy presence in this region threatened their land holdings in nearby Messenia, so they sent a small contingent of soldiers to confront the Athenians. The Athenian commander, Demosthenes, had dramatic success and cut off a force of Spartans on the island of Sphacteria, whereupon he sent word back to Athens, claiming that Sparta was seeking a truce. Nikias, elected *strategos* for the year, advocated a careful approach and, instead of leading an expedition to decide the issue, proposed sending a committee to study the problem.

His chief political opponent, Cleon, railed against Nikias' timidity, arguing for an immediate attack by reinforcements. Nikias offered to step aside and pass command of the operation to Cleon, thinking he would make his opponent look like a blowhard. After initially balking, Cleon realized his bluff had been called, so he accepted command and, to the laughter of his rivals, claimed he could win a victory in just twenty days. Unfortunately for Nikias, Cleon did just as he had promised; he and Demosthenes won a victory at Sphacteria and forced the Spartans to the peace table. Cleon's success was a political setback for Nikias and was a striking indication of both his tendency towards being overcautious and his political miscalculation:

> Nikias' reputation suffered dreadfully as a result of Cleon's success. For a soldier to abandon his shield is bad enough, but it seemed somehow worse, more disgraceful, for Nikias to have voluntarily resigned his command out of timidity, and to have handed over to his political enemy the opportunity to achieve such an important success by voting himself out of office.[7]

Nikias' actions had an effect throughout the entire polis. Nikias found himself the object of the comic playwright Aristophanes' satire in several productions.[8] Plutarch goes so far as to claim Nikias did great harm to his city by allowing the demagoguery of Cleon to become more acceptable as a political style among the citizenry. Athens's standards of what constituted acceptable behaviour by a leader were lowered and this would have disastrous effects in the coming years, when politicians like Alcibiades came to power.[9]

Subsequently, Nikias played a key role in negotiating a peace treaty with Sparta, bringing a long pause, if not a permanent settlement, to the Peloponnesian War. However, the peace proved fragile and looked like a bad deal the longer the truce lasted. In fact, Nikias' primary characteristic, fear of what the Athenian people and government would think of him, reared its ugly head.[10] As the chief opponent of peace, after Cleon's death at Amphipolis, just prior to the truce, Alcibiades became Nikias' main political rival. He succeeded in being elected general and leading a bold campaign to finish off Sparta once and for all, a bid that failed at the Battle of Mantinea (418 BCE).

In the aftermath, the young aristocrat Alcibiades and his faction continued to look for opportunities to use Athens's military power.

When it appeared that Sicily might fall under the sway of Syracuse, a democracy with ethno-cultural ties to Sparta, Athens considered intervention. It is in this crisis that strong evidence for the case of Nikias' incompetence can be found. Nikias found himself in public debate over a proposed expansion with an Athenian expedition to Sicily and attack on Syracuse. In a heated argument with Alcibiades, Nikias argued for the status quo but failed to convince the voters to avoid conflict with Syracuse. The assembly voted to send a task force to Sicily with Nikias in command, to attempt to influence events there. Nikias tried a rhetorical trick, claiming that in order to conduct the campaign properly so far from home, a much larger and more expensive force was required. He hoped this would scare the voters into avoiding an invasion. His tactic backfired, and instead of dissuading his fellow citizens, he inspired them to approve the much larger task force, appointing Nikias on the command team in charge of the expedition, despite his opposition.[11] On the expedition itself, the largest Athens would attempt during the war, Nikias' performance mirrored that of the Athenian military and naval forces: initially steady if hesitant, but continually weaker and more dissolute as the campaign extended until the final defeat, a defeat Thucydides cites as the major reason for Athens losing the war.[12]

Once any expedition was authorized by the Athenian assembly, a combination of conscription and volunteers was used to fit out the fleet and army. Even in the wildly popular expedition to Sicily in 415, some conscription was required.[13] Those who would embark on an expedition were normally required to arrive with their equipment and three days of rations.[14] The men assembled in a prominent public place in Athens; the Agora, the Pnyx and the Lyceum are just a few of the areas where troops would marshal.[15] Sailors would muster by their respective ships at Piraeus.[16] The generals elected to lead an expedition would select conscripted troops based on political sensitivities and military needs; in other words, a mix of youthful troops and seasoned veterans.[17] Presumably, in undertaking such a large amphibious operation as the Sicilian expedition, the generals would have taken some troops who had amphibious experience. Given the number of raiding expeditions over the first fifteen years of the Peloponnesian Wars, such experienced veterans would have been easy to find.

Clearly, generals experienced in expeditionary warfare were better for such an operation as well. While Alcibiades had not commanded a major amphibious expedition, both Nikias and Lamachus had such experience. Lamachus had been involved in two expeditions that travelled far distances to the Black Sea: one just before the Peloponnesian War began in about 431,[18] and the other in 424.[19] Nikias was a general on three separate expeditions to Melos and Boeotia, Cythera and Mende/Scione.[20]

Upon mustering the troops, equipping the vessels and embarking, the expeditionary force sailed to its destination. This route had three distinct parts: the voyage from Athens to Corcyra (390 nautical miles), the voyage from Corcyra to Rhegium (600 km/375 mi.), and the voyage from Rhegium to the objective area (135 km/85 mi.). The fleet first sailed from Athens and various locations to assemble at Corcyra. Thucydides is silent on the particulars of this part of the expedition. On previous voyages around the Peloponnese, Athenian vessels were faced with a hostile or vacant coastline and had to fend for themselves. Since no friendly towns would have provided markets for feeding a fleet, earlier expeditions must have carried enough food with them to reach friendly territory on the west coast, but would still have had to stop nightly for water and rest. Security of the Sicilian expedition, given the number of land forces accompanying the ships, would not have been a problem, but friendly sites would have helped.

Athens had sent a small expedition to Sicily at the very beginning of the Peloponnesian War. Subsequently, the Athenians had conquered Pylos, on the west coast of the Peloponnese, and Cythera, off the south coast. These two spots acted as way stations for Athenian naval movements around the Peloponnese. Athenian and allied contingents could have stopped at both places for water, and possibly food. Demosthenes built a fort opposite Cythera on the shore in 414 on his way to Sicily.[21] The total amount of time a trireme fleet would have taken to travel from Athens to Corcyra is estimated at around four days.[22]

The second part of the voyage occurred after the fleet's reorganization at Corcyra. Nikias and the two other generals divided the fleet into three portions to make logistics easier.[23] They sent a three-ship reconnaissance force to scout the southern coast of Italy and eastern coast of Sicily and to arrange stopping places for the expedition.[24] The fleet crossed by the most direct manner, via the 134 kilometres (84 mi.) from Corcyra to the Iapygian promontory and landed near Tarentum to form up again.[25] This stretch would have taken one very long day for the entire fleet to cross.[26] After spending the night near Tarentum, the expedition proceeded slowly from the heel to the toe of Italy.

Most of the towns along the southern coast appear to have refused access,[27] although Diodorus suggests that Thurii and Croton were more accommodating.[28] In any case, frequent stops by the fleet would have been necessary. The ships continued along the southern coast of Italy towards their goal of Rhegium. The slow rate of sail of the combined fleet of mixed ship types meant that the voyage took about six days.[29]

Logistics proved challenging. Each fast trireme had approximately 270 rowers and crew. The transport vessels' crews were smaller, but still a large number, and there were more than 6,000 soldiers riding aboard the ships. The large number of mouths to feed among the army and ships' crews necessitated a large fleet of supply vessels, which was unprecedented before the Sicilian expedition.

The logistical problem of supplying so many people became critical upon the expedition reaching Rhegium (now Reggio Calabria), on the southwest corner of Italy, across from Messina. Rhegium was employed as a base of operations due to ties between Leontini (a town hostile to Syracuse), Rhegium and Athens.[30] Athens had a treaty of mutual support with Rhegium dating from 440, renewed in 427 at the beginning of the war.[31] It was superbly situated to support operations along either the northern or eastern coasts of Sicily. However, perhaps due to the perceived threat of the much larger army that comprised the Sicilian expedition, compared to previous Athenian fleets that had put in to Rhegium, the city would only allow a marketplace for the expedition's use, while the fleet anchored along the coast.[32] The three-ship reconnaissance team arrived with more bad news: Egesta, ostensibly the town that had invited Athens to Sicily, was unable to provide any of the monetary, and thus military, support promised earlier.[33]

At this point the three Athenian generals held a council of war and decided upon their strategy for invading Sicily. Nikias advocated a show of force in support of their allies Selinus and Egesta, and then a rapid return home. Alcibiades recommended a probe with part of the force to build an alliance of Sicilian cities as a coalition against Syracuse. Lamachus suggested that Syracuse would still be unprepared for the Athenians and vulnerable to offensive action. He recommended an immediate attack against Syracuse proper, the first stage of which would include seizing a base of operations near the city. At first, Alcibiades' course was adopted.[34]

The final stage of the expedition's voyage was from Rhegium to a base of operations near Syracuse. Lamachus had advocated a landing site and base of operations at Megara Hyblaea, just north of Syracuse.[35] However, Nikias convinced the Athenians to use a stratagem and oust the pro-Syracusan government in Catana, and thus to gain control of this large port with an advanced force of sixty triremes as a close base of operations for the final assault on Syracuse.[36]

From Catana, the Athenians proceeded to secure naval supremacy. In essence, their sixty fast triremes had been securing control of the sea throughout the expedition's long voyage from the east coast of Greece to Sicily. Syracusan intervention along the way was not expected, but the possibility was not ignored as the Syracusan assembly had debated the idea of contesting the Athenians.[37] Hermocrates rightly judged that an amphibious expedition was most vulnerable when strung out on the voyage to its destination;[38] however, his recommendations were ignored, and when the Athenians reconnoitred Syracuse's harbour before advancing the main fleet to Catana, they found no warships capable of challenging their control of the sea. Due to the absence of any significant Peloponnesian fleet in the theatre and the unpreparedness of Syracuse, which lacked the warships to counter the Athenian threat, initially there was no naval opposition to the Sicilian expedition, which could prepare to land troops near Syracuse with impunity.[39]

The Athenian expedition had paused at Catana before making its final run south to Syracuse, distracted by the recall of Alcibiades and the attempt at executing Nikias' diplomatic strategy. Nevertheless, by the end of the campaign season of 415, the Athenians finally made their move. Although advancing by land was possible, this option was dismissed given the superior numbers of Syracusan cavalry.[40] An amphibious landing in the face of Syracusan opposition was also undesirable, and in fact ran counter to standard Athenian amphibious operations, developed in the period since the Persian Wars.

At Syracuse the Sicilian expedition used a *ruse de guerre* to draw away the Syracusan cavalry from the landing area up to Catana. While the cavalry was headed north and the rest of the Syracusan army's attention was also drawn in that direction, the Athenian and allied fleet sailed by cover of night from Catana and the troops were landed on the west edge of the Great Harbour of Syracuse without any opposition.[41] The landing area featured hilly terrain around the outpost of

Olympeium, a temple to Zeus, to the west, swampy terrain to the south and east, and the Anapus River to the north. The Athenians built a palisade around their fleet, destroyed the nearest bridge over the Anapus, and constructed a fort on their southern flank to guard against an attack from their rear.[42] With these precautions, the beachhead was quite secure from a direct assault, and particularly protected against cavalry. Since there would be no market to speak of for the purchase of food, the beachhead was an important place for the many supply ships to disgorge their stores and set up a travelling market for the land forces and ships' crews to use. Ships could have easily travelled back to Catana or other friendly Sicilian towns and transported more supplies, and reinforcements, back to the Athenian base.

After the Athenians landed their troops and built up their bridgehead, the Syracusan cavalry returned from Catana, formed up with the rest of their land forces and marched to the plains southeast of Syracuse and north of the Athenian position to offer battle.[43] The Athenians refused at first, perhaps to retain the initiative or perhaps to complete disembarking supplies and setting up their bridgehead. The next day, the Athenians moved out from their camp and their phalanx met the Syracusan phalanx in a pitched battle. The Athenians were still wary of the preponderance of Syracusan cavalry, some 1,400 strong, and so they deployed their forces in two parts, one an eight-rank-deep phalanx up forward, and the second a square to both protect the camp and act as a reserve. Given that they had brought only thirty cavalry with them to Syracuse, the Athenians were forced to rely on the geography of the area, their tactical dispositions, and the 1,400-odd slingers, archers and peltasts they had brought to counter the Syracusan horse.[44]

The pitched battle was an Athenian victory, with both the left wing and centre of the Syracusan army being defeated by the Argive and Athenian hoplites respectively.[45] However, the Athenian victory was not as decisive as it could have been; pursuit of the broken Syracusan infantry was impossible due to the large number of cavalry that screened the retreat back to the city.[46] Lack of cavalry in their expeditionary force was the ostensible reason the Athenians decided to withdraw into Catana for the winter without beginning siege operations around Syracuse.[47] They intended to acquire more cavalry both from allied Sicilian cities and from Attica; they were successful in doing so in time for the following campaign season.[48]

With Nikias and Lamachus in dual command, the Sicilian expedition at this point had achieved moderate success. The Athenians and their allies had assembled a large land army and fleet, with an enormous fleet of supply ships alongside. They had sailed nearly 1,600 kilometres (1,000 mi.) from the Aegean Sea to Syracuse without significant loss due to storms or hostile attacks. Though their logistical arrangements for a local base of operations at Rhegium went awry, after a delay they captured the far more useful base of Catana, much closer to their main opponent in Sicily, Syracuse. From Catana they had landed their entire army unopposed and secured a very strong bridgehead in the Great Harbour of Syracuse. Subsequently, they defeated the Syracusan army in a pitched battle and so ensured the viability of their expeditionary force. They then moved to Catana for the winter.

The following spring, the cavalry that the Athenians had managed to collect over the winter defeated the Sicilian cavalry patrolling on the Epipolae, a high plateau overlooking Syracuse to the south. The Athenian army then moved forward, spread out and began to encircle Syracuse with siege lines in order to cut the city off completely from the land.[49] The Syracusans attempted to thwart the Athenian entrenchments with counter-walls. In the skirmishes that arose where these two sets of walls intersected, Lamachus was killed, but Nikias managed to bolster the Athenian defences long enough to complete the siege lines.[50] The Athenian fleet trapped the newly built Syracusan fleet in the Great Harbour and blockaded Syracuse.

It was at this point that the Spartan general, Gylippus, who had been dispatched to Sicily with a small contingent of Peloponnesians, arrived on the scene. Despite the Athenian siege, he slipped past their defences without being seen.[51] Once he landed his forces and learned of the situation, he immediately directed the Syracusan army to attempt a counter-wall to break the Athenian siege lines again. The first attempt failed, but Gylippus persevered, taking the blame for the failure on himself, and launched a second attack, relying more on Syracusan light forces, one of the army's strengths. This time, with Nikias conducting a desultory defence, the Athenians were pushed back, their wall breached, and the siege was broken.[52]

At this point, Nikias read impending disaster in the setback he had suffered and sent word back to Athens, describing the situation as grim and requesting the expedition be pulled out of Sicily or that massive reinforcements be sent.[53] Nikias also requested being relieved of command, due to ill health.[54] The Athenians decided to double down on their operation and dispatched Demosthenes, their most experienced commander, with a second expedition, nearly as large as the first.[55]

Upon Demosthenes' arrival in Syracuse, the wily commander realized that swift action was necessary in order to prevent a debacle.[56] As his fleet arrived, the freshly constructed Sicilian fleet nearly defeated the Athenians in a naval battle. Demosthenes saw that the Athenian siege was on the edge of a precipice and knew only bold action could restore the operation and regain the upper hand. He led a risky night attack, but, while succeeding in taking part of the Syracusan counter-wall, he was forced to retreat in the face of the Sicilians' counter-attack.[57]

It was at this point that Demosthenes realized that Nikias had led the Athenian expedition into an unwinnable position. Despite the large number of fresh reinforcements he had brought with him, Demosthenes argued for retreating and withdrawing from Sicily altogether. The forces in Sicily could be better used to defend Athens from Spartan forays out of their new fortifications in Attica.[58] The hesitant Nikias balked at first, but acquiesced when fresh reinforcements arrived from Greece for Syracuse.[59]

Nikias' religious piety, however, hitherto considered a positive character attribute, betrayed him, as the gods would soon betray Athenian fortunes. As the Athenians were preparing to pull out, a lunar eclipse occurred and Nikias, after consulting his priests, decided to accept their recommendation and wait for the next moon in 27 days' time.[60] Subsequently, the Syracusan fleet, in a hard-fought series of battles, finally defeated the Athenian fleet and now it was the Athenians blockaded in the Great Harbour, not the Syracusans.[61] The Athenian army attempted to march out to another coastal location in the hopes of withdrawing, but in a long, chaotic retreat they were overwhelmed by the pursuing Syracusan army and cut to pieces. The surviving members of the expedition were enslaved and either sold off or forced to work in rock quarries in horrible conditions.[62]

Nikias' record shows that he does deserve to be considered one of the worst commanders in history for two reasons. First, while a list of tactically incompetent commanders in history is long indeed, battlefield performance alone can be of questionable utility in judging strategic competence. Consider Hannibal Barca or Robert E. Lee, whose tactical acumen disguised strategic myopia and doomed both Carthage and the Confederacy to catastrophic defeat. Likewise, American battlefield success in the Vietnam War proved strategically meaningless in the withdrawal of the United States from the conflict. In Nikias there was little tactical brilliance, but even more problematic, decisive failure at the operational and strategic levels.

A combination of tactical and strategic folly would seem to be the hallmark of true incompetence, particularly if the general is in a position to determine the strategic direction of the war as well as how the war will be fought. The impact of a strategic decision and its poor execution on campaign make for a double damnation for any commander responsible for such a debacle. Nikias' qualities of incompetence were exemplified in the utter catastrophe of the Sicilian expedition, which not only doomed Athens's strategic fortunes in the Peloponnesian War, but ended its Mediterranean empire and its hegemony in Greece.

In addition to the strategic impact of their military ineptitude, it is useful to measure commanders' competence, in any historical era, by a contemporary standard. While modern military histories and biographies are replete with judgements of generals' merits, a more systematic analysis will prove useful here. In *On the Psychology of Military Incompetence*, as mentioned in the introduction to this volume, Norman Dixon argues that the traditional view of a lack of intelligence explaining poor generalship is wrong and that a commander's personality, more than any other individual cause, holds better explanatory power. Applying Dixon's ideas to the examination of Nikias should show that he was, by modern standards, a hopelessly incompetent military commander.

Nikias exemplified Dixon's notion of wasting resources. During the political debate on whether to intervene in Sicily, Nikias' rhetorical stratagem to dissuade the Athenian demos from attacking Syracuse was to claim that an inordinately large and costly task force would be required for the mission to be successful.[63] The result was the demos deciding to double down on the decision, their excitement enflamed by the thought of such a large expedition. Nikias' political miscue here, not unlike his misplay with Cleon in the Pylos campaign, resulted in the dispatch of one of the largest expeditions ever mounted by Athens. Given Athens's other military needs and the resulting disaster in Sicily, this proved to be an enormous waste of resources and the antithesis of the economy of force. Athens's successful strategy hitherto had been to keep its fleet at hand, engaged in small expeditions directly against its opponents. Weaknesses that Sparta had previously exploited were the tenuous nature of the Delian League, a coalition held together largely by the threat of Athenian force, and the line of supply to the northern Aegean and beyond, essential for keeping Athens's large population fed. Launching more than half its navy and army far away from the main theatre of war was an uneconomic use of force. Nikias may have understood this in principle, but he failed to realize the Athenian voters did not and, more importantly, he failed to persuade them of the truth.

Nikias' handling of information is another key element of his incompetence. Failure to secure information or to utilize appropriate intelligence figures largely in this list. From its inception, the Sicilian expedition operated from a grotesque misunderstanding of information. Despite years of contact with towns in Sicily, the Athenian leadership in 415 either did not understand the geopolitical realities of the island or failed to explain them adequately to the sovereign power in the Athenian government, the assembly of the people or demos. A group of delegates had visited Segesta, the Sicilian town requesting Athenian assistance, but they were duped into believing the Segestans wealthier than they were in reality.[64] Promises of money and alliances with other Sicilian towns were given to the Athenians. Were Athens to come as liberators to Sicily, they would be greeted with open arms. Nikias' role in this folly was his failure to persuade the demos that sending an expedition against Syracuse would be a very bad idea.[65] Despite laying out a sound argument about Athens's positive but precarious strategic situation, Nikias badly misjudged the Athenian people and its demographic shift towards younger voters. One of these younger voices, Alcibiades, a combat veteran and aristocrat who had not yet had a chance at senior command, inflamed the Athenian people's desire for glory and profit.[66]

In a democracy, strategy is not simply ways and means or continual advantage or a plan of action; persuasion is the essential element of turning strategic ideas into political action. Any democratic strategist must be able to persuade those holding sovereignty of the correct action to take. In ancient Athens, a pure democracy, decisions were made directly by the assembled citizens. As a leading political figure, as well as a senior military commander, Nikias was responsible for persuading the demos on a wise strategic choice. He failed and it cost himself and his city dearly.

Although he was careful to collect information in advance of the expedition, and was rightly sceptical of some of the more optimistic accounts from locals about Sicilian assistance to Athens, his hesitant nature made him disregard information vital to the expedition's success. Upon arrival in the theatre, when it was apparent the Syracusans were caught by surprise and were unprepared, Lamachus advocated an immediate attack, calculating that the advantage of surprise and shock was fleeting.[67] Nikias wanted to land and conduct a demonstration, and then return to Athens.[68] Alcibiades advocated setting up a base of operations near Syracuse and spending a season collecting allies before attacking.[69] Alcibiades' choice prevailed, although he himself was recalled to Athens to face charges of impiety. Had Nikias understood the unpreparedness of Syracuse and the precarious nature of the supposedly friendly Sicilian towns, he would have realized Lamachus' bold suggestion could have provided a quick victory.

After establishing a base in which the expedition spent the winter, Nikias began to besiege Syracuse, slowly extending entrenchments across the Epipolae, the high ground north of town, in order to cut the city off from landward supplies. As the siege progressed, a Spartan commander, Gylippus, arrived and through Nikias' slow response was allowed entry into Syracuse, as was a subsequent relief force of Peloponnesian ships and soldiers.[70] Nikias knew what was happening, but chose to disregard the information because it ran counter to his preferred view of the operation, a cautious steady siege and his own diplomatic negotiations saving the day. This cognitive dissonance would feed Nikias' predilection for inactivity or hesitancy.

Nikias demonstrated obstinacy in the face of contrary evidence as a habit of command, most critically in his continued belief that he could convince an internal political faction in Syracuse to seize control and make terms with Athens, giving him a low-cost and easy victory. This obstinacy infected his conduct of military operations. In his direction of the siege of Syracuse, he decided on a double wall of circumvallation built close to the southern end of the city walls, rather than a single wall farther away. Running siege lines closer was easier and nearer to his supply lines. On the other hand, a wall farther away from Syracuse's city walls could have more rapidly cut off the city on its landward flank, the chief object of any siege lines. Nikias chose the slower, closer option because he firmly believed that his negotiating ability would convince one of the political factions in Syracuse to surrender. He continued to believe in this possibility almost until the end of the campaign, refusing to seize back the initiative from Syracuse and ignoring the impending disaster, continually believing that an internal coup would end the siege.[71]

It is perhaps Nikias' indecisiveness and subsequent failures to exploit any advantages or utilize the element of surprise that were the chief shortcomings in his leadership. Plutarch criticizes Nikias for his continued initial attempts to be removed as commander of the expedition and especially for his continued hesitant approach to planning and executing the operation, once the decision had been made:

> Once he had got nowhere either in his attempts to convince the Athenians to abandon the war or in his requests to be relieved of the command – once the Athenian people had, so to speak, picked him up, taken him and deposited him at the head of the expeditionary force – then his excessive caution and hesitation were out of place.[72]

His continued negative attitude towards the campaign had a depressing effect on his officers and men and 'sapped their energy for action'.[73]

Additionally, Nikias hesitated when the expedition first arrived in Sicily, declining Lamachus' advice to attack Syracuse immediately upon their arrival. Once the Athenian expeditionary force had established a firm beachhead, Nikias' slow and methodical nature characterized the conduct of the campaign. Even when the Athenians did achieve tactical success in their first major land battle, Nikias never followed up these victories, allowing Syracuse to retreat in order and revitalize their forces, while the Athenians retreated to Catana to be safe and sound over the winter.

The end of the Sicilian debacle illustrates two more of Nikias' personality flaws: his abuse of the truth about what was happening to the expedition when he communicated back to Athens, and his clinging to notions of supernatural intervention during the ill-timed lunar eclipse. In 414 Gylippus' leadership and the influx of Peloponnesian and Sicilian reinforcements began to have an effect on the campaign. Gylippus' tactics had brought the siege to a halt and the influx of veteran Corinthian triremes bolstered the Syracusan navy. It was as if the

Athenians were now the besieged army. Although Athens still retained command of the sea, it was growing more and more difficult to keep the opposing forces at bay. When Nikias realized that the course of the campaign had shifted, he wrote back to Athens, laying out the status of the expedition but absolving himself of any responsibility for the problems, blaming his army and navy's exhaustion on the long supply chain through Italy and the multi-year length of the campaign. Nikias told the Athenian assembly they needed to decide what to do next: either withdraw the current expedition or send another large force to reinforce Sicily. He also requested that he be relieved of his command, due to poor health.[74] Essentially, he was foisting a campaign-level decision onto his government, despite the fact that he had been appointed as the commanding general. His misinformation campaign was designed to avoid blame.[75] The most fraudulent part of his letter home was in failing to report any details about his shortcomings in command, about how he failed to prosecute the siege in a timely manner, failed to keep his ships in position to blockade properly, allowing Gylippus and a Corinthian fleet to sneak past his fleet. His claims that the logistic train back to Italy was the cause of his supply problems failed to mention that he had stockpiled everything at a base far from the front lines. A Syracusan raid would later capture or destroy most of the Athenian supplies and money.[76] It appeared that in offering the Athenian assembly a choice between recalling the expedition and sending another expensive task force, he was pushing them towards withdrawal, but in a way designed so that he could not be blamed for the decision. Once again, Nikias miscalculated the people's will; they decided to double down again, and dispatched another large force led by a crack commander, Demosthenes. As detailed above, this second expedition, rather than restoring Athens's fortunes, simply increased the overall cost of the campaign.

Nikias led his forces into a debacle that proved to be the peripeteia not only of the tragedy of the Sicilian expedition, but of the entire Peloponnesian War. Thucydides' concluding lines are some of the most poignant ever written by a historian:

> This proved the most significant occurrence in the whole of this war, and, it seems to me, in the whole of recorded Greek history – unparalleled triumph for the victors, and unparalleled disaster for the vanquished. This was, as they say, 'total

annihilation'. Beaten in every way on every front, extreme miseries suffered on an extreme scale, and army, fleet, and everything else destroyed, few out of all those many made their return home. Such were the events in Sicily.[77]

Two expeditions totalling more than five hundred ships and 40,000 troops, and the equivalent of millions of dollars in cash, were all lost. Athens still had the resources to hang on for another decade in the war, but its old enemy Persia leapt at the chance to remove the Athenian Empire from its doorstep by paying for a Spartan navy to defeat Athens's fleet, pry apart the Delian League, and bring down the democratic government. Athens would continue to be an important city in the Greek and Roman world, but it would never again rise to its former greatness. The strategic impact of Nikias' failure in leading the Sicilian expedition was catastrophic, and Nikias clearly and repeatedly demonstrated the characteristics of an incompetent military commander. He failed to understand his situation, from beginning to end. He was inept at logistics, at tactics and at operations. He hesitated constantly, missing many golden opportunities to take advantage of Syracusan weakness and allowing the city to recover, to be reinforced, and to turn the tide of near defeat into decisive victory. His indecisiveness was amplified by his fear of being blamed for the failure of the expedition. In the end, his incompetence did not just result in defeat on the battlefield, but in the annihilation of nearly every member of the Athenian army and fleet in Sicily, the flower of Athens's military forces and citizenry, a catastrophe that led to the fall of the Athenian Empire.

12
RAYMOND VI, COUNT OF TOULOUSE

Laurence W. Marvin

orn in 1156, Raymond vi was Count of Toulouse between 1195 and 1222.[1] He deserves placement in the pantheon of worst military leaders based on his conduct and performance during the greatest crisis his region ever faced: the era of the Albigensian Crusade (1208–29). His great-great-grandfather and illustrious namesake, Raymond iv, was the highest-ranking noble from the South of France to participate in the First Crusade (1095–9). Unlike his distant forebear or many of his contemporaries, Raymond vi made it to middle age without taking the cross for either the Third Crusade (1189–93) or the Fourth (1198–1204). Contrary to many other men of his station, Raymond never risked his life or sacrificed his time or treasure for his faith. He stayed home in southern France, participating in its regional politics and petty spats. At the time the region was neither culturally nor linguistically French, so modern historians typically call it 'Occitania' or 'Languedoc' after the Occitan language.[2]

The 'crusade era' (1095–1291) began after Pope Urban ii exhorted Latin Christians to assist their co-religionists in the Holy Land suffering under the Seljuk Turks and to liberate the city of Jerusalem from Muslim control. As an incentive the pope offered an indulgence – a remission of sins – for participants. Subsequent popes repeated and expanded the call from lands far away to those much closer to home.[3] Thus it was that in 1208 Pope Innocent iii called for military action against internal enemies in the heart of Latin Christian Europe, known as the 'Cathars' or 'Albigensians'.[4] The resulting Albigensian Crusade was distinctive for two reasons. For one, compared to crusades to the Middle East, where the goal coalesced around gaining or regaining

Christian control over Jerusalem, in Occitania there was no clearly demarcated objective beyond eradicating the heresy. Since the practitioners of Catharism were part of the culture they supposedly subverted, it was impossible to establish a military objective beyond pointing fingers at local political leaders who allowed Catharism to exist unchecked in lands they ostensibly controlled. Although Catharism in Occitania had concerned the papacy for decades, and there had even been a small military expedition against Cathars in the town of Lavaur in 1181, it was not until 1208, after the assassination of a papal official, Peter de Castelnau, that the papacy successfully motivated people to remove the heresy through concerted military activity.[5] The result of the pope's call was a two-decade bloody conflict.

A second reason making the Albigensian Crusade unique was how crusaders received an indulgence for their involvement. Between the First and Third Crusades the ways in which one could obtain an indulgence became increasingly flexible, but the Albigensian Crusade became infamous for the ease whereby one could do so.[6] In 1210 it appears that the papal legates (the pope's local representatives) in Occitania instituted a forty-day residency in the army rather than for specific actions or service.[7] This unintentionally boosted crusading domestically over the hazards one faced travelling the much longer distances to the Holy Land. The specific (and small) number of days encouraged crusaders to fulfil the requirement and no more, leading many to abandon the army at inconvenient times.[8]

The pope held Raymond VI responsible for Peter de Castelnau's murder or for ordering it because the murder occurred in Raymond's lands, even though no evidence has ever directly implicated him. Raymond had been unconcerned with heresy prior to 1208, and undoubtedly viewed papal preoccupation with it as unwarranted outside interference, which was a common attitude held by many other southern nobles towards the Church's attempts to stamp out heresy. In 1208, however, he was excommunicated: consequently the Albigensian Crusade was directed against Raymond himself as the region's figurehead and because of his alleged culpability in the legate's assassination.

Excommunication was the most serious penalty that the Church could throw at a person.[9] A ruler no longer in the Church's good graces potentially forfeited his right to rule. For example, in 1077 Pope Gregory VII excommunicated Emperor Henry IV and deprived him of his office. Henry faced such a widespread rebellion that he spent three days on his knees in the snow outside the pope's residence pleading for absolution.[10] By the early thirteenth century excommunicating sovereigns and suzerains was more common. At various times for various reasons the Church excommunicated greater contemporary figures than Raymond VI, among them King John of England and King Philip Augustus of France. Yet they continued to rule without many questioning the legitimacy of their reigns. Like John and Philip, Raymond appears to have cared little about his excommunication, especially since he had been excommunicated twice before, in 1196

Raymond VI announces the death of Simon of Montfort to the city of Toulouse, 1218, sculpture by Jules-Jacques Labatut in the Capitole de Toulouse, 1894.

and in 1207.[11] What made Raymond's 1208 excommunication different was that it came with the pope's call to invade Occitania to extirpate heresy with the promise of an indulgence. The prospect of concerted military action put unusual pressure not simply on Raymond of Toulouse, but all the nobles and people of the region.

Though excommunication was a penalty imposed upon individuals, there was more at stake than one man's life and lands. Since monarchs and prominent nobles might easily flout excommunication, the Church developed additional measures to place extra stress on excommunicated men. Among them was the issuing of an interdict at communities or territories controlled by the excommunicated. The interdict denied certain Christian services to those under it, including church burials and the celebration of the Mass.[12] It was deliberately designed to put public pressure on top of the personal excommunication of a ruler. In an era when people wore their religion on their sleeve, so to speak, the inability to receive basic Christian rites was taken seriously. Raymond's lands and the city of Toulouse, for example, were placed under interdict for several reasons during much of the Albigensian Crusade. In 1211 divine services were prohibited wherever Raymond was, a sort of roving interdict that increased his unpopularity in Toulouse.[13]

Raymond's title and authority as 'Count of Toulouse' was more ambiguous than it might suggest. Authority in Occitania, like many other regions of Western Europe at the time, existed in a grey zone based on one's individual charisma, reputation, energy and ability at enforcing it. Raymond did not enjoy sovereignty over the lands, territories or people associated with his title, family or person, but rather exercised suzerainty under both the English and French monarchs. His control waxed and waned depending on how vigorously he enforced it and it shifted depending on political, family or marriage alliances or squabbles. Maintaining suzerainty required constant vigilance or those subject to it either ignored it or filled the vacuum themselves. In Raymond's case, lands that theoretically fell under his suzerainty either by birth or marriage stretched across a wide swath of Occitania like pearls on a necklace. Within these territories many towns and nobles owed Raymond little to nothing and what they did owe he had to enforce. Parts of the Count of Toulouse's western territories, for example the Agenais, had recently fallen under his control after a long period of contestation with the English monarchy, settled only in 1196 by a marriage between Raymond and the king of England's sister, Joan.[14] In the Agenais Raymond had suzerainty only via his wife, and, after her death, on behalf of his son and heir, Raymond VII. The Toulousain region was by no means firmly in Raymond's hands either. Although Raymond was 'count' of Toulouse, the largest and most important city within his territories, he shared authority in the city with its municipal government and the Bishop of Toulouse. These three entities rarely got along.[15]

In the early summer of 1209 large numbers of men from northern France gathered to crusade in the south.[16] Raymond slowly realized that, far from a toothless punishment, his excommunication this time might lead to his deposition, or at the very least an invasion of his territories. In June 1209 some papal legates summoned Raymond to answer a list of charges. He was not directly accused of heresy, but rather of hiring mercenaries and not punishing heretics in his lands.[17] In exchange for absolution, Raymond turned over custody of several of his towns in his eastern possessions and received a ceremonial scourging in front of an audience of ecclesiastical dignitaries in his ancestral town of St Gilles.[18] By 22 June Raymond had taken the cross as a crusader but the crusade army's target still remained his western lands. As the army moved south Raymond met with its leadership and reconciled with it, aided by one of his cousins among the crusade leaders, Peter, Count of Auxerre.[19]

In an extraordinary turn that showed his keen sense of self-preservation, Raymond convinced the crusaders, determined to punish someone, to move against the lands of his nephew, Raymond-Roger Trencavel, Viscount of Béziers, Carcassonne and Albi. The two had never been close and did not get along, and when the stakes were high, Raymond cared little about family beyond his own heir.[20] To avoid being attacked many nobles and towns along the army's path made their peace with the crusade leadership, but when Raymond-Roger Trencavel refused, the crusaders invaded his lands. The subsequent storming of Béziers, the capitulation of Carcassonne, and the surrender, incarceration and death of Raymond-Roger Trencavel need not be recounted here other than to point out that Raymond VI, by urging the crusaders to attack his nephew's territories in order to save his own, had some culpability in his nephew's death.[21]

In the late summer or early autumn of 1209 a committee of bishops and nobles drawn from the crusade army chose a minor noble from northern France, Simon of Montfort, to lead a sustained multi-year effort to eradicate heresy in the south.[22] Simon replaced Raymond-Roger Trencavel as Viscount of Béziers, Carcassonne and Albi, but extended his efforts beyond these regions to mount military incursions into any area that had been 'infected' with heresy. Between 1209 and 1211 this expansion of the conflict brought crusader forces closer to Raymond's lands and in effect challenged his suzerainty. During this time Raymond VI theoretically supported the crusade but grew leery of the aggressiveness with which Simon pursued it. He did as little as possible to assist Simon of Montfort and this failure caused him once again to run afoul of the Church. In 1210 at a regional council held in St Gilles, Raymond was accused of not honouring papal instructions to root out heretics in his lands. At that council Raymond was again excommunicated, putting his position and his lands in jeopardy for a second time.[23]

As a political leader during the first two years of the crusade Raymond had appeared to be tone-deaf to Church authority, a dangerous trait in the early thirteenth century. As humiliating as it was to submit to papal directives, alienating the papacy or its officials without understanding the potential blowback it might cause showed a lack of strategic thought. During this time Raymond did little to cultivate or repair relationships with either the local clergy or, just as importantly, the cities and towns of the region.

At a series of meetings in 1211, attempts at reconciliation with Simon or with the Church failed. In early 1211 Raymond met Simon of Montfort for unknown reasons near the town of Albi. It was obvious that the two men disliked each other. Simon may have been looking for a pretext to continue expanding his mandate to eliminate heresy, which the Count of Toulouse clearly had not done. Raymond brought along some unnamed followers whom Simon believed wished him physical harm, and when Simon mentioned this at the meeting, Raymond denied he had brought them.[24] The meeting accomplished nothing other than intensifying the antipathy between the two men. Soon after, Raymond attended a council of prelates, abbots and papal officials at Narbonne where Simon of Montfort was present, along with King Peter II of Aragon, who had his own stakes in Occitania. According to the most specific source, Peter Vaux-de-Cernay, this council offered Raymond a reasonable way out of his excommunication, though his possible absolution was not specifically stated. Provided he expel heretics, the council promised him Church endorsement of his position and territories. The council told Raymond that he might even gain more direct control over some lordships in his territories whose holders were considered to be, or were, avowed heretics. He refused the deal and its conditions.[25] During a third meeting at either Arles or Montpellier, the council presented Raymond with a much harsher list of demands that seemed designed to ensure he would not accept them, hence legitimizing any subsequent military action against him.[26] Unsurprisingly, Raymond of Toulouse continued to risk invasion of his territories because of his failure to adapt to current political and religious realities.

Once the weather was good enough for campaigning, Simon of Montfort lost no time in seizing the initiative. In spring 1211 he besieged the town of Lavaur, a reputed Cathar refuge, which was only about 32 kilometres (20 mi.) east of Toulouse. Prior to the Albigensian Crusade, Raymond VI and Raymond-Roger Trencavel disputed suzerainty over Lavaur but generally Raymond-Roger was understood to have it. Now as Raymond-Roger's replacement as viscount, Simon tried both to enforce his own authority and to root out heresy there, but Raymond considered it a threat to his own suzerainty.[27] As effective a commander as Simon was, at the siege he was perennially short of troops and supplies, leaving him dependent on the surrounding regions for reinforcements and logistical assistance. Far from assisting Simon, Raymond secretly sent some of his men into Lavaur to help the defenders, who were discovered by Simon after the city fell.[28] Raymond VI appeared at the siege several times and discouraged anyone from within Toulouse from helping the crusaders, and prevented supplies from Toulouse reaching the siege.[29]

Toulouse's large and experienced civic militia could have been of great use to Simon of Montfort. The city itself, however, was divided by internal disputes between the city proper and its main suburb, mostly over whether to support the crusade or not. The zealously orthodox Bishop of Toulouse, Fulk of Marseilles, wished to assist the crusade but some in Toulouse disliked Fulk as much as they did Raymond VI. In 1210 Fulk had organized a separate militia known as the 'Whites' to combat heresy within the city and to support the crusade, but a rival militia, known as the 'Blacks', formed in opposition in one of the suburbs.[30] During the siege of Lavaur, Fulk ordered the White militia to go there and assist.[31] Raymond chose to hinder their progress openly.

As the militiamen prepared to depart, Raymond appeared among them and ordered them not to go. At the eastern exit of the city the count literally threw himself in front of the gate to physically prevent them from leaving, telling them they would have to break his arms in order to pass him. Temporarily obeying and acting as if to disperse, the White militiamen simply gathered at another gate and left the city anyway.[32] Sometime later Raymond again appeared at Lavaur and convinced some of the militiamen, now wavering in their support amidst the straitened conditions of a bitter siege, to depart early and return to Toulouse. Supplies from Toulouse dried up.[33]

Despite the lack of support, Lavaur fell to Simon of Montfort. After this success, he moved westward to campaign directly in the Toulousain. While the people of Toulouse and their titular count were by no means united in opposition to the crusade, Simon assumed as much and placed the city of Toulouse under siege. This was a different prospect than any other siege he had conducted so far, since Toulouse's size dwarfed all of his other previous targets. At this point Raymond of Toulouse felt obliged to defend the region. As Simon's army moved towards the city, Raymond, alongside a number of other southern lords and their men, some Toulousain militia and a band of Spanish mercenaries, skirmished with the crusade army about 5 kilometres (3 mi.) from Toulouse. This gory affair perhaps produced hundreds of casualties on both sides. Raymond's force, however, was unable to stop the approaching army and it retreated back into the city.[34] Under siege the city defended itself well, forcing Simon to abandon the effort after a brief time. Simon's aggressiveness, his own growing unpopularity, and his perceived weakness after the failed siege of Toulouse led towns and lords to renounce his authority. In turn this emboldened Raymond of Toulouse.

With Simon's military reputation tarnished and his army depleted as crusaders departed after serving their forty days, Raymond decided to take the offensive in the late summer of 1211. His operational and tactical goal was to find Simon's reduced army and defeat it even if strategically this would not help his standing with the papacy.[35] Like every other commander of the early thirteenth century, Raymond had no standing army to do this. The army he gathered consisted of men and lords from towns and territories across the region, together with the militia of Toulouse and a large contingent of more than 1,000 mounted Navarrese mercenaries.[36] This composite force served under

Raymond not because of his military reputation but because of his status as a senior noble and the threat that Simon of Montfort posed to all of them.

Initially, Simon withdrew to his capital of Carcassonne but, taking the advice of one of his advisers, Hugh of Lacy, he moved west towards Toulouse to make a stand at Castelnaudary. Castelnaudary was a weakly fortified town in a salient, but Simon gambled correctly that Raymond and his patchwork army would not pass up the chance to attack his much smaller army exposed in a deficient fortification. Simon's available forces, mostly denuded of northern crusaders who had served their forty days and then left, were minuscule compared to Raymond's. Even the people of Castelnaudary were hostile to the small crusader army, and the town's militia defected to Raymond.[37]

The resulting military activity in the autumn of 1211 offers a classic comparison between two different leaders and their personalities. Simon of Montfort was aggressive, confident and experienced after several years of intensive warfare, while Raymond revealed his inexperience in directing an army to achieve a tactical goal. Instead of closely investing the town or a portion of its walls, or imposing a blockade at the very least, Raymond constructed a fortified camp some distance away, seemingly more concerned with defending himself than besieging the crusaders.[38] Raymond's failure to impose a blockade allowed the crusaders to continue to resupply themselves from outside the town. When some nobles of his army attacked Castelnaudary's gates independently, the rest of Raymond's army slowly responded. By then their commander's military reputation was sinking fast.

Initially the besiegers shot rocks from a single mangonel (a stone-throwing machine) at Castelnaudary's fortifications, but the missiles shattered on impact rather than damaging the walls. After obtaining harder missiles this weapon did enough destruction to merit an unsuccessful sortie to destroy it, led by Simon himself. Nevertheless, without more machines to cause a breach in the walls followed by an assault, Raymond's army would exhaust its supplies and its loose cohesion would dissolve. As the days wore on, any respect his enemies may have had for Raymond or his army evaporated into contempt. The crusaders jeered at Raymond's siege crews and offered to fight them in the open. Perhaps most telling was the anecdote related by Peter Vaux-de-Cernay: a southern *jongleur* (a musical entertainer) in Raymond's army asked the count why he bothered to use missile weapons against Castelnaudary's defences when he refused to attack crusaders roving freely outside its walls.[39]

Soon after, one of the other senior commanders in Raymond's army, Raymond-Roger, Count of Foix, attacked a crusader supply train a few kilometres east of Castelnaudary on its way to resupply the town, while Raymond of Toulouse remained behind in the fortified camp. The Battle of St Martin la-Lande resulted in a decisive tactical victory for Simon of Montfort, who, at the height of the battle, left the defences of Castelnaudary with sixty men to assist in the supply train's rescue – proof yet again of Raymond's failure to blockade the town – and helped secure the victory.[40] The lopsided defeat dumbfounded Raymond of Toulouse and destroyed morale, despite the fact that his army still far outnumbered the crusaders. Soon after the defeat Raymond ended the siege. In its hurry, his army burned much of its equipment or left it behind, suggesting a near-panic, especially when it was so unnecessary.[41] Raymond's chance to prove himself the saviour of the south, or at the very least its defender, had ended in humiliation.

For the next year the Count of Toulouse did nothing to contest Simon of Montfort's continued expansion around his territory, even when crusaders raided very close to the city of Toulouse.[42] By the end of 1212 Raymond travelled to Aragon and requested assistance from his current brother-in-law, King Peter II of Aragon, who was concerned about the crusade's effects on his own Occitan lands and vassals.[43] In 1209 Peter had travelled north to mediate an amicable end to the siege of Carcassonne but failed. Events in Spain kept him preoccupied and out of Occitania except for brief visits until after 1212, when he helped to engineer the strategic defeat of the Muslim Almohads at the Battle of Las Navas de Tolosa.[44] This victory freed him to intervene militarily in the north to support Raymond and his own vassals in Occitania. As a bellicose, successful commander and sovereign possessing strong credentials as a crusader, Peter was a better match for Simon than the cautious Raymond, who in the coming campaign slipped to the status of a mere lieutenant. Peter's intervention was assisted by the fact that, because of Simon's successes and the pope's desire that crusade efforts be directed towards a new crusade to the Middle East, the indulgence for service on the Albigensian Crusade was withdrawn in the spring of 1213.[45] This permanently reduced Simon's army to a small rump of his personal followers.

In the summer of 1213 a coalition army, including Raymond and the militia of Toulouse, sortied out of the city to attack the Montfortian garrison at the small town and weak fortress of Pujol. There was no crusader field army in the vicinity to come to its relief. This much larger force managed to take the fortress and capture its garrison, fleeing ahead of a crusader flying column dispatched to relieve it.[46] This small tactical victory temporarily bolstered the southern cause, and constituted the first victory against the crusade in which Raymond played some part.

Later in 1213 King Peter brought his own Aragonese–Catalan army north to counter the crusade's continuous advances. Together with the Count of Toulouse, other southern lords and their followers and the civic militia of Toulouse, this most likely constituted the largest army ever to contest the crusade. It culminated in a showdown near the town of Muret, about 18 kilometres (11 mi.) south of Toulouse, in which yet again a force far superior in numbers confronted the ever-aggressive Simon of Montfort. Of great interest is Raymond's role prior to the battle, because it revealed his default strategic and tactical thinking and how little impact his advice had on Peter's decision to fight Simon of Montfort in the field. The combined army put Muret, a weak fortification with a small garrison, under siege like Pujol. Muret would likely have fallen except that Peter wanted to entice Simon of Montfort to rescue it, hoping that with his larger army he could defeat Simon in a pitched battle. At one of Peter's last war councils before the battle Raymond recommended that the king not seek open battle but rather that the coalition reinforce its fortified camp, not unlike what he had done at Castelnaudary in 1211. If Simon's forces attacked, the coalition army could use arrows and javelins to weaken or destroy the crusaders from protected positions.[47] An Aragonese noble, Michael of Luesia, derided this advice, essentially calling Raymond a coward for advocating anything less than a pitched battle. Peter refused to consider Raymond's plan, believing that the count had suggested it from 'fear or cowardice'.[48] Raymond's advice, based on his own inclinations and distilled through experience, yet so contemptuously discounted before the battle, demonstrated how little influence he had on military decision-making at the moment. The consequent Battle of Muret was a complete disaster for Peter, resulting in his death, the scattering of the Occitan, Aragonese and Catalan army, and the slaughtering of the militia of Toulouse. Raymond dutifully fought and retreated from the field back to Toulouse with the rest of the survivors without eliciting any positive or negative mention for his conduct during the battle.

After the battle the survivors considered their next step. Raymond recommended they now accept whatever terms were necessary to reconcile themselves to the Church. He intended to go to Rome to plead his case to the pope himself. Instead, he went to England, where he sought support from King John, who as Duke of Gascony was an important landholder in southern France.[49] After being expelled by a papal legate there, Raymond returned to Occitania by February 1214. That spring his younger half-brother Baldwin, who had been a loyal supporter of the crusade since 1209, was captured in the Agenais and brought to Montauban. Informed of this development, Raymond went there with several other southern lords. After consulting them he endorsed and witnessed Baldwin's hanging for his disloyalty in participating in the Battle of Muret on the crusader side.[50] Raymond and Baldwin had little in common, and in fact had not been raised together.[51] Had there been no crusade in Occitania, Baldwin would have lived the life of a younger son, dependent on whatever munificence his older brother might bestow. Raymond's continually dicey position after 1209 made Baldwin, a crusade loyalist, a potentially attractive replacement as count of Toulouse, or at the very least a rival. With so little brotherly affection existing between them, Raymond took the opportunity to put Baldwin out of circulation permanently; yet, this swift and final action further eroded Raymond's reputation. One of the major sources on the crusade, whose author supported Raymond's cause, omitted mention of Baldwin's capture or execution because no argument or justification could defend his murder. Other sources remark that even by the violent standards of the era what Raymond did was reprehensible, with one calling him a 'second Cain'.[52] While the thirteenth-century world was more brutal than the Western world of today, there were other ways in which Raymond could have dealt with Baldwin, such as having him executed by a more honourable or painless method than hanging, or after more time had elapsed, or simply incarcerating him. The quickness and method of Baldwin's death repulsed Raymond's contemporaries.

By the time the Fourth Lateran Council met in 1215, Raymond's fortunes had struck rock bottom. This huge ecumenical council discussed a great number of issues, among them deciding what to do about lands seized from Raymond by Simon of Montfort since 1211. Raymond and his son attended the council, though he did not personally plead his case. Others argued on his behalf that the count's personal religious beliefs had never been questioned and that his dispossession was unjust. According to the source most sympathetic to Raymond, the pope did not dispute Raymond's orthodoxy but recognized that the count had simply not done much to suppress heresy in his lands, while clearly Simon of Montfort would.[53] Eventually the pope acquiesced in allowing Simon to retain the majority of lands or suzerainty he had wrested from the Count of Toulouse.[54] By Lateran IV, Raymond was almost sixty years old and his plight had drawn little sympathy from anyone, although his teenaged son was another story. Raymond's inaction, poor choices and bad luck had caused his son to have lost almost everything.

Raymond appears to have recognized this, because in subsequent years he gave the younger count a more active role in the fight to regain his lands. In a series of meetings in the eastern part of Raymond's lands along the Rhône River, many of which had not been seized by Simon and had not been given to him by the provisions of Lateran IV, the two Raymonds secured the homage of many lords who feared a future Montfortian incursion and believed that Raymond and his son had been treated badly. After gaining pledges of loyalty and cash, in the spring of 1216 the two launched a surprise siege of the younger Raymond's birthplace, the city of Beaucaire. On the east bank of the Rhône, Beaucaire's Montfortian garrison was far from Simon's western power centres and its distance made it hard for him to respond quickly.[55] In a move that suggests the mantle of leadership had passed from father to son, Raymond VII directed the siege of Beaucaire while Raymond VI travelled to Spain to drum up further support and funds.[56] The younger Raymond had already proved himself to be more energetic and charismatic than his father, and the elder's track record as a commander was poor. If the younger lost at Beaucaire, it could be chalked up to youth and inexperience. Raymond VI had run out of chances.

Raymond the Younger showed the kind of drive, determination and tactical acumen that his father had not, and the siege of Beaucaire resulted in a major personal and symbolic military victory for him. The long and brutal siege thwarted Simon's relief efforts and shattered the aura of his invincibility when Beaucaire surrendered to Raymond VII. Far off in Spain, the elder Raymond shared no laurels in this victory. Simon's loss at Beaucaire led to his own poor strategic thinking when he moved against the city of Toulouse again, believing it was on the cusp of rebellion against his authority. Though it may have been, egged on by vague messages from Raymond vi from Spain, the people of Toulouse tried to reassure Simon that they were loyal, especially since the town's defences had been weakened by Simon in both 1215 and 1216.[57] To restore Simon's good faith, he demanded hostages and an exorbitant cash sum to be paid by the next year. At the same time, Raymond the Younger continued to build his reputation in eastern towns along the Rhône. In 1217 defections forced Simon to campaign in the eastern part of his domains, which took his attention away from Toulouse to the extent that its people openly rebelled against him for his exactions. In August 1217 Raymond vi returned from Spain and in September 1217 he entered the city of Toulouse with a small army.[58]

Raymond vi received a hero's welcome in Toulouse, something he could never have imagined had Simon's own bumbling and impatience not driven the people of the city to throw their support behind a man who less than a decade before they had largely despised. In the subsequent months Raymond assisted, but did not direct, the defence of the city against Simon, who vowed to take the city and punish its people. Raymond did not act as a commander-in-chief, but rather as a senior statesman. He endorsed the formation of a city government to help defend the city and advised that holding out against Simon would be difficult. He also wrote to his son in Provence, urging him to come to Toulouse.[59] During the siege Raymond acted as a symbol of southern resistance, but did nothing militarily to distinguish himself. The second siege of Toulouse lasted from September 1217 to late June 1218, ending shortly after a stone flung from a trebuchet killed Simon of Montfort. Although the crusade continued under Simon's son Amaury, its fortunes mostly fell after 1218.

Between Simon's death and his own, the sexagenarian Raymond vi played no role in the continuing southern counteroffensive, acknowledging that his day had passed and that it was up to his son to take back what was his. In 1222 Raymond vi died an excommunicant and was refused a church burial.[60] In the coming years the French crown became more directly involved in the region, especially since Amaury of Montfort wanted out from under leading the crusade and gave up his claims. By the treaty of Paris in 1229 Raymond vii retained the lands he had recaptured and passed them on to his heir, his daughter Jeanne, who was married to Alphonse, son of King Louis viii.[61]

The arrangement specified that should Alphonse and Jeanne die heirless, the lands of the Count of Toulouse would pass directly to the French crown, which duly happened in 1271. Thus in this once quasi-independent region with its own customs and language, French sovereignty replaced Occitan suzerainty.

Raymond VI was not evil, but craven and self-serving. In an era when political and military leadership were intertwined and loyalty was often given to a personality rather than an institution or state, he lacked the charisma to inspire and the ability to defend his lands while remaining in the good graces of the Church. As a war leader he largely failed to win the loyalty or trust of the towns, people and nobles of the region and was outclassed by his adversary Simon of Montfort. He did not see the danger in flouting the Church's zealousness against heresy until an army was virtually on his doorstep. Diverting the crusaders in 1209 against his nephew to save his own lands was recognized as a cynical act. Between 1209 and 1211 he ham-fistedly tried to slow down the crusade even while officially supporting it. His counter-campaign of 1211 was a humiliating mess that cemented his reputation as a timorous commander outclassed by an outnumbered foe. Besides the capture of Pujol in 1213 he had no substantive military or political accomplishments and whatever success he enjoyed after that belonged to his son.

Occitan secular elite culture put great store by the idea of *paratge* (peerage), a loose concept or quality that encompassed nobility of blood and spirit, largesse and the willingness to defend one's property.[62] Although the Occitan source called the *Song of the Cathar Wars* uses the term frequently, it would be a stretch to apply it to Raymond VI.[63] He poorly represented the qualities it was supposed to encompass and was no *beau idéal* of thirteenth-century martial and chivalric virtues. Raymond's deficient strategic and tactical judgement plagued what he did except in a few minor instances. Thus he deserves inclusion among the worst commanders in history because of his inability to exhibit much competency at any level of warfare either by thirteenth-century standards or modern ones.

PART 5

BUNGLERS

Nogi Maresuke.

13
NOGI MARESUKE

Danny Orbach

The worst policy of all is to besiege walled cities.
Sun Tzu, *The Art of War*, III.3

Military incompetence cannot be understood apart from historical context. Most military leaders are neither geniuses nor fools, but even if they are, external circumstances play a great part in their successes and failures. The triumphs of commanders known as 'brilliant', such as Napoleon, owed as much to luck, the mistakes of others, and structural advantages within their armies and the environments they operated in as to skill and wisdom. At the same time, generals who acquired bad reputations, such as Douglas Haig (of Somme and Passchendaele 'fame'), faced unprecedented problems that very few of their contemporaries knew how to solve.[1]

This chapter will investigate the performance of General Nogi Maresuke, the commander of the Imperial Japanese 3rd Army in the Russo-Japanese War, as a contextualized case of military incompetence. Nogi's management of the siege of Port Arthur (July 1904 to January 1905) was horrendous, notwithstanding his eventual victory. His incompetence was not only the result of individual characteristics, but a reflection of institutional constraints, external circumstances and the shortcomings of subordinates. However, instead of honestly facing Nogi's failures and deciphering the context that aggravated them, Japanese and foreign observers lionized him as a brilliant commander, an embodiment of Japan's martial spirit. This uncritical judgement perpetuated Nogi's mistakes beyond their historical context, turning them into timeless 'military lessons'. The result was a disaster with repercussions for both world wars.

The Russo-Japanese War began in 1904, after a long period of failed negotiations between the two empires over spheres of influence in East Asia. On 9 February Japan attacked the Russian Pacific Fleet in Chemulpo and Port Arthur in Korea and Manchuria. This surprise attack had mixed results. While the Japanese were able to destroy the ships in Chemulpo, they failed to annihilate the Port Arthur squadron or to seal the approach to the harbour by scuttling old steamships. The Russian vessels were damaged, but not destroyed. They could theoretically leave Port Arthur for the safer harbour of Vladivostok, but remained anchored due to the cautious attitude of the local commander, Admiral Vilhelm Vitgeft, who feared a disastrous engagement with the blockading Japanese Navy. It would be better, he argued, to preserve the ships for future action.

Landing in Chemulpo, forward elements of General Kuroki Tametomo's 1st Army quickly captured the Korean Peninsula. On 1 May, in the first major land engagement of the war, Kuroki's army crossed the Yalu River and soundly defeated the Russian defenders. In the battle of the Yalu, Japanese tacticians were at their best, executing difficult river crossings, surprise attacks and enveloping movements, with proper concentration of force and skilful use of terrain. Beaten and humiliated, Russia's forces withdrew northwards to their command centre in Liaoyang, leaving Port Arthur isolated. The 2nd Japanese Army, under General Oku Yasukata, landed on 5 May near Pitzuwo, and gave the Russians another beating in the battle of Nanshan, thus securing the narrow waist of the Liaodong Peninsula. The Japanese now dominated Liaodong, closing on Port Arthur from both land and sea.[2]

The original plan of the Japanese, developed by Field Marshal Ōyama Iwao, commander-in-chief of the Manchurian Army, and his chief of staff, General Kodama Gentarō, was to bypass Port Arthur. All they intended was to block the Russian forces in town with relatively few troops ('a bamboo palisade', in Kodama's words), using the rest of the army to drive northwards towards Liaoyang, and afterwards, maybe even Mukden and Harbin in Manchuria. By occupying these important centres, Japanese planners hoped to cut off eastern Siberia from the Russian Far East and force the tsar to the negotiating table.[3]

Things changed, however, due to the interference of the Imperial Navy. Admiral Tōgō Heihachirō, commander of the Combined Fleet, was concerned that in a few months the Russian Baltic Fleet might sail to the Far East, break the naval siege on Port Arthur, and unite with Vitgeft's squadron. Then the Japanese would lose their naval dominance, with disastrous consequences. Even when Tōgō destroyed most of the Russian fleet on 10 August, at the Battle of the Yellow Sea, faulty intelligence led him to believe that the wrecked squadron still posed a threat. Obsessed by the phantom of an enemy squadron that was, in fact, unseaworthy, Tōgō pressed the army to neutralize the danger by occupying Port Arthur from land.[4]

Facing repeated pleas from the navy, Ōyama and Kodama, the leaders of the Manchurian Army, changed their plans and decided to storm Port Arthur with a newly established 3rd Army, organized for the purpose. Command was given to General Nogi Maresuke, a semi-forgotten pensioner living in quiet retirement. Nogi's career was a mixed bag of victories and failures, one of which coloured his whole reputation. In the Satsuma Rebellion of 1877 he had recklessly driven his unit into encirclement and lost the imperial banner. He had asked for permission to commit suicide to atone for his disgrace, but received 'the gift of life' from the Meiji emperor. Emotionally, he never recovered. A man with a strong suicidal drive, Nogi also had no formal Japanese military education, but he did study for eighteen months in Germany. He had one important advantage, though. Originally from Yamaguchi Prefecture, Nogi was a former retainer of the Chōshū Clan, and thus close to Field Marshal Yamagata Aritomo, chief of the Imperial General Staff, and to the ruling clique of the army.[5]

Yamagata and the other leaders of the army did not think highly of Nogi's abilities as a strategist, but they believed that for the task of occupying Port Arthur he would be a good fit. In the First Sino-Japanese War (1894–5) Nogi himself had captured it in one day, with only one regiment and almost no resistance. Back then, however, the enemy commander-in-chief was quick to make his escape, so the Japanese faced nothing but a chaotic mob and a defenceless town with primitive fortifications. Now they had to deal with a modern, well-equipped and fortified army.[6] And yet, almost everyone expected Nogi to finish the job quickly. In Tokyo, residents even prepared festive lanterns and rehearsed for victory parades. But the lanterns would have to be stored far longer than anyone anticipated.[7]

Port Arthur was a formidable fort, partly anchored by the sea, with four lines of defence. Around the old town there was a wide ditch. Three and a half kilometres from the ditch there was a second line: the old Chinese city wall, fortified by modern earthworks and several permanent forts with interlocking fields of fire. The eastern forts, especially Pine Trees Hill, Twin Dragons (Erlong), Panlong, Cockscomb and Wantai, were especially formidable.[8] Then, there was a third line comprised of hurriedly fortified hills, hugging the town from both east and west. In the east, this line was weaker, stretching from Wolf's Hills (Fenghuang shan) in the north, to Great and Small Orphan Hills in the south. In the west, there were several important hills with makeshift fortifications, including 210-Metres Hill, Namako, Akasaka and 203-Metres Hill. The last was especially important, as it offered an unobstructed view of Port Arthur. Any occupant with heavy long-range artillery could bombard both port and fortress with impunity.[9]

Nogi, however, did not have such long-range guns. *Hitachi-Maru*, the navy ship that carried his 11-inch siege howitzers, was intercepted and destroyed by marauding Russian vessels from the Vladivostok Squadron on 17 June.[10] This would have serious repercussions, as heavy guns were needed to breach the thick Russian fortifications and to bombard the battleships in the harbour with any efficiency. Nogi was forced to shoot sparingly with the guns he did have, because the ammunition budget of the Japanese Army was extremely low. Some of Nogi's staff officers feared an impending disaster, as it was believed that attacks against fortified positions require massive preparatory bombardments.[11]

In late July and early August the 3rd Army was able to occupy the relatively weak third line of defence north and east of the fortress, and even defeat a Russian counter-attack. From their new positions on Big Orphan Hill, the Japanese began to shell the town and harbour. On 20 August they opened the first in a series of three general assaults against the Russian second line of defence.[12]

The General Staff in Tokyo advised Nogi to attack Port Arthur from the northwest, similarly to the line of advance in the First Sino-Japanese War. The commander of the 3rd Army, however, disagreed. He preferred to lead his first general assault against the northeastern sector, namely Twin Dragons, Cockscomb, Panlong and Wantai. This route was convenient, as it was close to the army's supply railhead.

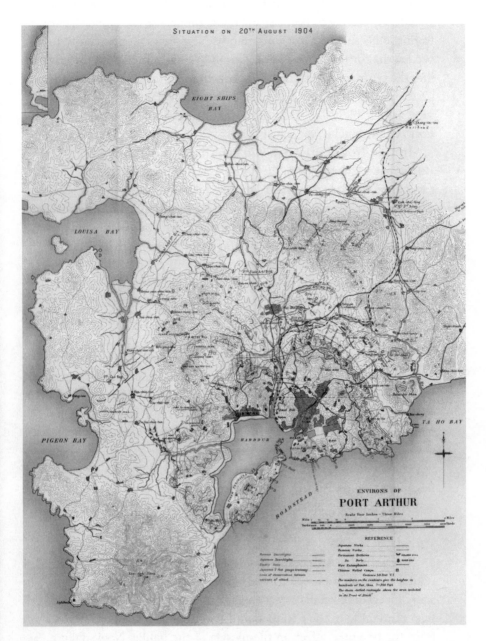

ENVIRONS OF
PORT ARTHUR

Scale Four Inches - Three Miles

REFERENCE

The environs of Port Arthur, 20 August 1904.

Furthermore, Nogi surmised, because the Japanese had attacked from the northwest during the First Sino-Japanese War, that the Russians would be expecting the same again. Better to surprise them, and charge from the northeast. Most importantly, Nogi saw an opportunity to occupy the fortress in one stroke. From Wantai, a ravine led directly into the centre of the old town. This direct route seemed most appropriate, as the 3rd Army had been ordered to occupy the fortress as soon as possible. Nogi was certain that he would be able to capture Port Arthur quickly, as he had in 1894.[13]

In fact, Nogi considerably underestimated the strength of the Russian permanent forts in the northeastern sector. He did not know, for starters, that a covered road connected them, allowing the Russians to quickly transfer soldiers, supplies and ammunition. Ignoring ample reconnaissance intelligence and several warnings from British military observers and Japanese officers, he also failed to realize that the fortified Russians had a 10:1 advantage in machine guns and artillery superiority of 465 to 364 guns. The Russians probably also had a spy inside Nogi's headquarters. Port Arthur's commander, General Anatoly Stoessel, learned about the direction of the general assault and was able to direct his forces accordingly.[14]

The general assault was an unmitigated disaster. On 24 August, after five days of hard fighting, Nogi lost 18,000 men (almost one-third of his force) without capturing his main target of Wantai. His soldiers charged in waves, as 'human bullets', in front of enemy machine guns, one of several suicidal attacks later described by veterans such as Sakurai Tadayoshi.[15] The Japanese in the surrounding hills were under constant fire from Wantai, and suffered appalling casualties, more than 30 per cent in many cases. Both armies were exhausted, and Nogi accepted his officers' recommendation to give up the fight for now. The general offensive would resume when reinforcements arrived.[16]

The assault was so costly and disastrous for the Japanese that its results had to be kept secret. Prudently, on the eve of the attack, Nogi's staff officers ordered all correspondents, Western and Japanese, not to report anything to their editors until Port Arthur had fallen.[17] Apart from the potential effect on the morale of the public, Nogi's failure disturbed the overall strategy of the Japanese. As the British official history of the war maintained, had Nogi's troops been freed of Port Arthur, Field Marshal Ōyama Iwao could have used them in the Battle of Liaoyang. With more power, he would have had a chance to destroy the Russian Army, not merely push it northwards, as happened.[18]

After the failure of the first general assault, Nogi tried to use tunnels, mines and saps in order to shelter the advance of his troops, and eventually blow up the fortresses from below. In September, the 3rd Army finally received 11-inch howitzers, dismantled from forts in mainland Japan – eighteen heavy guns in total. By 20 September the Japanese were able to capture the waterworks redoubt, and cut the water supply to Port Arthur. Now the Russians had to use Chinese wells inside the fortress.[19] One day later, in the west, Nogi's troops captured Namako Hill, north of 203-Metres Hill. From the top of that hill, they had a limited view of the port and could damage some of the ships with their guns. The price was 4,700 Japanese casualties. The 1st Division was even able to occupy the southern slope of 203-Metres Hill for a short while, but soon lost it to a Russian counter-attack.[20]

On 26 October Nogi launched a second general assault on the Russian forts along the eastern sector. His goal was to occupy the fort before the emperor's birthday on 3 November. This time the Japanese could use tunnels and saps they had created over months of back-breaking labour. The idea was to bombard the Russian positions for three days with the heavy guns, then fill the ditches surrounding them with soil to facilitate an attack. The Japanese knew their saps did not reach far enough, but hoped to storm the remaining 50 metres (164 ft) and overthrow the defenders with numerical superiority. Yet again, Japanese intelligence failed: the ditches were much wider than Nogi and his staff officers anticipated. They had been misled by the report of a dubious agent. The prolonged bombardment with the 11-inch howitzers damaged the Russian forts and taxed the nerves of their defenders, but could not destroy them. This disappointing result, a precursor to similar bombardments on the Somme and other First World War engagements, was due not only to technical problems in the howitzers, but to logistical difficulties. Lacking ammunition, the Japanese slackened their pace of fire, giving the Russians time to mend the forts. Even worse, the Japanese guns, their barrels distorted from continuous firing, lost their accuracy, sometimes missing their targets and killing their own men in droves.[21]

Thousands of Japanese soldiers were killed for no gain. It became difficult to replace casualties and the troops that did arrive were often inadequately trained. The defeat of the second general assault became a national scandal, as Port Arthur gained importance in the eyes of the public far exceeding its real strategic value. Mobs stoned Nogi's house in Tokyo, and senior generals in the army appealed for his removal. It is said that only the personal intervention of Emperor Meiji saved Nogi from the sack.[22]

The Navy and the Army's General Staff in Tokyo tried to convince Nogi to abandon his futile efforts in the northeastern sector and concentrate on the western outposts, such as 203-Metres Hill. From there, he could bombard and destroy the Russian Navy, the most important goal of the siege. Time was of the essence, as the Japanese Navy needed dry-docking for two months, at least, before being able to contend with the Baltic Fleet. Nogi's job was to free them from this task, and he failed to deliver. Still he refused to change his plans and was resolute about launching another, identical frontal assault against the forts in the northeastern sector.[23]

Unable to convince Nogi and his staff, the Navy and the Army General Staff now applied pressure on Ōyama and Kodama, leaders of the Manchurian Army. But to Tokyo's disappointment, Nogi's direct superiors backed their obdurate subordinate. On 9 November they advised that it would be unwise to change the direction of the attack midway or to divide the army's firepower between two targets. Instead, Ōyama and Kodama asked to reinforce Nogi's army with Japan's only remaining reserve division, the 7th, and to enlarge his ammunition allocation. The General Staff resisted for a while but finally gave in. Thus, in late November, Nogi launched a third general assault.[24]

On 26–27 November, the third general assault began to show signs of an impending debacle. The attack on the forts failed, yet again, at the cost of 3,800 casualties. Nogi was depressed and exhausted from lack of sleep. In a conversation with a staff officer from Tokyo, he even said he was more than ready to give his command to a more suitable person. Unsurprisingly, nobody volunteered.[25]

Now General Nagaoka Gaishi, army vice chief of staff, was finally able to convince Ōyama and Kodama that the continuation of present tactics would spell disaster. Instead of slamming his troops against the forts of the eastern sector, Nogi had to direct all of his efforts towards 203-Metres Hill. Accordingly, on 27 November Nogi ordered his troops to occupy the hill, whatever the cost, this time with the help of the newly arrived 7th division. The attack failed when Nogi ordered the infantry to proceed without adequate softening with his heavy artillery, and the inexperienced soldiers of the 7th were mowed down like grass. The artillery barrages were not that effective before, but proceeding without them was even more suicidal. In this way, the commander of the 3rd Army was consuming Japan's strategic reserves as quickly as his own troops.[26]

Field Marshal Ōyama, who had previously protected Nogi, now turned furiously against him. On 30 November he sent a scathing telegram to 3rd Army headquarters, accusing Nogi of grave tactical mistakes. Ōyama charged Nogi with keeping both senior officers and reserves too far from the front, where they were unable to react quickly to Russian counter-attacks. Ōyama also criticized Nogi for failing to take 203-Metres Hill, which was quite hypocritical, as Ōyama and Kodama had themselves supported him in this issue until a short while before. In any case, Ōyama dispatched his chief of staff, General Kodama, to Port Arthur, along with troop reinforcements (an infantry brigade) and orders to micromanage Nogi's army. Ōyama warned Nogi to obey Kodama in all things. In case of trouble, Kodama was authorized to relieve Nogi of his duties and take formal charge of the 3rd Army.[27]

Kodama reached Port Arthur on 30 November, tired and angry. With tears in his eyes, Nogi ceded all authority to him. Subsequently, Kodama treated Nogi and his officers as if they were trainees, hurling insults and commands. He ordered Nogi's staff to haul the 11-inch howitzers to the foot of 203-Metres Hill, taking care this time to allocate enough ammunition for the attack. On 5 December, after days of heavy shelling, with the help of saps and truly heroic perseverance, the 3rd Army was able to overcome the stout Russian defence and occupy 203-Metres Hill. Twelve thousand Japanese soldiers were killed in one of the bloodiest battles of the siege. The 1st and 7th Japanese Divisions, which bore the main brunt of the fighting, were virtually obliterated.[28]

From 203-Metres Hill the Japanese shelled the Russian fleet into pulp. As military historian Richard Connaughton writes, with the destruction of the fleet, the fortress lost its importance. The town also suffered immensely, as the Japanese could bombard almost any target from the top of 203. Ōba Jirō noticed that since the occupation of that crucial hill, the resistance of the Russian soldiers in the still-formidable eastern forts considerably slackened. Stoessel later admitted to Nogi that only after 203 was taken had he thought of surrender.[29]

On 18 December and 1 January, respectively, Twin Dragons and Wantai were finally occupied, through a combination of sapping and frontal assaults. Wishing to avoid street fighting and wholesale slaughter, General Stoessel surrendered Port Arthur to Nogi on 2 January. In the final account, the Russians lost 31,306 men, the Japanese more than 60,000.[30]

As a result, General Nogi, now free to join the battles in northern Manchuria with his army, became the hero of the day, virtually immune from sacking. Very few knew about his incompetence, or the fact that the successful fighting in early December was micromanaged by Kodama. Lieutenant Colonel Tanaka Giichi, one of Ōyama's staff officers, and the vice chief of staff, Nagaoka Gaishi, demanded Nogi be relieved, but Kodama refused. That would stain the reputation of the 3rd Army and sour the victory at Port Arthur.[31]

Nogi, however, sank even deeper into depression. The death of his two sons in Nanshan and Port Arthur, along with so many of his soldiers, broke his spirit. When he reported to the emperor, 'the words froze in his throat and his eyes welled with tears. When he did eventually finish, he pleaded to be allowed to die, to which the emperor replied that he should wait until the emperor's death.' Nogi wrote to Army Minister Terauchi, 'I have no excuse to offer to my sovereign and to my countrymen for this unscientific, unstrategical combat of brute force.' Being an incompetent general but a decent man, the burden of the fallen haunted Nogi until his eventual suicide on 13 September 1912.[32]

Nogi's performance in the siege of Port Arthur was desultory. But the individual weaknesses of a general turn into military incompetence only in combination with external circumstances. And Nogi was put into an unenviable situation that highlighted all of his personal weaknesses.

First of all, Nogi was pressured by both army and navy to occupy Port Arthur as soon as possible. Haste never contributes to sound judgement. It is important to note that Major General Ichiji Kōsuke, Nogi's chief of staff, warned the General Staff in Tokyo that premature attacks might lead to failure.[33] Then there was the problem of intelligence, which was poor in the extreme. The single map given to the 3rd Army did not include information on newly built Russian fortifications, and misrepresented the permanent fortifications on the eastern sector as makeshift. As a result, Nogi and his staff underestimated the strength of the Russian defences in their line of advance, as well as the height of the parapets and the width of the ditches. Some field commanders who witnessed the strength of the Russian fortress before the first general assault were reluctant to report and correct Nogi's underestimation, as such warnings could be interpreted as 'cowardice'. The culture in the Japanese Army dictated combative optimism, which encouraged a reckless underestimation of adversaries.[34]

Moreover, as a siege was not in the army's original plan, the General Staff failed to devote efforts to the study of modern siege warfare, and existing knowledge was hopelessly obsolete. Experiments with explosives on thick concrete were sparse, up-to-date techniques of sapping and mining were hardly studied, and even the budget for tunnelling equipment was cut by the General Staff's 5th (Fortification) Department. These institutional failures would likely have led to disaster, with or without Nogi. It must be mentioned that not only Nogi, but his superior, Field Marshal Ōyama, underestimated the difficulties of the siege and believed as late as August 1904 that Port Arthur could be occupied at one stroke.[35]

Crucial failures of logistics and supply, beyond Nogi's control, also ravaged his troops and sapped their fighting power. First of all, as noted, the allocation of ammunition to Nogi's army was absurdly inadequate. The same was true for food. Navy doctors had long observed that the terrible disease of beriberi plagued troops nourished mainly or exclusively with polished white rice. This could be remedied by green vegetables, or, lacking any, mixing the rice with barley. The medical department of the army, however, clung to obsolete theories according to which beriberi was caused by germs. Therefore it refused to supply barley rice, also because it was harder to transport. As a result, beriberi ravaged Nogi's corps throughout the siege.[36]

Finally, Nogi did not have a skilled staff to assist him. This was especially unfortunate, because in the Japanese Army, chiefs and vice chiefs of staff used to manage day-to-day affairs for their commanders. Like Nogi, however, many of the 3rd Army's senior officers were chosen according to clan, clique or personal loyalties.[37] Chief of staff Ichiji Kōsuke, an ineffective leader by almost all accounts, balanced Nogi's Chōshū credentials with his Satsuma descent. He was also a relative of Field Marshal Ōyama, commander-in-chief of the Manchurian Army. Notwithstanding his alleged expertise in artillery, Ichiji was completely ignorant of modern gunnery. Astoundingly, he initially refused to receive 11-inch siege howitzers, cabling the General Staff that they were 'unneeded'. These guns, which would finally destroy the Russian Pacific Fleet, were transferred to the 3rd Army mainly because of the dogged persistence of the Army Ministry and the General Staff.

Ōba Jirō, Ichiji's vice chief of staff, was, like Nogi, a former Chōshū retainer. Far from covering for Ichiji's incompetence, he was an overworked and mediocre officer. Constantly citing difficulties, Ōba defended the repetition of failed tactics. Instead of listening to the 3rd Army's critics, he denounced them as pencil pushers who undermine morale with detached, theoretical arguments.[38] Ichiji and Ōba did not have any background in military engineering and fortifications, a crucial skill given the central importance of tunnelling, sapping and mining in siege warfare. Major General Uehara Yūsaku, considered the army's foremost expert in such warfare, was not assigned to the 3rd Army. The General Staff, instead, dispatched him to the 4th Army, where his father-in-law, an extremely difficult personality, was in charge. It was assumed that only Uehara would be able to work with him. Where such personal considerations reign supreme, military incompetence is likely to proliferate like weed in an abandoned garden.[39]

Nogi had to work in difficult circumstances: a crushing schedule, incessant pressure from above, missing equipment, deficient doctrine, poor intelligence and a dysfunctional staff. He also faced resolute adversaries entrenched in formidable, modern fortifications with intensive firepower. In such conditions, armies need commanders with adequate political clout to question irrational orders from above and press the high command for more resources and support; commanders creative enough to improvise with what they have, and surprise their enemies with innovative tactics. Lacking the benefit of a competent staff, the commander of the 3rd Army also had to be an officer with deep understanding of siege warfare, military engineering and hilly topography. Nogi was none of these.

His list of weaknesses, faults and failures is almost endless, but it is best to begin with the most important quality of an army commander: strategic thinking. Strategy is the art of coordination between goals and means. What, in fact, was the goal of operations in Port Arthur? As Ōba Jirō, Nogi's vice chief of staff, wrote in his diary, two possible goals were to occupy the fortress and to destroy the Russian

Pacific Fleet.[40] Obtaining the first goal would also achieve the second one. With the occupation of the fortress, the fleet would either be overrun from the land, or forced to escape to sea – and it was not seaworthy after 10 August. However, it was also possible to destroy the fleet *without* occupying the fortress, through bombardment from the top of 203-Metres Hill. This became possible only in late September, with the arrival of the 11-inch siege howitzers.

Nogi's orders from the Manchurian Army and the General Staff were to occupy the fortress. However, it was well known that Port Arthur had little strategic value in itself, and the only reason for the siege was to destroy the fleet.[41] Nogi, who lacked strategic imagination, failed to understand that and stuck to the literal meaning of his orders. Until late November he did not attach any importance to 203-Metres Hill, because he was still looking for the shortest route to the fortress. Even when the General Staff made it clear that this interpretation was wrong, that destroying the fleet was his most important priority, Nogi refused to budge. He had received his formal orders, and that was that. Disastrously, he was supported by Ōyama and Kodama, his superiors from the Manchurian Army. When the General Staff was finally able to convince Nogi and his superiors to attack 203-Metres Hill, in late November, its occupation had become much more difficult, because the Russians had significantly reinforced their fortifications.[42]

Chōnan Masayoshi, Nogi's stoutest and most recent defender, has attempted to justify not only Nogi's unimaginative interpretation of his orders, but his decision to attack the fortress from the east rather than from northwestern elevations like 203-Metres Hill. Leaning heavily on diaries and memoirs of 3rd Army staff officers, Chōnan argues that the western side of the fortress was actually more fortified, and that Nogi had no other choice, given his meagre allocation of troops, ammunition and artillery.[43] But even if for the sake of argument one were to agree with Chōnan's interpretation, Nogi's performance would remain inexcusable.

Let us assume that Nogi absolutely had to attack the fortress from the northeast, without giving any attention to 203-Metres Hill and the destruction of the Russian fleet. Even in such a case, Nogi and his staff officers had to know that frontal attack against a fortress, without sufficient intelligence, heavy siege howitzers and adequate ammunition, was suicidal. The only way forward was to harass the fortress, dig saps and mines, and wait until they reached the Russian positions.

Only with a covered, subterranean approach did the Japanese have a chance to storm the eastern forts, or even better – blow them up from below. This work was admittedly difficult, because much of the ground was made of solid rock, which the low temperatures of the Manchurian autumn made even firmer.

It was only in mid-December that the saps reached far enough to allow a frontal assault in the eastern sector:

> The lives lost in August, October and November were for the most part thrown away to absolutely no purpose, for exactly the same result would have been obtained if no assaults had been delivered until the middle of December. The fortress would have fallen on the same date, and thousands of lives might have been saved.[44]

Indeed, the final occupation of Twin Dragons and the other eastern forts in December was achieved with the help of saps and underground explosions, combined with artillery and infantry assaults. That could not be done until mid-December.

As Nogi and his staff officers were ignorant about military engineering and siege warfare, they could not understand that in order to take over the fortress, they had to channel their efforts into tunnelling, sapping and mining. Benjamin Norregaard, reporter for the London *Daily Mail*, recalled that such work 'was too slow for him [Nogi], and it was taxing his tenacity and fortitude to a much higher degree than the most desperate attacks in the open. They [the Japanese soldiers] did not like it, and they did not understand it, and the majority of their officers shared their feelings.'[45] Ashmead-Bartlett maintained with justification that 'had the Japanese commander-in-chief taken up the most elementary book on engineering, and given his generals instructions to follow out its precepts, he could have captured Port Arthur in the same time with far less trouble and cost'.[46]

As some of his defenders maintain, Nogi began his campaign with intelligence that was faulty to non-existent. That, by itself, was not his fault.[47] And yet, as Lieutenant General Nagaoka Gaishi wrote in anger, Nogi did not make any effort to collect fresh intelligence. True, he frequently toured the front positions to inspire courage, but did not use his tours to assess the situation in person. Ichiji, his chief of staff, and other staff officers were reluctant to inspect the front line altogether. Instead, Nogi's staff sent inexperienced infantry officers to gather intelligence in the field. These officers were interested in heroic attacks more than in intelligence. As a result, only after three disastrous frontal assaults were they able to gather enough information on essentials such as fortress structure, the location of guns and concentrations of Russian troops.[48]

Due to his indifference to intelligence, as well as his unimaginative thinking, Nogi repeated the same mistakes over and over again, ignoring all pleas for reform. It seems the only tactical manoeuvre he knew was the frontal assault. Contrary to the arguments of Nogi's defenders, the standing orders of the General Staff did not force him to attack Port Arthur with frontal assaults or massed bayonet charges. Even the basic army textbooks offered alternative tactics.[49]

Nogi rarely intervened to manage the assaults he ordered; nor did he adjust them in tandem with battlefield conditions, which were always in flux. As a result he almost never tried tactics such as infiltration of weak points, or surprise attacks. His general assaults were almost always held at the end of each month: the first on 19 August, the second on 26 October and the third on 26 November. With such a predictable schedule, it is small wonder that Nogi failed to achieve surprise.[50] When he did try once to create a commando unit for a surprise nocturnal attack during the third general assault, against the advice of most of his staff officers, it ended in disaster. As Ōba warned, the soldiers who were picked from different divisions hardly knew one another and lacked cohesion. To make things worse, they wore *tasuki*, white headbands signifying determination, making them prime targets at night. Far from achieving its target, the unit was eliminated by the Russians on 26 November, the first night of the assault.[51]

Some of Nogi's defenders said that he was a highly effective, charismatic leader, beloved by his troops. That was essentially correct. The Reuters correspondent with the 3rd Army, for example, testified that Nogi 'commanded his army always, in the best possible meaning of the phrase. He possessed the confidence and affection of his officers, and he was universally loved by his men It was partly this that made his soldiers fight as they did.'[52] But that was a big part of the problem. A charismatic general may lead troops better into a direction of their choosing. When this direction is disastrous, charismatic leadership does more harm than good. Nogi's self-assurance deluded his officers. A lieutenant from the 1st Division, for example, wrote in his diary before the frontal attack of 20 August that he and his comrades would probably enter Port Arthur by the 22nd. Delusions of military leaders are always dangerous, and if they are charismatic and beloved, also contagious.[53]

Given such incompetence it is a wonder that Nogi eventually won, though at a terrible price. That could be partly explained by the nature of siege warfare. A fortress cut off from the outside will eventually fall, and, if all else fails, be starved out. Then, Kodama tutored Nogi in the final stage of the siege. And finally, General Stoessel, the Russian commandant of Port Arthur, was even more incompetent than Nogi. However, analysis of corresponding Russian failures (and they were numerous) is beyond the scope of the current chapter.

No one is devoid of weaknesses and blind spots, even generals deemed highly competent. Such weaknesses become 'incompetence' when battlefield conditions require the very skills that one lacks. If, for example, a particular officer is ignorant about naval tides but is well versed in mountain geography, he may shine on high elevations but cause terrible disasters at sea. Generals who have a tendency for nervous breakdowns may function well against conventional and expected adversaries, but crumble when an enemy acts 'off script'. At the same time, efficient institutional culture and competent staffs may mitigate or cover up particular weaknesses of top commanders. Conversely, dysfunctional institutions and unqualified subordinates may aggravate them.

In conventional battlefields, where bravery, persistence and 'on-script' work are rewarded, Nogi could have been just fine. With competent staff officers, he could have even inspired the troops with his leadership and charisma, leaving the daily work, in which he was not skilled, to his subordinates. However, battlefield conditions that required improvisation, flexibility and active involvement highlighted Nogi's weaknesses. The result was disaster.

Nogi's post-war reputation perpetuated this disaster. Even before the cannons had stopped, he had become an untouchable symbol. The newspapers, for example, expunged embarrassing sentences from his post-war report to the emperor 'on grounds of national security'.[54] Even the confidential in-house reports of the army applied self-censorship. Commanders bragged about their units' offensive spirits, underplaying boring details of coordination and logistics. Regimental histories did not elaborate about supply and munitions failures, which were endemic during the siege. Nogi was showered with honours, medals and pageantry in Japan and abroad. After his suicide in 1912, he was declared a 'war god' (*gunshin*), embodying the spirit of his soldiers and their bravery.[55]

Therefore it is unsurprising that the Imperial Army drew dangerous lessons from Nogi's performance. Popular veteran accounts such as Sakurai Tadayoshi's *Human Bullets* ascribed the victory in Port Arthur to the Japanese sacrificial spirit, and celebrated the triumph of elan over matter.[56] In the army, an increasingly strong military faction, identified with long-serving chief of staff Uehara Yūsaku (1915–23), looked down on technology and emphasized 'military spirituality'. As long as soldiers were imbued with mystical loyalty to the emperor and constant readiness to die in the line of duty, they could defeat better-armed, more numerous and stronger adversaries, as they had in Port Arthur.[57] Nogi, with all of his faults, never idolized his chosen tactics. He believed in elan and offensive spirit, like most Japanese (and foreign) commanders of the time, but engaged in frontal assault because he saw no other way. He even confessed (privately) that his tactics were 'unscientific and unstrategical'. His successors, making a virtue out of what even Nogi saw as necessity, blew the horns of military hubris that plagued the Japanese Army until the end of the Pacific War.

The lessons of Port Arthur were no less disastrous abroad. Nogi was venerated not only by Japanese, but by foreign military observers and war correspondents who should have known better. General Sir Ian Hamilton, chief of the British observing mission, famously wrote that Nogi was 'a man of great nobility of character, endowed with a philosophic heroism which penetrates through the mild dignity of his manners and appearance'.[58]

Accordingly, the consensus among military observers was that Nogi won due to the power of the 'Japanese spirit'.[59] After all, in the late nineteenth century a burning question among military professionals concerned the influence of modern firepower on future battlefields. The lessons of Port Arthur were used to silence dissenters who argued that 'old-school' massed infantry attacks are useless against modern fortifications, machine guns and artillery. As far as mainstream critics were concerned, Port Arthur proved that it *was* possible, as long as one possessed resolution, elan and morale.[60] The British official history of the Russo-Japanese War recognized the difficulty of storming fortified positions, but still mostly ascribed the failures of Nogi's general assaults to tactical mistakes, lack of coordination between the attacking forces, or simple misfortune. In the end, the report concluded that 'the siege and defence of a fortress is in essentials what it has always been, since success or failure depends mostly on the spirit shown by either side . . . the struggle will remain for all time as an example of heroic devotion and supreme valour.'[61]

Nogi's eventual victory, and that of Japan in the war, hammered one specific insight almost beyond debate. Just like in the Japanese Army, British and German military observers concluded that the 'spirit' of the attack was the trump card that won the war for Japan.[62] Because Nogi occupied Port Arthur in the end the cost of his victory was forgotten. Indeed, his 'spirited' assaults were praised as the root of his triumph. Very few had asked whether Nogi could have defeated his besieged foes faster and with fewer casualties. The fixation on 'offensive spirit' would trail these armies like a shadow until the disastrous frontal attacks of the First World War, and beyond.

14

ROMANUS IV DIOGENES

Andrew Holt

ew historical battles have been ascribed the significance of
the Battle of Manzikert, which took place in 1071 between
the forces of the Byzantine Empire and the Great Turkish
Empire.[1] The defeat of the Byzantine emperor Romanus IV
Diogenes by Sultan Alp Arslan resulted in a political crisis in
Constantinople, followed by a brief civil war, and opened up Anatolia
to Turkish conquest and settlement in the years that followed. These
circumstances led to Byzantine requests for Western military aid
and prompted Pope Gregory VII to propose in 1074 the creation of an
army of 50,000 Westerners, which he would lead personally, to aid
Eastern Christians in their conflicts with the Seljuk Turks.[2] Gregory's
proposed expedition never materialized, but in the 1090s Byzantine
requests for Western military aid once again intensified due to continued Turkish military threats to important and strategic Byzantine
cities and towns in western Asia Minor. These renewed requests for
military aid by the Byzantine emperor Alexius I Comnenus ultimately
prompted Pope Urban II's calling of the First Crusade in 1095 and,
with it, the birth of the broader crusading movement.[3]

Regardless of the significance of the Battle of Manzikert, the
purpose of this chapter is to argue that the military leadership of
Romanus IV Diogenes merits his inclusion in this volume of the worst
military leaders in history. Romanus belongs on such an ignoble list
due to an extraordinary number of both strategic and tactical errors
of judgement. To be clear, the fact that Romanus was defeated at
Manzikert and that such a defeat may have resulted in disastrous
consequences for the Byzantine Empire in the years that followed is

Alp Arslan humiliating Romanus IV, illumination from Giovanni Boccaccio,
Les Cas des nobles hommes et femmes, 15th century, Bibliothèque nationale de
France, MS Français 232, fol. 323.

not the reason for such a negative view of his military leadership. It is certainly true that sometimes even good military leaders, using sound and reasonable judgement, can nevertheless lose important military conflicts. Instead, Romanus made a series of easily categorized blunders, with greater and lesser degrees of culpability on his part, leading up to and during the battle that a wiser commander would not have made. Moreover, many of these blunders could well have represented the difference between victory and defeat.

The circumstances leading to Romanus' failure and the collapse of Byzantine authority in Asia Minor were set in motion decades before he came to power in 1068. Only 43 years earlier, the Byzantine Empire was at a high point in terms of military power and security at the end of the reign of Basil II (*r.* 976–1025). The lengthy reign of Basil the Bulgar-Slayer, as Basil II was known, had strengthened the empire and accelerated a process of expansion that began with his predecessors at least as early as 955. It was during this time that the empire prospered as a result of its superior military organization and competent administrative infrastructure, while its enemies were otherwise in decline.[4] During this time the Byzantine Empire expanded into three disparate regions, including Bulgaria, the Georgian and Armenian east, and Muslim areas to the southeast.[5] Byzantine soldiers prided themselves on their order and discipline, and were inspired by emperors like Basil II, who often personally took command of armies in the field.[6]

Although experiencing much success from the mid-tenth century until 1025, the traditional Byzantine military organization emphasizing provincial theme armies, raised from the various administrative districts, underwent significant changes during this period as well, which would also have the unintended effect of helping to usher in a period of decline in the wake of Basil II's reign.[7] During the latter part of the tenth century, the Byzantine army embraced a much more offensive tactical structure, corresponding with the needs of the previously mentioned territorial expansion. These efforts required professional soldiers who could operate more effectively than the only seasonally available theme armies.[8] New organization, competent leaders, effective logistics and the tactical capabilities offered by the recruitment of professional mercenary soldiers initially led to many military successes for the Byzantine Empire in the latter half of the tenth century and the early eleventh.[9]

Yet, as such efforts to incorporate and rely on new elements of professional mercenaries, both foreign and indigenous to the empire, into the Byzantine army continued, the theme armies were increasingly neglected, especially after Basil II's death in 1025.[10] By the middle of the eleventh century, Byzantine forces had become a mix of mercenary units, older thematic forces and foreign units. The Varangian Guard, for example, established during the reign of Basil II to act as his bodyguard, represented a corps of mercenaries from Russia, Scandinavia and, by the eleventh century, the British Isles.[11] Although ably managed under rulers like Basil II, this situation brought about varying levels of discipline, allegiance and commitment to service that would troublingly manifest themselves in the era leading up to the Battle of Manzikert in 1071.

Additionally, there were two other major causes of military decline or weakness during the period from 1025 to 1071, namely the debilitating effects of extensive civil–military strife and the loss of Armenia as a military stronghold and buffer for Byzantine holdings in Asia Minor. During the period following Basil II's rule, Byzantine emperors and their ambitious generals were often distrustful of each other as they battled for authority and popularity, an issue that intensified during the reign of Constantine IX from 1042 to 1055. In addition to relying on mercenaries, emperors sought to reduce the authority of generals, deprived their armies of funds, and replaced otherwise capable commanders with less capable ones who were considered to be more loyal to the crown.[12]

Moreover, during the period following Basil's reign, wasteful spending in an effort to reclaim control over Italy, as well as building projects and court largesse, depleted imperial finances and impacted Byzantine security in Asia Minor. During the reign of Constantine IX, for example, the emperor had to debase the gold coinage, which lowered the value of military pay, hurting morale among the troops. Even more significantly, to save money, in 1053 Constantine demobilized 50,000 thematic troops who were protecting the Armenian frontier and serving as a buffer to Turkish expansion into Asia Minor. Only two years later, by 1055, the Seljuk Turks during the reign of Tughril Beg would take advantage of this situation to raid into Armenia and Eastern Anatolia with little opposition.[13]

The Armenian chronicler Matthew of Edessa, who despised the Byzantines, described such circumstances in grim terms, claiming they were the cause of Armenian weakness and defeat during the eleventh century. He noted, for example, how the 'effeminate' Byzantines had disbanded the brave soldiers who had been defending Armenia and replaced them with 'eunuch generals and troops', who were presumably more loyal to the emperors. According to Matthew,

> whenever they [Byzantine leaders] found a brave and mighty man, they blinded him or threw him into the sea and drowned him ... [they also transformed] brave young men into eunuchs ... [who] spoke meekly and softly just like women ... Thus, because of them, all the faithful were subjected to servitude.[14]

Consequently, as historian Albert Friendly has noted, at the end of this destructive process the Byzantine civil leadership had nothing to fear from its military, but then, neither did its enemies.[15]

The decline in Byzantine military effectiveness took place at a crucial time when new threats emerged in the eleventh century that would further complicate matters for the Byzantines. Besides the Seljuk Turks, they also included the Normans, who by the mid-1050s were challenging the Byzantine provinces of Apulia and Calabria, and the Pechenegs, a Turkic threat from the steppe lands north of the Black Sea.[16] Yet, in consideration of Romanus and his military leadership here, the rise of the Turks represented the most pressing concern for the Byzantine Empire. Indeed, as historian Anthony Kaldellis has argued, 'The Seljuk conquests represented the most pivotal moment in the history of the Near East since the Arab conquests of the seventh century.'[17]

Although the Byzantines were able to negotiate a treaty with the Turks in 1055, it failed to stop raids into Asia Minor and nearby areas. In the years that followed, numerous Byzantine cities, including Melitene, Sebasteia and Ani, were attacked and sacked by Turkish forces.[18] Yet, Turkish efforts in Byzantine areas up to this point, although often experiencing success, were not as focused as they might have been. Such raids were mostly carried out by nomadic Turcoman soldiers, who supplemented the Seljuk armies. Turkish rulers like Tughril tried to pacify such warriors by allowing them to wander and raid the edges of the Turkish Empire, and the Byzantine territories represented those edges. It is unlikely that the Seljuk leaders could have entirely controlled them anyway and may have only begun to lead occasional Turcoman raids primarily as a means of gaining greater influence over them, giving them opportunities for large-scale raiding.[19] During this period the Seljuks were far more concerned with the Fatimids in Egypt than they were with the Byzantines in Asia Minor, but from the Byzantine perspective, the Turkish raids came to represent a major security concern requiring drastic action.[20]

Alp Arslan first came to power as the second sultan of the Seljuk Empire in 1063, after his uncle Tughril died the same year. Early in his reign he focused on securing his position as sultan of the Seljuks against the claims of another uncle and his brother, as well as maintaining control over his nomadic Turcoman followers, whom he otherwise depended on militarily.[21] Alp Arslan often led his Turcoman troops on campaigns against the Christian kingdoms of the Caucasus, including Georgia and Armenia. He did so in an effort to keep the Turcomans both busy and content with raiding opportunities, as well as to direct their efforts in ways that he felt would help secure the frontiers of his empire while he focused on his primary opponent, the Fatimids. Such efforts, led by a Turkish Sunni Muslim sultan, were presented by contemporary Muslim sources as jihad, providing Alp Arslan an opportunity to both demonstrate his religious commitment and help legitimize his authority.[22] One of the more notable Turkish attacks on Byzantine holdings came in 1067, when the Seljuks reached and sacked Caesarea, pillaging the town, desecrating its cathedral and causing alarm throughout the empire.[23] The call for something to be done to address the Turkish threat increased, but Emperor Constantine x died the same year, thereby putting the pressure to respond on his successor, Romanus iv Diogenes.

Romanus, a popular general from a wealthy and distinguished family, married the widow of the emperor and came to the throne in January 1068.[24] Once in power, Romanus immediately set about restoring order to the empire and security and control in Asia Minor, but his efforts were hindered by various factors. The Byzantine contemporary historian Michael Attaleiates, who served as an important adviser to Romanus and is the best surviving source for his reign, describes, for example, how huge numbers of relatives sought to advise and influence the emperor to their own ends.[25] Additionally, Romanus had to deal with the hostility of considerable portions of the military, especially among foreign troops and mercenaries, on whom the empire depended. The Varangian Guard, for example, resented Romanus' favouritism towards native Byzantine troops, and such hostility and distrust between the emperor and his troops would lead to many problems during Romanus' reign, as he embarked on a series of military campaigns against the Turks.[26]

When Romanus came to power, he was an experienced military campaigner and was confident in his ability to develop a plan to restore Byzantine security. Unlike his predecessors, Romanus sought to take the fight to the Turks, outside of Byzantine frontiers, rather than maintaining a defensive posture, and this strategy was reflected in the three campaigns he led personally from 1068 to 1071.[27] In the case of the first campaign from 1068 to 1069, Romanus initially headed for Armenia in an effort to reverse Turkish military gains, but during the expedition he became concerned over the situation in Syria and focused his efforts there. His efforts in Syria strengthened some key strategic areas, such as Antioch, but contemporary sources also suggest that there were a number of missed opportunities and poor performances by the Byzantine army. Attaleiates, who as a member of the military tribunal accompanied Romanus on his campaigns, and who is perhaps among the most sympathetic of contemporary sources towards the emperor for the period, condemned the cowardice, ineptness and lack of motivation of the troops during the campaign.[28]

In the second campaign in 1069, Romanus had fewer achievements than during his first. Among his chief goals was to put down a rebellion in Armenia led by a European mercenary named Krispinos, who had previously fought well for the Byzantine Empire, but felt unappreciated and under-compensated.[29] Krispinos sought to reconcile with Romanus, but the emperor refused, resulting in the exile of a capable commander and his forces, who in response then took to raiding and further weakening the region.[30] The emperor's engagements with the Turks during this campaign proved entirely ineffective, with embarrassing episodes at times involving the retreat and desertion of many of his troops at the sight of Turkish forces, even allowing their equipment to fall into the hands of the enemy.[31] At one point, when Romanus became aware that Turks were pushing into Cappadocia, targeting the city of Iconium (now Konya), he abandoned his efforts in Armenia to head back to Cappadocia. Romanus arrived too late to prevent the sacking of Iconium and even failed to cut off the slow-moving Turks, weighed down with plunder, as they escaped through the mountains of Cilicia. With nothing left to do, a discouraged Romanus led his army back to Constantinople. Romanus' efforts during both campaigns were heavily criticized by the politically influential eleventh-century monk, court adviser and historian Michael Psellus, a major critic of Romanus' reign and a political enemy. Psellus noted that the second campaign was especially unproductive, resulting in thousands of Byzantine deaths for the capture of only a small number of enemy prisoners.[32]

Although Romanus had led two campaigns during the first two years of his reign, he was prevented from doing so in 1070 on account of the manoeuvring of his political opponents in the capital.[33] Yet, as emperor, Romanus was still expected to provide security for Byzantine holdings in the east, and so had to entrust his generals with the task. Romanus appointed as general Manuel Comnenus to lead eastern armies against the Turks and initially Manuel won acclaim for his effectiveness. Attaleiates suggests that this provoked envy on the part of Romanus, who then ordered a significant part of Manuel's forces to be sent to Syria to relieve the besieged city of Hierapolis (now Manbij).[34] This significantly depleted Manuel's forces, leading to Manuel's defeat and humiliating capture at Sebasteia by the Turkish leader Erisgen, who was a rebellious relative of the sultan Alp Arslan. During his captivity, Manuel convinced Erisgen to take him to Constantinople, where they could negotiate an alliance against Alp Arslan. In response, the sultan sent his emir Afsin to demand that the empire turn over the rebel Erisgen, and if they did not it would invalidate an earlier Byzantine–Seljuk treaty that had prevented mass plundering in Asia Minor. Romanus refused and the Turks then attacked Byzantine possessions, devastating many areas.

Afsin returned to Alp Arslan in the spring of 1071, reporting that the Byzantines had no way to defend against his forces and that Asia Minor would be essentially his for the taking if he chose to do so. Fortunately for the Byzantines, the sultan had no desire to capture Asia Minor at that time, as his focus was instead on his Fatimid enemies and preparations for an invasion of Egypt. Setting out from Khurasan in either late 1070 or early 1071, the sultan likely sought to guard his rear from attack by capturing Manzikert (now Malazgirt) and other Armenian or Byzantine cities as he headed south.[35] These actions caused considerable worry in Constantinople, and prompted Romanus to act by leading his third, and final, campaign to the east.

Although in 1070 Romanus had made strategic decisions from Constantinople that hindered the ability of his generals, such as

Manuel Comnenus, to carry out their duties against the Turks, he nevertheless made some efforts during this period to improve the morale and effectiveness of the Byzantine army. Among these efforts, he made sure that soldiers were compensated for any overdue pay they deserved, upgraded some military equipment, implemented new training regimens for the troops and recruited additional mercenaries for his army. Romanus' first two campaigns in 1068 and 1069 had convinced him of the need for such reforms and more professional soldiers, and so the mercenary ranks of his army swelled.[36] To his eventual detriment, Romanus would come to rely on these non-Byzantine troops of often-questionable loyalty during the Manzikert campaign.

Romanus also allowed his concerns about political circumstances in Constantinople to factor into his military preparations for the Manzikert campaign. His rivals included Michael Psellus, who had influence over the young co-emperor Michael VII, and members of the wealthy and powerful Doukas family, which included John Doukas, who served as caesar and member of the Byzantine senate. Romanus made the decision to take Andronikos Doukas, John Doukas' oldest son, on his Manzikert campaign, making him a general in his forces. He probably did this only so Andronikos could serve as a hostage, making the Doukas family less likely to initiate a coup during his absence. Yet assigning a political enemy wishing to see the emperor's downfall to such an important role in his army's leadership would prove to be a major mistake.

It was under these circumstances that Romanus, confident of the effectiveness of his reforms of the Byzantine army, finally headed out on his third and final campaign in March 1071. Only a month earlier, Romanus had agreed to a truce with the sultan Alp Arslan, which gave the emperor a little more time to prepare for his campaign against the Turks and led the sultan to believe he could focus on his primary enemy, the Fatimids. Romanus' goal was to secure the border between Anatolia and Armenia from Turkish penetration and possibly to secure the Lake Van region as a potential staging ground for future conflicts with Alp Arslan's forces.[37]

Various figures have been provided for the size of Romanus' army, once its parts came together, with modern historians typically estimating a figure between 40,000 and 48,000, excluding camp followers, and medieval Byzantine sources suggesting far higher, but certainly inflated, figures in the hundreds of thousands.[38] Whatever the final number, the army was quite large for the time and would have been comprised of imperial tagmata, thematic troops from Anatolia and Syria, private levies of Anatolian landholders, Armenian troops and numerous foreign troops led by their own commanders.[39]

As Romanus travelled across Asia Minor, gathering levies of troops, the campaign was beset by problems. The effort to collect the Anatolian levies was hindered by the fact that Turkish raiding had flushed conscripts out of the cities into the countryside, making it hard to round them up efficiently. Once the army reached the Byzantine base at Cryapege, undisciplined Frankish mercenaries began raiding the surrounding areas, forcing Romanus to intervene, resulting in the vanquishing of the Frankish contingent by the remainder of Romanus' army. Moreover, while travelling from Sebasteia to Theodosiopolis (now Erzurum), Romanus' troops witnessed the still-exposed corpses of Byzantine soldiers who had died fighting in Manuel Comnenus' failed efforts a year earlier, which damaged morale and confidence. They also had to deal with the logistical hardships of travelling through lands that had been devastated by warfare and Turkish raiding that had destroyed agricultural elements of those areas, requiring the Byzantine army to carry enough supplies to provision tens of thousands of troops daily.[40] These challenges aside, Romanus and his forces were able to arrive in the Lake Van region in late August, a little over five months after they had embarked from Constantinople.

Once at Lake Van, Romanus made the fateful decision to divide his troops, sending an estimated 25,000 of his best troops under the command of the general Joseph Tarchaneiotes to retake the city of Chliat (now Ahlat), while Romanus continued on to Manzikert with the remaining 23,000 troops. This decision was based in part on intelligence reports claiming that Alp Arslan, who had been besieging Aleppo until he heard of Romanus' actions, was making haste to the Armenian frontier to confront Romanus' forces, but along the way his army had been severely diminished due to a dangerous river crossing and desertion.[41] In response, Romanus sought to secure control of both Chliat and Manzikert quickly, before the sultan arrived with whatever forces he could muster. Romanus and his forces quickly retook the walled fortress city of Manzikert from a small garrison that included Seljuk soldiers, then they camped outside the city overnight with the plan of linking up with the remainder of his army in Chliat, about 47 kilometres (29 mi.) away, the next day.

The intelligence on which Romanus based his decisions while at Lake Van was faulty, as Alp Arlsan still commanded a sizeable force and it would swell as he incorporated thousands of additional Muslim forces as he moved into Armenian territory. While camped outside Manzikert, Byzantine forces foraging in the area were surprised by a Seljuk force, whom they initially believed were only Turcoman raiders, but were actually the vanguard of Alp Arslan's army. In response, Romanus sent Nikephoros Bryennios with a force to deal with what the emperor understood to be merely a small force of raiders. When Bryennios found the Seljuk force much more formidable than he expected, he called on Romanus to send reinforcements. Romanus initially declined, accusing his general of cowardice, before eventually relenting and sending a relief force that succeeded in temporarily dispersing the Turks, but paid a heavy price for their efforts. The leader of the relief force, Vasilak Basilakes, was captured in the effort and surviving Byzantine troops returned from the engagement with heavy injuries.[42] This finally alerted Romanus to the seriousness of the situation. He assembled his troops to mount a counter-attack, but by then the Turks had dispersed. Romanus returned to his camp, where he and his forces would suffer harassment from Seljuk forces overnight.

The harassment of Romanus' troops began when Uze mercenaries left the fortified camp during the night to buy provisions from local merchants. The Seljuks attacked the Uze troops, forcing them to rush back to the Byzantine camp, where some of them were then attacked by Byzantine forces, who mistook them for Turks. The Turks then spent the remainder of the night making noise and shooting arrows into the Byzantine encampment.[43] During this night about a thousand Uze mercenaries also defected to the Seljuks, turning on their former Byzantine masters and undoubtedly providing them with valuable information on the size and capabilities of Romanus' army.[44] This event caused concern about the loyalty of the many other mercenary troops that Romanus was counting on and the overall effectiveness of the Byzantine army at this stage.

Regardless of these concerns, Romanus believed that he had significant reserve forces at Chliat, around 25,000, that could make their way to aid his slightly smaller force at Manzikert, and so he wanted to engage the Turks quickly. So confident was he in this assumption that Romanus even rejected a late and surprising peace offer made by an envoy of the Abbasid caliph Al-Qaim, extended with Alp Arslan's agreement, likely in an effort to avoid derailing the sultan's planned efforts against the Fatimids.[45] The campaign had been very expensive and Romanus would need something substantial to show for his efforts if he were to fend off the criticisms of his political enemies in Constantinople, and having the opportunity of engaging directly in battle with the army of the sultan represented a rare opportunity. Consequently, Romanus wanted war, but what the emperor did not know was that Tarchaneiotes and his forces had abandoned their efforts when they became aware of the arrival of Alp Arslan and his troops at Lake Van, heading back to Anatolia and abandoning Romanus and his forces at Manzikert. On 25 August Romanus sent messengers to Chliat in an unknowingly futile effort to recall his now non-existent reserve forces and prepared the troops he had under his direct command to fight the Seljuks on the next day. Romanus wanted to move quickly, believing that the sultan was trying to avoid such a conflict, likely to stall for time to allow for more reinforcements to arrive.[46] On the morning of Friday 26 August both armies prepared for battle, with the Byzantines marching out of their camp and initiating the conflict.[47]

Historian Brian Todd Carey has argued that the precise location of the Battle of Manzikert is hard to pin down due to the 'fluid nature' of the conflict, but that modern historians believe it took place somewhere within a 103 square-kilometre (40 sq. mi.) area of the steppe to the south or southeast of the city.[48] Whatever the size of Romanus' army by this time, perhaps somewhere between 20,000 and 22,000 troops, it was likely, to some degree, larger than the forces Alp Arslan had collected up to this point, which could also partly explain both the reluctance of Alp Arslan and the eagerness of Romanus to engage. Various elements of the battle are uncertain or unclear from the sources, which can be contradictory at times. For example, information is inexact regarding at what time of day the battle took place, how many skirmishes took place before the primary battle, or how long Byzantine and Seljuk forces engaged each other during their primary battle.[49]

Historians have constructed essentially two different accounts of the Battle of Manzikert based on primary sources.[50] One version, dependent on the claims of Michael Attaleiates, was that Romanus led his forces in an effort to chase retreating Turks, but only served to draw Byzantine forces away from their now largely unguarded camp. Romanus, fearing an ambush, gave the order to turn around, but this was misinterpreted by his troops as a call to retreat, which suggested the emperor had fallen and caused a panic. Attaleiates claimed Andronikos Doukas started this rumour and ordered the troops under his command back to the camp, leaving the emperor out in front of the army with few troops to protect him, leading to his capture by the Turks.[51] In this version, no major engagement took place between the two forces due to the blunders of Byzantine forces or the treachery of their leaders. The other version describes a more formal battle between Turkish and Byzantine forces, with the Turks defeating the right wing of the Byzantine forces at Manzikert, but ends in the same result, with the capture of Romanus and the retreat of the forces under his general Andronikos.[52] In both versions, the bulk of the Byzantine army is with Trachaneiotes and not present for the battle as a result of Romanus' earlier decision to split up the army.

One small glimmer of good fortune for Romanus, in the wake of his capture by the sultan, is that Alp Arslan was still focused on his Fatimid enemies, viewing his engagement with the Byzantines as a distraction, so he made no demands for Byzantine territory and ultimately released the emperor in exchange for a moderate ransom.[53] Nevertheless, even with such a favourable response by the sultan, things did not end well for Romanus or the Byzantine Empire. While the emperor was a prisoner, Michael Psellos and the Doukas family conspired to have Michael VII Doukas proclaimed the legitimate emperor, resulting in a civil war between the rival emperors. Romanus was ultimately defeated, overthrown and blinded by his enemies, before dying in August 1072.[54]

At this point, it seems worthwhile to recap the various errors and mistakes that took place under Romanus' leadership prior to and during the Manzikert campaign that would influence its outcome. These mistakes and errors of judgement might be divided into three often overlapping categories. They include Romanus' poor political leadership and judgement, fundamental strategic errors, and poor tactical decisions on the battlefield.

A number of problems stemmed from Romanus' poor political leadership or judgement. This includes the appointment of Andronikos Doukas as a general in his forces. The Doukas family was powerful politically and a major rival of Romanus', and therefore would have been happy to see Romanus fail. While the emperor likely thought that having Andronikos along gave him the equivalent of a hostage to help limit the political scheming or manoeuvring of the Doukas family in Constantinople, it also planted a dedicated enemy among his higher ranks.[55] Bringing him on the campaign, and assigning him an important strategic role in it, proved to be a very poor choice at Manzikert, as Andronikos and the forces he led betrayed the emperor at a key moment during the conflict.

Romanus also made the mistake of relying on many foreign troops of questionable loyalty and dedication. Although the use of foreign troops had become normalized under past emperors, their use during the mid-eleventh century contributed to the neglect of the theme armies. Yet past emperors like Basil II had been able to manage such troops effectively, in a way that would not be repeated by later emperors like Romanus. Rather than reforming Byzantine forces to significantly lessen his dependence on foreign troops and mercenaries, Romanus simply continued with the framework of his immediate predecessors, even expanding his efforts for the recruitment of mercenaries and swelling his ranks with Armenians, Georgians, Arabs, Bulgars, Rus, Khazars, Uze, Pechenegs, Normans and Franks.[56] As a result, by the time of the Battle of Manzikert in 1071, Byzantine forces were a mix of troops significantly dependent on mercenary and foreign forces, which were often hostile to Romanus as a result of his clear favouritism towards Byzantine troops, and thus also often troublemaking and unmotivated.

These issues played out during the Manzikert campaign on multiple occasions. As noted earlier, unruly Frankish mercenaries had to be put down by the remainder of Romanus' army soon after their arrival at Cryapege, but the emperor's most significant problems with foreign troops were caused by the Uze mercenaries. Although the administration of an oath of loyalty to the Byzantine cause had been given to Uze mercenaries in 1071, it appears to have meant little to them at key points during the campaign, leading up to the overnight defection of a thousand troops to the Seljuk cause before Manzikert.[57] Why the Uze troops defected is not certain, but could have been the result of their exposure to Turkish forces that night and concern over their strength, anger over attacks by Byzantine forces upon their return to camp or, as historian Jonathan Harris has implied, their shared racial and ethnic background with the Turks, or some overlapping combination of these reasons.[58]

Perhaps the most notable political miscalculation contributing to the Byzantine failure at Manzikert was Romanus' rejection of peace initiatives offered by Alp Arslan at a time when military circumstances were far from ideal for the emperor, with only half of his forces at his command. As described earlier, the sultan had not initially set out to confront the Byzantines and sought to make peace so that his focus could return to the Fatimids, and so he offered peace to the emperor prior to the Battle of Manzikert. Although Romanus was likely unaware of how close the sultan's forces were at the time he considered the peace offer, he reportedly declined it because he was concerned about how it might look in Constantinople if he returned, after so much time and expense, without having engaged the enemy in battle.[59] Unfortunately for Romanus, the rejection of the peace offer and continuation of the conflict would result in far greater humiliation as a result of his defeat and capture.

Romanus also made a number of key strategic and tactical errors that led to his failure at Manzikert. For example, the emperor failed to listen to the counsel of his leading generals, Tachaneiotes and Nicephoris Bryennius, who advised him not to leave Theodosiopolis during the campaign, which they thought was a more favourable place to fight. Instead, Romanus aggressively pushed east with the goal of recapturing the fortresses of Manzikert and Chliat.[60] Perhaps most notably, once at Manzikert, Romanus incautiously decided to divide his army based on poor intelligence, sending more than half of his troops to Chliat, apparently unaware of the proximity of the sultan's forces. Indeed, throughout the Manzikert campaign, Romanus seems to have relied on faulty intelligence, and his failure to either create a better system for gathering accurate information or, at the least, demonstrate more caution in accepting and operating with the poor intelligence available to him, is Romanus' fault alone.

Once engaged in battle, Romanus' forces were also poorly led, poorly disciplined and often confused. Turkish forces employed a crescent formation during the battle, feigning a retreat that drew Byzantine forces out of their fortified positions to give chase, resulting in their near encirclement by the Turks, who then employed cavalry to further carve the Christian army into smaller groups made vulnerable to annihilation. When Romanus ordered his forces to retreat, the imperial standard was turned around to communicate this intention, but the sign was misinterpreted by many of his troops to mean the emperor had been defeated or killed, resulting in panic in the Byzantine ranks and disaster on the battlefield. In desperation, Romanus ordered the troops to turn around to fight again, at which point the rearguard led by Andronikos Doukas abandoned the battlefield, demoralizing the rest of the Byzantine army as the Turks could now attack from the rear and plunder the Byzantine camp for booty.[61]

In the end, regardless of the problems Romanus inherited when he became emperor, his inability to properly recognize and reform institutional failings in the Byzantine military, assemble loyal officers and committed troops around him, and gather useful intelligence and adjust his strategy accordingly during the campaign were all failures of leadership on his part. Although he was an experienced military commander, his troops were, nevertheless, ineffectively managed and poorly disciplined under his leadership on the battlefield, contributing to problems that a more careful and competent commander could have foreseen and avoided.

15

LORD WOLSELEY

Joseph Moretz

T he reputation of Field Marshal Viscount Garnet Wolseley stood so high in his day that the commonplace 'All Sir Garnet' required no explanation to a nineteenth-century British public blessed with many heroes. Hartington, the Secretary of State for War, without resorting to irony, could refer to 'our only General' when writing to Granville, the Foreign Secretary.[1] Behind such accolades remained an officer of singular fortune demonstrating vision and valour in the varied locales where the British Army served, be it Crimea, China, India, Canada, the Gold Coast and, most recently, Egypt. That by itself was not unusual for a Victorian officer, but that he commanded several of these expeditions perhaps was. Asked to explain his success, Wolseley remarked, 'I never fight unless I know that I am certain to win.'[2]

Discernment, then, set him apart from contemporaries and, allowing that General Sir William Butler was far from an unbiased observer, his conclusion that Wolseley 'was the best and most brilliant brain I ever met in the British army' attests to an officer of unique abilities.[3] Given to reflection, he had already published a history of Britain's war with China and, more importantly, *The Soldier's Pocket-book for Field Service.*[4] That he sought as much in others is demonstrated by those members of his inner circle known as the 'Ashanti Ring' who had passed through the Staff College, including Field-Marshal Sir Evelyn Wood and Major General Sir Herbert Stewart.[5] Moreover, Wolseley displayed those qualities of paternal care over subordinates that have become a trademark of British officership. Purchasing pipes from his own funds for the troops engaged in the Sudan and recommending soldiers receive double pay for every day spent south of Aswan or in the Suakin environ suggest an officer who, if playing favourites, also favoured those who mattered. As such, writing to his wife, Wolseley paid his warmest tribute to the individual redcoat, remarking, 'I turn my back upon Khartoum with a sinking heart, and, as I look back at the events of the last four months, my mind dwells upon one bright spot only, the splendid conduct of the private soldier: he is a splendid fellow.'[6] This was more than professional pride: when not looking after his men, Wolseley lent a kindly hand to a spendthrift brother, a spinster sister and an ageing, widowed mother. Clearly, there was much about Wolseley worthy of admiration.

Yet, the campaign planned, organized and commanded by Wolseley to rescue Major General Charles Gordon, conducted in the autumn of 1884 and culminating with the fall of Khartoum in January 1885, was a terrible failure. If Wolseley escaped immediate blame for the debacle, he nevertheless bears responsibility for orchestrating events. His disbandment of the Egyptian Army in September 1882 following the defeat of Colonel Ahmed Urabi's forces at Tel el-Kebir created the space for the Mahdi's rebellion in the Sudan to prosper. Responding to the unrest created, Britain first dispatched Gordon, and, when that proved insufficient, Wolseley commanding thousands of soldiers. Returning home in July 1885, Wolseley never experienced active service again, though continuing to serve the army he loved for another fifteen years.[7]

It had all been so different three years previously. Then, careful planning and prior reconnaissance by the Admiralty and the War Office had mapped Egyptian defences, and, armed with this information, a plan dating from 1875 for securing the Suez Canal and other key points was updated.[8] Thus the landings of August may have been rushed, but they were never rash. Final success at Tel el-Kebir following a brilliant night march led by the then 49-year-old Wolseley concluded a brief, but highly significant, campaign: to wit, Urabi and the Nationalists were banished, Khedival authority was restored, and Britain stood supreme in Egypt. Not without justification, Wolseley returned to England a hero to receive a barony and the gift of £30,000.[9]

As Wolseley resumed his duties as adjutant general at the War Office, Egypt's problems in Sudan increasingly were becoming Britain's as the latter assumed paramount authority. The reasons were

Garnet Wolseley,
1st Viscount
Wolseley, *c.* 1884.

financial, for while Egypt may have been willing to intervene in Sudan, it was also bankrupt. Thus, an appeal to the Sultan, Egypt's nominal sovereign, to restore control in Sudan following an uprising led by Muḥammad Aḥmad ibn al-Saiyid ʿAbd Allāh, a religious warrior cum Sunni prophet forever known as the Mahdī, advanced no further owing to Cairo's inability to meet the costs of deploying Turkish troops. Here, British disbandment of the Egyptian Army, a move overseen by Wolseley in 1882, presented a complicating factor. While the Khedive, Méhémet Tawfiq, would have liked to employ his own army, presently it was being reformed under Valentine Baker, a cashiered British officer in the employ of the Sultan.[10]

Strategically and economically, retention of Sudan made perfect sense given the centrality of the Nile to Egypt's economy. Still, it was a proposition Egypt could not afford in the near term. Emphasizing the finance factor, Sir Evelyn Baring, scion of the famous banking house, arrived in Cairo in September 1883. Very much London's man, Baring served as Consul General to the Khedive and remained the power behind the throne. As for evacuating Sudan, retention of its Red Sea ports persisted as an important British aim. Thus it was a qualified evacuation that London insisted upon. For the Khedive, that remained a surrender too far. Unable to send an army, he sent an officer.

Enter Lieutenant-Colonel William Hicks, late of the Bombay Staff Corps. He proceeded to Khartoum in February 1883 to reorganize Egypt's Sudanese garrisons before tackling the Mahdi's rebellion. Hicks Pasha aimed to defeat the rebels in the Kordofan, a desolate, scorching environment southwest of Khartoum. If the region lacked few sources of water, then it possessed a surfeit of adherents to the Mahdi's cause.[11] Beginning well in a number of minor skirmishes, Hicks and 11,000 troops were annihilated at Shaykan in November 1883.[12] More drubbings were in store for the Khedive and, from these failures, the call to send Gordon to Sudan followed.[13]

Ostensibly Gordon's mission was to specify how Egypt's Sudanese garrisons might be evacuated. That fig leaf may be discounted for one did not need to send a general to render such an assessment.[14] A fair conclusion is that Gordon's mission undertaken in January 1884 was from the beginning designed to assume command of Khartoum's forces. General Gordon's initial thoughts were to evacuate all via the town of Berber on the Nile and the port of Suakin on the Red Sea.[15] Unfortunately, between Gordon's London departure and his arrival in Khartoum on 18 February, further misfortunes ensued. Most prominently, Baker, leading a ragtag collection of troops, was routed at El Teb.[16] This moved Wolseley to argue for the despatch of British reinforcements. Reluctantly, the Cabinet authorized the deployment of a brigade from those British troops occupying Egypt.[17]

The expanding military crisis gave vent to a political crisis, for British Near East policy appeared to be in tatters. Direct intervention remained unpopular in many European capitals, including London, with the Tories charging that Gladstone's actions towards Egypt were feckless, if not dishonest and illegal.[18] Ensuring the safety of the Suez Canal had brought British forces to Egypt. Disengaging, though, proved exceedingly difficult. Egypt's continuing instability was one reason, but another was aspects of prestige that anchored British rule in India. Matters of prestige weighed heavily on Wolseley, but so too did the worsening situation confronting Gordon, who had yet to reach Khartoum. By announcing that it would not fight for Sudan, Wolseley held that Britain was forfeiting the support of tribes not aligned with the uprising. With British forces also besieged at Suakin, Wolseley desired to see a protectorate proclaimed over eastern Sudan. Otherwise, Gordon, the presumed rescuer, would require rescuing himself. To be sure, Wolseley was not guaranteeing even this would be successful. It merely offered the chance of forestalling a greater failure at a much higher cost later.[19]

Implicit in the decision to send an officer of Gordon's stature was that Britain would send others if necessary. In April Wolseley proposed a Nile autumn advance by 6,500 British troops. The Cabinet, however, remained deeply divided. If publicly London remained firmly against rescuing Gordon, then change was discernible. Reluctantly, Gladstone accepted a commitment in the summer of 1884 from which he had shrunk the previous winter. Sudan may not yet have been an imperial interest, but Egypt certainly was and, ever the more so, was British standing in the East.[20]

A campaign in Sudan was never going to be easy given the 'primitive regional infrastructure, vast distances, hostile environmental conditions, poorly understood geography and a determined enemy' to be overcome.[21] Accordingly, it called for a rigorous analysis of alternatives. Failure might yet ensue, especially as the one requiring rescue – Gordon – was such a mercurial commodity. Time was the great unknown and it remained for Wolseley to fashion a plan respecting this critical element. Yes, the politicians had dithered, but that only emphasized the need for alacrity once the decision had been rendered.[22] Wolseley, however, discounted any approach to Khartoum not anchored on the Nile, notwithstanding the arguments of those serving in Egypt with General Sir Frederick Stephenson and Major General Sir Andrew Clarke, commander of the Royal Engineers, at the forefront. The latter proposed constructing a rail line from Suakin to Berber, from whence the Nile and subsequently Khartoum could be reached.[23] At £1.2 million, its cost alone was one barrier to pursuing the endeavour. That the railway's course had not been surveyed remained another.[24] Still, those considerations were no less true after Gordon's demise when the government sanctioned a Suakin–Berber approach. It would have been better to have adopted a Nile approach employing the British Army and a Suakin–Berber advance using elements of the Indian Army. Success might not have ensued, but it would have forced the Mahdī to meet two distinct threats. Exactly why Wolseley did not adopt such a plan is unknown, but two considerations must be noted. First, Wolseley saw the problem as a replay of his 1870 Canadian Red River advance. Second, Wolseley dared not risk another general beating him to Khartoum.

Though the government had yet to commit to an expedition, measures proceeded apace with British troops moving south to Aswan. On 16 May Hartington proposed a joint Admiralty and War Office Working Group. Gladstone deflated the initiative by insisting the War Office settle its own affairs first.[25] Thus in the absence of formal concurrence and minus an approved plan, the War Office began laying the groundwork for both Nile and Suakin–Berber operations. Yet the failure of the Cabinet to address Sudan matters in a timely fashion doomed the prospect of Suakin–Berber operations.

In late July word arrived in London that Berber had fallen to the rebels on 26 May. This invalidated the assumption that a Suakin-centred force could be held back until a rail line was completed. More significantly, the window to construct a rail line had evaporated with the onset of the African summer. Hartington thus wired Stephenson that a Nile-anchored approach was likely. Still, Stephenson persisted in touting the advantages of a Suakin–Berber route. Such advocacy did Stephenson little credit and for his pains he was jettisoned as the presumptive commander for the expedition and replaced by Wolseley.[26]

Stephenson's advocacy of a Suakin–Berber advance exasperated Hartington and Wolseley. That it required troops Britain did not have is one explanation. That Wolseley believed a full-scale expedition could yet be avoided remains another. That belief, however, assumed that a compliant Gordon would not merely wait to be rescued.[27] Meanwhile, Wolseley proceeded to Egypt. His departure represented another halfway choice, for the decision to save Gordon had not yet been made. Once in Egypt, Wolseley assessed how Khartoum might be relieved before the end of the year. Agreeing now to provide the necessary troops, the War Office advised their employment beyond Dongola remained to be sanctioned. Here, bluff and self-deception were on display. Wolseley argued that the deployment 'of a fairly imposing British force' might forestall the need for any serious fighting. Hartington, parroting Wolseley, trusted it was so. Subtracting those forces required to maintain and protect the expedition's lines of communication, three infantry battalions were deemed adequate for extracting Gordon. That misunderstood the nature of the enemy to be faced. Fired by a deep fanaticism and the righteousness of their cause, the rebels had shown a willingness to brave superior fire and suffer inordinate losses. Doubtlessly, Wolseley thought the training and fire-discipline of British troops would be the vital factor. Still, the more practical reason why Wolseley would advance with three battalions was because this was the limit of what could be sustained.[28]

In September nine battalions of infantry were detailed for service in Egypt and Sudan. They were joined by a body of mounted troops under Brigadier General Sir Herbert Stewart. Coming from selected cavalry and infantry volunteers stationed in Britain and from those already serving in Egypt, the Camel Corps represented an elite body and mirrored an approach Wolseley had aimed to implement against the Ashanti in 1873.[29]

Necessarily, a Nile advance required shallow-draught boats. To that end, Wolseley tasked Colonel William Butler and Lieutenant Colonel James Alleyne to work with the Admiralty and find the required craft. Eventually, eight hundred 35-foot shallow-draught whalers were secured. Manned by Canadian *voyageurs*, Egyptian conscripts and naval ratings, the boats' crews were certainly eclectic. Some were *very* old, while others lacked skills and rejected military discipline. Even if those drawbacks had not existed, the whalers were not the only craft plying the Nile and its rapids. Steamers from Thomas Cook brought the Egyptian Army, which had been tasked with maintaining the expedition's lines of communication. In hindsight, Butler lamented the congestion present on the Nile. The greater problem though was the lack of an overall plan specifying the loading of boats and the relative priority of men and material. Yet, even if all had been correct, Butler believed all were working to a lethargic pace.[30]

Such shortfalls reflected the ad hoc nature of the War Office practice of acquiring items only when needed. It also reflected the lack of doctrine in joint operations. As for the pace of operations, it was impossible for Wolseley to be everywhere. Extending telegraphs and employing more staff officers might have alleviated problems, but the fundamental failure was the lack of a clear, enunciated plan that all elements of the team could follow. It was not Wolseley's responsibility to write such a plan; it was his responsibility to see that such a plan existed.

In late November Wolseley proposed creating a Naval Brigade from the personnel already supporting the expedition. While it did not approximate what a military officer thought of when speaking in terms of a brigade, the body under Captain Lord Charles Beresford did bring unique capabilities to an expedition operating on and serviced by the Nile.[31] Foremost, the personnel were subject to military discipline and familiar with boats, launches and skiffs not unlike the civilian steamers and *nuggars* (large sailing boats) plying the Nile in support of the expedition's logistics. Unfortunately, forming the brigade at the eleventh hour came with a steep price as the personnel forming its ranks were scattered along the lines of communication.[32] Thus, time, already a scarce commodity, elapsed as officers and ratings were collected. Worse was to follow.

One of the immediate problems encountered was the lack of coal to support the advance. Major General Redvers Buller, Wolseley's chief of staff, blamed Major General the Hon. James Dormer, chief of staff to British Forces in Egypt, as the chief culprit for this lapse. Wolseley believed the error to be Buller's, but he incurs not a little blame for assuming all was correct with the establishment's logistics.[33] Allowing that errors occurred, a key consideration must be afforded the lack of political direction. Failing to define its object beforehand, when the size of the expedition was doubled in September and its mission narrowed to retrieving Gordon, the logistical assumptions of April proved false. In addition to the lack of coal, the commercial steamers being used proved unreliable.[34] Privately, Buller calculated there was insufficient time to move the supplies required for the 10,000 troops now engaged before Gordon's own wherewithal had been expended. Accordingly Buller pressed for reducing the proportions of the expedition. Wolseley acceded to a point: he cancelled the orders of two battalions still in Britain.[35]

Help for Gordon needed to make progress more quickly if a greater tragedy were not to ensue. Writing to Gordon in early November, Wolseley now appreciated the limitations of a Nile advance. It might reach Khartoum. It was not, however, likely to reach Khartoum in time. Consequently, Wolseley informed Gordon that 1,500 mounted troops would cross the desert and avoid the reverse course the Nile ran between Korti and Abu Hamed. That measure conformed with Gordon's plan to hold five steamers at Metemmeh for the approaching expedition. Dividing his force, Wolseley sent one body under Major General William Earle along the Nile, while Herbert Stewart's mounted troops bypassed the Fourth and Fifth Cataracts. Unfortunately, though Wolseley reached Korti on 16 December, the balance of his command remained miles behind.[36]

Stewart departed on 8 January 1885 for the 290-kilometre (180 mi.) trek to Metemmeh. The delay was entirely due to the preparations still required; the lack of coordination between Wolseley and Buller, who remained separated by a large distance, and the need to collect the Naval Brigade at Korti.[37] The Naval Brigade would be key to what followed for the Desert Column represented only a reconnaissance in force. Aiming to cross the Bayūda Desert to seize Metemmeh as an advance base, Stewart's body sought to restore contact with Gordon, hence the presence of Colonel Wilson, the expedition's intelligence officer, who would give Gordon a letter. Its exact contents remain unknown, but it likely advised Gordon not to expect relief until April.[38]

Meanwhile, the progress of the Desert Column became measured in days, then in weeks. This owed everything to logistics as intermediate waypoints needed to be established along the line of march.[39] If the delay was unavoidable, how some responded was not: many officers now toured the historical sites dotting the way.[40] Though the days began warm with a mild breeze present, heat ruled the afternoons while the nights were cold. Stewart's column marched, rested and marched again at night. Men and beasts began to suffer as they advanced. Now the provision of water became acute. Much of it simply evaporated, and, when wells were found, many proved inadequate to the demands of such a large body. Stewart pressed ever forward hoping the next well would suffice. Under such circumstances, discipline suffered. Wilson was critical of the manner of march, believing more would have been achieved if the column had marched by day and slept by night.[41]

In Khartoum, Gordon was facing dwindling supplies. Rations were cut, but, unable to increase supplies, he aimed to reduce demand, allowing 5,000 non-combatants to quit the city.[42] Stewart's difficulties, meanwhile, were compounded by the Mahdists, who held the wells of Abu Klea. There a sharp action followed on 17 January, with an enemy of at least 8,000 under Abu Safia breaching British lines before the square could be formed. Among the British 92 wounded and 75 dead, a key casualty was Colonel Frederick Burnaby of the Royal Horse Guards. Wilson wrote of Abu Klea that he 'felt when it was over that we had a narrow escape'.[43] A mixed force of bluejackets, infantry and cavalry – British and Egyptian – that had not trained together suffered numerous breakdowns in their weapons. None could fault the elan of the attacking Sudanese, however: more than eight hundred fell defending the wells that now belonged to Stewart.[44]

With the Nile still miles and days away, Stewart had wanted to rest his command but acted otherwise, knowing Gordon, too, faced desperate times. Thus a very tired column resumed its trek to Metemmeh.[45] Tragically, the column suffered a further reverse when it was forced to engage the enemy anew on 19 January near Abu Kru, suffering nearly 25 killed and more than one hundred wounded, including a gravely wounded Stewart.[46] Anticipating the possibility, Wolseley had promised the War Office that either Buller or himself would see matters through.[47] Of course, for that to occur both needed to be nearby. They were not. Command now transferred to the ranking officer, Charles Wilson, a sapper of singular scientific talents but lacking command experience. Wilson turned to Colonel the Hon. Edward Boscawen, Lieutenant Colonel Percy Barrow, Major Wardrop and Captain the Earl of Airlie for guidance.[48] In this, some viewed Wilson as a bit of an 'old woman', but Snook is surely correct that the approach adopted was more akin to a commander wisely employing the staff and subordinate commanders present.[49]

The Desert Column continued its advance, albeit slowly, as many wounded were present and horse and camel, absent fodder and water, were spent from overwork. Indeed, so weakened had the column become that Wilson deprecated attacking Metemmeh, fearing it could not be held once taken. Believing even a successful action would produce only more casualties, Wilson established his force on the Nile above Metemmeh proper.

By 22 January the prospects of reaching Gordon were fast slipping away. Omdurman, a bastion covering Khartoum's approach, was known to have fallen. With Stewart gravely injured, Burnaby dead, and all the officers of the Naval Brigade killed or wounded save a very ill Beresford, the only thing seemingly remaining of the original plan was the object. Still, Wilson did not despair. A cavalry patrol reported the way clear, and Wilson, Beresford and accompanying infantry cautiously boarded steamers to conduct a reconnaissance as far as Shendy.[50]

Following yet another delay, and with Breresford now incapacitated, it was not until 24 January that Wilson set out with the steamers *Tel El-Howein* and the *Bordein*. The force comprised Wilson, three officers, 240 Sudanese troops, a handful of ratings and twenty British soldiers in scarlet tunics. The tunics, Wolseley's idea for the final advance, were meant to overawe the enemy, but the gesture was wasted on the likes of the Mahdī and shows Wolseley's essential misunderstanding of the foe.[51] In fact, Khartoum had fallen on 26 January 1885, the anniversary of Gordon's Cairo departure, following a siege of 317 days.[52] Two days later Wilson sighted Khartoum but could approach no closer than the confluence of the White and Blue Niles, for a hot reception forestalled reaching the city proper. Capturing the drama, Wilson recalled:

> The sight at this moment was very grand: the masses of the enemy with their fluttering banners near Khartum [*sic*]; the long rows of riflemen in the shelter-trenches of Omdurman; the numerous groups of men on Tuti [Island]; the bursting shells, and the water torn up by hundreds of bullets and occasional heavier shot, – made an impression never to be forgotten. Looking out over the stormy scene, it seemed almost impossible that we should escape.[53]

They did, but only in the most harrowing of ventures.

Elsewhere, Earle's column advanced methodically along the Nile. Even without facing resistance, getting beyond the Fourth Cataract proved difficult enough. At Berti, on 3 February, word arrived of Khartoum's fall. The news reached London two days later.[54] With Parliament in recess, the Cabinet did not meet until 6 February, but concrete facts were still lacking. Thus Earle continued to advance before meeting 1,500 Mahdists holding Kirbekan. The general elected to attack. Gaining the position, Earle, a battalion commander, and ten others did not survive. It remained for Brigadier General Henry Brackenbury to assume command. The River Column continued its advance for initial reporting only told of Khartoum's fall and did not provide news of Gordon's fate. The expedition now assumed the proportions of a punitive expedition against the tribes. Notwithstanding such brutishness, hope remained that Gordon might still be alive.[55] The news soon said otherwise and on 24 February Wolseley ordered Brackenbury to retire.[56]

Culturally, the death of Gordon proved a seminal moment and boded ill for Gladstone's fortunes. If any silver lining existed, then it must be that while Gordon held Khartoum, the Mahdī dare not move on Egypt. With that hindrance gone, British forces were singularly exposed. Retreat became a necessity where before it had been merely a virtue. If Wolseley's army was tactically successful during the advance, then it had been severely bloodied: both William Earle and Herbert Stewart had fallen and many a lesser officer too. More problematic, insufficient troops were present to meet a Mahdī no longer tethered to Gordon and Khartoum, all while the hottest period of the year approached. Accordingly Buller evacuated Abu Kru, so recently won, on 13 February.[57]

Throughout the affair Wolseley castigated his staff and the capabilities of senior officers, excepting, of course, Herbert Stewart. Those officers were not blameless, but they had been under Wolseley's command and were the product of his preferment. Wilson received an extra dose of venom, with Wolseley holding him and Gladstone responsible for the failure of the relief expedition. Gladstone's sin was one of omission, or more precisely, failing to act in a timely manner, thus time lost at the beginning could not be made good. Wilson's error was that of an officer who was not equal to his calling, with General Gordon paying the price for the inadequacy.

Those views were entirely self-serving. Accepting Wilson might have reached Khartoum before its fall, his ability to alter the outcome of events approached nil. As for Gladstone, his reluctance to send an expedition was known to Wolseley from the beginning. Rather than prod a superior to adopt a course of action he did not want to follow, would it have been better to accept the constraint and act accordingly? At no time in the drama had Wolseley simply recommended Gordon be ordered to vacate Khartoum. Thus more significant than the failings of subordinates and superiors were the failings of Wolseley. He failed to ensure enough camels and coal were on hand to support his force and had insisted on making an advance anchored on the Nile to the exclusion of all other possibilities. For these failings, Wolseley need look no further than the confines of his own tent for the officer responsible.[58]

News of Khartoum's fall reached London on 4 February. With Parliament in recess, it remained for newspapers to give vent to the grief and outrage felt. Ironically, it was the failures of statesmen, not soldiers, that weighed heavy in the balance. This was but natural as British soldiers were still engaged in combat. Hence, the failures of strategy loomed larger than any failure in tactics. Surveying events, *The Times* concluded:

The fall of Khartoum is instinctively felt to mean much more than the loss of a battle, the collapse of a garrison, or even the loss of a heroic soldier who has so long maintained the honour of his country against tremendous odds. It is the *reductio ad absurdum* of a whole policy, a disaster not only pregnant with instant dangers to our scattered troops, but carrying with it dangerous possibilities of disturbance in the remotest corners of the Empire.[59]

Such risk was inherent when imperial rule rested more on prestige than on consent. Gladstone at last responded in an address to the House of Commons on 19 February, reminding all that Egyptian policy in Sudan and, consequently, that of Britain, had been one of evacuation. A change was now signalled. With the Mahdī having gained Khartoum and Mahdism running rampant, evacuation no longer sufficed as a policy.[60] Wolseley was directed to begin a fresh offensive from Suakin with the aim of breaking the power of Osman Digna. In view of the logistical problems associated with sustaining an offensive in eastern Sudan, the construction of a rail line between Suakin and Berber became the first order of business.

Events elsewhere quickly forced a volte-face. A dispute over the Afghan border gave rise to the Penjdeh (Panjdah) crisis and the possibility of war with Russia. Thus the War Office warned Wolseley on 13 April that operations directed towards Khartoum would probably be terminated. A week later, the order was confirmed.[61] Wolseley, however, argued otherwise, believing Britain must crush Mahdism now or face having to do so later at a much higher cost.[62] The consideration had merit, but the British Army was not equipped to fight campaigns in multiple theatres. Of course, a personal motive existed for Wolseley. Evacuating Sudan would fail to redeem Gordon. More importantly, it would fail to redeem the reputation of Wolseley. Writing to his wife, Wolseley lamented, 'I have had a bad time of it, have gone through all the drudgery of a hard campaign without even tasting any drop of war's pleasures – an experience I have never had before, and, pray God, I may never again be exposed to.'[63] In the sorry affair that was the Gordon relief expedition, one prayer would be answered: though Wolseley would eventually secure a field marshal's baton and become commander-in-chief of the British Army, never again would he command in battle. The accolades owed everything to his administrative ability, the agendas of others and timing: Queen Victoria's third son, the Duke of Connaught, was deemed too inexperienced when the post of commander in chief became vacant in 1895.[64]

Wolseley was a methodical, thoughtful soldier. In short, he was held to be a 'scientific soldier'.[65] These would be sound qualities for most occasions, but if Gordon were to be saved, then a saviour possessing a modicum of dash was required, certainly more dash than Wolseley had shown.[66] Arrogant, bitter and vain, he badly underestimated the nature of the Mahdī and the movement that was Mahdism. Wolseley also held Gladstone in contempt: not a sin, perhaps, but working against the known inclinations of established civilian authority assuredly was. This was not all Wolseley's doing, for, at this hour, Britain's structures of military oversight had form but lacked substance. Absent a General Staff and a supervising body of control, too much was expected from British generals. Another war in South Africa would prove this conclusively with reform of the army and the War Office and the creation of the Committee of Imperial Defence following. To be sure, Cabinet oversight existed in theory, but Parliament worked to a schedule divorced from foreign and strategic affairs: Parliament stood in recess in January 1884 when Gordon departed for Sudan; it was in recess again in January 1885 when Gordon departed forever.

Finally, time, space, operational capability and logistics are elements to be dismissed at one's peril. Willpower is a critical factor but when pressed too far merely lapses into hope. Such was Wolseley's failing. Tactically the army had performed well; administratively, it had been found wanting. This was not all Wolseley's fault; systemic problems existed. Still, the essential errors were his. It was Wolseley who had sponsored Gordon. When that step faltered, it was Wolseley who pressed for a relief force to be sent. Few generals are given the chance to redeem an earlier failure. Wolseley was one. Conceiving, organizing and commanding the expedition launched in the autumn of 1884, only a greater failure ensued. Wolseley, as a commander, never faced a first-class enemy. This alone precludes him from being considered a great captain, notwithstanding a reputation won through many a hard-fought campaign and burnished at Tel el-Kebir in 1882. That he failed in his last expedition is the lament of many a commander and testifies to his limitations as a military leader.

REFERENCES

INTRODUCTION

1 Michael Howard, 'The Use and Abuse of Military History', RUSI *Journal*, CVII/625 (1962), pp. 4–10.
2 Niccolò Machiavelli, *The Prince*, trans. Hill Thompson (Norwalk, CT, 1955), p. 113.
3 Alan Clark, *The Donkeys* (New York, 1962).
4 John Laffin, *British Butchers and Bunglers of World War One* (Godalming, 1998).
5 Norman F. Dixon, *On the Psychology of Military Incompetence* (London, 1976); Robert Pois and Philip Langer, *Command Failure in War: Psychology and Leadership* (Bloomington, IN, 2004).
6 Pois and Langer, *Command Failure in War*, p. 2.
7 Eliot Cohen and John Gooch, *Military Misfortunes: The Anatomy of Failure in War* (New York, 2006), p. 232.
8 John Keegan, *The Face of Battle* (London, 1988), p. 263.
9 Stephen Roskill, *Admiral of the Fleet Earl Beatty: The Last Naval Hero* (Annapolis, MD, 2018).

I ROMAN FEDEROVICH VON UNGERN-STERNBERG

1 Leonid Iuzefovich, *Samoderzhets Pustyni: Fenomen Sud'by R.F. Ungern-Shternberga* (Moscow, 1993), pp. 18–19; Canfield F. Smith, 'The Ungernovščina - How and Why?', *Jahrbücher für Geschichte Osteuropas*, XXVIII/IV (1980), pp. 593–4.
2 Iuzefovich, p. 19; Evgenii Belov, *Baron Ungern fon Shternberg: Biogragiia, Ideologiia, Voennye Pokhody 1920–1921 g.g.* (Moscow, 2001), pp. 17–18; N. N. Kniazev, *Legendarnyi Baron* (Harbin, 1942), p. 8.
3 Iuzefovich, *Samoderzhets Pustyni*, p. 19; Belov, *Baron Ungern*, p. 18; Smith, 'The Ungernovščina - How and Why?', p. 591.
4 Peter Wrangel, *The Memoirs of General Wrangel, the Last Commander-in-Chief of the Russian National Army* (London, 1930), p. 7.
5 Ibid.; Boris Volkov, 'About Ungern: From the Notebook of a White Guard', typescript trans. Elena Varneck, pp. 45–6, Hoover Institution

Archives, Stanford University; Smith, 'The Ungernovščina – How and Why?', p. 591.

6 Robert A. Rupen, *Mongols of the Twentieth Century* (Bloomington, IN, 1964), p. 50.

7 Gerard M. Friters, *Outer Mongolia and Its International Position* (Baltimore, MD, 1949), pp. 54–6.

8 Rupen, *Mongols*, p. 61.

9 Ibid.

10 Grigorii Semenov, *O Sebe: Vospominaniia, Mysli, i Vyvody* (Harbin, 1938), pp. 10–11.

11 Kniazev, *Legendarnyi Baron*, p. 10; Volkov, 'About Ungern', p. 46.

12 Belov, *Baron Ungern*, pp. 19–21.

13 David Footman, *Ataman Semenov*, St Antony's Papers on Soviet Affairs (Oxford, 1955), p. 4.

14 Semenov, *O Sebe*, pp. 42–5.

15 Ibid.

16 Footman, *Ataman Semenov*, pp. 6–7; Semenov, *O Sebe*, pp. 57–63.

17 Semenov, *O Sebe*, pp. 63–7.

18 Ibid., pp. 66–9.

19 Ibid., pp. 79–80.

20 Footman, *Ataman Semenov*, p. 17.

21 Ibid., pp. 17–30.

22 Ibid., pp. 33–5, 43–50.

23 Ibid., pp. 33–5, 38–41.

24 Semenov, *O Sebe*, pp. 136–7.

25 Footman, *Ataman Semenov*, pp. 55–7.

26 Semenov, *O Sebe*, pp. 81–2; Footman, *Ataman Semenov*, pp. 33–5, 46–9.

27 Urajiostoku Hakengun Sanbōbu, 'Baron Ungerun'gun sentōryoku narabi jikyū nōryoku no handan ni kansuru shiryō', 1 May 1921, pp. 4–5, Japanese Military Archives, Library of Congress Microfilm Reel 117, no. 1061; Volkov, 'About Ungern', pp. 46–7; Victorin M. Moltchanoff, *The Last White General: An Interview Conducted by Boris Raymond* (Berkeley, CA, 1972), pp. 107–8.

28 Hakengun Sanbōbu, 'Baron Ungerun'gun', pp. 2–3.

29 'Ungeru'gun sonawaretaru Nihonjin no kōdō shimatsu', Attachment in Qiqihar Consul General Yamazaki to Foreign Minister Uchida, 7 November 1921, 'Rōkoku kakumei ikken, (bessatsu) Ungerun no Uruga no kōgeki', Japanese Foreign Ministry Archives, 1-6-3-24-13-28-1.

30 Footman, *Ataman Semenov*, pp. 42–3; Smith, 'The Ungernovščina – How and Why?', pp. 594–5.

31 Smith, 'The Ungernovščina – How and Why?', pp. 594–5; Volkov. 'About Ungern', pp. 12–13, 48–50; A. S. Makeev, *Bog Voiny – Baron Ungern: Vospominaniia bybshago ad'iutanta Nachal'nika Aziatskoi Konnoi Divizii* (Shanghai, 1934), pp. 13–14.

32 Makeev, *Bog Voiny*, p. 13.

33 Hilel Salomon, 'The Anfu Clique and China's Abrogation of Outer Mongolian Autonomy', *Mongolia Society Bulletin*, X/1 (1971), pp. 67–70; Footman, *Ataman Semenov*, pp. 36–7; Thomas E. Ewing, 'Russia, China, and the Origins of the Mongolian People's Republic,

1911–1921: A Reappraisal', *Slavic and East European Studies*, LVIII (1980), p. 407.

34 Salomon, 'Anfu Clique', pp. 76–80.

35 D. P. Pershin, 'Baron Ungern, Urga, and Altan Bulak: An Eyewitness Account of the Troubled Times in Outer (Khalka) Mongolia during the First Third of the Twentieth Century', typescript trans. Elena Varneck, pp. 3–4, 8, 14–18, D. P. Pershin Papers Box 1, Hoover Institution Archives, Stanford University; M. I. Kazanin, 'Through Mongolia by Cadillac in 1920', *Canada–Mongolia Review*, II/1 (1976), pp. 38–9.

36 Kniazev, *Legendarnyi Baron*, p. 31; Makeev, *Bog Voiny*, p. 14.

37 Kniazev, *Legendarnyi Baron*, pp. 30–34.

38 Smith, 'The Ungernovščina – How and Why?', pp. 593–4; Belov, *Baron Ungern*, pp. 101–11.

39 Pershin, 'Baron Ungern', pp. 43–4.

40 Kniazev, *Legendarnyi Baron*, pp. 41–6.

41 Ibid., pp. 46–7.

42 Volkov, 'About Ungern', pp. 27–8.

43 Ibid.

44 Ibid.

45 Pershin, 'Baron Ungern', pp. 45–6.

46 Ibid., pp. 44–6.

47 Ibid., pp. 48–52, 56–7, 70; Kniazev, *Legendarnyi Baron*, pp. 58–65.

48 Volkov, 'About Ungern', pp. 14–15; *North China Herald*, 16 April 1921, p. 156; 'A Letter of Ungern to General Lu Chang-Kuu, 16 February 1921', Special Delegation of the Far Eastern Republic, *Letters Captured from Baron Ungern in Mongolia Reprinted from Pekin and Tientsin Times* (Washington, DC, 1921), p. 15, Hoover Institution Archives, Stanford University.

49 Riabukhin (Ribo), 'The Story of Baron Ungern', pp. 3–10; V. Sokolnitskii, 'Kaigorodovshchina', typescript trans. Elena Varneck, p. 29, Hoover Institution Archives, Stanford University.

50 Riabukhin (Ribo), 'The Story of Baron Ungern', p. 6.

51 'A Letter of Baron Ungern to General Lu Chang Kuu, No. 489', 2 March 1921, Far Eastern Republic, *Letters Captured from Baron Ungern*, pp. 10–12; see also Belov, *Baron Ungern*, pp. 101–11.

52 Pershin, 'Baron Ungern', pp. 79–80.

53 *North China Herald*, 23 April 1921, p. 234; Rodney Gilbert, 'The Mongolian Campaign Farce', *North China Herald*, 18 June 1921, pp. 794–5.

54 Hakengun Sanbōbu, 'Baron Ungerun'gun', pp. 4–8.

55 'A Letter of Baron Ungern to His Agents in Peking No. 986', 20 May 1921, 'A Letter of Baron Ungern to General Lu Chang Kuu, No. 489', 2 March 1921, Far Eastern Republic, *Letters Captured from Baron Ungern*, pp. 10–12.

56 Volkov, 'About Ungern', pp. 9–12, 15–16.

57 Ibid., pp. 16–21.

58 Ewing, 'Russia, China, and the Mongolian People's Republic', pp. 414–20.

59 Kniazev, *Legendarnyi Baron*, p. 30.

60 Iuzefovich, *Samoderzhets Pustyni*, pp. 230–32; Belov, *Baron Ungern*, pp. 33–4.

61 Iuzefovich, *Samoderzhets Pustyni*, p. 232.

62 Riabukhin (Ribo), 'Story of Ungern', pp. 12–23.

63 Ibid., pp. 23–5.

64 Ibid., pp. 26–40.

65 Pershin, 'Baron Ungern', pp. 105–13.

66 Iuzefovich, *Samoderzhets Pustyni*, pp. 204–9, 234–9.

67 Smith, 'The Ungernovščina – How and Why?', p. 595.

2 NATHAN BEDFORD FORREST

1 John Scales, *The Battles and Campaigns of Confederate General Nathan Bedford Forrest, 1861–1865* (El Dorado Hills, CA, 2017), p. xi; Williamson Murray and Wayne Wei-Siang Hsieh, *A Savage War: A Military History of the Civil War* (Princeton, NJ, 2016), p. 301; Shelby Foote, *The Civil War: A Narrative*, 3 vols (New York, 1958–74).

2 Andrew Lytle, *Bedford Forrest and His Critter Company* (New York, 1960).

3 Brian Steel Wills, *A Battle from the Start: The Life of Nathan Bedford Forrest* (New York, 1992), pp. xv, 1.

4 As just one example of the former, see Lochlainn Seabrook, *A Rebel Born: A Defense of Nathan Bedford Forrest, Confederate General, American Legend* (Franklin, TN, 2010), a literal case of ancestor worship.

5 Wills, *A Battle from the Start*, p. 22.

6 Ibid., pp. xv, 16, 26, 363, 380; James Webb, *Born Fighting: How the Scots-Irish Shaped America* (New York, 2004); Grady McWhiney, *Cracker Culture: Celtic Ways in the Old South* (Tuscaloosa, AL, 1988); James G. Leyburn, *Scotch-Irish: A Social History* (Chapel Hill, NC, 1962); Henry Jones Ford, *The Scotch-Irish in America* (Princeton, NJ, 1915); Wills, *A Battle from the Start*.

7 On Yancey, see Eric Walther, *William Lowndes Yancey and the Coming of the Civil War* (Chapel Hill, NC, 2006).

8 The *New York Times* reported on 28 June 1863 that Forrest stabbed Gould, who then produced his pistol and fired in self-defence. Most Forrest apologists claim that Gould fired at Forrest unprovoked, forcing Forrest to pull a penknife and lunge at his attacker in self-defence. Lytle, *Bedford Forrest and His Critter Company*, pp. 165, 340; Wills, *A Battle from the Start*, pp. 77, 144–5, 161, 260, 288.

9 Wills, *A Battle from the Start*, pp. 7–102, 104–8, 290.

10 David A. Powell, *Failure in the Saddle: Nathan Bedford Forrest, Joe Wheeler, and the Confederate Cavalry in the Chickamauga Campaign* (El Dorado Hills, CA, 2010).

11 Ibid., p. 208.

12 Ibid., p. 210.

13 Ibid., p. 211.

14 Ibid., p. 152.

15 Ibid., pp. 205, 207.

16 Earl Hess, *Braxton Bragg: The Most Hated Man of the Confederacy* (Chapel Hill, NC, 2016).

17 For a detailed discussion of the alleged incident, see Powell, *Failure in the Saddle*, pp. 318–27.

18 See John Cimprich, *Fort Pillow, a Civil War Massacre, and Public Memory* (Baton Rouge, LA, 2005); and Brian Steel Wills, *The River Was Dyed with Blood: Nathan Bedford Forrest and Fort Pillow* (Norman, OK, 2014).

19 See Tom Parson, *Work for Giants* (Kent, OH, 2014).

20 For a reassessment of Lee's greatness, see Alan T. Nolan, *Lee Considered: General Robert E. Lee and Civil War History* (Chapel Hill, NC, 1991).

21 U.S. War Department, *The War of the Rebellion: A Compilation of the Official Records of the Union and Confederate Armies* (Washington, DC, 1880–1901), ser. 1, vol. XXXIX, pt. 2, p. 121. Hereafter, OR.

22 See James Picket Jones, *Yankee Blitzkrieg: Wilson's Raid through Alabama and Georgia* (Athens, GA, 1976).

23 Wills, *A Battle from the Start*, pp. 71–2.

24 For just two examples, see Scales, *The Battles and Campaigns of Confederate General Nathan Bedford Forrest, 1861–1865*; and Major Charles McDaniel, USAF, 'Lt Gen Nathan Bedford Forrest (CSA): Great Captain or Just Another Confederate General?', master's thesis, Air Command and Staff College, 2006.

25 See Cathal Nolan, *The Allure of Battle: A History of How Wars Have Been Won and Lost* (Oxford, 2017).

26 Wills, *A Battle from the Start*, pp. 146, 192, 327, 336, 349, 358.

27 OR, ser. 1, vol. XLIX, pt. 2, p. 1290.

28 Court Carney, 'The Contested Image of Nathan Bedford Forrest', *Journal of Southern History*, LXVII/3 (August 2001), p. 603.

29 Neil S. Edmond, 'An Analysis of the Leadership of Nathan Bedford Forrest, C.S.A'. (unpublished MS, Command and General Staff College, 1934), Combined Arms Research Library, Fort Leavenworth, KS, pp. 1, 31, 40, 42; Wills, *A Battle from the Start*, p. 302; McDaniel, 'Lt Gen Nathan Bedford Forrest (CSA)', p. 20.

30 Carney, 'The Contested Image of Nathan Bedford Forrest', p. 618.

31 Ibid., p. 603.

3 JOHN M. CHIVINGTON

1 'The Battle of Sand Creek', *Rocky Mountain News* (December 1864), repr. in *The Sand Creek Massacre: The Official 1865 Congressional Report with James P. Beckwourth's Additional Testimony and Related Documents*, ed. Bill Yenne (Yardley, PA, 2015), pp. 56–8; Captain Silas S. Soule to Major E. W. Wynkoop, letter, 14 December 1864, in *Sand Creek Papers: Documents of a Massacre (Annotated)* (Bellevue, WA, 2016); Lieutenant Joseph A. Cramer to Major E. W. Wynkoop, letter, 19 December 1864, ibid.

2 Mark Grimsley and Clifford J. Rogers, eds, *Civilians in the Path of War* (Lincoln, NE, 2002), p. 141.

3 Gary L. Roberts, *Massacre at Sand Creek: How Methodists Were Involved in an American Tragedy* (Nashville, TN, 2016), p. 69; Steven Hahn, *A Nation without Borders: The United States and Its World in an Age of Civil Wars, 1830–1910* (New York, 2016), pp. 144–5, 234, 280–82; Yenne, ed., *The Sand Creek Massacre*, p. 7.

4 Hahn, *A Nation without Borders*, p. 282.

5 Grimsley and Rogers, eds, *Civilians in the Path of War*, pp. 139–42; Reginald Horsman, *Race and Manifest Destiny: Origins of American Racial Anglo-Saxonism* (Cambridge, MA, 1981), p. 191.

6 Hahn, *A Nation without Borders*, pp. 283–4; Yenne, *The Sand Creek Massacre*, p. 6; Stan Hoig, *The Sand Creek Massacre* (Norman, OK, 1961), pp. 3–4.

7 Roberts, *Massacre at Sand Creek*, pp. 69–73; Carol Turner, *Forgotten Heroes and Villains of Sand Creek* (Charleston, SC, 2010), p. 53.

8 Roberts, *Massacre at Sand Creek*, pp. 76–8, 123; Colonel John P. Slough report, 29 March 1862, *War of the Rebellion Official Records of the Union and Confederate Armies,* ser. 1, vol. IX, part 1, chapter XXI, p. 533, www. collections.library.cornell.edu; Colonel John P. Slough report, 30 March 1862, ibid., pp. 534–5; Yenne, ed., *The Sand Creek Massacre,* p. 17; Colonel John M. Chivington to Lieutenant Colonel Samuel F. Tappan, letter, 23 October 1862, folder 3, MS collection 617, Samuel Tappan Papers, Stephan H. Hart Library and Research Center, Denver, CO; Soule to Wynkoop, letter, 14 December 1864; Cramer to Wynkoop, letter, 19 December 1864; Hoig, *The Sand Creek Massacre,* pp. 19–20; Hahn, *A Nation without Borders*, p. 266; Lieutenant Colonel Samuel F. Tappan to Colonel John Chivington, letter, January 1863, Samuel Tappan Papers.

9 Roberts, *Massacre at Sand Creek*, pp. 76–8, 123; Roster/Roll-Call of the Department of Kansas, 31 January 1864, *War of the Rebellion Official Records of the Union and Confederate Armies,* series 1, vol. XXXIV, part II, chapter XLVI, p. 206, www.collections.library.cornell.edu; Colonel John M. Chivington, testimony, in *The Sand Creek Massacre*, ed. Yenne, p. 101; Lieutenant Colonel Samuel F. Tappan to Colonel John Chivington, letter, January 1863, Samuel Tappan Papers.

10 Roberts, *Massacre at Sand Creek*, pp. 77–8.

11 Hoig, *The Sand Creek Massacre*, pp. 18–28; Major General S. R. Curtis to Major General H. W. Halleck, correspondence, 23 July 1864, in *The Sand Creek Massacre,* ed. Yenne, p. 62; Major General S. R. Curtis to Major General H. W. Halleck, correspondence, 8 August 1864, ibid., pp. 62–3.

12 Messrs. J. S. Brown, D. C. Corbin and T .J. Darrah to Captain J. S. Maynard, Acting Assistant Adjutant General, letter, 13 June 1864, *War of the Rebellion Official Records of the Union and Confederate Armies*, series 1, vol. XXXIV, part IV, chapter XLVI, p. 354, www.collections.library.cornell. edu; Lieutenant Clark Dunn, 1st Colorado Cavalry, report, 18 April 1864, *War of the Rebellion Official Records of the Union and Confederate Armies,* series 1, vol. XXXIV, part 1, chapter XLVI, p. 884, www.collections.library. cornell.edu; Major General S. R. Curtis to Major General H. W. Halleck, correspondence, 10 August 1864, in *The Sand Creek Massacre*, ed. Yenne, p. 63; Major General H. W. Halleck to Major General S. R. Curtis, correspondence, 13 August 1864, ibid., p. 63.

13 Curtis to Halleck, correspondence, July 23, 1864; Colonel John M. Chivington to Major S. C. Charlot, Assistant Adjutant General, Department of Kansas, report, June 11, 1864, *War of the Rebellion Official Records of the Union and Confederate Armies*, series 1, vol. XXXIV, part IV, chapter XLVI, pp. 318–19, www.collections.library.cornell.edu.

14 Governor John Evans to Secretary of War Edwin Stanton, correspondence, 18 August 1864, *War of the Rebellion Official Records*

of the Union and Confederate Armies, series I, vol. XLI, part II, chapter LIII, p. 765, www.collections.library.cornell.edu; Governor John Evans to Secretary of War Edwin Stanton, letter, 10 August 1864, ibid., p. 644; Governor John Evans to Honorable W. P. Dole, Commissioner of Indian Affairs, letter, 10 August 1864, ibid., p. 644; Major S. C. Charlot to Colonel John M. Chivington, 13 August 1864, ibid., p. 695; Colonel John M. Chivington to Major S. C. Charlot, letter, 18 August 1864, ibid., p. 766; Major Scott J. Anthony to Acting Assistant Adjutant General, letter, August 1864, ibid., p. 926; 'Chivington's Address on Sand Creek', *Denver Republican,* 6 October 1894, box 3, folder 13, Carey Papers, University of Denver; 'Statement from Col. Chivington in Regard the Battle of "Sand Creek"', *Daily Free Press,* 26 June 1866, box 3, folder 13, Carey Papers, University of Denver; Governor John Evans to Commissioner of Indian Affairs, Department of the Interior, letter, 15 October 1864, in *Sand Creek Papers: Documents of a Massacre (Annotated);* Governor John Evans to Secretary of War Edwin Stanton, letter, 22 August 1864, *War of the Rebellion Official Records of the Union and Confederate Armies,* series I, vol. XLVI, part II, chapter LIII, p. 809, www.collections.library.cornell.edu; Major General H. W. Halleck to Major General S. R. Curtis, letter, 3 September 1864, in *The Sand Creek Massacre,* ed. Yenne, p. 66; Major General S. R. Curtis to Major General H. W. Halleck, letter, 28 August 1864, ibid., p. 66; Governor John Evans to Secretary of War Edwin Stanton, letter, 7 September 1864, ibid., p. 66.

15 'Chivington's Address on Sand Creek', *Denver Republican,* 6 October 1894.

16 Roberts, *Massacre at Sand Creek,* p. 120; Soule to Wynkoop, letter, 14 December 1864; Cramer to Wynkoop, letter, 19 December 1864.

17 Colonel John M. Chivington to Major General S. R. Curtis, correspondence, 8 August 1864, *War of the Rebellion Official Records of the Union and Confederate Armies,* series I, vol. XLI, part II, chapter LIII, pp. 613–14, www.collections.library.cornell.edu.

18 Roberts, *Massacre at Sand Creek,* p. 123.

19 Lieutenant Colonel Samuel F. Tappan to Colonel John Chivington, letter, January 1863, Tappan Papers.

20 Major General S. R. Curtis to Colonel John M. Chivington, letter, 28 September 1864, *War of the Rebellion Official Records of the Union and Confederate Armies,* series I, vol. XLI, part III, chapter LIII, p. 462, www. collections.library.cornell.edu; Colonel John M. Chivington to Major C. S. Charlot, letter, 26 September 1864, ibid., p. 399; Major General S. R. Curtis to Major General H. W. Halleck, letter, in *The Sand Creek Massacre,* ed. Yenne, p. 67.

21 General Field Orders No. 1, 27 July 1864, in *The Sand Creek Massacre,* ed. Yenne, p. 75; Governor John Evans to Commissioner of Indian Affairs, Department of the Interior, letter, 15 October 1864, in *Sand Creek Papers: Documents of a Massacre (Annotated).*

22 Charles E. Mix, Acting Commissioner of Indian Affairs to Governor Evans, letter, 23 June 1864, ibid.; Governor John Evans to Major S. Colley, letter, 12 July 1864, ibid.

23 Governor John Evans to Commissioner of Indian Affairs, Department of the Interior, letter, 15 October 1864, ibid.; Governor John Evans,

Proclamation, 11 August 1864, ibid.; Governor John Evans, Proclamation, 27 June 1864, ibid.

24 Colonel John M. Chivington to Secretary of War Edwin Stanton, letter, 19 September 1864, in *The Sand Creek Massacre*, ed. Yenne, p. 68; Major General H. W. Halleck to Colonel John M. Chivington, letter, 20 September 1864, ibid., p. 68; Colonel John M. Chivington to Major General H. W. Halleck, letter, 22 September 1864, ibid., p. 68; Major General H. W. Halleck to Colonel John M. Chivington, letter, 23 September 1864, ibid., p. 68.

25 'Chivington's Address on Sand Creek', *Denver Republican*, 6 October 1894; Roberts, *Massacre at Sand Creek,* pp. 123–4.

26 Black Kettle to Major Colley, letter, 29 August 1864, Sand Creek Papers, Special Collections, Tutt Library, Colorado College, Colorado Springs, CO, www.libraryweb.coloradocollege.edu; Major E. W. Wynkoop, testimony, 15 January 1865, in *The Sand Creek Massacre*, ed. Yenne, p. 81; Major Scott J. Anthony, report, 7 November 1864, folder 9, MS collection 695, Edward Wynkoop Papers, Stephan H. Hart Library and Research Center, Denver, CO.

27 Colonel John M. Chivington to Major C. S. Charlot, Aide to Major General S. R. Curtis, letter, 26 September 1864; Major E. W. Wynkoop, testimony, 15 January 1865; Major General S. R. Curtis to Colonel John M. Chivington, letter, 28 September 1864.

28 Major E. W. Wynkoop, testimony, 15 January 1865; United States Congress, *Sand Creek Massacre: Report of the Secretary of War* (Washington, DC, 1867), pp. 215, 217.

29 Ibid.

30 Ibid.

31 Ibid., p. 87; Cramer to Wynkoop, letter, 19 December 1864; Major Scott J. Anthony, report, 7 November 1864, Edward Wynkoop Papers; Major Scott J. Anthony, report, 6 November 1864, in *The Sand Creek Massacre*, ed. Yenne, p. 70; Major Scott J. Anthony, testimony, 14 March 1865, *Massacre of the Cheyenne Indians, Report of the Joint Committee on the Conduct of War at the Second Session Thirty-Eighth Congress*, ibid., p. 18.

32 Opening Statement, *Massacre of the Cheyenne Indians, Report of the Joint Committee on the Conduct of War at the Second Session Thirty-Eighth Congress,* ibid., pp. i–ii.

33 Major General S. R. Curtis to Brigadier General J. H. Carleton, Commanding Department of New Mexico, letter, 28 November 1864, *War of the Rebellion Official Records of the Union and Confederate Armies*, series I, vol. XLI, part IV, chapter LIII, p. 709, www.collections.library.cornell.edu.

34 Major E. W. Wynkoop, testimony, 15 January 1865; Major Scott J. Anthony, testimony, 14 March 1865, *Massacre of the Cheyenne Indians*, in *The Sand Creek Massacre*, ed. Yenne, pp. 16, 18; Mr John S. Smith, testimony, 14 March 1865, *Massacre of the Cheyenne Indians*, ibid., pp. 7–8.

35 Colonel John M. Chivington, second report on Sand Creek, 16 December 1864, *War of the Rebellion Official Records of the Union and Confederate Armies*, series I, vol. XLI, part I, chapter LIII, pp. 948–50, www.collections.library.cornell.edu; 'Chivington's Address on Sand Creek', *Denver Republican*, 6 October 1894.

36 United States Congress, *Sand Creek Massacre*, pp. 116–17; Major Scott J. Anthony, testimony, 14 March 1865, *Massacre of the Cheyenne Indians*, p. 23.

37 Soule to Wynkoop, letter, 14 December 1864; Cramer to Wynkoop, letter, 19 December 1864; Major Scott J. Anthony, testimony, 14 March 1865, *Massacre of the Cheyenne Indians*, pp. 20–21, 29; Major Scott J. Anthony to Lieutenant A. Helliwell, Acting Assistant Adjutant General, report, 28 November 1864, *War of the Rebellion Official Records of the Union and Confederate Armies*, series I, vol. XLI, part IV, chapter LIII, p. 708, www. collections.library.cornell.edu; Colonel John M. Chivington, second report on Sand Creek, 16 December 1864, pp. 948–50; 'Chivington's Address on Sand Creek', *Denver Republican*, 6 October 1894.

38 Soule to Wynkoop, letter, 14 December 1864; Cramer to Wynkoop, letter, 19 December 1864; David Louderback, affidavit, 27 January 1865, in Hoig, *The Sand Creek Massacre*, p. 181.

39 Colonel John M. Chivington, first report on Sand Creek, 29 November 1864, *War of the Rebellion Official Records of the Union and Confederate Armies*, series I, vol. XLI, part I, chapter LIII, p. 948, www.collections. library.cornell.edu; Colonel John M. Chivington, second report on Sand Creek, 16 December 1864, pp. 948–50; Major Scott J. Anthony, report, 1 December 1864, *War of the Rebellion Official Records of the Union and Confederate Armies*, series I, vol. XLI, part I, chapter LIII, pp. 951–2, www.collections.library.cornell.edu; Samuel Colley, testimony, in Hoig, *The Sand Creek Massacre*, p. 177; James A. Cramer, affidavit, ibid., p. 185; Soule to Wynkoop, letter, 14 December 1864; Cramer to Wynkoop, letter, 19 December 1864.

40 Lieutenant James Olney, affidavit, 20 April 1865, folder 6, MS collection 695, Edward Wynkoop Papers, Stephen H. Hart Library and Research Center, Denver, CO; Soule to Wynkoop, letter, 14 December 1864; Cramer to Wynkoop, letter, 19 December 1864; John S. Smith, testimony, in Hoig, *The Sand Creek Massacre*, pp. 178–9; James D. Cannon, affidavit, 16 January 1865, ibid., p. 179; David Louderback, affidavit, 27 January 1865, ibid., pp. 180–81; Lucien Palmer, affidavit, ibid., p. 185; United States Congress, *Sand Creek Massacre*, pp. 71, 143, 145, 150, 180; Mr John S. Smith, testimony, 14 March 1865, *Massacre of the Cheyenne Indians*, p. 9.

41 Major Scott J. Anthony, testimony, 14 March 1865, *Massacre of the Cheyenne Indians*, pp. 22–3; Yenne, ed., *The Sand Creek Massacre*, p. 15; 'Chivington's Address on Sand Creek', *Denver Republican*, 6 October 1894; Roberts, *Massacre at Sand Creek*, p. 134.

42 Soule to Wynkoop, letter, 14 December 1864.

43 Ibid.; Cramer to Wynkoop, letter, 19 December 1864; Samuel Colley, testimony, pp. 177–9; Jacob Downing, affidavit, 21 July 1865, in Hoig, *The Sand Creek Massacre*, p. 183; John S. Smith, affidavit, 15 January 1865, ibid., p. 179; 'Evidence Taken at Denver and Fort Lyon by a Military Commission, Ordered to Inquire into the Sand Creek Massacre, November, 1864', James P. Beckwith's Testimony, 6 March 1865, Senate Executive Document No. 26, 39th Congress, 2nd session, in *The Sand Creek Massacre*, ed. Yenne; Presley Talbott, affidavit, in Hoig, *The Sand Creek Massacre*, p. 183; United States Congress, *Sand Creek Massacre*, pp. 77, 142.

44 Major Scott J. Anthony, testimony, 14 March 1865, *Massacre of the Cheyenne Indians*, p. 16; Soule to Wynkoop, letter, 14 December 1864; 'Chivington's Address on Sand Creek', *Denver Republican*, 6 October 1894.

45 Samuel Colley, testimony, p. 178; Major Scott J. Anthony, testimony, 14 March 1865, *Massacre of the Cheyenne Indians*, pp. 26–7; Mr John S. Smith, testimony, 14 March 1865, ibid., p. 9; James D. Cannon, affidavit, 16 January 1865, ibid., p. 180; David Louderback, affidavit, 27 January 1865, ibid., pp. 180–81; L. Wilson, affidavit, in Hoig, *The Sand Creek Massacre*, p. 182; Asbury Bird, affidavit, ibid., p. 184; United States Congress, *Sand Creek Massacre*, pp. 23, 71, 77, 142, 145, 150; Dr Caleb S. Burdsal, affidavit, in Hoig, *The Sand Creek Massacre*, p. 184; Cramer to Wynkoop, letter, 19 December 1864; Soule to Wynkoop, letter, 14 December 1864.

46 Cramer to Wynkoop, letter, 19 December 1864; Soule to Wynkoop, letter, 14 December 1864; Colonel John M. Chivington, second report on Sand Creek, 16 December 1864, pp. 948–50.

47 Colonel John M. Chivington, first report on Sand Creek, 29 November 1864, p. 948.

48 Roberts, *Massacre at Sand Creek*, pp. 145–51; Major E. W. Wynkoop to Messrs Hollister and Hall, 20 April 1865, folder 7, MS collection 695, Edward Wynkoop Papers, Stephen H. Hart Library and Research Center, Denver, CO.

49 Colonel John M. Chivington, testimony, 26 April 1865, in *The Sand Creek Massacre*, ed. Yenne, pp. 101–8; 'Chivington's Address on Sand Creek', *Denver Republican*, 6 October 1894; 'Statement from Col. Chivington in Regard the Battle of "Sand Creek"', *Daily Free Press*, 26 June 1866.

50 Major General S. R. Curtis to Major General H. W. Halleck, letter, 12 January 1865, in *The Sand Creek Massacre*, ed. Yenne, p. 75; Major General S. R. Curtis to Governor John Evans, letter, 30 January 1865, ibid., pp. 76–7; General Field Orders No. 1, 27 July 1864.

51 Major General H. W. Halleck to Major General S. R. Curtis, letter, 11 January 1865, in *The Sand Creek Massacre*, ed. Yenne, p. 74.

52 Robert C. Carriker, *Fort Supply Indian Territory: Frontier Outpost on the Plains* (Norman, OK, 1970), p. 3; Major General S. R. Curtis to Major General H. W. Halleck letter, 12 January 1865; Colonel J. A. Hardie to Major General H. W. Halleck, correspondence, 11 January 1865, in *The Sand Creek Massacre*, ed. Yenne, p. 74; Roberts, *Massacre at Sand Creek*, pp. xv, 143; Hahn, *A Nation without Borders*, p. 283.

53 Subscription list, Colonel John M. Chivington portrait, State Historical and Natural History Society, 24 August 1898, folder 3, MS collection 994, John M. Chivington Papers, Stephen H. Hart Research and Library Center, Denver, CO; The Lee Kinsey Implement Company to Will C. Ferrill, curator, subscription submission, 26 August 1898, folder 2, MS collection 994, John M. Chivington Papers, Stephen H. Hart Research and Library Center, Denver, CO; Roberts, *Massacre at Sand Creek*, p. 162.

54 Opening Statement, *Massacre of the Cheyenne Indians*, p. v; Hoig, *The Sand Creek Massacre*, p. 168.

55 Ibid., p. 175.

4 DAVID BEATTY

1 Indeed, the best-known of Beatty's biographers hailed him as the 'the last naval hero' despite his performance at Jutland. Stephen Roskill, *Admiral of the Fleet Earl Beatty: The Last Naval Hero* (Barnsley, 2018).

2 Winston Churchill, *The World Crisis*, 6 vols (New York, 1923–31), vol. I, p. 89.

3 Ibid., vol. III, p. 106.

4 Roskill, *Admiral of the Fleet Earl Beatty*, pp. 20–21.

5 Ibid., pp. 22–3.

6 Andrew Lambert, *Admirals: The Naval Commanders Who Made Britain Great* (London, 2009), p. 339.

7 Robert Massie, *Castles of Steel* (New York, 2003), p. 86.

8 Roskill, *Admiral of the Fleet Earl Beatty*, pp. 32–3.

9 Massie, *Castles of Steel*, p. 87.

10 Roskill, *Admiral of the Fleet Earl Beatty*, p. 42.

11 Churchill, *The World Crisis*, vol. I, p. 88.

12 Ibid.

13 Bernard Ireland, *Jane's Battleships of the 20th Century* (New York, 1996), p. 68.

14 Ibid., p. 100.

15 Ibid., p. 115.

16 Churchill, *The World Crisis*, vol. I, p. 89.

17 Ireland, *Jane's Battleships of the 20th Century*, p. 104.

18 Ibid., p. 109.

19 Norman Friedman, *The British Battleship, 1906–1945* (Annapolis, MD, 2015), p. 62.

20 James Holmes, 'The U.S. Navy Has Forgotten How to Fight,' *Foreign Policy*, 13 November 2018, https://foreignpolicy.com.

21 Roger Keyes to Chief of the War Staff, letter, 23 August 1914, in *The Keyes Papers: Selections from the Private and Official Correspondence of Admiral of the Fleet Baron Keyes of Zeebrugge*, ed. Paul G. Halpern (London, 1979), p. 9.

22 James Goldrick, *Before Jutland: The Naval War in Northern European Waters, August 1914–February 1915* (Annapolis, MD, 2015), p. 114.

23 Roger Keyes to Chief of the War Staff, letter, 29 August 1914, in *Keyes Papers*, p. 12.

24 David Beatty to Keyes, letter, 18 September 1914, in *Keyes Papers*, p. 28.

25 Jack Sweetman, ed., *The Great Admirals: Command at Sea, 1587–1945* (Annapolis, MD, 1997), p. 354.

26 Goldrick, *Before Jutland*, pp. 265–6.

27 Ibid., p. 268.

28 Archibald Moore, After Action Report, 25 January 1915, in *The Beatty Papers: Selections from the Private and Official Correspondence of Admiral of the Fleet Earl Beatty*, ed. B. McL. Ranft, 2 vols (London, 1989), vol. I, p. 207.

29 Sweetman, *The Great Admirals*, p. 354.

30 Churchill, *The World Crisis*, vol. I, p. 89.

31 Beatty to John Jellicoe, letter, 8 February 1915, in *The Jellicoe Papers: Selections from the Private and Official Correspondence of Admiral of the Fleet Earl Jellicoe of Scapa*, ed. Temple Patterson, 2 vols (London, 1966), vol. I, p. 144.

32 John Jellicoe to Beatty, letter, 23 March 1915, ibid., vol. I, p. 152.

33 Julian Corbett, *History of the Great War Naval Operations, Based on Official Documents* (London, 1923), vol. III, p. 318.

34 Andrew Gordon, *The Rules of the Game: Jutland and British Naval Command* (Annapolis, MD, 2012), pp. 54–8.

35 Corbett, *History of the Great War Naval Operations*, vol. III, pp. 333–4.

36 Ibid., p. 334.

37 Ibid.

38 Gordon, *The Rules of the Game*, p. 613.

39 Eric Grove, Introduction to Roskill, *Admiral of the Fleet Earl Beatty*.

40 Gordon, *The Rules of the Game*, p. 2.

41 Corbett, *History of the Great War Naval Operations*, vol. III, pp. 355–6.

42 Rear Admiral Pakenham to Margaret Strickland-Constable, letter, 9 June 1916, East Riding Archives and Records Service, DDST/1/8/1/17. Quoted in David Stevens, *In All Respects Ready: Australia's Navy in World War One* (South Melbourne, Vic, 2014), p. 215.

43 Lambert, *Admirals*, p. 366.

44 Corbett, 'Introduction', *History of the Great War Naval Operations*.

5 GIDEON J. PILLOW

 1 General order No. 349, Headquarters of the Army, 12 November 1847, in Cadmus M. Wilcox, *History of the Mexican War* (Washington, DC, 1892), p. 583; Thomas W. Cutrer, ed., *The Mexican War Diary and Correspondence of George B. McClellan* (Baton Rouge, LA, 2009), p. 119.

 2 Ulysses S. Grant, *Memoirs and Selected Letters* (New York, 1990), p. 196.

 3 Nathaniel Cheairs Hughes Jr and Roy P. Stonesifer, *The Life and Wars of Gideon Pillow* (Chapel Hill, NC, 1993), pp. 4–7.

 4 Ibid., pp. 8–9.

 5 Ibid., pp. 9–11; Robert P. Wettemann Jr, *Privilege vs. Equality: Civil–Military Relations in the Jacksonian Era, 1815–1845* (Santa Barbara, CA, 2009), pp. 44–71; Samuel P. Huntington, *The Soldier and the State: The Theory and Politics of Civil–Military Relations* (Cambridge, MA, 1957), pp. 8–18, 202–11.

 6 Hughes and Stonesifer, *Gideon Pillow*, pp. 32–4.

 7 James K. Polk to Gideon Pillow, 29 June 1846, in *Correspondence of James K. Polk*, ed. Wayne Custler (Knoxville, TN, 2009), vol. XI, pp. 231–2; Polk to Pillow, 2 July 1846, ibid., pp. 233–4.

 8 Timothy D. Johnson, *For Duty and Honor: Tennessee's Mexican War Experience* (Knoxville, TN, 2018), pp. 66–7; William Hugh Robarts, *Mexican War Veterans: A Complete Roster of the Regular and Volunteer Troops in the War between the United States and Mexico, from 1845 to 1848* (Washington, DC, 1887), pp. 72–3.

 9 Wilcox, *History of the Mexican War*, pp. 113–14; Earl J. Hess, *Field Armies and Fortifications in the Civil War: The Eastern Campaigns, 1861–1864* (Chapel Hill, NC, 2005), pp. 6–9.

10 General Zachary Taylor to Dr Wood, quoted in Felice Flanery Lewis, *Trailing Clouds of Glory: Zachary Taylor's Mexican War Campaign and His Emerging Civil War Leaders* (Tuscaloosa, AL, 2010), p. 108.

11 St George L. Sioussat, 'The Mexican War Letters of Colonel William Bowen Campbell, of Tennessee, Written to Governor David Campbell of Virginia, 1846–1847', *Tennessee Historical Magazine*, 1 (June 1915), p. 161.

12 Allan Peskin, *Volunteers: The Mexican War Journals of Private Richard Coulter and Sergeant Thomas Barclay, Company E, Second Pennsylvania Infantry* (Kent, OH, 1991), pp. 47–8.

13 K. Jack Bauer, *The Mexican War, 1846–1848* (New York, 1974), pp. 282–6.

14 Justin H. Smith, *The War with Mexico* (New York, 1919), vol. II, p. 44.

15 Johnson, *For Duty and Honor*, pp. 142–3.

16 Ibid., pp. 144–5.

17 Ibid., p. 146.

18 Ibid., pp. 146–8.

19 Ibid., pp. 148–9.

20 Ibid., pp. 149–55; Cutrer, ed., *The Mexican War Diary and Correspondence of George B. McClellan*, p. 119.

21 Winfield Scott, *Memoirs of Lieutenant General Scott, Written by Himself* (New York, 1864), p. 440; George B. McClellan to Sen. Daniel Sturgeon, 20 October 1847, in *The Mexican War Diary and Correspondence of George B. McClellan*, ed. Cutrer, p. 136.

22 Timothy D. Johnson, 'A Most Anomalous Affair: Gideon Pillow and Winfield Scott in the Mexico City Campaign', *Tennessee Historical Quarterly*, 66 (Spring 2007), pp. 8–9; Scott, *Memoirs of Lieutenant General Scott*, p. 440.

23 Nathaniel Cheairs Hughes Jr and Timothy D. Johnson, eds, *A Fighter from Way Back: The Mexican War Diary of Lt. Daniel Harvey Hill, 4th Artillery, U.S.A.* (Kent, OH, 2002), pp. III, 121.

24 Johnson, 'A Most Anomalous Affair', pp. 10–11.

25 Johnson, *For Duty and Honor*, pp. 190–91.

26 Hughes and Stonesifer, *Gideon Pillow*, pp. 95–6.

27 Johnson, *For Duty and Honor*, pp. 192–3.

28 Johnson, 'A Most Anomalous Affair', pp. 13–15.

29 Ibid., p. 12.

30 General Order No. 349, in Wilcox, *History of the Mexican War*, p. 583.

31 Johnson, *For Duty and Honor*, pp. 193–200; Timothy Johnson, *Winfield Scott: The Quest for Martial Glory* (Lawrence, KS, 1998), p. 1.

32 Hughes and Stonesifer, *Gideon Pillow*, pp. 124–30.

33 Ibid.

34 Ibid., pp. 156–208; John Y. Simon, 'Grant at Belmont', *Military Affairs*, 45 (December 1981), pp. 161–6.

35 Hughes and Stonesifer, *Gideon Pillow*, pp. 209–17; Grant, *Memoirs*, p. 196.

36 Hughes and Stonesifer, *Gideon Pillow*, pp. 217–39; Benjamin Franklin Cooling, *Forts Henry and Donelson: The Key to the Confederate Heartland* (Knoxville, TN, 1987), pp. 200–223.

37 Larry J. Daniel, *Battle of Stones River: The Forgotten Conflict between the Confederate Army of Tennessee and the Union Army of the Cumberland* (Baton Rouge, LA, 2012), p. 185; David Evans, *Sherman's Horsemen: Union Cavalry Operations in the Atlanta Campaign* (Bloomington, IN, 1996), pp. 143–5.

38 Hughes and Stonesifer, *Gideon Pillow*, pp. 300–322.

6 ANTONIO LÓPEZ DE SANTA ANNA

1 Will Fowler, *Santa Anna of Mexico* (Lincoln, NE, 2007), pp. 109–13, 133–42.
2 Ibid., pp. 154–5.
3 Stephen L. Hardin, *Texian Iliad: A Military History of the Texas Revolution, 1835–1836* (Austin, TX, 1994), pp. 120–21.
4 Fowler, *Santa Anna of Mexico*, p. 143.
5 Hardin, *Texian Iliad*, p. 127.
6 Ibid., pp. 136–49.
7 Ibid., p. 157.
8 Ibid., pp. 173–4.
9 Ibid., p. 202.
10 Ibid., pp. 209–10.
11 Ibid., pp. 210–12.
12 Ibid., pp. 216–17.
13 Fowler, *Santa Anna of Mexico*, pp. 189–90.
14 Jack Bauer, *The Mexican War, 1846–1848* (Lincoln, NE, 1974), pp. 10–12.
15 Fowler, *Santa Anna of Mexico*, pp. 253–5.
16 Bauer, *The Mexican War*, pp. 206–10.
17 Timothy Henderson, *A Glorious Defeat: Mexico and Its War with the United States* (New York, 2007), pp. 164–5.
18 Ibid., p. 165.
19 Fowler, *Santa Anna of Mexico*, pp. 263–5.
20 Ibid., pp. 266–7.
21 Bauer, *The Mexican War*, pp. 260–61.
22 Fowler, *Santa Anna of Mexico*, pp. 268–9.
23 Henderson, *A Glorious Defeat*, p. 167.
24 Fowler, *Santa Anna of Mexico*, p. 275.
25 Henderson, *A Glorious Defeat*, pp. 169–70.
26 Fowler, *Santa Anna of Mexico*, pp. 272–3.
27 Ibid., pp. 280–81.

7 FRANZ CONRAD VON HÖTZENDORF

1 Samuel R. Williamson Jr, 'The Origins of the War', in *The Oxford Illustrated History of the First World War*, ed. Hew Strachan (Oxford, 1998), p. 16; Holger Herwig, *The First World War: Germany and Austria–Hungary, 1914–1918* (London, 1997), p. 9.
2 The common contemporary term for the Austro-Hungarian Army was the *k.u.k.*, an abbreviation of *kaiserlich und königlich*.
3 Lawrence Sondhaus, *Franz Conrad von Hötzendorf: Architect of the Apocalypse* (Boston, MA, 2000), p. 243.
4 For more on the Italian army in the First World War, see John Gooch, *The Italian Army and the First World War* (New York, 2014).
5 Claudia Reichl-Ham, 'Conrad von Hötzendorf, Franz Xaver Josef Graf', *International Encyclopedia of the First World War*, 8 October 2014, https://encyclopedia.1914-1918-online.net, accessed 6 March 2021.
6 Ibid.

7 Ibid.

8 Sondhaus, *Franz Conrad von Hötzendorf*, p. 99; Holger Herwig's assessment is offered in his review of Sondhaus, *Franz Conrad Von Hötzendorf: Architect of the Apocalypse*, in *Central European History*, xxxv/1 (2002), pp. 121–3.

9 Herwig, *The First World War*, p. 9; Herwig, review, *Central European History* (2002), pp. 121–3.

10 Sondhaus, *Franz Conrad von Hötzendorf*, p. 82.

11 Herwig, *The First World War*, p. 10.

12 Ibid.

13 Carl von Clausewitz, *On War*, ed. and trans. Michael Howard and Peter Paret (Princeton, NJ, 1989), p. 87.

14 Sondhaus, *Franz Conrad von Hötzendorf*, p. 82.

15 Herwig, *First World War*, p. 9.

16 Ibid., p. 10.

17 Sondhaus, *Franz Conrad von Hötzendorf*, p. 96.

18 Herwig, *First World War*, p. 10.

19 Graydon A. Tunstall Jr, *Planning for War against Russia and Serbia: Austro-Hungarian and German Military Strategies, 1871–1914* (New York, 1993), pp. 92, 128; Sondhaus, *Franz Conrad von Hötzendorf*, p. 122.

20 Herwig, *First World War*, p. 52.

21 Tunstall, *Planning for War*, p. 262.

22 That is, 'war, war, war'. Samuel R. Williamson Jr, *Austria–Hungary and the Origins of the First World War* (New York, 1991), p. 192.

23 Herwig, *First World War*, pp. 9–10.

24 Ibid., p. 11.

25 Herwig, review, *Central European History* (2002), p. 123.

26 From a letter of 28 July 1914, cited in Herwig, *First World War*, pp. 10–11. For a particularly engaging, though somewhat sensationalist, examination of the link between Conrad's romantic obsession with Gina and the start of the war, see Franz-Stefan Gady, 'The Scandalous Love Affair that Started World War 1', *National Interest*, 12 June 2014, https://nationalinterest.org, accessed 6 March 2021.

27 Sondhaus, *Franz Conrad von Hötzendorf*, p. 1.

28 Williamson, 'The Origins of the War', pp. 16–17.

29 Herwig, *First World War*, p. 18.

30 Ibid., p. 22.

31 Ibid., p. 13.

32 Norman Stone, *The Eastern Front: 1914–1917* (London, 1975), p. 71.

33 Sondhaus, *Franz Conrad von Hötzendorf*, p. 2.

34 Tunstall, *Planning for War*, p. 183; for a different view, see Günther Kronenbitter, 'Austria–Hungary', in *War Planning 1914*, ed. Richard F. Hamilton and Holger H. Herwig (New York, 2010), pp. 35–9.

35 Herwig, *First World War*, p. 53.

36 Ibid.

37 Some scholars disagree as to whether any Austro-Hungarian pre-war plans included an option for mobilization against both Serbia and Russia that called for an attempt to crush Serbia first before redeploying forces to the Russian front. For differing views, see Herwig, *First World*

War, p. 53; Tunstall, *Planning for War*, pp. 160–62; Stone, *Eastern Front*, p. 72.

38 Herwig, *First World War*, pp. 51–2; Tunstall, *Planning for War*, p. 162.

39 Ibid., pp. 143–53.

40 Herwig, *First World War*, p. 53.

41 Tunstall, *Planning for War*, pp. 143–53; Herwig, *First World War*, pp. 54–5.

42 Tunstall, *Planning for War*, pp. 160, 162, 184.

43 Ibid., pp. 165, 167–70; Herwig, *First World War*, pp. 54–5; Stone, *Eastern Front*, pp. 76–7.

44 Herwig, *First World War*, p. 54.

45 Tunstall, *Planning for War*, p. 219; Kronenbitter, 'Austria–Hungary', p. 46.

46 Tunstall, *Planning for War*, pp. 166–7.

47 Ibid., p. 138.

48 Herwig, *First World War*, p. 90; Graydon Tunstall, *Blood on the Snow: The Carpathian Winter War of 1915* (Lexington, KS, 2010), p. 15.

49 Stone, *Eastern Front*, pp. 78–9.

50 Herwig, *First World War*, pp. 87–9.

51 Stone, *Eastern Front*, pp. 79–80.

52 Graydon A. Tunstall, *Written in Blood: The Battles for Fortress Przemyśl in WWI* (Bloomington, IN, 2016), pp. 26–7.

53 Herwig, *First World War*, p. 56.

54 Stone, *Eastern Front*, pp. 79–80; Herwig, *First World War*, p. 90.

55 Stone, *Eastern Front*, pp. 84–5.

56 Ibid., pp. 85–7.

57 Ibid., pp. 88–9.

58 Ibid., pp. 89–90; Herwig, *First World War*, pp. 92–3; Tunstall, *Written in Blood*, pp. 40, 48.

59 Herwig gives casualties of 500,000, while others state 400,000. Herwig, *First World War*, p. 52; Stone, *Eastern Front*, p. 91.

60 Tunstall, *Planning for War*, p. 239.

61 Herwig states that 'Conrad quickly pinned responsibility for defeat on railroad technicians, Viennese diplomats, and the German ally. The truth is more complex and it lies with Conrad.' *First World War*, p. 52.

62 According to Herwig, he also 'confided to his dinner circle the "dreadful thought" that a lost war could cost him the comfort of his beloved "Gina"'. Ibid., p. 92.

63 Tunstall, *Written in Blood*, p. 138.

64 Herwig, *First World War*, pp. 107–8; Tunstall, *Written in Blood*, p. 110; Stone, *Eastern Front*, pp. 97–9.

65 Herwig, *First World War*, p. 120.

66 Ibid., pp. 108–9; Richard L. DiNardo, *Breakthrough: The Gorlice–Tarnow Campaign, 1915* (Denver, CO, 2010), p. 13.

67 Herwig, *First World War*, p. 78.

68 Tunstall, *Blood on the Snow*, p. 6.

69 DiNardo, *Breakthrough*, p. 23.

70 Tunstall, *Blood on the Snow*, p. 10.

71 Ibid., p. 5.

72 Tunstall, *Written in Blood*, pp. 212–15; Herwig, *First World War*, pp. 136–7; DiNardo, *Breakthrough*, pp. 23–5.

73 Tunstall, *Written in Blood*, p. 259; Tunstall, *Blood on the Snow*, pp. 163–208.
74 Tunstall gives the figure of 'at least' 800,000, while DiNardo gives a figure of 600,000. See DiNardo, *Breakthrough*, p. 25; Tunstall, *Blood on the Snow*, pp. 12, 212.
75 Tunstall, *Written in Blood*, p. 288; DiNardo, *Breakthrough*, p. 25.
76 Tunstall, *Written in Blood*, pp. 22, 114, 138.
77 Tunstall, *Blood on the Snow*, p. 160.
78 Herwig, *First World War*, p. 140.
79 Ibid., p. 141.
80 Ibid., pp. 143–4.
81 DiNardo, *Breakthrough*, p. 42; Herwig, *First World War*, pp. 143–4, 146.
82 Ibid., p. 146.
83 DiNardo, *Breakthrough*, pp. 31, 137.
84 For an example of this in the 1915 Serbian campaign, see Herwig, *First World War*, pp. 158–9. For an example from the Italian front, see ibid., pp. 204–7, 242; and DiNardo, *Breakthrough*, p. 86. For an example from the Romanian campaign, see Herwig, *First World War*, p. 218.
85 For Conrad's poor management of the Italian front, see Herwig, *First World War*, pp. 204–7; for his mismanagement of the Eastern Front in 1916 see ibid., pp. 209–12.
86 Ibid., pp. 214–16.
87 Ibid., pp. 242–3.
88 Ibid., p. 243.
89 Ibid., p. 344.
90 Ibid., p. 366.
91 Ibid., p. 372.
92 Ibid., p. 373.
93 See Franz Conrad von Hötzendorf, *Aus meiner Dienstzeit, 1906–1918*, 5 vols (Vienna, 1921–5).
94 Sondhaus, *Franz Conrad von Hötzendorf*, p. vii.
95 Eugene of Savoy, or Franz Eugen Prinz von Savoyen-Carignan (1663–1736), was an Austrian field marshal who fought in the Austro-Turkish wars, the War of the Grand Alliance, the War of Spanish Succession and the War of Polish Succession. He is widely regarded to have been 'the foremost general of his time' and one of the great commanders of all time. Trevor N. Dupuy et al., *The Harper Encyclopedia of Military Biography* (New York, 1995), pp. 242–3; Herwig, *First World War*, p. 43.
96 Tunstall, *Blood on the Snow*, p. 14; Herwig, *First World War*, p. 43.

8 LEWIS BRERETON

1 Christopher M. Rein, *The North African Air Campaign: U.S. Army Air Forces from El Alamein to Salerno* (Lawrence, KS, 2012), p. 178.
2 Wesley F. Craven and Jame L. Cate, eds, *The Army Air Forces in World War II*, vol. III: *Europe: Argument to V-E Day, January 1944 to May 1945* (Chicago, IL, 1951), pp. 230–34; David Eisenhower, *Eisenhower at War, 1943–1945* (New York, 1986), pp. 375–81. On 24 July, 9th Air Force P-47s mistakenly strafed U.S. positions after a botched weather recall, and on the 25th many

of Brereton's medium bombers dropped short of their targets, killing more than one hundred infantrymen from the 30th Infantry Division.

3 Kenneth P. Werrell, 'Friction in Action: Revisiting the u.s. Army Air Forces' August 1943 Raid on Ploesti', *Journal of Military History*, LXXXIII/2 (April 2019), pp. 509–40.

4 Stephen Taaffe, *Marshall and His Generals: u.s. Army Commanders in World War* II (Lawrence, KS, 2011).

5 Phillip S. Meilinger, *Hoyt S. Vandenberg: The Life of a General* (Bloomington, IN, 1989), p. 49.

6 Roger G. Miller, 'A "Pretty Damn Able Commander" – Lewis Hyde Brereton: Part I', *Air Power History*, XLVII/4 (2000), pp. 7–11.

7 Ibid., pp. 14–20.

8 Ibid., p. 24. Orders and Assignments, Brereton Personnel File, National Archives and Records Administration, St Louis, MO.

9 Lewis H. Brereton, *The Brereton Diaries: The War in the Air in the Pacific, Middle East and Europe, 3 October 1941 – 8 May 1945* (New York, 1946), p. 3; Christopher R. Gabel, *The u.s. Army Maneuvers of 1941* (Washington, DC, 1991), pp. 179–81.

10 Brereton, *The Brereton Diaries*, p. 5.

11 Samuel Limneos, 'Death from Within, the Destruction of the Far East Air Force: Strategy vs. Feasibility', *Army History*, 104 (Summer 2017), pp. 17–18.

12 William H. Bartsch, *December 8, 1941: MacArthur's Pearl Harbor* (College Station, TX, 2007), p. 409.

13 Brereton, *The Brereton Diaries*, pp. 38–9.

14 Bartsch, *December 8, 1941*, p. 415.

15 Rein, *The North African Air Campaign*, p. 168.

16 Wesley F. Craven and Jame L. Cate, eds, *The Army Air Forces in World War* II, vol. II: *Europe: Torch to Pointblank, August 1942 to December 1943* (Chicago, IL, 1949), pp. 477–8.

17 Rein, *The North African Air Campaign*, pp. 176–7.

18 Werrell, 'Friction in Action', p. 531.

19 Brereton, *The Brereton Diaries*, p. 192.

20 Craven and Cate, eds, *The Army Air Forces in World War* II, vol. II, p. 477.

21 H. H. Arnold, *Global Mission* (New York, 1949), p. 494.

22 Brereton, *The Brereton Diaries*, p. 214.

23 Meilinger, *Hoyt S. Vandenberg*, p. 49. Meilinger explains that Bradley and several other senior officers found Brereton to be uncooperative, while Arnold and Spaatz were likely 'disenchanted' with his performance.

24 Eisenhower, *Eisenhower at War*, p. 375.

25 Craven and Cate, eds, *The Army Air Forces in World War* II, vol. III, p. 230.

26 Ibid., pp. 230, 234. Brereton's figures from his *Diaries* differ, pp. 313–16.

27 Craven and Cate, eds, *The Army Air Forces in World War* II, vol. III, p. 234.

28 Brereton, *The Brereton Diaries*, p. 314.

29 Ibid., pp. 316–17; Robert M. Citino, *Blitzkrieg to Desert Storm: The Evolution of Operational Warfare* (Lawrence, KS, 2004), p. 110, quoting Omar Bradley in *A Soldier's Story*, p. 358.

30 Alfred M. Beck, ed., *With Courage: The u.s. Army Air Forces in World War* II (Washington, DC, 1994), p. 244.

31 Ibid.; Charles B. MacDonald, 'The Decision to Launch Operation
Market-Garden', in *Command Decisions*, ed. Kent R. Greenfield
(Washington, DC, 1960), p. 435; George H. Brett and Lewis H. Brereton,
Interview, 8 November 1962, Marshall Foundation Research Library,
p. 5.

32 Meilinger, *Hoyt S. Vandenberg*, p. 49.

33 Cable FWD 13765, Eisenhower to Senior Commanders, 4 September 1944,
in *The Papers of Dwight David Eisenhower: The War Years*, ed. Alfred D.
Chandler (Baltimore, MD, 1970), vol. IV, p. 2115. Brereton was an addressee.
The cable started with 'Enemy resistance on the entire front shows signs
of collapse.'

34 Martin Middlebrook, *Arnhem 1944: The Airborne Battle* (London, 1994),
pp. 438–40.

35 Charles B. MacDonald, *The U.S. Army in World War Two: The Siegfried
Line Campaign* (Washington, DC, 1963), p. 442.

36 Headquarters IX Troop Carrier Command, *Air Invasion of Holland, IX
Troop Carrier Command Report on Operation Market*, 2 January 1945, Annex
5i, Maneuver Center of Excellence Library, Fort Benning, GA; Craven and
Cate, eds, *The Army Air Forces in World War II*, vol. III, pp. 602–4.

37 Ibid., p. 602.

38 MacDonald, *The U.S. Army in World War Two*, pp. 138–9.

39 *Air Invasion of Holland, IX Troop Carrier Command Report*, p. 72.

40 Martin Wolfe, *Green Light: A Troop Carrier Squadron's War from
Normandy to the Rhine* (Washington, DC, 1993), p. 276; Middlebrook,
Arnhem 1944, p. 16; Sebastian Cox, 'Air Power in Operation Market-
Garden', *Air Clues*, 4 (April 1985), p. 152; Antony Beevor, *The Battle of
Arnhem: The Deadliest Airborne Operation of World War II* (New York, 2018),
p. 33.

41 Wolfe, *Green Light*, pp. 384–5; Beevor, *The Battle of Arnhem*, p. 33. Brereton
would choose to use double tow during the last major airborne operation
of the war, Operation VARSITY, where distances from bases to the landing
zones were much shorter than in MARKET.

42 Beevor, *The Battle of Arnhem*, p. 144.

43 Ibid., pp. 206, 246.

44 Brigadier General Floyd Parks to Family, 17 September 1944, Floyd Parks
Papers, Box 5, Eisenhower Library. Parks was Brereton's chief of staff at
FAAA.

45 Craven and Cate, eds, *The Army Air Forces in World War II*, vol. III,
pp. 608–9.

46 Efficiency Report on Lewis Brereton, General D. D. Eisenhower, 10
January 1945, Brereton Personnel File, NARA.

47 Brereton to Lieutenant General Barney M. Giles, Chief of the Air Staff,
HQ USAAF, 27 October 1944, Brereton Personnel File, NARA.

48 John Abbatiello, 'The First Allied Airborne Army in Operation Varsity:
Applying the Lessons of Arnhem', master's thesis, King's College
London, 1995.

49 'Lieutenant General Lewis Hyde Brereton', U.S. Air Force, www.af.mil,
accessed 18 March 2018.

50 Brereton Personnel File, NARA.

51 Ibid.
52 Phillip S. Meilinger, *Airmen and Air Theory: A Review of the Sources* (Maxwell Air Force Base, AL, 2001), p. 47.
53 Joint Publication 1-02, *Department of Defense Dictionary of Military and Associated Terms*, 15 February 2016, Washington, DC, p. 40.

9 GEORGE A. CUSTER

1 Duane Schultz, *Custer: Lessons in Leadership* (New York, 2010), p. 1.
2 Evan S. Connell, *Son of Morning Star: Custer and the Little Bighorn* (San Francisco, CA, 1984), p. 106.
3 Schultz, *Custer: Lessons in Leadership*, pp. 3–4.
4 Edward G. Longacre, *Custer: The Making of a Young General* (New York, 2018), p. 10.
5 Edward Caudill and Paul Ashdown, *Inventing Custer: The Making of an American Legend* (New York, 2015), pp. 21–2.
6 Longacre, *Custer*, pp. 46–55; Schultz, *Custer: Lessons in Leadership*, pp. 13–17.
7 Longacre, *Custer*, pp. 77–81.
8 Ibid., pp. 84–5; Schultz, *Custer: Lessons in Leadership*, p. 21.
9 Ibid., p. 2.
10 Longacre, *Custer*, pp. 118–27; Frederic F. Van de Water, *Glory-Hunter: A Life of General Custer* (Lincoln, NE, 1988), pp. 47–8.
11 Jeffry D. Wert, *Custer: The Controversial Life of George Armstrong Custer* (New York, 1996), p. 73.
12 Longacre, *Custer*, pp. 144–51.
13 Schultz, *Custer: Lessons in Leadership*, p. 2.
14 Longacre, *Custer*, pp. 170–76.
15 Wert, *Custer*, pp. 176–83.
16 Ibid., pp. 186–98.
17 Caudill and Ashdown, *Inventing Custer*, pp. 146–51.
18 Ibid., pp. 49–52; Wert, *Custer*, pp. 231–4.
19 Wert, *Custer*, pp. 235–6.
20 Ibid., pp. 236–43.
21 Caudill and Ashdown, *Inventing Custer*, pp. 56–62.
22 Ibid., pp. 88–92.
23 Ibid., p. 93; Van de Water, *Glory-Hunter*, p. 175.
24 Van de Water, *Glory-Hunter*, p. 183.
25 Bill Yenne, *Indian Wars: The Campaign for the American West* (Yardley, PA, 2006), pp. 107, 129.
26 Wert, *Custer*, pp. 270–77.
27 Ibid., pp. 277–8.
28 James Welch, *Killing Custer: The Battle of the Little Bighorn and the Fate of the Plains Indians* (New York, 1994), pp. 81–9.
29 Yenne, *Indian Wars*, pp. 177–8.
30 Ibid., pp. 179–80.
31 Welch, *Killing Custer*, pp. 113–23.
32 Van de Water, *Glory-Hunter*, p. 323; Schultz, *Custer: Lessons in Leadership*, p. 163.

33 Yenne, *Indian Wars*, pp. 193–6.
34 Welch, *Killing Custer*, pp. 152–3; Wert, *Custer*, pp. 337–9; Schultz, *Custer: Lessons in Leadership*, pp. 166–7.
35 Welch, *Killing Custer*, p. 127.
36 Yenne, *Indian Wars*, pp. 196–7.
37 Wert, *Custer*, pp. 345–8.
38 Schultz, *Custer: Lessons in Leadership*, p. 170.
39 Ibid., pp. 172–3.
40 Ibid., pp. 173–4; Yenne, *Indian Wars*, p. 206.
41 Schultz, *Custer: Lessons in Leadership*, p. 4.

10 MARCUS LICINIUS CRASSUS

1 Plutarch, *Crassus*, 31.1–7. The molten-gold story is perhaps apocryphal but reported in Cassius Dio, 40.27.3, and Florus, *Epitome*, 1.46.11. The author wishes to thank Jonathan Abel, John Hosler, Nicholas Murray and Benjamin L. Price for their feedback on this chapter Any errors are, of course, my own.
2 Plutarch, *Crassus*, 32.1–4.
3 Eliot A. Cohen and John Gooch, *Military Misfortunes: The Anatomy of Failure in War* (New York, 1990), p. 8.
4 See Gareth C. Sampson, *The Defeat of Rome in the East: Crassus, the Parthians, and the Disastrous Battle of Carrhae, 53 BC* (Philadelphia, PA, 2008), p. 146, *passim*. Sampson argues that Surenas' brilliance was the primary cause of the outcome of the battle. Sampson's book is the most comprehensive work available on the background, execution and significance of the Carrhae campaign. I referred to it frequently while composing this chapter.
5 Plutarch, *Crassus*, 6.1, 6.6.
6 Barry Strauss, *The Spartacus War* (New York, 2009), p. 117.
7 Ibid.
8 Plutarch, *Crassus*, 7.2.
9 Ibid., 2.3.
10 Ibid., 2.5–6.
11 Ibid., 2.1.
12 Ibid., 3.1–3.
13 Ibid., 2.2.
14 Plutarch, *Crassus*, 15.1–5.
15 Sampson, *The Defeat of Rome in the East*, p. 95.
16 Plutarch, *Crassus*, 16.1–2; Cassius Dio, 40.12.1.
17 Sampson, *The Defeat of Rome in the East*, pp. 95–6.
18 Jonathan P. Roth, *The Logistics of the Roman Army at War (264 BC–AD 235)* (Leiden, 2012), p. 67. Roth estimates that a full ration weighed between 2.2 and 2.85 pounds. My estimate is based upon 34,000 times the lower figure of 2.2 pounds.
19 Plutarch, *Crassus*, 17.1.
20 Rose Mary Sheldon, *Intelligence Activities in Ancient Rome: Trust in the Gods, but Verify* (London, 2005), p. 88.

21 Ibid., pp. 86–97.
22 Sampson, *The Defeat of Rome in the East*, pp. 100–101.
23 Ibid.
24 Ibid., p. 103.
25 Plutarch, *Crassus*, 17.4.
26 Sheldon, *Intelligence Activities in Ancient Rome*, p. 4.
27 Plutarch, *Crassus*, 18.4.
28 Sheldon, *Intelligence Activities in Ancient Rome*, p. 88.
29 Plutarch, *Crassus*, 19.1–3.
30 Ibid., 19.2.
31 Sampson, *The Defeat of Rome in the East*, p. 107.
32 Plutarch, *Crassus*, 21.5.
33 Ibid., 18.1–2.
34 Sampson, *The Defeat of Rome in the East*, pp. 112–13.
35 Plutarch, *Crassus*, 20.1; Sampson, *The Defeat of Rome in the East*, p. 108. Estimates of the size of the Roman army vary. Crassus may have marched into Parthia with as few as 35,000 men.
36 Ibid., pp. 109–11.
37 Plutarch, *Crassus*, 22.1–6.
38 Sampson, *The Defeat of Rome in the East*, p. 110.
39 Plutarch, *Crassus*, 21.4.
40 Ibid., 20.1.
41 For an in-depth examination of the battle and its aftermath, see Sampson, *The Defeat of Rome in the East*, pp. 124–47.
42 Plutarch, *Crassus*, 23.3.
43 Ibid., 23.4.
44 Ibid., 23.5.
45 Ibid., 23.6–24.3.
46 Ibid., 24.4.
47 Ibid., 24.4–26.6.
48 Ibid., 25.1.
49 Ibid., 25.2.
50 Ibid., 25.2–12.
51 Ibid., 26.3.
52 Ibid., 26.4–27.1.
53 Ibid., 27.3–8.
54 Ibid., 28.1–31.7.
55 Ibid., 28.1–31.7.
56 Ibid., 21.7.

II NIKIAS

1 Plutarch, 'The Life of Demetrius', *Lives*, vol. IX, trans. Bernadotte Perrin (Cambridge, MA, 1920), 1.6.
2 Plutarch, 'Nicias', *Greek Lives*, trans. Robin Waterfield (Oxford, 1998), 2.1.
3 Thucydides, *History of the Peloponnesian War*, ed. M. I. Finley, trans. Rex Warner (Oxford, 1972), 4.53–4, 4.129–31, 3.51, 4.42–4 and 3.91.
4 Plutarch, 'Nicias', 2.3 and 2.4.

5 Plutarch, 'Comparison of Nicias and Crassus', *Lives*, vol. III, trans. Bernadotte Perrin (Cambridge, MA, 1916), 3.4.
6 Description of Pylos campaign is from Thucydides, *Peloponnesian War*, 4.3–41.
7 Plutarch, 'Nicias', 8.2–4.
8 Ibid., 8.5–6.
9 Ibid., 8.8.
10 Ibid., 10.9.
11 Thucydides, *Peloponnesian War*, 6.24.
12 Ibid., 2.65.
13 M. R. Christ, 'Conscription of Hoplites in Classical Athens', *Classical Quarterly*, LI/2 (2001), p. 399.
14 Ibid., p. 403.
15 Ibid., p. 407.
16 Vincent Gabrielsen, *Financing the Athenian Fleet* (Baltimore, MD, 1994), p. 72.
17 Christ, 'Conscription of Hoplites', p. 409.
18 Plutarch, 'Pericles', *Greek Lives*, trans. Waterfield, 20.1.
19 Thucydides, *Peloponnesian War*, 4.75.1–2.
20 Ibid., 3.91.1–3, 4.53.1 and 4.129.2–3.
21 Ibid., 7.26.2.
22 John S. Morrison and John F. Coates, *The Athenian Trireme* (New York, 2000), p. 105. The authors present a very convincing re-creation of the duration, path and particulars of the Sicilian expedition's naval voyage.
23 Thucydides, *Peloponnesian War*, 6.42.1.
24 Ibid., 6.42.2.
25 Ibid., 6.44.2.
26 Morrison and Coates, *The Athenian Trireme*, p. 105.
27 Ibid.
28 Diodorus Siculus, *The Persian Wars to the Fall of Athens*, trans. Peter Green (Austin, TX, 2010), 13.3.4.
29 Morrison and Coates, *The Athenian Trireme*, p. 105.
30 Thucydides, *Peloponnesian War*, 3.85–8.
31 *Inscriptiones Graecae*, IG 12: *Inscriptiones Atticae*, 2nd edn, ed. Friedrich Hiller von Gaertringen (Berlin, 1924), IG 12.51, 52.
32 Thucydides, *Peloponnesian War*, 6.44.3.
33 Ibid., 6.46.
34 Ibid., 6.48–9.
35 Ibid., 6.49.4.
36 Ibid., 6.51.
37 Ibid., 6.50.4–5.
38 Ibid., 6.34.4–6.
39 Ibid., 1.100.2 (at Naxos) and 1.116.1–2 (at Samos).
40 Ibid., 6.64.1.
41 Ibid., 6.65.3.
42 Ibid., 6.66.2-3; An excellent re-creation of the topography of Syracuse is in Saverio Cavallari, *Zur Topographie von Syrakus* (Strasburg, 1845).
43 Thucydides, *Peloponnesian War*, 6.66.3.
44 Ibid., 6.22.1.

45 Ibid., 6.70.3.
46 Ibid., 6.70.3.
47 Ibid., 6.71.1–2.
48 Ibid., 6.88.6, 6.94.4.
49 Ibid., 6.97.1–4.
50 Ibid., 6.101.
51 Ibid., 7.2.
52 Ibid., 7.5–6.
53 Ibid., 7.8, 11–15.
54 Ibid., 7.15.2.
55 Ibid., 7.16.
56 Ibid., 7.42.
57 Ibid., 7.43.
58 Ibid., 7.47.
59 Ibid., 7.48.
60 Ibid., 7.50.
61 Ibid., 7.71–3.
62 Ibid., 7.78–81.
63 Ibid., 6.24.
64 Ibid., 6.8.1.
65 Ibid., 6.8.5.
66 Ibid., 6.16–18.
67 Ibid., 6.49.
68 Ibid., 6.47.
69 Ibid., 6.48.
70 Ibid., 7.2.
71 Ibid., 7.49.1.
72 Plutarch, 'Nicias', 14.5.
73 Ibid., 14.6.
74 Thucydides, *Peloponnesian War*, 7.11–15.
75 Donald Kagan, *The Peloponnesian War* (New York, 2003), pp. 294–5.
76 Thucydides, *Peloponnesian War*, 7.23.
77 Ibid., 7.87.

12 RAYMOND VI, COUNT OF TOULOUSE

1 My thanks to Matthew G. Stanard and Lydia Burton for their comments on earlier drafts.
2 Xavier de Planhol, *An Historical Geography of France*, trans. Janet Lloyd (Cambridge, 1994), pp. 133, 313–15.
3 Rebecca Rist, *The Papacy and Crusading in Europe, 1198–1245* (London, 2009), pp. vii, 3–9.
4 Peter of les Vaux-de-Cernay, *The History of the Albigensian Crusade*, trans. W. A. Sibly and M. D. Sibly (Woodbridge, 1998), pp. 10–14, hereafter abbreviated as PVC; Malcolm Barber, *The Cathars: Dualist Heretics in Languedoc in the High Middle Ages* (Harlow, 2000), p. 7.
5 William of Puylaurens, *The Chronicle of William of Puylaurens*, trans. W. A. Sibly and M. D. Sibly (Woodbridge, 2003), pp. 11–12, 27;

Élie Griffe, *Les Débuts de l'aventure Cathare en Languedoc (1140–1190)* (Paris, 1969), pp. 124–8.

6 Ane L. Bysted, *The Crusade Indulgence: Spiritual Rewards and the Theology of the Crusades, c. 1095–1216* (Leiden, 2015), pp. 45–6, 67–9, 161.

7 Laurence W. Marvin, 'Thirty-Nine Days and a Wake-Up: The Impact of the Indulgence and Forty Days Service on the Albigensian Crusade, 1209–1218', *The Historian*, LXV/1 (2002), pp. 75–94.

8 Ibid., pp. 91–2.

9 Elisabeth Voldola, *Excommunication in the Middle Ages* (Berkeley, CA, 1986), pp. 36, 45–7.

10 Paul of Bernried, *The Life of Pope Gregory VII*, in *The Papal Reform of the Eleventh Century: Lives of Pope Leo IX and Pope Gregory VII*, trans. I. S. Robinson (Manchester, 2004), p. 327; Uta-Renate Blumenthal, *The Investiture Controversy: Church and Monarchy from the Ninth to the Twelfth Century* (Philadelphia, PA, 1988), p. 123.

11 C. Devic and J. Vaissète, ed., *Histoire générale du Languedoc*, vol. VIII, 2nd edn, rev. A. Molinier (Toulouse, 1879), cols 436–8; Elaine Graham-Leigh, *The Southern French Nobility and the Albigensian Crusade* (Woodbridge, 2005), pp. 48–9; Walker Reid Cosgrove, 'Pierre's Crossing: Violence and Assassination in the South of France at the Turn of the Thirteenth Century', in *Ecclesia et Violentia: Violence against the Church and Violence within the Church in the Middle Ages*, ed. Radosław Kotecki and Jacek Maciejewski (Newcastle upon Tyne, 2014), p. 33.

12 Peter D. Clarke, *The Interdict in the Thirteenth Century: A Question of Collective Guilt* (Oxford, 2007), pp. 1–2.

13 PVC, p. 114; Clarke, *Interdict in the Thirteenth Century*, pp. 164, 173, 243–4.

14 *The Chronicle of William of Puylaurens*, p. 18; Claire Taylor, 'Innocent III, John of England and the Albigensian Crusade', in *Pope Innocent III and His World*, ed. John C. Moore (Aldershot, 1999), pp. 206–8; Richard Benjamin, 'A Forty Years War: Toulouse and the Plantagenets, 1156–1196', *Historical Research*, 61 (1988), pp. 270–85.

15 John Hine Mundy, *Liberty and Political Power in Toulouse, 1050–1230* (New York, 1954), pp. 30, 43, 45–7, 50; Walker Reid Cosgrove, 'Clergy and Crusade: The Church in Southern France and the Albigensian Crusade', PhD diss., St Louis University, 2011, pp. 96, 98.

16 Daniel Power, 'Who Went on the Albigensian Crusade?', *English Historical Review*, CXXVIII/534 (2013), pp. 1047–85.

17 PVC, p. 43; 'Processus negotii Raymundi comitis Tolosani', *Patrologiae cursus completus* 216, ed. J. P. Migne (Paris, 1891), cols 89–98.

18 PVC, pp. 44–5.

19 Ibid., p. 48.

20 *The Song of the Cathar Wars*, trans. Janet Shirley (Burlington, VT, 1996), p. 15; Graham-Leigh, *Southern French Nobility*, pp. 28–9.

21 PVC, pp. 48–9; *Chronicle of William of Puylaurens*, p. 32; Laurent Macé, 'La quarantaine du comte de Toulouse durant l'été 1209', in *En Languedoc au XIIIe siècle: Le temps du sac de Béziers*, ed. Monique Bourin (Perpignan, 2010), pp. 147–8.

22 PVC, p. 54.

23 Ibid., pp. 88–9.

24 Ibid., pp. 101–2.

25 Ibid., p. 102; *Song of the Cathar Wars*, pp. 37–8.

26 *Song of the Cathar Wars*, pp. 38–9.

27 *Chronicle of William of Puylaurens*, p. 38.

28 PVC, pp. 113–14.

29 Ibid., p. 112.

30 Laurence W. Marvin, 'The White and Black Confraternities of Toulouse and the Albigensian Crusade, 1210–1211', *Viator*, XV/1 (2009), pp. 133–50.

31 PVC, p. 114.

32 *Chronicle of William of Puylaurens*, p. 39.

33 PVC, p. 112.

34 *Song of the Cathar Wars*, pp. 45–6; *Chronicle of William of Puylaurens*, p. 41.

35 Laurence W. Marvin, *The Occitan War: A Military and Political History of the Albigensian Crusade, 1209–1218* (Cambridge, 2008), pp. 116–17.

36 *Song of the Cathar Wars*, pp. 48–9; PVC, pp. 130–31; Laurent Macé, *Les comtes de Toulouse et leur entourage: Rivalités, alliances et jeux de pouvoir XIIe–XIIIe siècles* (Toulouse, 2000), pp. 237–8.

37 *Song of the Cathar Wars*, p. 50; Daniel Brown, *Hugh de Lacy, First Earl of Ulster: Rising and Falling in Angevin Ireland* (Woodbridge, 2016), p. 120.

38 PVC, pp. 131–2.

39 PVC, p. 133; Linda Paterson, *The World of the Troubadours: Medieval Occitan Society, c. 1100–c. 1300* (Cambridge, 1993), pp. 111–14.

40 Marvin, *Occitan War*, pp. 122–7.

41 PVC, pp. 139–40; *Song of the Cathar Wars*, pp. 54–5; *Chronicle of William of Puylaurens*, pp. 42–3.

42 PVC, p. 168.

43 *Song of the Cathar Wars*, pp. 64–5.

44 Damian J. Smith, *Crusade, Heresy and Inquisition in the Lands of the Crown of Aragon (c. 1167–1276)* (Leiden, 2010), pp. 33–6.

45 PVC, p. 308.

46 *Chronicle of William of Puylaurens*, pp. 43–4; PVC, pp. 197–8.

47 *Song of the Cathar Wars*, pp. 69–70; *Chronicle of William of Puylaurens*, pp. 47–8.

48 *Song of the Cathar Wars*, pp. 69–70; *Chronicle of William of Puylaurens*, p. 48.

49 Taylor, 'Innocent III', p. 210; Marvin, *Occitan War*, pp. 196–7; *Song of the Cathar Wars*, p. 71.

50 *Chronicle of William of Puylaurens*, pp. 50–51; PVC, pp. 222–5.

51 *Chronicle of William of Puylaurens*, p. 31; Macé, *Les comtes de Toulouse*, pp. 74–86.

52 PVC, p. 225; *Chronicle of William of Puylaurens*, pp. 50–51.

53 *Song of the Cathar Wars*, pp. 72–9.

54 PVC, pp. 311–12; Constantin Fasolt, trans., 'Eyewitness Account of the Fourth Lateran Council (1215)', in *Medieval Europe*, ed. Julius Kirshner and Karl F. Morrison (Chicago, IL, 1986), vol. IV, p. 371.

55 *Song of the Cathar Wars*, pp. 83–7.

56 Ibid., pp. 86–7; *Chronicle of William of Puylaurens*, p. 55.

57 Marvin, *Occitan War*, p. 260.

58 *Song of the Cathar Wars*, pp. 119–20; *Chronicle of William of Puylaurens*, p. 59; PVC, p. 270.

59 *Song of the Cathar Wars*, pp. 122–7, 139.
60 *Chronicle of William of Puylaurens*, pp. 67–8.
61 Ibid., pp. 138–44.
62 C. P. Bagley, '*Paratge* in the Anonymous *Chanson de la Croisade Albigeoise*', *French Studies*, XXI/3 (1967), pp. 195–204, esp. pp. 195, 197; Paterson, *World of the Troubadours*, pp. 20, 64, 70–71, 288; Catherine Léglu, Rebecca Rist and Claire Taylor, eds, *The Cathars and the Albigensian Crusade: A Source Book* (New York, 2014), pp. 83, 181.
63 Bagley, '*Paratge*', p. 195. As Bagley noted, the word is used around fifty times in the poem's section written by an anonymous author.

13 NOGI MARESUKE

1 Cathal J. Nolan, *The Allure of Battle: A History of How Wars Have Been Won and Lost* (New York, 2017), pp. 251–3; Stephen D. Biddle, *Military Power: Explaining Victory and Defeat in Modern Battle* (Princeton, NJ, 2004), pp. 31–3. For a biographical, psychological approach to military incompetence, see Norman F. Dixon, *On the Psychology of Military Incompetence* (London, 1976).
2 For a survey of operations in the Russo-Japanese War until the beginning of the siege on Port Arthur, see Richard M. Connaughton, *Rising Sun and Tumbling Bear: Russia's War with Japan* (London, 2003), pp. 37–106.
3 Tani Hisao, *Kimitsu Nichi-rō senshi* (Tokyo, 1966), p. 197; Yoshihisa Tak Matsukata, 'Human Bullets, General Nogi and the Myth of Port Arthur', in *The Russo-Japanese War in Global Perspective: World War Zero*, ed. John W. Steinberg et al. (Leiden and Boston, MA, 2005–7), p. 182; Tōgawa Yukio, *Nogi Maresuke* (Tokyo, 1968), p. 231.
4 Kuwada Etsu, 'Ryojun yōsai no kōryaku', in *Kindai Nihon sensō-shi*, vol. I, ed. Kuwada Etsu and Okumura Fusao (Tokyo, 1995), pp. 508, 510, 516; Denis Warner and Peggy Warner, *The Tide at Sunrise: A History of the Russo-Japanese War, 1904–1905* (London, 1975), pp. 343–4.
5 Doris G. Bargen, *Suicidal Honor: General Nogi and the Writings of Mori Ōgai and Natsume Soseki* (Honolulu, HI, 2006), pp. 43–52, 62–3.
6 Kuwada, 'Ryojun', pp. 508, 511; Warner and Warner, *Tide at Sunrise*, pp. 299–301; Tōgawa, *Nogi*, pp. 228–9.
7 Erwin Baelz, *Awakening Japan: The Diary of a German Doctor* (New York, 1972), p. 288; Warner and Warner, *Tide at Sunrise*, p. 382.
8 Joseph E. Kuhn, 'Report on the Russo-Japanese War', in *Reports of Military Observers attached to the Armies in Manchuria during the Russo-Japanese War*, ed. U.S. War Department (Washington, DC, 1906), vol. III, p. 122.
9 Kojima Noboru, *Nichi-rō sensō* (Tokyo, 1990), vol. III, pp. 138–9; Tōgawa, *Nogi*, pp. 233–4; Kuhn, 'Report on the Russo-Japanese War', pp. 153–71.
10 Imperial General Staff, *Official History (Naval and Military) of the Russo-Japanese War* (London, 1920), vol. III, p. 67; Edward Diedrich, 'The Last Iliad: The Siege of Port Arthur in the Russo-Japanese War, 1904–1905', PhD diss., New York University, 1978, p. 292.
11 Chōnan Masayoshi, ed., *Nichi-ro sensō dai-san gun kankei shiryōshū: Ōba Jirō nikki, Inoue Ikutarō nikki de miru Ryojun, Hōten-sen* (Tokyo, 2014),

pp. 676–7; Kuhn, 'Report on the Russo-Japanese War', p. 190; Matsukata, 'Human Bullets', pp. 184, 187; General Shiroi's testimony, quoted in Takakura Tetsuichi, *Tanaka Giichi Denki* (Tokyo, 1957), vol. I, p. 307; Tōgawa, *Nogi*, p. 233.

12 Tōgawa, *Nogi*, pp. 229–30.

13 Tani, *Kimitsu Nichi-ro senshi*, pp. 202, 204; Chōnan, *Dai-san gun*, p. 673; Imperial General Staff, *Official History*, vol. III, pp. 62–3; Kuwada, 'Ryojun', p. 511; Warner and Warner, *Tide at Sunrise*, pp. 341–4; Furuya Tetsuo, *Nichi-ro Sensō* (Tokyo, 1966), p. 119; Tōgawa, *Nogi*, pp. 228–9.

14 Tani, *Kimitsu Nichi-ro senshi*, p. 229; Tōgawa, *Nogi*, p. 232; Diedrich, 'Last Iliad', p. 321; H. v. Müller, *Geschichte des Festungskrieges von 1885–1905* (Berlin, 1907), p. 230.

15 Tadayoshi Sakurai, *Human Bullets: A Soldier's Story of the Russo-Japanese War*, trans. Matsujiro Honda (Lincoln, NE, 1999).

16 Kojima, *Nichi-rō sensō*, vol. III, pp. 304–5, 329–32; Furuya, *Nichi-ro sensō*, p. 119; Warner and Warner, *Tide at Sunrise*, p. 374.

17 Kojima, *Nichi-rō sensō*, vol. III, p. 168.

18 Imperial General Staff, *Official History*, vol. III, pp. 36–7.

19 Ellis Ashmead-Bartlett, *Port Arthur: The Siege and Capitulation* (Edinburgh and London, 1906), p. 154; Furuya, *Nichi-ro sensō*, p. 128.

20 Tani, *Kimitsu Nichi-ro senshi*, pp. 205, 208; General Satō Kōjirō's testimony, quoted in *Tanaka Giichi Denki*, vol. I, p. 309; Kuhn, 'Report on the Russo-Japanese War', p. 184; Warner and Warner, *Tide at Sunrise*, pp. 381–3; Furuya, *Nichi-ro sensō*, pp. 124, 128.

21 'Ōba Jirō Nikki', entry 30 October 1904, in Chōnan, *Dai-san gun*, p. 48; Chōnan Masayoshi, *Shin shiryō Nichi-ro sensō rikusenshi: kutsugaesareru tsūsetsu* (Tokyo, 2015), pp. 735–6; Ashmead-Bartlett, *Port Arthur*, pp. 207–8, 223–4; Kuhn, 'Report on the Russo-Japanese War', p. 183; Müller, *Geschichte des Festungskrieges*, pp. 240–41; Imperial General Staff, *Official History*, vol. III, pp. 68–9. On the ineffectiveness of extended preparatory bombardments in the First World War, see John Keegan, *The Face of Battle: A Study of Agincourt, Waterloo and the Somme* (London, 2004), p. 236.

22 See data in Ōe Shinobu, *Nichi-ro sensō no gunjishiteki kenkyū* (Tokyo, 1976), p. 224; 'Ōba Nikki', entry 10 November 1904, in Chōnan, *Dai-san gun*, p. 51.

23 Ibid., p. 50.

24 Tani, *Kimitsu Nichi-ro senshi*, pp. 205–6, see especially the letter from Nagaoka to Iguchi Shogo, 6 November 1904, and the reply of Manchurian Army Headquarters dated 9 November 1904, Yamagata to Ōyama, 24 November 1904, Ōyama to Yamagata, 16 November 1904, Yamagata to Kodama, 16 November 1904, as well as other related telegrams, all reproduced on pp. 213–23. The 7th Division arrived on 11 November, as described in Chōnan, *Dai-san gun*, pp. 685–6.

25 Tani, *Kimitsu Nichi-ro senshi*, p. 210; General Ōzawa's testimony, ibid., p. 227; Kuhn, 'Report on the Russo-Japanese War', pp. 131–4; Furuya, *Nichi-ro sensō*, p. 135.

26 'Ōba Nikki', entries 27 and 28 November 1904, in Chōnan, *Dai-san gun*, pp. 57–8, and see also Chōnan's analysis on pp. 686–7.

27 General Ōzawa's testimony, Ōyama to Nogi, 30 November 1904, in Tani, *Kimitsu Nichi-ro senshi*, pp. 227, 234–5; Ōyama to Kodama, 29 November 1904, in Chōnan, *Dai-san gun*, p. 691; Kuwada, 'Ryojun', p. 515.

28 Tani, *Kimitsu Nichi-ro senshi*, pp. 235–7; Kuhn, 'Report on the Russo-Japanese War', pp. 137–8; *Tanaka Giichi Denki*, vol. I, pp. 304–7.

29 Connaughton, *Rising Sun and Tumbling Bear*, pp. 202–3; 'Ōba Nikki', entries 5–7, 25 December 1904, in Chōnan, *Dai-san gun*, pp. 60, 62; Müller, *Geschichte des Festungskrieges*, p. 246.

30 'Ōba Nikki', entries 18 December 1904, 1–2 January 1905, in Chōnan, *Dai-san gun*, pp. 61, 65–6; Ōe, *Nichi-ro sensō*, pp. 318–19; Warner and Warner, *Tide at Sunrise*, pp. 439–40; Müller, *Geschichte des Festungskrieges*, p. 247.

31 Kodama to Nagaoka, 1905 (precise date unclear), in *Nichi-ro sensō jūgun shōhei tegami*, ed. Ōhama Tetsuya (Tokyo, 2001), p. 511; Bargen, *Suicidal Honor*, p. 59.

32 Connaughton, *Rising Sun and Tumbling Bear*, p. 278; Bargen, *Suicidal Honor*, pp. 58–60.

33 Iguchi Shogo's diary, quoted in Tani, *Kimitsu Nichi-ro senshi*, p. 203; Matsukata, 'Human Bullets', pp. 184, 187; Kuwada, 'Ryojun', p. 513.

34 Tani, *Kimitsu Nichi-rō senshi*, pp. 196–7; Chōnan, *Dai-san gun*, pp. 670–72; Diedrich, 'Last Iliad', pp. 317, 400; Kuwada, 'Ryojun', p. 513; Warner and Warner, *Tide at Sunrise*, p. 346.

35 Chōnan, *Dai-san gun*, p. 678; Tani, *Kimitsu Nichi-ro senshi*, pp. 197–8; Kojima, *Nichi-rō sensō*, vol. III, pp. 139–41; Tōgawa, *Nogi*, p. 230; Kuwada, 'Ryojun', p. 506; Imperial General Staff, *Official History*, vol. III, pp. 69, 74.

36 Alexander R. Bay, *Beriberi in Modern Japan: The Making of a National Disease* (Rochester, NY, 2012), pp. 74–7, 80–83.

37 Ōe, *Nichi-ro sensō*, pp. 14–18, 317–18.

38 'Ōba Nikki', entries 24 October, 10 and 22 November 1904, in Chōnan, *Dai-san gun*, pp. 46, 50–51, 55; Chōnan, *Shin shiryō*, p. 732.

39 Tani, *Kimitsu Nichi-ro senshi*, pp. 199, 209–10 (Ichiji is quoted on p. 209); Ōe, *Nichi-ro sensō*, pp. 221–2, 318–19, 326; Matsukata, 'Human Bullets', p. 186. For Ōba's state of mind, see his reasoning for not shifting the direction of the main effort to 203-Metres Hill, in Chōnan, *Dai-san gun*, pp. 684–5.

40 'Ōba Nikki', entry 10 November 1904, in Chōnan, *Dai-san gun*, p. 50.

41 Furuya, *Nichi-ro sensō*, p. 125.

42 Yamagata Aritomo to Ōyama Iwao, 24 November 1904, in Tani, *Kimitsu Nichi-rō senshi*, pp. 220–21. See especially the letter from Nagaoka (Imperial General Headquarters) to Iguchi (Manchurian Army Headquarters), 6 November 1904, and the reply of Manchurian Army Headquarters, dated 9 November 1904, Yamagata to Ōyama, 24 November 1904, Ōyama to Yamagata, 16 November 1904, Yamagata to Kodama, 16 November 1904, as well as other related telegrams, all reproduced on pp. 213–23, as well as the excerpt from General Ōzawa's memoirs (p. 227), and 'Ōba Nikki', entry 10 November 1904, in Chōnan, *Dai-san gun*, pp. 50–51.

43 Chōnan, *Dai-san gun*, pp. 673, 684–5.

44 Ashmead-Bartlett, *Port Arthur*, p. 349. Ashmead-Bartlett's observations are supported by the conclusions of the British military observers; see Imperial General Staff, *Official History*, vol. III, pp. 74–5.

45 Quoted in Connaughton, *Rising Sun and Tumbling Bear*, p. 186. See also Diedrich, 'Last Iliad', pp. 351–2; Warner and Warner, *Tide at Sunrise*, p. 376.

46 Ashmead-Bartlett, *Port Arthur*, p. 349.

47 Chōnan, *Dai-san gun*, p. 672.

48 See Nagaoka's notes from 28 and 30 October, respectively, in Matsukata, 'Human Bullets', pp. 192–3; and also Tani, *Kimitsu Nichi-ro senshi*, pp. 227, 229–30, 235; Ashmead-Bartlett, *Port Arthur*, p. 87. Kuwada and Okumura, *Kindai Nihon Sensō-shi*, vol. I, p. 153; Furuya, *Nichi-ro sensō*, p. 135.

49 Matsukata, 'Human Bullets', p. 187. For the newest study that defends Nogi on such grounds (among other arguments), see Chōnan, *Dai-san gun*, p. 678.

50 Tani, *Kimitsu Nichi-ro senshi*, p. 210. See also Ashmead-Bartlett, *Port Arthur*, pp. 86–8, 302, 306.

51 'Ōba Nikki', entries 20, 22 and 26 November 1904, in Chōnan, *Dai-san gun*, pp. 53–5, 57; Diedrich, 'Last Iliad', pp. 414, 419. See also Nagaoka's notes from 28 and 30 October, respectively, in Matsukata, 'Human Bullets', pp. 192–3.

52 Quoted in Connaughton, *Rising Sun and Tumbling Bear*, pp. 169, 196. See also the testimony of Tanaka Kunishige on Nogi's leadership, in Ōe, *Nichi-ro sensō*, p. 384, note. For further analysis see Chōnan, *Dai-san gun*, p. 705; and Bargen, *Suicidal Honor*, p. 50.

53 One of Nogi's senior staff officers gave similar assurances to the foreign correspondents. Both sources are quoted in Kojima, *Nichi-rō sensō*, vol. III, pp. 173–4, 183; and see also Tani, *Kimitsu Nichi-ro senshi*, p. 228.

54 Edward J. Drea, *Japan's Imperial Army: Its Rise and Fall, 1853–1945* (Lawrence, KS, 2009), p. 122.

55 Bargen, *Suicidal Honor*, pp. 59–60; Drea, *Japan's Imperial Army*, pp. 122–3.

56 Sakurai, *Human Bullets*, pp. 37–8.

57 Matsukata, 'Human Bullets', pp. 198–9.

58 Quoted in Connaughton, *Rising Sun and Tumbling Bear*, p. 168.

59 Kuhn, 'Report on the Russo-Japanese War', pp. 231–2.

60 Gary P. Cox, 'Of Aphorisms, Lessons, and Paradigms: Comparing the British and German Official Histories of the Russo-Japanese War', *Journal of Military History*, LVI/3 (1992), pp. 392–3, 400; Michael Howard, 'Men against Fire: The Doctrine of the Offensive in 1914', in *Makers of Modern Strategy: From Machiavelli to the Nuclear Age*, ed. Peter Paret (Princeton, NJ, 1986), pp. 511–22.

61 Imperial General Staff, *Official History*, vol. III, pp. 69–71, 80.

62 Cox, 'Aphorisms', pp. 396–8.

14 ROMANUS IV DIOGENES

1 See, for example, Alfred Friendly, *The Dreadful Day: The Battle of Manzikert, 1071* (London, 1981), p. 57; and Carole Hillenbrand, *Turkish Myth and Muslim Symbol: The Battle of Manzikert* (Edinburgh, 2007), p. 3.

2 Gregory VII, 'Gregory VII assures King Henry IV of Germany of his sincere love and informs him about his planned expedition to help Eastern Christians, Rome: 7 December, 1074', in *The Register of Pope*

Gregory VII, 1073–1085, ed. and trans. H.E.J. Cowdrey (Oxford, 2002), pp. 122–3.

3 For an overview of the Byzantine origins of the First Crusade, see Peter Frankopan, *The First Crusade: The Call from the East* (Cambridge, MA, 2012).

4 Anthony Kaldellis, *Streams of Gold, Rivers of Blood: The Rise and Fall of Byzantium 955 AD to the First Crusade* (New York, 2017), p. 142.

5 Ibid., p. 142–5. See also Mark Whittow, *The Making of Byzantium: 600–1025* (Berkeley and Los Angeles, CA, 1996), pp. 374–90.

6 John Haldon, *Warfare, State and Society in the Byzantine World, 565–1204* (London and New York, 1999), p. 209. On Basil II taking command of armies in person, see Kaldellis, *Streams of Gold*, p. 9.

7 Warren Treadgold, *Byzantium and Its Army, 284–1081* (Stanford, CA, 1995), pp. 115–17.

8 John Halden, *Byzantium at War, AD 600–1453* (Oxford, 2002), p. 49.

9 Ibid., p. 49.

10 Ibid., p. 51.

11 Frankopan, *The First Crusade*, p. 28.

12 Friendly, *The Dreadful Day*, pp. 91–2; and Brian Todd Carey, *Road to Manzikert: Byzantine and Islamic Warfare, 527–1071* (Barnsley, 2012), p. 121.

13 Ibid.

14 Matthew of Edessa, *Armenia and the Crusades, Tenth to Twelfth Centuries: The Chronicle of Matthew of Edessa*, trans. Ara Edmond Dostourian, 2nd edn (Belmont, MA, 1993), pp. 96–7.

15 Friendly, *The Dreadful Day*, p. 97.

16 Frankopan, *The First Crusade*, p. 30.

17 Kaldellis, *Streams of Gold*, p. 196.

18 Jonathan Harris, *Byzantium and the Crusades* (London and New York, 2003), p. 33.

19 Carey, *Road to Manzikert*, p. 122; and Kaldellis, *Streams of Gold*, p. 198.

20 Michael Attaleiates, *The History*, trans. Anthony Kaldellis and Dimitris Krallis (Cambridge, MA, 2012), p. 183. See also Harris, *Byzantium and the Crusades*, p. 33.

21 Hillenbrand, *Turkish Myth and Muslim Symbol*, p. 6.

22 Ibid.

23 See Harris, *Byzantium and the Crusades*, p. 33; and Frankopan, *The First Crusade*, p. 30.

24 See Frankopan, *The First Crusade*, p. 30; and Friendly, *The Dreadful Day*, pp. 151–2.

25 See Attaleiates, *History*, p. 187; and Michael Psellus, *Fourteen Byzantine Rulers: The Chronographia of Michael Psellus*, trans. E.R.A. Sewter (New York, 1966), p. 351.

26 Friendly, *The Dreadful Day*, p. 153.

27 Hillenbrand, *Turkish Myth and Muslim Symbol*, p. 7.

28 Attaleiates, *History*, pp. 207, 209.

29 Friendly, *The Dreadful Day*, pp. 157–8. See also Attaleiates, *History*, p. 225.

30 Attaleiates, *History*, p. 229.

31 Friendly, *The Dreadful Day*, pp. 158–9.

32 Psellus, *Fourteen Byzantine Rulers*, p. 353.

33 Carey, *Road to Manzikert*, pp. 135–6.

34 Attaleiates, *History*, pp. 253–5.

35 Friendly, *The Dreadful Day*, p. 162.

36 Carey, *Road to Manzikert*, pp. 134–5.

37 Ibid., p. 136.

38 Ibid.; Friendly, *The Dreadful Day*, pp. 174, 178; and Kaldellis, *Streams of Gold*, p. 246.

39 Carey, *Road to Manzikert*, pp. 136–7; and Treadgold, *Byzantium and Its Army*, p. 41.

40 Ibid., pp. 137–8.

41 Ibid., p. 139.

42 Ibid., pp. 139–40.

43 Attaleiates, *History*, pp. 285–7.

44 Carey, *Road to Manzikert*, p. 142.

45 Attaleiates, *History*, p. 291.

46 Carey, *Road to Manzikert*, pp. 142–3.

47 Hillenbrand, *Turkish Myth and Muslim Symbol*, p. 14.

48 Carey, *Road to Manzikert*, pp. 143–4.

49 Hillenbrand, *Turkish Myth and Muslim Symbol*, p. 10.

50 Kaldellis, *Streams of Gold*, pp. 247–8.

51 Attaleiates, *History*, p. 293.

52 Kaldellis, *Streams of Gold*, pp. 247–8.

53 Harris, *Byzantium and the Crusades*, pp. 33–4.

54 Ibid., p. 34; and Hillenbrand, *Turkish Myth and Muslim Symbol*, p. 13.

55 Carey, *Road to Manzikert*, pp. 135–6.

56 Ibid., pp. 134–5.

57 Harris, *Byzantium and the Crusades*, p. 58.

58 Ibid., p. 40.

59 Hillenbrand, *Turkish Myth and Muslim Symbol*, pp. 8–9.

60 Ibid., pp. 7–8.

61 Ibid., p. 12.

15 LORD WOLSELEY

1 Bernard Holland, *The Life of Spencer Compton, Eighth Duke of Devonshire* (London, 1911), vol. 1, p. 483.

2 Wolseley, cited in Frederic Villiers, *Peaceful Personalities and Warriors Bold* (London, 1907), p. 177.

3 W. F. Butler, *Sir William Butler: An Autobiography* (London, 1911), p. 113.

4 Lieutenant Colonel G. J. Wolseley, *Narrative of the War with China in 1860* (London, 1862); and General Viscount Wolseley, *The Soldier's Pocket-book for Field Service* (London, 1886).

5 George Arthur, ed., *The Letters of Lord and Lady Wolseley, 1870–1911* (London, 1922), p. 123.

6 Ibid., pp. 154, 213 and 219.

7 Untitled leader, *The Times*, 30 November 1900, p. 9.

8 Richard Harrison, *Recollections of a Life in the British Army during the Latter Half of the 19th Century* (London, 1908), pp. 251–3; Alexander Bruce

Tulloch, *A Soldier's Sailoring* (London, 1912), pp. 200–201; and 'Journal, 1881–1884', pp. 36–9, Viscount Esher Papers, Churchill Archives Centre, Cambridge, CAC/ESHR/2/6.

9 Brian Bond, *The Victorian Army and the Staff College, 1854–1914* (London, 1972), p. 127. In current value, the grant equals nearly £2 million.

10 Earl of Cromer, *Modern Egypt* (New York, 1916), vol. I, pp. 379–87; and E. J. Montagu-Stuart-Wortley, 'My Reminiscences of Egypt and the Sudan (from 1882 to 1889)', *Sudan Notes and Records*, XXXIV/I (June 1953), p. 18. Colonel Baker, brother of the famed African explorer Sir Samuel Baker, had been convicted of sexual assault against a lady in a first-class rail carriage in 1875. See 'Colonel Baker's Case', *The Times*, 8 July 1975, p. 11.

11 Awad Al-Sid Al-Karsani, 'The Establishment of Neo-Mahdism in the Western Sudan, 1920–1936', *African Affairs*, LXXXVI/344 (July 1987), p. 386.

12 Charles Royle, *The Egyptian Campaigns, 1882 to 1885* (London, 1900), pp. 236–44; Lord Edmond Fitzmaurice, *The Life of Granville George Leveson Gower, Second Earl Granville, K.G., 1815–1891* (London, 1905), vol. II, p. 319; Butler, *Autobiography*, p. 266; and Alfred Milner, *England in Egypt* (London, 1902), pp. 70–71.

13 Lord Elton, *General Gordon* (London, 1954), pp. 326–7.

14 Colonel Donald Hamill Stewart had already been sent to the Sudan in late 1882 to report on the conditions then existing. His report did not make for pleasant reading.

15 The National Archives (hereafter TNA), Kew, Richmond, Surrey, United Kingdom, CAB[inet Papers] 37/14/11, Hamilton, 'General Gordon's Mission in the Soudan', 21 February 1885.

16 Cromer, *Modern Egypt*, vol. I, pp. 399–404.

17 *Hansard*, House of Commons debate, 11 February 1885, v. 284, cc4419.

18 Ibid., House of Lords debate, 5 February 1884, v. 284, cc18–29.

19 Holland, *Spencer Compton*, vol. I, pp. 425–7.

20 Ibid., pp. 478–9.

21 Mike Snook, 'Wolseley, Wilson and the Failure of the Khartoum Campaign: An Exercise in Scapegoating and Abrogation of Command Responsibility?', PhD diss., Cranfield University, 2014, p. 33.

22 E. A. de Cosson, *Days and Nights of Service with Sir Gerald Graham's Field Force at Suakin* (London, 1886), p. 321.

23 E. J. Montagu-Stuart-Wortley, 'My Reminiscences of Egypt and the Sudan (from 1882 to 1899) (Continued)', *Sudan Notes and Records*, XXXIV/2 (December 1953), p. 173; Holland, *Spencer Compton*, vol. I, p. 439; and 'Death of Sir Andrew Clarke,' *The Times*, 1 April 1902, p. 8.

24 TNA CAB 37/12/28, Clarke to Hartington, memorandum, 19 May 1884.

25 Holland, *Spencer Compton*, vol. I, pp. 459–60; and Count Gleichen, ed., *The Anglo-Egyptian Sudan: A Compendium Prepared by the Officers of the Sudan Government* (London, 1905), p. 248.

26 TNA CAB 37/13/37, R. Molyneux to Admiralty, signal of 8:25 a.m., 20 July 1884; Holland, *Spencer Compton*, vol. I, p. 473; R. H. Vetch, *Life, Letters, and Diaries of Lieut.-General Sir Gerald Graham V.C., G.C.B., R.E.* (Edinburgh, 1901), p. 275; Charles M. Watson, *The Life of Major-General Sir Charles Wilson* (London, 1909), p. 272; and Royle, *Egyptian Campaigns*, pp. 314–15.

27 TNA CAB 37/13/40, Northbrook to Gordon, letter, 8 October 1884; Spencer Childers, *The Life and Correspondence of the Rt. Hon. Hugh C. E. Childers*, vol. II, pp. 185–6; and Willoughby Verner, *The Military Life of H.R.H. George, Duke of Cambridge*, vol. II: *1871–1904* (London, 1905), pp. 265–77.

28 TNA W[ar] O[ffice Papers] 32/6109, Wolseley to Hartington, letter, 11 September 1884 and Hartington to Wolseley, letter, 17 September 1884.

29 Brian Parritt, *The Intelligencers: British Military Intelligence from the Middle Ages to 1929* (Barnsley, 2011), p. 108.

30 C. H. Melville, *Life of General the Right Hon. Sir Redvers Buller V. C., G.C.B., G.C.M.G.* (London, 1923), vol. I, pp. 195–206; Royle, *Egyptian Campaigns*, p. 315; TNA ADM[iralty Papers] 196/36 (F. Boardman); 'Sir William Butler', *The Times*, 8 June 1910, p. 9; Butler, *Autobiography*, pp. 277–87; and William F. Butler, *The Campaign of the Cataracts* (London, 1887), pp. 215 and 231.

31 TNA WO 32/6108, Wolseley to Hartington, signal No. 78 of 22 November 1884; and *London Gazette*, 28 April 1885, No. 25465, p. 1913.

32 TNA WO 32/6106, 'Report of Proceedings of Naval Brigade from 26 November last to 8 March 1885'.

33 Wolseley, however, held Dormer to be a very effective officer and requested his presence after the wounding of Herbert Stewart. See Verner, *Cambridge*, vol. II, p. 288.

34 Adrian Preston, ed., *In Relief of Gordon: Lord Wolseley's Campaign Journal of the Khartoum Relief Expedition, 1884–1885* (London, 1967), pp. 67 and 93; Bernard Holland, *The Life of Spencer Compton, Eighth Duke of Devonshire* (London, 1911), vol. II, p. 6; and Arthur, ed., *Wolseley*, p. 128.

35 Melville, *Buller*, vol. I, pp. 199–200.

36 TNA WO 32/6112, Wolseley to Gordon, letter, 7 November 1884 and WO 32/6113 Gordon, letter to 'The English', 4 November 1884.

37 Melville, *Buller*, vol. I, pp. 208–9; Preston, ed., *In Relief of Gordon*, p. 67; and Charles W. Wilson, *From Korti to Khartum: A Journal of the Desert March from Korti to Gubat, and of the Ascent on the Nile in General Gordon's Steamers* (Edinburgh, 1886), pp. xvii–xxii.

38 Montagu-Stuart-Wortley, 'My Reminiscences of Egypt and the Sudan', p. 39; Wilson, *From Korti to Khartum*, pp. 113 and 301; and Alfred E. Turner, *Sixty Years of a Soldier's Life* (London, 1912), p. 99.

39 Wilson, *From Korti to Khartum*, pp. xxii–xxiii.

40 Turner, *Sixty Years*, pp. 90–91.

41 Wilson, *From Korti to Khartum*, pp. 9–11.

42 Julian Symons, *England's Pride: The Story of the Gordon Relief Expedition* (London, 1965), p. 230.

43 Wilson, *From Korti to Khartum*, p. 32.

44 *London Gazette*, 20 February 1885, No. 25444, p. 755.

45 Ibid., 24 February 1885, No. 25446, p. 855.

46 Ibid., p. 853. Stewart received special promotion to major general before succumbing to his wounds.

47 Verner, *Cambridge*, vol. II, p. 279.

48 Ibid., p. 286; 'British Victory Near Metammeh', *The Times*, 29 January 1885, p. 5; John Adye, *Soldiers and Others I Have Known: A Volume of Recollections* (London, 1925), p. 125; and Melville, *Buller*, vol. I, pp. 213–18.

49 Snook, 'Wolseley, Wilson and the Failure of the Khartoum Campaign', pp. 231–2.

50 *London Gazette*, 10 April 1885, No. 25460, pp. 1667–8; Wilson, *From Korti to Khartum*, pp. 92–117; and Butler, *Autobiography*, p. 297.

51 Wilson, *From Korti to Khartum*, pp. 128–9.

52 Ibid., p. 287.

53 Ibid., pp. 174–5.

54 Royle, *Egyptian Campaigns*, p. 394.

55 *London Gazette*, 10 April 1885, No. 25460, pp. 1663–6; and Esher Papers, CAC/ESHR/2/7, Brett to Hartington, letters, 5 and 6 February 1885.

56 Royle, *Egyptian Campaigns*, p. 400.

57 Ibid., p. 388; *London Gazette*, 25 August 1885, No. 25505, p. 4039; and 'Sir Reginald Talbot', *The Times*, 16 January 1929, p. 17.

58 Arthur, ed., *Wolseley*, p. 155.

59 *The Times*, 6 February 1885, p. 9.

60 *Hansard*, House of Commons debate, 19 February 1885, v. 294, cc873–9.

61 'Naval and Military Intelligence,' *The Times*, 2 June 1885, p. 6; and William Galloway, *The Battle of Tofrek* (London, 1887), pp. 320–21.

62 M. P. Hornik, 'The Mission of Sir Henry Drummond-Wolff to Constantinople, 1885–1887,' *English Historical Review*, LV (October 1940), pp. 601–2.

63 Arthur, ed., *Wolseley*, p. 211.

64 Halik Kochanski, *Sir Garnet Wolseley: Victorian Hero* (London, 1999), pp. 213–14.

65 Andrew Syk, ed., *Military Papers of Lieutenant-General Frederick Stanley Maude, 1914–1917*, Army Records Society 32 (Stroud, 2012), p. 97.

66 Elton, *General Gordon*, p. 405.

BIBLIOGRAPHY

Bauer, Jack, *The Mexican War, 1846–1848* (Lincoln, NE, 1974)

Beevor, Anthony, *Arnhem: The Battle for the Bridges, 1944* (London, 2019)

Brereton, Lewis H., *The Brereton Diaries: The War in the Air in the Pacific,
Middle East and Europe, 3 October 1941–8 May 1945* (New York, 1946)

Clark, Alan, *The Donkeys* (New York, 1962)

Cohen, Eliot A., and John Gooch, *Military Misfortunes: The Anatomy of Failure
in War* (New York, 1990)

Connaughton, Richard M., *Rising Sun and Tumbling Bear: Russia's War with
Japan* (London, 2003)

Diodorous Siculus, *Historical Library*, Books XII and XIII

Dixon, Norman F., *On the Psychology of Military Incompetence* (London, 1976)

Donovan, James, *A Terrible Glory: Custer and the Little Bighorn – the Last Great
Battle of the American West* (New York, 2008)

Fowler, Will, *Santa Anna of Mexico* (Lincoln, NE, 2007)

Friendly, Alfred, *The Dreadful Day: The Battle of Manzikert, 1071*
(London, 1981)

Goldrick, James, *Before Jutland: The Naval War in Northern European Waters,
August 1914–February 1915* (Annapolis, MD, 2015)

Gordon, Andrew, *The Rules of the Game: Jutland and British Naval Command*
(Annapolis, MD, 2012)

Graham-Leigh, Elaine, *The Southern French Nobility and the Albigensian
Crusade* (Woodbridge, 2005)

Haldon, John F., *Warfare, State and Society in the Byzantine World, 565–1204*
(London and New York, 1999)

Hardin, Stephen, *Texian Iliad: A Military History of the Texas Revolution
1835–1836* (Austin, TX, 1994)

Henderson, Timothy, *A Glorious Defeat: Mexico and Its War with the United
States* (New York, 2007)

Herwig, Holger, *The First World War: Germany and Austria–Hungary, 1914–1918*
(London, 1997)

Hillenbrand, Carole, *Turkish Myth and Muslim Symbol: The Battle of Manzikert*
(Edinburgh, 2007)

Hoig, Stan, *The Sand Creek Massacre* (Norman, OK, 1961)

Howard, Michael, 'The Use and Abuse of Military History', RUSI *Journal*, CVII/625 (1962), pp. 4–10

Hughes, Nathaniel Cheairs, and Roy P. Stonesifer, *The Life and Wars of Gideon Pillow* (Chapel Hill, NC, 1993)

Kaldellis, Anthony, *Streams of Gold, Rivers of Blood: The Rise and Fall of Byzantium, 955 AD to the First Crusade* (New York, 2017)

Keegan, John, *The Face of Battle* (London, 1988)

Kochanski, Halik, *Sir Garnet Wolseley: Victorian Hero* (London, 1999)

Laffin, John, *British Butchers and Bunglers of World War One* (Godalming, 1998)

Lambert, Andrew, *Admirals: The Naval Commanders Who Made Britain Great* (London, 2009)

Lewis, Felice Flanery, *Trailing Clouds of Glory: Zachary Taylor's Mexican War Campaign and His Emerging Civil War Leaders* (Tuscaloosa, AL, 2010)

Luckett, Richard, *The White Generals: An Account of the White Movement and the Russian Civil War* (New York, 1974)

Marvin, Laurence W., *The Occitan War: A Military and Political History of the Albigensian Crusade, 1209–1218* (Cambridge, 2008)

Massie, Robert, *Castles of Steel* (New York, 2003)

Matsukata, Yoshihisa, 'Human Bullets, General Nogi and the Myth of Port Arthur', in *The Russo-Japanese War in Global Perspective: World War Zero*, ed. John W. Steinberg et al., 2 vols (Leiden and Boston, MA, 2005–7)

Michno, Gregory F., *The Three Battles of Sand Creek: In Blood, in Court, and as the End of History* (El Dorado Hills, CA, 2017)

Miller, Roger G., 'A "Pretty Damn Able Commander": Lewis Hyde Brereton, Part I', *Air Power History*, XLVII/I (2000), pp. 4–27

——, 'A "Pretty Damn Able Commander": Lewis Hyde Brereton, Part II', *Air Power History*, XLVIII/I (2001), pp. 22–45

O'Neill, Connor T., *Down Along with that Devil's Bones: A Reckoning with Monuments, Memory, and the Legacy of White Supremacy* (Chapel Hill, NC, 2020)

Pegg, Mark Gregory, *A Most Holy War: The Albigensian Crusade and the Battle for Christendom* (New York, 2008)

Plutarch, 'Nicias', *Greek Lives*, trans. Robin Waterfield (Oxford, 1998)

Pois, Robert, and Philip Langer, *Command Failure in War: Psychology and Leadership* (Bloomington, IN, 2004)

Powell, David A., *Failure in the Saddle: Nathan Bedford Forrest, Joe Wheeler, and the Confederate Cavalry in the Chickamauga Campaign* (El Dorado Hills, CA, 2010)

Preston, Adrian, ed., *In Relief of Gordon: Lord Wolseley's Campaign Journal of the Khartoum Relief Expedition, 1884–1885* (Rutherford, NJ, 1967)

Roberts, Gary L., *Massacre at Sand Creek: How Methodists Were Involved in an American Tragedy* (Nashville, TN, 2016)

Roskill, Stephen, *Admiral of the Fleet Earl Beatty: The Last Naval Hero* (Annapolis, MD, 2018).

Rupen, Robert A., *Mongols of the Twentieth Century* (Bloomington, IN, 1964)

Sampson, Gareth C., *The Defeat of Rome in the East: Crassus, the Parthians, and the Disastrous Battle of Carrhae, 53 BC* (Philadelphia, PA, 2008)

Schindler, John R., *Fall of the Double Eagle: The Battle for Galicia and the Demise of Austria–Hungary* (Lincoln, NE, 2015)

Smith, Canfield F., 'The Ungernovščina – How and Why?', *Jahrbücher für Geschichte Osteuropas*, XXVIII/IV (1980), pp. 590–95

Sondhaus, Lawrence, *Franz Conrad von Hötzendorf, Architect of the Apocalypse* (Boston, MA, 2000)

Strauss, Barry, *The Spartacus War* (New York, 2009)

Symons, Julian, *England's Pride: The Story of the Gordon Relief Expedition* (London, 1965)

Thucydides, *History of the Peloponnesian War*, ed. M. I. Finley, trans. Rex Warner (Oxford, 1972)

Tōgawa Yukio, *Nogi Maresuke* (Tokyo, 1968)

Turner, Carol, *Forgotten Heroes and Villains of Sand Creek* (Charleston, SC, 2010)

Utley, Robert, *Custer: Cavalier in Buckskin* (Norman, OK, 2001)

Warner, Denis, and Peggy Warner, *The Tide at Sunrise: A History of the Russo-Japanese War, 1904–1905* (London, 1975)

Watson, Alexander, *Ring of Steel: Germany and Austria–Hungary in World War I* (New York, 2014)

Wawro, Geoffrey, *A Mad Catastrophe: The Outbreak of World War I and the Collapse of the Hapsburg Empire* (New York, 2014)

Wert, Jeffrey, *Custer: The Controversial Life of George Armstrong Custer* (New York, 1996)

Wills, Brian S., *The Confederacy's Greatest Cavalryman: Nathan Bedford Forrest* (Lawrence, KS, 1998)

CONTRIBUTORS

JOHN J. ABBATIELLO

John Abbatiello is Chief, Research, Integrationand Assessment Division, Center for Character and Leadership Development (CCLD), at the USAF Academy. Upon completing his PhD at Kings College London in 2004, he returned to the USAF Academy Department of History as the Deputy Department Head. He is the author of *Anti-submarine Warfare in World War I: British Naval Aviation and the Defeat of the U-Boats* and numerous articles and book reviews on air power, sea power and military affairs.

SIR JEREMY BLACKHAM

Vice Admiral Sir Jeremy Blackham, RN (Retired) had four sea commands during his 41-year career: *Beachampton, Ashanti, Nottingham* and *Ark Royal* (when he commanded the first RN Task Group off Bosnia). Ashore, he filled important staff appointments, including Commandant of the Royal Navy Staff College, Director of Naval Plans, Director General Naval Personnel Strategy, Assistant Chief of Naval Staff and Deputy Fleet Commander, and was the first Deputy Chief of Defence Staff (Capability).

Leaving the RN in 2002, he spent three years with EADS, as UK Country President, before becoming an independent consultant, adviser and mentor. He is a former chairman of several consultancy companies, and was Chair of the Blackheath Conservatoire of Music and the Arts from 2000 to 2007. He is a former Non-executive Director of Airbus Helicopters UK and a former member of the UK Chief of Defence Staff's Strategic Advisory Panel. He was Vice President, Trustee and Associate Fellow of the Royal United Services Institute for Defence and Security between 1996 and 2008 and Editor of the *Naval Review* from 2002 to 2017 and is a frequent writer on defence.

GATES BROWN

Gates Brown is an Assistant Professor of military history in the Department of Military History at the u.s. Army Command and General Staff College in Fort Leavenworth, Kansas. His main research focus is the early Cold War period with a focus on u.s. nuclear and defence policy. He currently has a manuscript under review concerning President Eisenhower's deployment of intermediate range ballistic missiles to Western Europe.

MARK GROTELUESCHEN

Mark Grotelueschen is a Professor at the u.s. Air Force Academy. He received his undergraduate degree in history from the u.s. Air Force Academy, MA in military and diplomatic history from the University of Calgary, and doctorate from Texas A&M University. An internationally renowned scholar on the First World War, Mark Grotelueschen is the author of *The AEF Way of War: The American Army and Combat in World War I* and *Doctrine under Trial: American Artillery Employment in World War I*. He is the editor of *The Officer's Companion to Military History* and *Forged by Fire: Military History for the Profession of Arms* and is the author of numerous other shorter works.

ANDREW HOLT

Andrew Holt is Professor of History at Florida State College at Jacksonville. He holds a PhD from the University of Florida and is a medieval historian who specializes in the crusading era. He is co-editor (with James Muldoon) of *Competing Voices from the Crusades, Seven Myths of the Crusades* with Alfred J. Andrea, and *Great Events in Religion: An Encyclopedia of Pivotal Events in Religious History*, 3 vols, co-edited with Florin Curta. He is also the sole author of a two-volume encyclopaedia on the crusades for Greenwood Press (2019) and editor of the crusades section of the Oxford Bibliographies Online (offered by Oxford University Press), and serves as a series editor for Hackett Publishing's Myths of History Series.

GREGORY HOSPODOR

Gregory S. Hospodor is an Associate Professor in the Department of Military History at the u.s. Army Command and General Staff College. During the 2017 academic year, he served as Visiting Distinguished Professor in the u.s. Air Force Academy's Department of History. He holds a PhD from Louisiana State University, an MA from the University of Mississippi and a BA from the College of William and Mary, all in history. His current research project deals with the combat operations of the First Infantry Division (u.s.) during the 1943 Sicily campaign and what it reveals about the so-called American Way of War.

JOHN M. JENNINGS

John M. Jennings is Professor of History at the u.s. Air Force Academy, where he specializes in modern Japanese history. He received his master's and doctoral degrees from the University of Hawaii at Manoa, and he has been a visiting researcher at Sophia University and International Christian University in Tokyo. He is the author of *The Opium Empire: Japanese Imperialism and Drug Trafficking in Asia, 1895–1945*, as well as numerous shorter works. He is currently researching Japanese Army operations in Siberia from 1918 to 1922.

LAURENCE W. MARVIN

Laurence W. Marvin is Professor of History at Berry College in Mount Berry, Georgia. He received his PhD in 1997 from the University of Illinois at Urbana–Champaign. He is the author of *The Occitan War: A Military and Political History of the Albigensian Crusade, 1209–1218*. In 2018 his co-edited volume *Louis VII and His World* was published by E. J. Brill. Among his publications are articles in *War in History* and *War and Society* as well as other articles, book chapters and reviews. Currently he is writing a military history of the Fifth Crusade.

DAVID MILLS

David Mills served in the u.s. Army for almost ten years, then worked in corporate America for eight years. He earned his bachelor's degree in history from Frostburg State University, his master's degree in history from Minnesota State University, Mankato, and his PhD from North Dakota State University. He taught for a number of years at Minnesota West Community College, and is now an Assistant Professor of History at the u.s. Army Command and General Staff College at Fort Leavenworth. He is the author of two books, *Cold War in a Cold Land: Fighting Communism on the Northern Plains* and *Operation Snowbound: Life behind the Blizzards of 1949*. He is working on another manuscript that examines America's role in feeding post-war Europe and the Soviet Union.

JOSEPH MORETZ

Joseph Moretz is a 1979 graduate of Frostburg State College in Frostburg, Maryland. In 1989 he graduated with distinction from the Command and Staff College of the u.s. Naval War College and proceeded to King's College London, where in 1990 he was awarded an MA and in September 1999 a PhD in war studies. An independent researcher and writer, he is the author of *The Royal Navy and the Capital Ship in the Interwar Period, Thinking Wisely, Planning Boldly: The Higher Education and Training of Royal Navy Officers, 1919–1939* and *Towards a Wider War: British Strategic Decision-Making and Military Effectiveness in Scandinavia, 1939–40*. He is a member of the British Commission for Military History, the Society of Military History, the Army Records Society (uk) and the Navy Records Society (uk). He is presently completing a study on the British experience of amphibious operations and the development of its associated doctrine for the period 1882–1916.

DANNY ORBACH

Danny Orbach is an Associate Professor in the departments of history and Asian studies at the Hebrew University of Jerusalem. He is a military historian, who published on subjects such as military resistance, war atrocities and freelance military adventurers. His two latest books are *The Plots against Hitler* and *Curse on This Country: The Rebellious Army of Imperial Japan.* Currently, he works on the history of intelligence in the early Cold War.

CHRISTOPHER REIN

Christopher Rein is the Managing Editor at Air University Press, Maxwell Air Force Base, Alabama. He holds a PhD in history from the University of Kansas, where his dissertation and first book, published as *The North African Air Campaign,* argued for an operational use of air power rather than strategic pursuits that have dominated the USAF for most of its history. His second book, *Alabamians in Blue,* examines the linkages between environmental history and southern dissenters in northern Alabama during the Civil War. He has served as a Naval ROTC Instructor at Southern University in Baton Rouge, Louisiana, and as an Associate Professor of history at the U.S. Air Force Academy in Colorado Springs, where he taught and directed a number of courses in military and American history, including courses on the Civil War and the Second World War.

COURTNEY SHORT

Courtney A. Short holds a PhD in history from the University of North Carolina, Chapel Hill. She served as the Deputy Department Head and as an assistant professor in the History Department at the U.S. Air Force Academy where she taught military history, the Second World War and the history of unconventional warfare. Her research focuses on race and identity during the occupation of Okinawa, 1945–6. She is the 2017 Honorable Mention of the Edward M. Coffman Society for Military History First-Manuscript Prize for her work *The Most Vital Question': Race and Identity in Occupation Policy Construction and Practice, Okinawa, 1945–1946.* She is the author of *Uniquely Okinawan: Determining Identity During the U.S. Wartime Occupation.*

CHUCK STEELE

Chuck Steele is an Associate Professor of history at the U.S. Air Force Academy. He has served as the course chair for USAFA's offerings in naval history, military thought, technology and warfare; the core and scholar's courses in modern military history; and the history of the First World War. He earned his BA in history at the University of California, Berkeley (1987), his MA in war studies from King's College London (1990) and his PhD in history at West Virginia University (2000). He served as the first Defence Editor of *Rotor and Wing* magazine, and subsequently worked as an Assistant Professor of history at the U.S. Military Academy (2002–6). He is the book reviews editor for the *International Journal of Naval History* and has written on naval affairs for *Naval History*, the *Journal of the Australian Naval Institute* and the UK's *Naval Review*. An ocean enthusiast, he is a PADI-certified Divemaster with elementary training in nautical archaeology from Britain's Nautical Archaeology Society.

JAMES TUCCI

James Tucci is Professor of Strategy and Security Studies at the School of Advanced Air and Space Studies (SAASS). He is a graduate of Augustana College in Rock Island, Illinois, where he read Greek and Latin for a Bachelor's degree. He also holds an MA in history from the University of Missouri at Columbia and a PhD in comparative world history from the University of Wisconsin–Madison. During his 22-year USAF career, he served as an ICBM Flight Commander, flew over 1,000 hours in both USAF and U.S. Navy aircraft, and was Director of Military History in the USAF Academy History Department. He has taught history, strategy, literature, classical language and security studies at the U.S. Air Force Academy, the USAF Air Command and Staff College, Auburn University, the Netherlands Defense College, the United Arab Emirates Defense College and SAASS.

DEREK VARBLE

Derek Varble holds a doctorate in history from Oriel College, University of Oxford, where he researched twentieth-century diplomacy. He also completed an undergraduate degree in history at the U.S. Air Force Academy and a graduate degree in history at the George Washington University. He lives in Colorado.

ROBERT P. WETTEMANN JR

Robert Wettemann is Associate Professor of history at the U.S. Air Force Academy. He received his BA in history from Oklahoma State University, and his MA and doctoral degrees in history from Texas A&M University. He is the author of *Privilege vs. Equality: Civil–Military Relations in the Jacksonian Era, 1815–1845* and numerous articles and other shorter publications.

ACKNOWLEDGEMENTS

First and foremost, we would like to thank our contributors for their enthusiastic participation in this project and chapters that comprise the resulting volume: John Abbatiello, Gates Brown, Mark Grotelueschen, Andrew Holt, Gregory Hospodor, Laurence Marvin, David Mills, Joseph Moretz, Danny Orbach, Christopher Rein, Courtney Short, James Tucci, Derek Varble and Robert Wettemann. We literally could not have done this without them. As several of the authors are employed by the u.s. Air Force Academy or other institutions within the u.s. Department of Defense, we offer the following disclaimer: the views expressed in this volume are those of its authors and do not necessarily represent the official policy or position of the u.s. Air Force Academy, the Air Force, the Department of Defense or the u.s. Government.

We would also like to express our gratitude to Sir Jeremy Blackham for graciously contributing a thought-provoking Foreword.

In addition to our contributors, the following individuals generously shared their time and expertise: Joseph Barry, Ronald Bulatoff, Elena Danielson, John Dunn, Daniel Franke, Colleen Galloway, Yagil Henkin, Mark Honnen, Michael Klimenko, Rotem Kowner, Jia Lu, Margaret Martin, Patricia Polansky, John Roche, Timothy Romans, John Stephan and Robert Valliant.

We are also sincerely grateful for the assistance of the staffs of the following institutions for their support: Azrieli Foundation and the Truman Institute for the Advancement of Peace, Hebrew University of Jerusalem; Hamilton Library, University of Hawaii at Manoa; Hoover Institution Archives and Library, Stanford University; McDermott Library, u.s. Air Force Academy; and the Stephen H. Hart Library and Research Center at the History Colorado Center in Denver.

The staff at Reaktion Books have been of great assistance in the preparation of this volume. In particular, we wish to thank the publisher Michael Leaman for his (sorely tried) patience and support during the long process of transforming a concept into a book, along with his assistant, Alex Ciobanu, and our desk editor, Amy Salter, for their invaluable production expertise.

Last but by no means least, we would like to extend our deepest gratitude to our family and friends for their unwavering support during the writing and editing of this volume. Any errors are our responsibility alone.

PHOTO ACKNOWLEDGEMENTS

The editors and publishers wish to express their thanks to the below sources of illustrative material and/or permission to reproduce it:

Bibliothèque nationale de France, Paris: p. 254; photo Didier Descouens (CC BY-SA 4.0): p. 219; from *Kinsei Meishi Shashin* (Photographs of Modern Notables), vol. 1 (Osaka, 1935), photo National Diet Library, Tokyo: p. 234; Library of Congress, Prints and Photographs Division, Washington, DC: pp. 53 (Brady-Handy Collection), 153 (FSA/OWI Collection), 166 (Civil War Photographs, 1861–1865); from Brantz Mayer, *Mexico; Aztec, Spanish and Republican: A Historical, Geographical, Political, Statistical and Social Account of that Country from the Period of the Invasion by the Spaniards to the Present Time*, vol. 11 (Hartford, CT, 1853), photo Smithsonian Libraries, Washington, DC: p. 118; National Archives at College Park, MD: p. 103; Naval History and Heritage Command, Washington, DC: p. 84; The New York Public Library: p. 200; courtesy The Stephen H. Hart Library & Research Center, Denver, CO: p. 66; Thorvaldsens Museum, Copenhagen: p. 182.